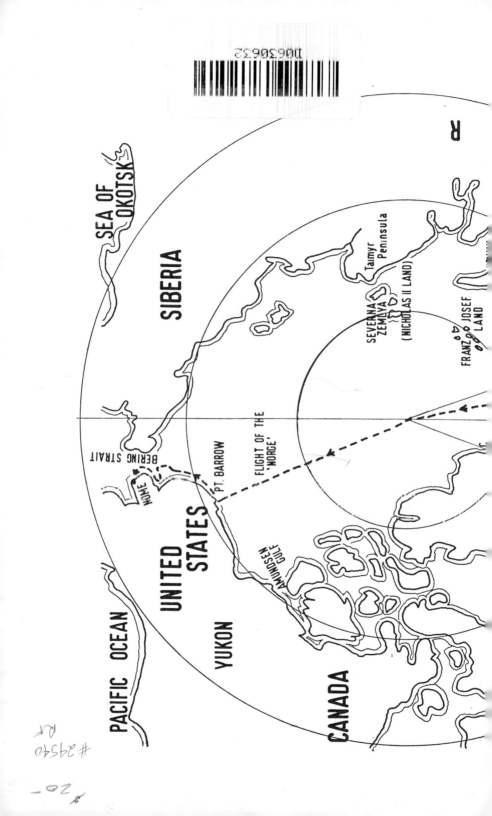

ICE CRASH

ICE CRASH

by

Alexander McKee

SOUVENIR PRESS

CONTENTS

6   CONTENTS

LIST OF ILLUSTRATIONS

ACKNOWLEDGEMENTS

IN Italy, my thanks must go first to General Umberto Nobile and his charming wife, Signora Gertrud Nobile, not only for a lengthy interview in Rome but for an extended correspondence spanning more than a year. After the General's death, Signora Nobile was kind enough to look through the draft MS of this book and make a number of helpful suggestions.

My thanks also to a colleague of Umberto Nobile, General Francesco Pricolo, a former commandant of Rome airport; to the editor of *Corriere della sera*, Milan; and to Rear-Admiral G. Benini, the Italian Defence and Naval attaché in London.

In Norway, I am indebted to the late Rolf S. Tandberg who, just before he was admitted to the hospital where he later died, was kind enough to send me a copy of his booklet, which corrects many persistent errors regarding the *Italia* expedition. I should like to thank also Reidar Lunde, chief editor of *Aftenposten*, Oslo, who put me in touch with Mr. Tandberg.

In Denmark, I was fortunate to find a real expert on Arctic aviation who moreover has made a hobby out of collecting documentation on the *Italia* tragedy. Ove Hermansen, air traffic controller at Kastrup airport, Copenhagen, was most generous in guiding me past some of the pitfalls which await the researcher in this subject. He, too, like Signora Nobile, was kind enough to read the MS in draft form and make very many valuable suggestions.

In Sweden, Lieutenant-Colonel Nils Kindberg of the Flygstaben information office put me in touch with an officer uniquely able to assist me. Lieutenant-Colonel Rolf Westerberg, a former air attaché in Washington, and an expert on the Swedish rescue operations in the Arctic, 1928, was then preparing a study for Svensk Flyhistorisk Förening, the Swedish Aviation Historical Society, to be published on the fiftieth anniversary in 1978.

Colonel Westerberg was kind enough to provide much information, answer many queries, and send me a copy of the study when it was published.

In Finland, I was assisted by my old friend Ora Patoharju, well known in the contrasted sphere of underwater exploration. Through him I got in touch with Pentti Laakso of Helsinki, who is a member of the Finnish Aviation Museum Society, the American Aviation Historical Society, and the International Plastic Modellers Society; with Eino Ritaranta; and with Jalmar Tiusanen, who was a wireless operator at Vaasa in 1928.

For help with Russian aspects of the story, I must acknowledge the assistance of *Soviet Weekly*, the Society for Cultural Relations with the USSR, and the Arctic & Antarctic Research Institute.

For insights into relevant aspects of early aviation, I contacted Air Marshal Sir Edward Chilton, who came to know Italo Balbo professionally while piloting VIPs round the Schneider Trophy course at Calshot (I still have my own souvenir programme for the 1931 contest containing a foreword by Balbo); and Group Captain G. E. Livock, author of *To the Ends of the Air*, who took part in the famous formation flight of four Supermarine Southamptons to Australia in 1927–1928.

For their assistance with documentation, I should like to thank the librarians of the Royal Geographical Society, the Royal Aeronautical Society, the Scott Polar Research Institute, the British Library Newspaper Library, the Portsmouth Central Library, and, once again, the kind and painstaking staff of the Hayling Library. I must not forget, for their invaluable help in purchasing books long out of print, Lynge & Son's international antiquarian bookshop of Copenhagen, and Damms Antikvariat of Oslo.

The bulk of the evidence has never been available in English and therefore I must acknowledge with particular gratitude the work of those who kindly translated in full or in summary a number of books and articles: Liliane Evans (Italian), Ilse McKee (German), Leena Riley (Finnish), Mary Templeman and V. Webber (Russian). I found particularly helpful the discussions I had with Liliane Evans (who was born in Florence) regarding this period in Italian history.

For help with obtaining photographs I have to thank the late General Nobile, Lieutenant-Colonel Nils Kindberg, Eino Ritoranta; and for drawing the endpaper maps, Michael Coobmer.

If, in spite of the above, there are errors, the fault is mine.

PLACE-NAMES AND SPELLINGS

THERE is no uniformity of spelling, either of personal names or place-names, in the books, articles and documents which form the bulk of the evidence for the story of the Italian polar airships. This is not surprising, as nine different languages are involved – Italian, Norwegian, Swedish, Finnish, Dutch, French, Czech, English and Russian. In Russian, of course, a different alphabet is used and there is no 'correct' spelling of Russian words in English. And in English there are sometimes alternative spellings – Spitsbergen and Spitzbergen, for instance. The latter has been used here because it seems more evocative of the place.

To complicate matters further, the Norwegians have given the Spitzbergen area a new name – Svalbard – and altered most of the old names, many of which were English, to a Scandinavian equivalent. And to confuse utterly, two adjacent capes (Bruun and Bergström) have swapped names. Because the new, Norwegian names are those which have a future, it seems proper to provide a comparison list.

Names Used Here	New Norwegian Names
Amsterdam Island	Amsterdamøya
Bear Island	Bjørnøya
Beverly Sound	Beverlysundet
Brandy Bay	Brennevinsfjorden
Broch Island	Brochøya
Cape Bergström	Bergströmodden
Cape Bruun	Kapp Bruun
Cape Leigh Smith	Kapp Leigh Smith
Cape Platen	Kapp Platen
Cape Wrede	Kapp Wrede
Charles XII Island	Karl XII Øyane

Names Used Here	*New Norwegian Names*
Danes Island	Danskøya
Dove Bay	Duvefjorden
Foyn Island	Foynøya
Green Harbour	Grønfjorden
Grey Hook	Gråhuken
Hinlopen Strait	Hinlopenstretet
King Charles Land	Kong Karls Land
Kings Bay	Kongsfjorden
Lady Franklin's Bay	Lady Franklinfjorden
Liefde Bay	Liefdefjorden
Mossel Bay	Mosselbukta
New Aalesund	Ny Ålesund
North Cape	Kordkapp
North-East Land	Nordaustlandet
Prince Charles Land	Prins Karls Forland
Rijps Bay	Rijpforden
Scoresby Island	Scoresbyøya
Seven Islands	Sjuøyane
Spitzbergen	Spitsbergen
Verlegen Hook	Verlegenhuken
Virgo Bay	Virgohamna
White Island	Kvitøya
Wood Bay	Woodfjorden

LIST OF PRINCIPAL CHARACTERS

ITALY

Nobile, Umberto	: Colonel, *Norge*, 1926; General, *Italia*, 1928.
Nobile, Dr. Amedeo	: his brother, Professor of Physics.
Crocco, Arturo Valle, Giuseppe Usueli, Celestine	} with Nobile, the 'brains' of the airship factory.
Bonzani, Alberto	: Under Secretary for Air, 1926.
Balbo, Italo	: Under Secretary for Air, 1928.
Pricolo, Francesco	: Commandant, Rome Airport.
Mercanti, Arturo	: Milanese supporter, *Italia* project.
Mussolini, Benito	: Fascist dictator of Italy since 1922.
Cecioni, Natale	: Motor mechanic, *Norge* & *Italia*.
Arduino, Ettore	: Motor mechanic, *Norge* & *Italia*.
Caratti, Attilio	: Motor mechanic, *Norge* & *Italia*.
Pomela, Vincenzo	: Motor mechanic, *Norge* & *Italia*.
Alessandrini, Renato	: Foreman Rigger, *Norge* & *Italia*.
Pontremoli, Dr. Aldo	: Prof. of Physics, Milan Univ., *Italia*.
Mariano, Adalberto	: Commander, RN 1st officer, *Italia*.
Zappi, Filippo	: Commander, RN 2nd officer, *Italia*.
Viglieri, Alfredo	: Lieutenant, RN 3rd officer, *Italia*.
Trojani, Felice	: Engineer *Italia*.
Ciocca, Calisto	: Motor mechanic *Italia*.
Pedretti, Ettore	: W/T Operator *Italia*.
Biagi, Giuseppe	: W/T Operator *Italia*.
Tomaselli, Francesco	: Journalist, *Corriere della Sera*, *Italia*.
Lago, Ugo	: Journalist, *Popolo d'Italia*, *Italia*.
Giudici, Davide	: Journalist, *Corriere della Sera*, *Krassin*
Romagna Manoja, Giuseppe	: Captain of the *Città di Milano*.
Baldizone, Francesco	: Commander, 2 i/c. *Città di Milano*.
Baccarini, Ugo	: Chief W/T Officer *Città di Milano*.
Cendali, Guido	: Medical Lieutenant, *Città di Milano*.
Franceschi, Gian	: Priest.
Sora, Gennaro	: Alpini ski-instructor.
Albertini & Matteoda	: University skiers.
Maddalena, Umberto	: Major, pilot of S-55.
Penzo	: Major, pilot of S-55; Dornier Wal.

13

CZECHOSLOVAKIA

Behounek, Dr. Frantisek : Professor, Prague University, Electric. & radio activity, *Italia*.

NORWAY

Amundsen, Roald : NW Passage, 1903–5; S. Pole, 1911; *Norge*, 1926.
Amundsen, Leon : his brother.
Amundsen, Gustav : his nephew, shore crew, *Norge*, 1926.
Dietrichson, Leif : Lt. RN, Dornier, 1925; Latham, 1928.
Riiser-Larsen, Hjalmar : 1st Lt. RN, Dornier, 1925; nav. *Norge*, 1926.
Omdal, Oscar : Fl. Lt. RN, Dornier, 1925; mech. *Norge*, 1926.
Horgen, Emil : navigator   *Norge*, 1926.
Wisting, Oscar : Hunter, S. Pole 1911, helmsman *Norge*, 1926.
Gottwald, Birger : W/T Operator   *Norge*, 1926.
Storm-Johnsen, Frithjof : W/T Operator   *Norge*, 1926.
Ramm, Fredrik : Journalist, *Norge*, 1926.
Arnesen, Odd : Journalist, *Aftenposten*, 1926 & 1928.
Thommessen, Dr. Rolf : Ed. *Tidens Tegn*, President Aero Club.
Lutzow-Holm, Finn : Lt. RN, pilot of rescue aircraft, 1928.
Nansen, Fridtjof : Polar explorer, *Fram*.
Sverdrup, Otto : Captain of the *Fram*.
Hoel, Dr. Adolf : Oslo University expert on Svalbard.
Gran, Major Tryggve : Polar explorer.

Dog Teams
Tandberg. Rolf S. : Coal Company, Spitzbergen.
Nöis, Hilmar : Trapper.
Varming, Ludwig : a Dane.
Dongen, Sjef van : a Dutchman.
Kraemer, Waldemar : Trapper.

SWEDEN

Andrée, Salomon August : Arctic balloonist, died 1897.
Malmgren, Dr. Finn : Prof. Uppsala Univ., meteorologist, *Norge* & *Italia*.
Tornberg, Egmont : Capt., Cdr. of Air Group, 1928.
Christell, Einar : Lt., observer, Air Group, 1928.
Lundborg, Einar : Lt. pilot, Air Group, 1928.
Schyberg, Birger : Lt., pilot, Air Group, 1928.
Nilsson, Viktor : Civilian pilot, Air Group, 1928.

FINLAND

Lihr, Gunnar : Civilian pilot, Aero Co, 1928.
Backman, Uno : Civilian mechanic, Aero Co, 1928.
Sarko, Olavi : Lieutenant, Finnish Air Force, 1928.

SOVIET UNION

Samoilovich, Prof. Rudolf	: Pres., Inst. Arctic Studies,	*Krassin.*
Tchukhnovsky, Boris	: Air group commander	*Krassin.*
Eggi, Karl	: Ship captain	*Krassin.*
Oras, Paul	: Ship Commissar	*Krassin.*
Alexandrowitsch, Xenia	: Waitress	*Krassin.*
Woronzowa, Ljubow	: Journalist	*Krassin.*
Babuskin, M. S.	: Airman	*Malygin.*
Schmidt, Nicholas	: Farmer & radio 'ham', Archangelsk.	

FRANCE

Guildbaud, Rene	: Commandant, pilot of Latham, 1928.
Cuverville, Albert de	: Lieutenant, co-pilot of Latham, 1928.
Valette, Emile	: W/T Operator, of Latham, 1928.
Brazy, Gilbert	: Mechanic, of Latham, 1928.

UNITED STATES

Ellsworth, Lincoln	: Dornier, 1925; *Norge*, 1926. Antarctic, etc.
Eilson, Carl Ben	: Lt., US Army, Arctic aviation pioneer.
Byrd, Richard	: Lt., USN, claimed 1st North Pole flight, 1928.
Peary, Robert E.	: Comdr., USN, claimed 1st North Pole on foot, 1909.
Cook, Dr. Frederick A.	: claimed 1st North Pole on foot, 1908.

AUSTRALIA

Wilkins, George H.	: Captain, Arctic aviation pioneer.

CANADA

Stefansson, Vilhjalmur	: Explorer, author 'The Friendly Arctic'.

GREAT BRITAIN

Scott, G. H.	: Major, airship pilot, died R.101, 1930.
Scott, Robert Falcon	: Captain, RN, died Antarctic, 1912.
Franklin, Sir John	: Rear-Admiral, RN, died Arctic, 1847.

PROLOGUE

THE General's gaze took in only half the scene. The monument by the lake, ready for unveiling the names of the dead; the drilled ranks of uniformed men drawn up on parade; the more casual group in formal civilian clothes, the foreign diplomatic corps. The French, the Russians, the Finns, the Norwegians, the Swedes, the Danes, the Dutch . . . yes, they were all there. Representatives of all those nations which had taken part in that great sea and air rescue operation in the Arctic half a century ago. 22 aeroplanes, 15 ships, 1,500 men, so it was said.

Now the General's mind was almost wholly focused on the past, remembering. The General was 93, but some things old men did not forget. Physically, he was present at a ceremony organised by the Chief of Air Staff at the Museum of Military Aviation at Vigna di Valle on Lake Bracciano, north of Rome. Physically, he was confined to a wheel-chair; small, frail, immobile, and half-ashamed to appear thus in public. But mentally, Umberto Nobile was sharply alert, nearer to those far-off days than he had been for many years.

This was the 24th of May, 1978, the day of his ultimate vindication, but the old man's thoughts went back to the years of indignity and disgrace, of vilification, of exile abroad. And beyond them, to the exploits of a younger, more vigorous man – the man he had been fifty years before – in the time of his triumphs, when his flights were world news, his Arctic airships the spectacularly successful vehicles which were opening a new phase of Polar exploration, flying over the unknown top of the world.

It had been four o'clock in the morning, fifty years ago, when the final flight of them all had begun. Father Gian Franceschi had said a brief prayer. The General had ordered 'Let go!' The ground crew had released their hold on the mooring ropes that kept the airship tethered to the icy landscape, nose down. A hundred and fifty voices had shouted: 'Hurrah!' The roars of their cheering had mingled with the thunder of engines, as the General had ordered them speeded up. The 348-foot long dirigible has lifted her bulk into the frozen sky and nosed towards Cape Mitra at the entrance to King's Bay, Spitzbergen. A flock of gulls busy picking over the camp midden, had risen screaming at the disturbance, their shrieks sounding like lost souls.

PART ONE
THE NORGE

Chapter 1

RUINED IN THE WALDORF ASTORIA

ROALD AMUNDSEN was near to black despair. Alone in his room at the Waldorf-Astoria, not the cheapest hotel in New York, he felt himself irrevocably a ruined man. Fifty-four and finished. He flinched at any knock on the door, in case it was another creditor. His recent lecture tour of the United States had been a financial flop, while his articles in the American press had brought meagre rewards. His debts were huge, so there was no hope of paying them off even in a year or two. And since he would not talk to them, some of his creditors had taken to slipping their bills under his door.

But after all this was more or less how he had begun in 1903. On the eve of his three-year voyage to find the North-West Passage, the goal of seamen for four centuries, a creditor had given him twenty-four hours to pay up. Otherwise, he threatened to seize the expedition's vessel and prosecute the young explorer for fraud. Rather than see his dream destroyed, Amundsen had convinced his six companions that they must escape from Norway; and escape, they had, vanishing into a rain-storm, as light-hearted as pirates.

On his successful return, a richer Amundsen had paid those old debts; but the pattern remained. In 1911, he had become the first conqueror of the South Pole, but only by deceiving his friends and associates, to get the use of the ice-ship *Fram*. That ship was the creation of Fridtjof Nansen, the pioneer of exploration by polar drift. Amundsen had copied his methods and those of Peary the American with brilliant success. But now he prided himself on being an innovator, also – in his own opinion, the first man to grasp that the time of dog teams was done and that the era of aviation had begun. He had realised this as early as 1909 and in 1914 had actually bought a French Farman biplane and learnt to fly it. After the Great War, in 1921 and 1922, he had

21

carried out his first flights in the Arctic with two German Junkers and an American Curtiss; and had lóst two of them without achieving his aims. His latest bid, planned for next year, 1925, was to have been a flight over the North Pole with German Dornier Wal flying boats now being built under licence at Marina di Pisa in Italy. Unfortunately, he could not afford to pay for them.

This was doubly distressing because his fund-raiser had ordered three of the big machines, instead of the two Amundsen had asked for. Amundsen blamed the whole affair on this man's failure to manage the promotional side of the expedition properly. Nor were these the only debts outstanding. So serious had matters become that even his own brother, Leon Amundsen, who was his business manager, had taken fright and fearing that he himself would never be repaid by Roald, had tried to sell the explorer's house over his head. A most unsavoury court case had ensued, with some people believing that he and Leon were in collusion to defraud their joint creditors. But Roald himself had furiously attacked Leon, speculating publicly as to what weird aberration might have made his own brother do this thing to him. It could hardly be that he had inherited unsavoury characteristics, for their father and mother were the finest and most honest people in the world. Perhaps it was marriage, that state he himself had avoided? But who could tell?

The telephone rang.

Amundsen flinched at the sound. Reluctantly, he picked up the receiver. Another creditor? Another man suggesting an immediate settlement – or brusquely delivering a summons?

'Captain Amundsen? I met you several years ago – in France, during the war, if you recall,' said an unknown voice. 'I'd like to come up and talk.'

A ruse? A creditor cleverer than the rest? Amundsen suspected so and gave a gruff, non-committal reply. He certainly did not recognise the man's voice. But the stranger, whoever, he was, would not be put off. He went on, purposefully.

'I'm an amateur interested in exploration, and I might be able to supply some money for another expedition.'

Amundsen could hardly believe what he was hearing.

'My name is Lincoln Ellsworth,' went on the caller.

It soon became clear that the visitor was fortunate to have a rich father who was prepared to indulge his son's ambitions to become prominent in Arctic exploration. He agreed to put up the sum of 85,000 dollars, which paid comfortably for two Dornier Wals. By May, 1925, the Amundsen-Ellsworth Polar Expedition was preparing at King's Bay, Spitzbergen, for an epic flight – the first to the North Pole. It was going to be terribly risky, with no margins for headwinds, navigational lapses, or the vagaries of the compass when flying so close to the magnetic pole.

All aeroplanes, even the most modern, had extremely limited range and with cruising speeds of around 100 m.p.h. were much affected by strong winds. For this reason, more aviators had fallen into the Atlantic than had crossed it – and the few who had succeeded had flown the easy way, from America to Europe, pushed by the prevailing tailwinds. No aeroplane had yet succeeded in crossing in the other direction, although an airship had – the British airship R.34 had made the double crossing in 1919. A German zeppelin had also crossed, without publicity, on a delivery flight in 1924. Airships were slow – slower even than motor cars – but they could fly non-stop for thousands of miles, which the aeroplane could not do, and if they suffered engine trouble they could stay up while repairs were carried out; whereas an aeroplane came down at once, regardless of whether it was flying over mountains, cornfields, forests, water, or ice. Whether it force-landed safely then depended in part on whether it was fitted with wheels, floats or skis.

Some of those who experienced it tend to regard this era as having been the 'golden age' of aviation. The first machines were too primitive – either underpowered boxkites or un-navigable balloons; they were hardly practical vehicles. Nowadays of course private flight for pleasure is regulated and restricted, while much passenger flying is an experience closely akin to that of a sardine – except that the sardine is dead and does not know what is being done to it. The period of freedom was in the 1920s and 1930s.

In 1925, the aeroplane was less than twenty-five-years-old, effectively; the airship and practical radio had a history hardly longer. In 1903 the first 'hops' by a powered aeroplane were made by Wilbur and Orville Wright in America; and in the same year an Italian inventor, Guglielmo Marconi, had supervised the first radio transmission between England and America. The two inventions were to be intimately connected. For a million years or more, man had been a land animal, dreaming of flight. Then, all at once, within a generation, the dream became reality. In split-seconds, one could speak between continents; or in a matter of weeks, fly round the world. But the flying had not yet become routine, and the radio was not entirely reliable. Yet the hazards were cheerfully accepted and many airmen secretly dreaded the inevitable coming of the aerial bus-driver. Joyfully, they knew that his time was not quite yet. There was pioneer work still to do.

Even with that background of challenge and daring, Amundsen's Polar Sea project seemed foolhardy. It could be contemplated only by men who were at home in the Arctic, for whom a forced landing was not final; men who could live off the Arctic and walk out over the ice to safety. Some men of the North, men like the Icelandic Canadian Vilhjalmur Stefansson, had written of the 'Friendly Arctic'; Amundsen was not so sanguine, but he had trained himself from youth to endure cold, privation and great physical exertion, had become skilled and knowledgable in all the arts of survival in snow and ice. He was fiercely proud of his exceptional physical performance in polar conditions; and this 'ace' mentality must have been a vital factor in the planning and execution of such appallingly hazardous ventures as his dash to the South Pole to forestall Scott. Captain Scott, the British amateur, had died with all the men of his sledge party in Antarctica; Amundsen, the Norwegian professional, had got there first by the wide margin of a month, and he had brought back all his men in good health.

In aviation, however, it was Amundsen who was the amateur; maker of elementary mistakes. His extremely bold plan was to fly two Dorniers in formation, lightly loaded with three men in each, so that if it looked as if they would run out of petrol (which failing a strong tailwind was a virtual certainty), both could land and transfer petrol from one machine to the other, into which the crew of the Dornier to be abandoned would crowd. Admittedly, the Dorniers were capable of taking off and landing from smooth ice as well as water, but even so there might be jumbled pack-ice below them or the machines might be flying blind in one of those frequent Arctic fogs which make navigation so difficult and an economical straight-line course virtually impossible to follow.

Amundsen and Lincoln Ellsworth were to be the two navigators. Both the pilots were drawn from the Norwegian Navy – First-Lieutenant Hjalmar Riiser-Larsen and Lieutenant Leif Dietrichson. Of the two engineers, Flight-Lieutenant Oskar Omdal was also a Norwegian Navy man, but the other engineer, Feucht, was German. Riiser-Larsen was a pipe-smoking giant, seemingly placid, with a keen brain. In 1921 he had gone to England at his own expense to attend a course in airship theory, and had then worked briefly on the problem of mooring-masts for dirigibles. It was he who, at the first flight conference Amundsen held at Spitzbergen in 1925, made the critical suggestion which was to lead to a new era in polar exploration. While they were discussing what was clearly a perilous enterprise with the Dorniers, he startled them all by saying that he had heard of an airship going cheap for not more than 100,000 dollars.

Admittedly, it was second-hand but of recent construction. It was the Italian semi-rigid airship N.1, designed by the brilliant Italian engineer Umberto Nobile, whose factory had a reputation for turning out very practical and economical dirigibles, and selling them all over the world. This tested ship, he had heard, was for sale, too.

Airships had a false but glamorous image of strength and power stemming from their gigantic size, dwarfing the gnat-like aeroplanes. The great rigid airships were as large as ocean liners, six or seven hundred glittering feet long, or even more. To see such an enormous silvery structure in flight over one's head was perhaps the most impressive aerial spectacle of the century. Yet they had their characteristic drawbacks and weaknesses, not apparent to a layman. The practical Italian N-class ships were not so enormous as the German Zeppelins had been or their current British imitations; but they were impressive enough and certainly better suited to long-distance flying than the Dorniers.

Immediately, Lincoln Ellsworth was convinced. He promised there and then to buy the N.1 for 100,000 dollars, if it really was available at that price. They would do a continent-to-continent flight in her next year, 1926. This year, they could be more cautious and attempt only that proving flight to the North Pole and back.

The decision probably saved all their lives, for even the less ambitious programme brought them to the edge of disaster. The flying boats had a cruising speed of 90 m.p.h. and a range in still air of 1,500 miles. As the Pole was 761 statute miles from where King's Bay lies in 79° North, the enormity of the risks Amundsen was taking were obvious, even if all went well. In fact, when they were 600 miles out towards the Pole, one Dornier had engine failure – and by the wildest of lucky chances there was a large open stretch of water below them at that moment. What followed became an epic. The two flying boats came down on the water, the water froze, but with incredible exertion in three weeks they cleared a take-off runway on the ice, crowded into one Dornier flown by Riiser-Larsen, and by the tiniest of margins got off and returned to Spitzbergen after having been regarded as lost for twenty-five days. The Arctic expertise of the Norwegians had been vital to their survival, but Amundsen had had a sharp lesson in flight planning. As soon as they got back to Norway, a telegram was sent to Colonel Umberto Nobile, asking him to come to Oslo to discuss the possible purchase of the airship N.1.

Nobile was born in 1885 at Lauro di Nola near Naples in Southern Italy. The town is set in the hinterland of the volcanic gulfs of Naples and Salerno, famous for the pre-1944 silhouette of the twin summits of Vesuvius and Monte Somma looking down over the partly excavated ruins of Pompei and Herculaneum, which were overwhelmed by the eruption of A.D. 79. Pompei had been a new, brash, vulgar, Roman intrusion on an area basically Greek for almost a thousand years. Many overlords in their turn succeeded the Romans, including Goths, Normans, Spaniards, Austrians, French and British. The modern result is an exciting mix of peoples remarkable for their exuberance and gaiety. To walk into one of the Neapolitan towns from the countryside is an audible encounter, not of motor car engines or industrial machinery, but with a roar of language, of men and women talking, laughing and bargaining at the tops of their voices. A grave Roman might turn up his nose, and many do, but it is difficult not to absorb some of the colourful lightheartedness of the place and its people.

This was the background of Umberto Nobile, born fifth in a family of three sons and four daughters, his father an official in the ministry of finance. To an Italian woman he would seem a man of flashingly romantic and flamboyant temperament, immensely attractive. And not to an Italian woman only, but to women of all nationalities perhaps. To his relatives and particularly his wife, Nobile conveyed a different but not necessarily contradictory impression, of a man immensely concerned with the importance of his work and sacrificing much of what should have been his leisure time to it. A graduate of the University of Naples, he had obtained diplomas in industrial and electrical engineering and had at first found a post in the state railways where his work was mainly concerned with electrified lines.

In 1911, however, he turned to aeronautical engineering in its most complex and experimental form – the structure of rigid airships. The success of these huge and vulnerable vehicles depended essentially on the weight-to-strength ratio of the design and construction, because that determined the payload. When Italy entered the Great War on 24 May, 1915, on the side of the Allies, Nobile after being three times turned down for military service on medical grounds, was forced to accept that his contribution must be in the field of scientific engineering. With three other engineers, Arturo Crocco, Giuseppi Valle and Celestine Usueli, he founded the Stabilimento di Construzione Aeronautiche to design and build dirigibles of all types. He was mostly concerned with the small semi-rigid airships of the M-class which Italy found so useful for bombing operations against Austria-Hungary on land and for long scouting flights over the Adriatic. After the war the group split up, because while the other men wanted to go on to build large rigid airships, Nobile had come to accept that the smaller and simpler semi-rigid was more practical for Italy.

In 1919 he became director of the military airship works near Rome while still only thirty-four, and in 1921 designed a larger and much improved version of the M-class semi-rigids which he designated N.1. But designing and building are two different things. He did not obtain authorisation to go ahead with the construction of this new class of naval airship until 1923, and that official decision was closely tied up with political events. On 28 October, 1922, Benito Mussolini had seized power after the March on Rome. From that time on, there were opportunities for ambitious men, or those with exciting plans, but they were almost equally matched by the slipperyness of the ground underfoot.

In the same year, a corps of aeronautical engineers was brought into being as part of the armed forces, so Nobile's first military rank was Lieutenant-Colonel, with swift promotion to full Colonel. Three years later this was to bring him under a newly-appointed Under Secretary for Air, the dramatically-bearded air force officer, Italo Balbo, one of the Quadrumviri, the four top men of Fascism. Nobile resented Balbo, calling him 'a professional Fascist'. That is, a man who was determined to make his career out of and by Fascism. He was even younger for his position than Nobile, having been twenty-six at the time of the March on Rome. Balbo's ideas on the future of aviation were opposed to those of Nobile; he believed in the aeroplane and that the way to prove its usefulness and reliability lay in the carrying out of dramatic long distance flights by large formations. He saw himself as the air leader, not merely the planner of the enterprise, but the pilot of the lead machine. The hero, in fact.

Nobile's attitude was different originally; it was the engineering problems of flight which interested him. So it was not until 1924, after having made hundreds of airship flights as passenger or pupil that he began to actually command the airships he had designed; and the following year obtained a test pilot's licence in order to carry out his own research and development work. To one of his colleagues in aviation at this time, the commandant of Rome airport, Nobile appeared 'a very cultured man, ambitious, eager to rise to the top.' Among the Capronis, the famous family of aircraft designers and manufacturers, he was regarded as a brilliant aeronautical engineer of great promise.

In contrast to Amundsen, an athlete and sportsman who from youth had slept with the window open even in winter in order to harden himself for the great tasks ahead, Nobile was basically a scientist and university professor. For many years he lectured at the School of Engineering at the University of Naples; he created the Institute of Aerodynamics. His *Elementi di Aerodinamica* in two volumes became a classic textbook and he was to publish many treatises on scientific and technical subjects. His academic attainments were on quite a different level from those of the Norwegian explorer, who did, however, possess a ruthless quality of logical planning and leadership which was to bring him astounding success many times. While Nobile made a pet of a dog, which usually flew with him, Amundsen based his exploration techniques on expendable huskies to draw the sledges and be slaughtered for food in any emergency or indeed as an essential element in the planning.

Nobile arrived in Oslo to meet Amundsen on 25 July, 1925. A thousand miles north of Rome and refreshingly cool when compared to the 90 degrees in the shade normally experienced around the bay of Naples at that time of the year, the Norwegian capital sheltered at the base of black mountain ranges at the head of an immense fjord reaching inland 100 kilometres from the open sea. For many months of the year the waters of the fjord appeared black and bottomless, reflecting the snow-streaked mountain ridges towering to grey and wintry skies. Clearly, it was easier in Norway to travel by water than by land.

The memory of the Vikings was particularly present at this time, Oslo being the old name of the Norwegian capital, going back to about 1050 and that King Harald Hardrada who figures so frequently as a name of dread in English history books. However, there had been a period of 300 years when Norway had come under the Swedish crown and its capital was called Christiana. That period of comparative subjection had ended at last on 31 December, 1924. Oslo had been Oslo again for a matter of seven months. A revival of national feeling was taking place – it was in the air all over Europe – and in Oslo it was centred on the Viking ship discoveries; there was an intense desire to establish a national museum where the 'longships' and their associated finds could be comprehensively displayed. In England a similar impulse was leading to the preservation of the great three-decker H.M.S. *Victory* at Portsmouth and her eventual restoration to her state at the time of the battle of Trafalgar in 1805. And in 1927 Mussolini was to drain Lake Nemi, south of Rome, in order to expose two giant pleasure vessels built for the Roman emperor Caligula and then put them on display under cover.

None of the Norwegian Viking ship discoveries were recent. The first, at Borre, had been discovered and then destroyed by road-making as early as 1850–52. The next three had been excavated and preserved as well as possible – the Tune ship in 1867; the Gokstad ship in 1880; the Oseberg ship in 1904. All had been found on the shores of the great fjord south of Oslo, but under Swedish rule not a great deal had been done to display these remarkable survivals from the Viking age in Norway. Now a combined Viking ship museum was planned. The first wing of the permanent building was already under construction and was due to be opened to the public next year, 1926.

A separate Maritime Museum was to display the ice-drift ship *Fram*, associated with Nansen, Sverdrup and Amundsen; and eventually Amundsen's little *Gjöa* and Thor Heyerdahl's *Kon-Tiki*.

So the first meeting between the Italian airship designer and the Norwegian explorer was very much in Amundsen's territory, at his house just outside Oslo, still rather a sleepy provincial town. As usual, Amundsen had an aide to back him, the giant Hjalmar Riiser-Larsen, whose genial 15½ stone compared to the slightly-built Italian's 9½ stone (the weights of the crew were to be an important factor soon, because of the airship's tiny payload). Also present was a representative of the Aero Club of Norway, whose participation would be crucial in providing many of the necessary base facilities in Oslo the capital, at Vadsoe on the north coast and at Spitzbergen, without which the airship could not operate. Fuel, gas, mooring masts, hangars – all would have to be transported or constructed.

The President of the Norwegian Aero Club was Dr. Rolf Thommessen, editor and owner of the large-circulation daily newspaper *Tidens Tegn* of Oslo. Like a great many people in those days, he was an admirer of Mussolini and of what he thought Mussolini was trying to do. Consequently, he was prepared to give the Italians a fair crack of the whip, as far as credit was concerned, commensurate with the size of the Italian participation in the enterprise. Neither he nor the other Aero Club officials were ready to swing in behind Amundsen automatically, and this was to lead to a breach within the Norwegian camp.

There already was a breach in the Italian camp, although that word is too crude to catch the delicacy of the relationships involved; only those who actually took part could really grasp them. Like Thommessen, Nobile seems to have admired Mussolini; and for the same reasons – he got things done. Without Mussolini, Nobile felt, perhaps there might have been an Italian participation in Polar exploration, but on the whole he felt that unlikely. Certainly, under some other regimes of which he had experience, decisions would not have been taken so swiftly, nor put into effect so expeditiously, as with Il Duce. Furthermore, he did not waver; once he had decided to do something, he put his weight behind it so that matters moved. Of course, there was a penalty. Mussolini had to take the credit, or at least the major part of it, so as to boost his regime and his own position in it; but this sort of thing happens under all kinds of governments, although rarely perhaps so blatantly as with Benito Mussolini. But then, this small man was the first Italian prime minister who was of working class origins, and that might explain a lot. What he favoured were projects which would tend to create a bold, daring, even reckless image of a reinvigorated Italy, worthy of the Caesars. The Fascists intended, if they could, to alter the world's preconceived ideas of Italians as 'Wops', 'maccaroni-eaters', 'ice-cream merchants', 'organ-grinders', or fat opera singers.

A flight by an Italian-designed and piloted airship across the Arctic Ocean via the North Pole would very much assist this policy; and therefore Colonel Nobile carried with him very favourable financial terms, combined with certain conditions.

The technical omens for airships were good then, and for the smaller types of airship, very good. In this same month of July, 1925, the Goodyear company in America launched the non-rigid airship *Pilgrim*; Goodyear had had German advice and had also consulted Nobile, who had spent some time in America during the period between designing his semi-rigid N.1 and receiving belated authorisation to build. It was widely believed that airships would operate all the long-distance ocean routes; that the aeroplane had no future in long-range flying. The poor performance of the airship was not then obvious, by comparison. Most aeroplanes of the time were biplanes with an array of struts and wires which made them look like flying bird-cages and which truly represented built-in air-brakes. Only with the introduction of the streamlined monoplane did the performance of the heavier-than-air machine forge ahead and, for any given engine-power, make it much more efficient. And, of course, the aeroplane lacked the extreme vulnerability of the airship, with its vast bulk, to strong winds and storms. Nevertheless, at this time, at this particular stage of aviation development, the accident rate for lighter-than-air ships was comparatively low, while that for aeroplanes was high.

The Germans, innovators of the great rigid ships, had suffered few peacetime losses before the outbreak of war in 1914. The post-war pattern was less clear, because for a time the Germans had been forbidden to build large airships (or aeroplanes) which could be converted into bomb carriers. There had been a definite run of post-war accidents involving either surrendered German Zeppelins or foreign copies of a Zeppelin design. In 1921, the British R.38, crudely and shoddily copied for the U.S. Navy from a shotdown wartime Zeppelin, broke up when carrying out a simple turning manoeuvre with the loss of 44 men (16 of them Americans) from its 50-man crew. In 1923, the surrendered Zeppelin L.Z. 114, taken over by the French and renamed *Dixmude*, disappeared over the Mediterranean in a storm with the loss of all the 50 men aboard. And in 1925 the American *Shenandoah*, which was a Zeppelin copy based on L.49 (L.Z. 96) broke up in mid-air in a squall with the loss of 14 men. The Germans certainly were not accepting these mishaps as reflecting on their design or the future of airships generally. They were planning to construct a supership some 776 feet long (236.8 metres) which was to be launched in 1928 as the *Graf Zeppelin*, the most phenomenally successful rigid of all time.

Nobile's airship N.1 was much smaller; less than half the length and with a comparatively insignificant payload. But it was a simpler ship because it did not rely on an elaborate, highly-stressed metal framework. Nobile's design was basically just a large gasbag, with a keel from which the control cabin and engine gondolas were slung. Length was 347.8 ft. (106 metres), diameter was 64 ft. (19.5 metres), the useful load it would carry was 18,243 lbs. (8,275 kg.) The three 245 h.p. six-cylinder Maybach engines produced a maximum speed of around 70 m.p.h. (113 km/hr), giving a cruising speed in still air of 50 m.p.h.

These figures, and many others less easy to grasp, were crucial to the first meeting in Oslo between Nobile and the Norwegians. The purpose of the discussions was exploratory: to sketch the general outlines of the project, to see if it was possible with an existing airship, and if so at what cost; how much each of the parties would contribute, and on what terms.

It was Amundsen who laid down the objective: the establishment of a forward refueling and gas-replenishment base at King's Bay in West Spitzbergen, part of a new Norwegian possession called the Svalbard. From this Norwegian base a flight would be made via the North Pole to Point Barrow in Alaska, passing to one side of the Magnetic Pole which is in the Canadian Arctic some 1,300 miles from the geographical pole. The flight path of the airship would cover an immense region of the globe which had never been seen by any living man, let alone explored. There might be only frozen sea below them, but there could also be new lands to discover and to name. It was this thought which really drove Amundsen; at the back of his mind was a picture of himself, landing from an airship to take possession of newly-found territory for Norway. That would indeed be a fitting climax to a great Polar career.

Nobile said that his first airship N.1 was incapable of the flight. The payload was too small. The reason was that she had had to be built of the materials in stock at the time, many of which were too heavy, so there was a fundamental drawback. However he had a similar but much improved version of the prototype under construction which, when completed, would have the necessary range to cross the Polar Sea.

Amundsen said that he could not wait. The expedition must take place the following spring, in 1926, which meant that he must have the N.1. Nobile pondered as to how he could lighten N.1 so that she could carry the necessary weight of petrol to cover a distance of some 2,500 miles. The load N.1 would lift was absolutely governed by her comparatively small volume of 654,000 cubic feet of hydrogen gas. For comparison, a rival Norwegian-German Polar expedition – which might trump Amundsen's Norwegian-Italian project – had for its planning basis a large rigid airship of 4,768,000 cubic feet, seven times that of the small semi-rigid N.1. Nobile had to do a number of rapid sums, subtracting what weights he could remove safely from N.1 – such as the luxury accommodation for 25 passengers – but adding the extra weight which would be needed for strengthening the ship to permit her to use mooring masts, a necessity in the case of this particular flight, but not used at home where she was housed in a shed. Airships moored to masts have been known to stand on their noses in some high wind conditions, so there was nothing theoretical about this calculation. Nobile concluded that in all, after a lot had been subtracted and something had been added, he must have a net gain in payload of just 3,500 lbs. to make the Polar flight possible. He thought he could do it. But the comparative insignificance of this weight in terms of modern aviation shows graphically how small their safety margin was, how great were the risks these pioneers were prepared to accept; and above all, why Nobile was always worrying about what seemed to Amundsen negligible factors, such as the weight of the clothing each man wore, and even as to whether he could carry sixteen or seventeen men or must reject some unfortunate crew member at the last moment. The reason for this uncertainty was the awkward fact, common to all lighter-than-air craft, that temperature affects the lifting powers of the gas because heat causes it to expand while cold makes it contract.

The problem is very similar to that of ballasting in a submarine, where what appear to be small weights are actually quite critical. In the one, the inrush of a small amount of water; and in the other the loss of a small amount of lift by tearing of the envelope directly or by a change in temperature, can cause the vehicle to sink uncontrollably. The margins between positive and negative

2

buoyancy are tiny; and neutral buoyancy difficult to achieve. For instance, if the gas heats too much the airship will rise fast and then large amounts of gas must be valved off to bring her down again; but when this has been done, should the airship then grow cold and sink, some ballast must be dropped and eventually there may be insufficient ballast left to jettison so as to stop her from falling. Amundsen seems not to have grasped that in changing so blithely from the aeroplane to the airship, that he was merely swapping one set of technical problems for a different set of technical problems, and that he must rely heavily upon the judgement of the aviation experts he chose.

In his youth, he had intelligently noted how necessary it was in the days of Polar voyages by sea for the chief explorer also to be the captain of the ship. For if they were two different men, two rival groups would promptly appear among the crew. The explorers and scientists would form round the exploration leader, while the seamen and engineers would back the captain in any dispute and what could be merely a technical difference of opinion became at once a political matter – who held the real power? To avoid such divisions in his own expeditions, Amundsen far-sightedly put himself out to obtain the necessary seamanship qualifications to be master of his own ship in both meanings of the word; and thereafter all disputes were amicably settled between, on the one hand Amundsen the chief explorer, and on the other hand, Captain Amundsen, master of the exploration vessel. But what he was doing now, was to introduce a rival captain into his team – Nobile, the captain of the airship, whose role Amundsen could not take over. The Norwegian hoped to keep the Italian in a subordinate position by regarding the Colonel as a 'hired pilot'; but it was not going to work. Nobile was an officer in the armed forces of a foreign power; he was not a self-effacing Norwegian aide-de-camp prepared to stay in the background; as pilot of an aircraft, his was the final responsibility.

Amundsen was also by the same token entering the field of international politics and diplomacy, although he claimed not to have realised this. Lincoln Ellsworth, although a foreigner, was a private individual; Nobile was not. Amundsen recollected at being surprised when, he said, Nobile offered the N.1 as a free gift to him, provided that the airship flew the Italian flag during the enterprise. Amundsen assumed, probably correctly, that some-one in the Italian government thought it might be possible to gain favourable publicity for Italy and her new regime (which Amundsen detested) by holding on to the coat-tails of the famous Norwegian. Well, that was what Lincoln Ellsworth had done, bought himself worldwide fame by financing a famous man; and Amundsen had not complained. But the idea of having the Italian colours substituted for the Norwegian flag (although it *was* an Italian airship) irritated the old explorer beyond measure. He turned it down.

Instead, he asked what price the Italians were asking outright for the unconditional sale of N.1. Nobile replied that as she was two years old, the price would be the equivalent of £15,000 rather than the £20,000 she had cost originally; and that would include the necessary modifications required for a Polar flight. Amundsen was delighted, because in terms of American currency, this sum was $25,000 less than the $100,000 he had been promised by Ellsworth.

What it amounted to was that Italy contributed the airship at less than cost, Ellsworth paid, the Norwegian Aero Club would help the Italians prepare bases and supply all the special Polar kit they recommended, and Amundsen would give his name, which was renowned, and a few days of his time (for he was shortly due to leave on a lecture tour of the United States which would prevent him taking part in the preparations personally).

It seemed to be a bargain for everyone. So much so, that it was decided to work out the details, commit them to paper in a formal agreement, and sign them in Rome the following month. The final signature would be that of Benito Mussolini, his first act as Minister for Aviation, a new post he had granted himself. His support would be important, for there were many voices in Italy and elsewhere to be raised, saying that the N.1 was incapable of leaving Italy, let alone flying over the North Pole. Others again attacked the choice of Nobile as pilot, there being many experienced airship officers eager and available to seize this plum job of a Polar flight, some of them senior to Nobile. In the small world of aviation at this time and afterwards there was sometimes an atmosphere of professional jealousy which could often arouse feelings of that intensity which men like to think only women possess.

Into this pool of Roman intrigue, in the August of 1925, came Amundsen and Riiser-Larsen, the former zealously guarding his Polar status and determined to be sole commander of this Polar expedition, (despite some lip service to the invaluable Ellsworth). And then, quite unexpectedly, not even in half-quarrel during a conference, but fortuitously during a mere pleasure excursion, Amundsen was forced to experience the most nerve-racking doubts as to Nobile's competence in what must soon be for all of them, a matter of triumphant life or sordid death.

Chapter 2

A TRIP TO THE SEASIDE

THERE were no autostrada then, but even in 1925 the road from Rome to Anzio was a good one, with few bends. For the two Norwegians, and particularly Amundsen, it was a nightmare. He was sitting in the front of Nobile's Fiat, with the giant Riiser-Larsen occupying most of the back seats. All was well on the straights, but Amundsen had to hold on convulsively on each corner, as Nobile accelerated round the bend, braking quickly if another car came in sight, and to Amundsen's fevered mind, appeared to be continually on the point of over-turning the Fiat. Instead of conveying his apprehension directly to Nobile, who was sitting beside him, the old explorer turned round and, speaking in Norwegian, asked Riiser-Larsen if he, Riiser-Larsen could not do something to stop this lunatic killing them all.

Amundsen was not the first, and he certainly will not be the last foreigner to register a high degree of terror at his introduction to Italian driving. Normally, it takes half a week to realise that the Italians, from long experience, have it all weighed up and in addition, most of them have an extraordinary quickness of reaction which must have saved the lives of hundreds of thousands of pedestrians. Nobile, who has never had a motor accident (he was still driving at 88), had then been driving some 15 years, since 1910 in fact. He knew the car, the road, and the traffic. Amundsen, on the other hand, was more used to dog sleds than mechanically-propelled vehicles. If the Fiat had had paws instead of wheels at each corner, he might have been better capable of judging the driver.

After they had had their sea bathe at what Amundsen thought was Ostia, but Nobile says was Anzio, and the two Norwegians were safely back at their hotel in Rome, Amundsen turned to Riiser-Larsen and in shaken tones asked him to consider that, if this was how the man they had engaged to pilot their dirigible acted on the ground, how could they trust him when he was in the air? It was utter rubbish, of course, for it was Nobile's dirigible really; and Riiser-Larsen rejected Amundsen's proposition entirely, but in such a way as not to offend him. He retorted that it did not follow. Some of the calmest pilots he knew were, on the ground, just as excitable and apparently erratic as Nobile seemed to be; they had exactly the same nervous characteristics. But once in the air they became perfectly steady and were as calm in the face of danger as the best of more phlegmatic types. In effect, Riiser-Larsen was telling Amundsen: 'Don't talk rot!' And because Amundsen was very easily influenced, he accepted the correction and the final negotiations were concluded. *

These negotiations were taking place in Rome during August and developed into something of a battle, Amundsen wanting as many of his Polar-trained Norwegians as possible in the crew of the airship while Nobile wished to retain as many of his trained Italian airshipmen, who were already used to the N.1 and understood her, as he could make Amundsen accept. Neither got what he wanted, but instead a half-and-half compromise of Norwegians and Italians with the addition of one Swedish scientist (Malmgren, a former associate of Amundsen), one Russian radio operator (Olonkin, who had also been with him on the *Maud* expedition), and naturally the American Lincoln Ellsworth. The common language for orders would be English, but it wasn't all that common. Naturally, each leader wanted to enlist at least his own key men on whom he knew, from past experience, he could rely for certain given tasks; he would know their capabilities exactly. Strangers, and foreigners, too, could not be summed up with precision until they had been known so long that they had ceased to be either strange or foreign. By having each leader bring along his own retainers, so to speak, Amundsen was risking not only rivalry between two already established groups, but of national rivalry as well as ordinary formed-group rivalry. Only very high professional standards could prevent it.

* When, the following year, Amundsen's nephew Gustav came to Rome, his reactions to Italian driving were the same as his uncle's. 'We took something between a flying-trip and a motor-trip,' he wrote. 'I reckoned our speed to be about seventy or eighty kilometres an hour.' That is, a steady 45-50 m.p.h. down the Appian Way to Ciampino. 'It is rather fascinating,' he went on, 'to rush along a straight country road at a dizzying speed.'

It was probably the memory of these days of burning heat in Rome at high summer, while he argued with Nobile, that caused Amundsen afterwards to jeer at the Italians as 'a semi-tropical race', and to write them off entirely as likely Polar material. On the other hand it is true that many northerners have unrealistic ideas as to what the Italian climate is actually like. During the war which was to come, for instance, many an English soldier freezing quietly in the ice and snow and biting wind high up on an Italian mountain was to promise himself that if ever he got back home, after the war he would sue every travel agent in England who had ever tried to sell him 'Sunny Italy' as a holiday destination.

Possibly also it was the irritation of these negotiations in the heat which either turned Amundsen anti-Italian or confirmed a bias already there. He was to write that while he was prepared to share the honours of the flight with his American friend, Lincoln Ellsworth, he was not prepared to share anything with the Italians. Yet the Italian contribution was at least as important, and arguably much more so. Anyway, at this point Ellsworth had to remain in America because his father had died and Amundsen, who had to earn his living and also try to pay off some of his huge debts, had to start his lecture tours. The bulk of the work, and it was very exacting, fell on Nobile and the Italians; with the Aero Club of Norway helping where possible. The intricate weight and stress calculations necessary to make N.1 into a proper Polar vehicle were entirely the responsibility of Nobile. If this work was done sloppily, or not at all, as with the British R.38, then N.1 would probably kill them.

There were three basic types of dirigible (that is, balloons capable of being directed while in flight, not condemned merely to drift or to fly tethered). At one extreme there was the rigid airship, usually of great size, usually shaped like a cigar. This was constructed of a series of rings, or cylindrical girders, held together by a framework of fore-and-aft girders or longerons. Inside the girder framework were a number, usually a large number, of lifting bags or gas cells. Outside the girder framework again was the envelope, pressed against the girders and plainly showing their rigid pattern. All the great weight-carriers were of this type, which was almost universally believed at the time to be the destined long-distance transport of the future.

At the other end of the scale was the small airship of the non-rigid type. The early versions were simply an elongated balloon with an aeroplane fuselage, complete with engine, slung below it on wires. When deflated, complete collapse followed; like a child's toy balloon, they just went flat on the grass. Apart from having an engine and being steerable, they were little different from the 'kite' balloons used for battlefield observation in the Great War of 1914–18 or the anti-aircraft 'barrage' balloons of the Second World War. The best story of how they got their unofficial name of 'blimp' is the English one which goes, that under Army nomenclature they were designed as Type B (Limp). Hence 'Blimp' (also the nickname for the British infantry's image of the pot-bellied staff officer of uncertain temper and habits). Simple airships of this type were used in the Great War for bombing, but more usually for convoy work with their respective navies. After the war, virtually only one role could be found for them, and that was in America as flying advertisement hoardings. When the Second World War broke out, again it was only America which could use them, mainly over coastal waters far from hostile aeroplanes and submarines.

The 'limp' airships all had ballonnets or internal air bladders to maintain the shape of the envelope and compensate for loss of gas. They fulfilled a function not too unlike that of the inner-tube of a car or bicycle tyre. Sunlight shining on the envelope of an air-ship causes the gas to expand; if this happened, then initially, the ballonnets could be deflated, so that the dirigible lost replaceable compressed air, not irreplaceable lifting gas. But if, in extremes, gas had to be valved off at height, then on descending again the airship would lose its shape, its aerodynamic form, and become inefficient and even hazardous to fly. In this case compressed air was forced into the ballonnets, so that the hull retained its shape although the hydrogen gas content was less and the hull had reduced lifting powers.

The semi-rigid dirigible came midway between the blimp and the rigid airship, both in size and type of construction. There was a rigid but flexible 'keel' running the full length of the ship to take the weight of the loads she had to carry, both internally and externally in the way of control cars, engine gondolas and so on. In the case of N.1, there was a rigid nose cone as well and the keel was built in several sections to increase flexibility. The usual system of ballonnets was employed, but with a semi-rigid the exact pressure state of the internal air bladders was less critical. The Italians believed that this type of medium-sized construction had greater give in it and that such an airship was less likely to break up in storms than the fully rigid type.

While Nobile was stripping N.1 of her passenger fittings, from her kitchen to her saloon furniture, so as to gain the 3,500 lbs. of lift he needed for the extra petrol, a number of rival airship experts within the Air Ministry went to Mussolini and warned him that a disaster was impending; it was impossible to reach the North Pole with an airship so small as N.1, with its comparatively tiny payload. They were, of course, very nearly right. Indeed, if Nobile did not succeed in appreciably lightening the ship, they would be entirely right. Mussolini did not hesitate. He sent for General Alberto Bonzani, the Assistant Secretary for Aviation, and told him to expedite everything concerned with the Polar project. He had entered into an agreement with the Norwegians and he was not going to go back on it.

These preparations included the setting up of mooring masts and major refuelling and repair bases at Vadsoe in northern Norway and at King's Bay, Spitzbergen; and a less important mast at Oslo, which would be visited only in order to show off the airship over the Norwegian capital. At two other stopping points on the long route to the north, in England and in Russia, full airship facilities already existed. The Norwegian Aero Club was erecting a large, three-walled but roofless hangar at Spitzbergen, to protect the airship from the Polar storms which can be unbelievably severe.

Italian critics of the venture pointed to another weakness. Because of Amundsen's understandable desire to ship as many of his 'old buddies' aboard as possible, only one trained airship officer would be flying with N.1 – and that would be Nobile. Amundsen had refused to have an all-Italian crew and so Nobile had had to pare down his men to the absolute bare minimum of five technicians.

There was Natale Cecioni, a thirty-nine-year-old Florentine, as chief motor mechanic. Twenty years in workshops, including fifteen years flying experience. He grumbled, he was rude, he spoke an atrocious Tuscan dialect – and he was tirelessly efficient. A big, bulky man almost as heavily built as the Norwegian giant, Riiser-Larsen, he was phlegmatic. When Nobile asked him if he wanted to take part in the first-ever flight over the North Pole, with a 50/50 chance of coming back (or not coming back, if one looked at it the other way), he said, 'Yes.' And that was all.

As the number two to Cecioni there was Ettore Arduino from Verona. A dozen years flying experience as engine mechanic, decorated for valour in the war. A calm, quiet man who, in contrast to Cecioni, never grumbled.

Then there was Attilio Caratti, thirty-years old, an experienced airship mechanic from Brescia. He very nearly did not make the trip because at his medical examination the doctor found that he had previously suffered from acute rheumatism in his joints which might recur on such a long and arduous flight. But when Nobile told him that, on medical grounds, he could not go, Caratti was so obviously distressed that Nobile reversed his decision. In a way, this was a weakness in Nobile; that he would try to be kind when sometimes it was not desirable. Amundsen, too, had a matching characteristic – that he tended to look after his old comrades, perhaps excessively so on occasion.

The only Southern Italian among them was another motor mechanic, Vincenzo Pomella; but he was not southern in looks, for he had fair hair and blue eyes.

Finally there was Renato Alessandrini, from Rome. A rigger by trade, his job was to assemble airships and then check the finished structure, both on the ground and in flight, by clambering around inside them and wriggling into the most inaccesible places. He knew N.1 literally inside out, having helped put the ship together. He brushed aside Nobile's attempt to outline the risks of the enterprise. 'You're going, so I'm going!'

Five men were few enough to handle a three-engined airship on a long and tiring flight; and there was only one officer, the sixth man – Nobile.

So Amundsen's 'old buddies', the Norwegians, would have to be used. And this meant that, with only a month to go, they would have to be trained. The only one of them with any airship experience at all was Riiser-Larsen, an aeroplane pilot who had attended a course in airship theory and made a few flights in British dirigibles; but he was a navigator as well, and so this was one of the tasks he could carry out in N.1. Another Norwegian, Oscar Omdal, was a motor mechanic who had flown in one of Amundsen's Dornier Wals, so he could be useful in this capacity. Yet another Norwegian, Birger Gottwaldt, could handle the wireless, together with the young Russian, Olonkin. The Arctic hunter Oscar Wisting was there because, as he had accompanied Amundsen to the South Pole, the old explorer thought he should be with him as he passed over the North Pole. Nobile decided to train Riiser-Larsen, Wisting, and another Norwegian, Emil Horgen, to handle the directional controls – the rudder and the elevators.

As meteorologist, they were to be joined by the young Swedish scientist, Finn Malmgren, professor of the University of Uppsala, who had served as meteorologist in Siberia with the *Maud* expedition. Nobile had first met him a few months previously when he had stopped at Oslo during a journey he was making to check the Russian airship facilities at Leningrad and to liaise with the Soviet officials, including the Red Air Force general, Zinovief, and the Foreign Minister, Emanuel Litvinoff. Malmgren's forecasts and observations, given the sudden severities of the Arctic weather, would be important and might be critical. Nobile was relieved to find him a level-headed young man, ready to face up to the risks. Malmgren told him, judiciously, 'I think the probability of success in this flight is about fifty per cent. But of course our own chances of survival are greater than that.'

On the first stage of the ferry flight there would be a French Air Force officer, Lieutenant Mercier, in case N.1 had to come down in France. Some of the critics suggested that Nobile's airship was not capable of getting even that far. Major G. H. Scott, the leading British airship pilot, would also fly the first stage to help with the landing at the British airship base of Pulham in Lincolnshire. Scott was to survive the N.1 in 1926 but not the R.101 in 1930.

Test flying of the modified N.1 began on 27 February, 1926. To show his confidence, King Victor Emmanuel was on board for one of the flights; but privately spoke to Nobile about the risks of icing, which he understood might be serious. The N-class were a successful type, with a number on order for foreign countries, including Japan, but Arctic flying was something else again. As for flying actually over the North Pole, no one had ever done that before, so the hazards could not be accurately assessed. Nobile's wife was so worried that as the time of final departure came near, she became unable to sleep at night. The only person who was not at all anxious, it seemed, was their eight-years-old daughter, Maria. On asking daddy where he was going, and being shown a map by her father, who pointed to Spitzbergen, Maria

instantly piped up: 'There? – Oh, there's nothing in that. You'll
be there in a moment!' In fact, Spitzbergen was rather more than
halfway, in a direct line, between Rome and Alaska. They would
not in fact be flying direct, but via some of the few bases in
Europe capable of handling airships.

However, Nobile had found that his calculations had come out
right. When the modifications had been done, and assuming that
there were no more than 16 people on board, the planned extra
lift of 3,500 lbs. was actually there. It would be enough, with a
small margin, to take the airship across the Arctic Sea from
Spitzbergen to the north coast of Alaska.

So, on 29 March, 1926, at Ciampino airport outside Rome, the
formal ceremony of handing over an Italian airship to yet another
foreign purchaser took place. Those were the days of grass airfields and petrol engines of no great power. Of canvas coverings
more often on wooden frameworks than metal. Of leisured flight,
more often from open cockpits than enclosed cabins. There was
a tangible smell of grass, petrol and oil in the open air, with the
breeze lazily lifting the windsock. And yet a pioneer atmosphere
of challenge, achievement, and risk.

Amundsen, in his best, knife-creased suit was there, with
Ellsworth; Amundsen wore a large bowler on top of an already
large head, so that he seemed top-heavy, as if the weight would
drive his tapered legs into the earth and anchor him there. But
he would wear these unsuitable formal clothes on such occasions
and for public photographs, rather than the serviceable leggings,
hunter's shirt and soft cap he used more frequently.

Mussolini, the Italian officers noted with relief, was also
correctly dressed, with bowler hat, wing-collar, and dark suit;
moreover, he had shaved that morning. Il Duce, having achieved
the foremost position in his own country, liked to be comfortable.
Sometimes he wore a Fascist black shirt, formal striped diplomatic trousers – and spats (they kept his feet warm). Sometimes
he did not shave for several days and was content to turn up in
the evening at some glittering ceremonial occasion, with stubble
on his cheeks. His wife rarely accompanied him, she felt herself
too obviously to be a peasant woman and very much out-of-place.

Nobile, of course, wore the uniform of a Colonel in the
Engineers. Italian officers' uniforms of this period tended to be
more flattering to male vanity than those of British officers, for
instance, although their pay was less. It was an arrangement

which suited them, while the opposite scheme seemed to satisfy the British. What was readily noticeable, however, was that the uniforms doled out to the ordinary British soldier, sailor or airman were so drab and ill-fitting as to be not merely disgusting but damaging to national prestige when abroad. They stated not merely the existing differences between officers and other ranks, but said a great deal more concerning the exact degree of regard in which the armed forces were held in England at this time. However, there existed a school of international thought which regarded Italian uniforms in general as hilarious comic opera. Amundsen, as it happened, shared this view.

Amundsen was surprised to find that the dirigible which was now to be handed over still bore the legend 'N 1' at bow and stern, with Italian colours unobtrusively painted on. Dr. Rolf Thommessen, who as president of the Norwegian Aero Club was formally accepting the airship from the Italians, had agreed to this. On the sides of the envelope, however, in tall lettering blazed the airship's new name, *Norge*. Formally, the N.1 was now the 'Norway'. The red-white-green banded flag of Italy was lowered and then the red-white-and-blue crossed flag of Norway was raised. The Italian flag was given to Mussolini who handed it to Nobile with the words, 'This is to be dropped on the ice at the Pole.' As the crowds cheered excitedly, he added, 'I'll come and see you off.'

Internally, the *Norge* looked 'distinctly picturesque', as Nobile put it. Room had had to be found for the masses of specialised stores which the airship had not been built to carry, and so they had been placed on the various girders. Then there was the personal kit and Arctic clothing of the crew to be embarked, so that there was hardly room to move, even in the control cabin. The most prominent new feature of the re-organised accommodation were two velvet-covered chairs made of light steel tubing, intended for the two masterminds, Amundsen and Ellsworth. Amundsen really worked at the business of command, and this was just another of his many measures taken to ensure that the project remained the AMUNDSEN-ELLSWORTH POLAR EXPEDITION and not the AMUNDSEN-ELLSWORTH-NOBILE POLAR EXPEDITION. He had told Nobile so personally; now he was saying it in steel and velvet.

3 April, 1926, the day appointed for the actual start, was dull and with rising winds threatened a storm. Mussolini was there to

see them go, as he had promised, but he was pale and his face was bandaged. The previous day he had narrowly survived an attempted assassination, the second. The first time, in 1925, the man had been arrested before he could shoot. This time the gun had been fired and the bullet had grazed Mussolini's nose, a very close call indeed. The would-be killer was an Irish revolutionary, the Hon. Violet Gibson. 'Fancy! A woman!' Mussolini had said afterwards, with apparent unconcern.

Nobile was desperately sorry that in these circumstances, and with everyone assembled, that he should have to cancel; but the weather, steadily worsening, threatened a disaster. Eventually, having made up his mind, he went over to Mussolini and told him that he was putting off their departure. 'Good! You're quite right,' replied Mussolini. 'It's better not to take the risk.' And as he said goodbye, he told Nobile, 'You'll succeed. I'm sure of it. You'll go – and come back victorious.'

It was a week more before the *Norge* got away at last. Amundsen and Ellsworth had left long ago, by train, for Oslo; and would later go on to Spitzbergen by ship to make sure the hangar and other facilities were ready to receive the airship on time. Including Major Scott, Lieutenant Mercier and an Italian journalist, there were 21 people on board – and one dog. The flying dog was Nobile's pet, Titina, ten inches high and weighing 12 lbs. Amundsen was to complain that Nobile, on grounds of weight, had refused to let the Norwegians bring with them some flying suits made specially for them in Berlin, while carrying unnecessary passengers. Of course, there are pressures in cases like this, and it may be that little Titina was Nobile's one real indulgence.

For the real start on 10 April, Nobile was at Ciampino airfield by seven o'clock. There were few spectators. His wife had promised to turn up later to see him off, but Nobile was worried that there would be a tearful scene to make the parting more difficult. She knew the risks very well, because his brothers had pointed them out, when asking her to stop him from making the flight at all. Nobile had not denied the hazards and had explained how he would like Maria brought up, supposing that he did not return. She had faced up to this with courage. It was only as the days passed and only 48 hours remained before the start, and then 24 hours and then 12 hours that her worry had made her utterly unable to sleep. At about nine o'clock she arrived with Maria, looking amazingly serene, trying to smile. She gave him a parting kiss and whispered, 'Go away happy!'

At 9.30 Nobile went on board. The airship was now held to the earth only by the muscles of the ground crew who were hanging on to the mooring ropes like a tug-of-war team. The three engines were slowly ticking over. Nobile signalled: 'Let go!' and the men who were pulling on the ropes released their hold. The *Norge*, with the Italian tricolour fluttering from the control cabin, rose slowly and majestically, the engines revving faster. The cheers, the shouts of farewell died away as the airship climbed and after parading over Rome turned out over the Tyrrhenian Sea and set course for France.

They were over the sea all day until dusk when they sighted the south coast of France. All night they were over France, at first speeding north with a violent wind reaching 36 m.p.h. behind them, blowing the airship onwards; then with a similarly strong wind against them, reducing their 50 m.p.h. cruising speed to a crawl over the actual ground. Nobile ordered higher revs, but an indicated airspeed of 58 m.p.h. gave only a small gain. In four-and-a-half hours they covered only 102 miles, from Angers to Rochefort. By dawn, the wind was not merely strong but squally and with a lot of up-or-down draughts which caused the airship to pitch and roll alarmingly. Nobile took her down towards the ground hoping for slower and stiller air at low altitude. It was mid-afternoon before the *Norge* had crossed the Channel and reached the British East Coast airship station at Pulham, where the landing proved difficult in spite of Major Scott being on hand.

While Colonel Nobile was being introduced to the waiting dignitaries who included the Crown Prince of Norway and the British Minister for Air, Sir Samuel Hoare, Titina was whining her heart out in prison. Although the English had allowed her to land, they had shut her away in a small storeroom as a temporary quarantine measure, and there she stayed all night, in great distress at being parted from her master. She would not even eat the food put before her. Next morning, one of the Italian crew members of the *Norge* went to comfort the dog and found that she had torn her collar in a desperate effort to get free. He let her out for a run and she promptly found Nobile and raced up to him. Then, exulting at her freedom, she tore away across the airfield and into a neighbouring field.

Shortly afterwards, a tall and impressive man in black uniform came up to Nobile. It was a senior police officer. If Titina was let out, he said, the law provided that she could be destroyed and her owner fined £200 into the bargain. So the dog went back to prison, where she whined continually, in spite of the attempts of her English gaolers to feed her sweets and give her a new collar.

Nobile's intended route had been a tour of Scandinavian capitals – Oslo, Stockholm and Helsinki – on the way to Gatschina near Leningrad where the *Norge* could be safely housed until such time as the forward bases at Vadsoe and King's Bay had been made ready. The significance of Leningrad was not merely that it possessed nearby that rare construction – an airship hangar – but that it housed in a former Czarist palace the Soviet Arctic Institute, a repository of knowledge many times larger than any comparable organisation anywhere in the world. The reason for this interest was, and is, that Russia occupies half the perimeter of the Arctic Circle.

Indeed, Amundsen's pride notwithstanding, it was a Czarist Russian officer, Lieutenant Nagurskiy of the Imperial Army who first flew over the Arctic. In the summer of 1914 he had made five rescue flights over the Barents Sea and Novaya Zemlya in a French Farman biplane fitted with floats and powered by a 70 h.p. Renault engine. This was the same year in which Amundsen bought the same type of machine and learnt to fly it, but was unable to make an actual Arctic flight. However, the outbreak of the Great War in August, 1914, brought all this to an end. The Russian aviator went to the front, while Amundsen gave his machine to the Norwegian Government for war purposes (although Norway was not involved). And, regardless of Amundsen's claims, the Soviet Government in the post-war years had helped pioneer practical Arctic aviation. In 1924 a German Junkers flown by Boris Tchukhnovsky (sometimes spelled Tschucknowski) had reconnoitred the North-East passage in advance of the shipping movements for the season, selecting the best route for the ships across the Kara Sea.

For the 705-mile flight from Pulham to Oslo the forecast of calm weather proved correct; but it was accompanied by fog. The *Norge* averaged 57 m.p.h. over the ground, which was good, but in Oslo the meteorologists warned Nobile that a depression was coming in from the Atlantic and advised that he leave before it arrived. Consequently, Nobile decided to cut short the rejoicings in the Norwegian capital, cancel his projected visits to the capitals of Sweden and Finland, and instead make direct for Gatschina airfield, outside Leningrad, passing over the Baltic states. Riiser-Larsen had trouble with his navigation and thought they were over Finland when in fact the airship was on the opposite side of the Baltic, above Esthonia and Lithuania. But the *Norge* reached Gatschina, 25 miles south of Leningrad, after a seventeen-hour flight covering 738 miles. Nobile had not slept, or even closed his eyes, for sixty hours – the penalty for being the only airship officer on board. But the date was 15 April, 1926, the exact day he had given to the Russians as a pure estimate some four months earlier. Now they merely had to wait for the other teams to complete the work at Vadsoe and King's Bay.

It was an ideal opportunity to get to know the Russians better and to hear what they had to say about aviation in the Arctic, indeed a continuation of the work of his preliminary visit back in January. The Soviet Government had rebuilt the hangar and equipped it as an airship base, so that necessary repairs and maintenance could be carried out on the *Norge*. The people themselves were extremely interested and friendly. The high point of the visit was a reception for the Italians, held at the Academy of Sciences, where Nobile met many of the most prominent men then working in this field. Basically, they were pessimistic about the prospects for the *Norge* expedition.

The degree of pessimism varied from individual to individual, Professor Rynin of the Institute of Aerial Communications, Leningrad, being particularly worried. It was the Arctic weather which bothered them, with its liability to snow-squalls and sharp drops in temperature. They assumed that ice or snow would form or accumulate on the airship and as the weight of it steadily grew, so it would force the airship down. They cited one particularly striking case they had encountered with a tethered 'kite' balloon. The balloon on its steel cable had risen into a freezing cloud. Within minutes, they said, a layer of ice an inch thick had formed round the steel mooring cable and brought the balloon to earth. Nobile had to listen in silence. This was the same idea, but delivered now with a wealth of experience behind it, which he had encountered from the King of Italy during the test flights of N.1 two months ago. There was no real answer but to fly over the Pole and find out.

At home in Italy, he had been resentful of criticism, suspecting (probably with reason) that internal politics lay behind the arguments; and this tended to obscure the fact that there was some substance in what the critics said, that N.1 was too small, her reserves of power and fuel insufficient for safety. One gambit his opponents had played was to enlist the aid of Gabriele d'Annunzio, Italy's poet-hero, to promote the idea of a rival and much larger semi-rigid airship which was to be designed by General Gaetano Arturo Crocco and Celestine Usuelli and piloted by General Giuseppe Valle. Nobile had had little difficulty in convincing other officers that a semi-rigid of the great size postulated was then a practical impossibility.

But the fact remained that the argument of his Italian opponents, that the N.1 class was not man enough for the job, served only to reinforce the Russian argument he was hearing now – that a Polar airship, by implication, must have a great deal of reserve lift and power to combat the weight of ice or snow which might form on the envelope during flight. At the back of many people's mind must have been the experience of Major G. H. Scott of the British Royal Air Force, when he had commanded R.34 in the first east-west crossing of the Atlantic in 1919. R.34 was a large rigid airship of 1,950,000 cubic feet, 643 feet long, with five engines of 250 h.p., based on the German Zeppelin L.33. Once committed to the flight, Scott discovered he had two stowaways on board. One was a small cat of no consequence, the other was a former crew member who had been stood down so that instead of his 200 lbs. weight, the same amount of extra fuel might be carried. The result was that R.34 reached New York with only two hours flying time left after a journey of 108 hours, a comparatively tiny margin.

The impractical giant semi-rigid to have been designed by General Crocco would have had a capacity of 120,000 cubic metres. The large rigid R.34 had a capacity of 53,218 cubic metres. The semi-rigid N.1 had a capacity of only 19,000 cubic metres, a sobering figure indeed. The great difference made by the R.34's stowaway, the nearly critical results of loading an extra 200 lbs., may have been in Nobile's mind when, in the weeks ahead, he was to take hurtful decisions concerning who could, and who could not, come on the epic flight across the Polar Sea.

What he could not alter were the command decisions as to when the flight was to be made and under what conditions the attempt might be aborted; he had attempted to obtain decisive status here, but Amundsen would only agree to 'consult' the Italian airship designer. The Norwegian relied heavily upon Riiser-Larsen and effectively regarded himself as the Commander and Riiser-Larsen as the Second-in-Command, with the only airship expert present being regarded purely as a chauffeur. It was going to be an awkward arrangement and must have worried Nobile a lot, particularly at moments like this, when the Russians were building objections and it was becoming clear that the *Norge* might have to turn back or be forced down. All the same, the irony of it was that he owed virtually everything to Amundsen and Riiser-Larsen, for it was they who had insisted on buying a particular airship, the N.1, and on employing a particular individual, its designer Umberto Nobile, to fly it for them. Had it not been for their stipulations, some other experienced airship man would most certainly have been chosen. Possibly General Valle, perhaps Colonel Pricolo.

In the last week of April a severe blizzard brought work on the King's Bay base to a halt, although Vadsoe was ready, and Amundsen cabled Nobile suggesting that the flight be put off until June. Nobile was exasperated. April was the last month of winter in the Arctic and by June the higher temperatures would reduce the airship's lift and make it impossible to fill the *Norge*'s tanks with enough petrol to make the long flight to Point Barrow of some 3,000 miles or more. Amundsen's additional idea, that in June the danger of icing might be less, ignored the fact that they had consulted the Arctic weather men and chosen the best time of the year, fog and airship technicalities taken into account, to ensure success: that is, mid-April to mid-May. Nobile cabled back that it was May now, or not at all, and Amundsen changed his mind again. Vallini, the Italian officer responsible for the work on the mooring mast and hangar at Spitzbergen telegraphed that both would be ready by 4 May, and so Nobile prepared to leave Leningrad.

At nine o'clock on the morning of 5 May, 1926 the *Norge* was brought out of the hangar at Gatschina. A strong wind was blowing and would be against them but the forecast for the route was generally favourable. In the Arctic, fog was the main hazard to fliers; but over the Barents Sea it was sudden cyclones of hurricane force, which might tear an airship in two. At 9.30 Nobile ordered the ground party to let go the ropes, someone shouted: 'Viva l'Italia!', the Russian soldiers cheered, and a Russian band struck up the Italian national anthem.

It was twenty-five miles to Leningrad from the airship base to the south, and for all twenty-five of them the *Norge* pitched and rolled like a ship in a storm, rose suddenly and as swiftly dropped again in the bumpy air. The Neva was blue, flecked with white specks of ice. Following the river at 700 feet, the *Norge* flew over the Winter Palace and along the Nevsky Prospect, cleanly glittering in the cold sunshine of a stormy spring day. No suggestion at all of the bloody events which had made these names symbolic of world drama in October, 1917, barely ten years before. And even as low as 700 feet, they were still too high to note the faces of the people, pinched, anxious in the aftermath of the Revolution.

Beyond the still-great city stretched the white, monotonous plain to the icy shores of Lake Ladoga. The air was calmer over the lake, because of the constant temperature of the surface of the blue water, and they had a respite from the bumping although the headwind was still strong. Crossing the far shore they flew on with constant buffeting from the squalls over an immense plain, streaked with dark trees, with stretches of stagnant water, and with snow. This was Karelia, partly in Finland, partly in Russia.

Inside the *Norge*, it was dark and cold, some of the crew stamping their feet to keep warm. Outside the sun was bright all day until it was almost sunset. Then the sky became grey and remained grey throughout the night until dawn; there was no actual darkness. The dark was behind them, to the south; they were flying north towards the eternal light of the Arctic summer. It was an odd sensation for Italians, although the Norwegians understood it well enough.

Shortly after four o'clock on the morning of 6 May they were at 2,200 feet, still over land, when the port engine began to run irregularly; finally it stopped. Examination showed that the crankshaft had snapped, a matter too serious to be repaired in flight. At 5.30 they were over Vadsoe, a pretty little Norwegian village sited on a long inlet of the sea, with the borders of Finland and Russia only a few miles away. While the ships in the harbour below blew off their sirens happily, Nobile moored to the mast which had been put up for them on a small island, and refuelling began. He decided not to wait to carry out the engine repair here, in case the weather should deteriorate for the critical crossing of the Barents Sea ahead of them. There are 780 miles of sea between

Vadsoe and King's Bay, the only land between being Bear Island at nearly the halfway point.

The land and sea area between (and including) Bear Island and Spitzbergen was known as the Svalbard. Spitzbergen itself consisted of two main islands (there are many smaller ones), of which one, confusingly, was called West Spitzbergen (Vestspitsbergen) and the other North-East Land (Nordaustlandet). There was no such place as East Spitzbergen. Many of the place names then were English, although Norwegian spellings are now more common. Almost everyone spoke of the airship's destination as King's Bay rather than Kongsfjorden, for instance. This was an arm of the sea surrounded by mountains reaching over 4,000 feet in height, not really a good site for a landing ground. However, on the southern arm of the bay was located the small settlement of Ny Aalesund (New Aalesund), grouped between the coal wharf and the coal mines which provided the reason for habitation in the first place. A few small colliers plied between the mines and the Norwegian ports. A handful of hunters had shacks along the coasts of Spitzbergen and made a living by killing bears, foxes and other animals for their pelts. It was a desolate place, gripped by ice, covered in snow. There was no airfield as such, only an open space near the newly-built hangar.

This was the goal of the Italians when at 3 p.m. Central European Time they slipped from the Vadsoe mooring mast and followed the Norwegian coast as far north as they could, before heading out over the ocean. Now the sky was clouding over, white horses began to appear on the backs of the grey, seemingly stationary waves, and a sudden hail of rain engulfed the airship, swiftly turning to snow. Remembering the warnings the Russian aviation experts had given him about the dangers from damp snow accumulating on the upper surfaces of the envelope, Nobile sent his chief rigger, Alessandrini, up top to check and report. But all was well – the snow was not sticking. Several times after that they flew through snow flurries without any build-up of weight on the envelope. Nobile became confident that there was nothing to fear from this hazard at this time.

It was just as well that the snow was not accumulating because, a few hours after flying over their first iceberg, the airship, labouring on over the sea on two engines, suffered yet another engine breakdown. Nobile drove the *Norge* on to the north on one engine for the two hours that it took to repair the trouble.

As if to assist him, the wind had dropped and the vicious buffeting and bumping motions had stopped. Having been on his feet for 40 hours, Nobile was exhausted and curled up in his sleeping-bag for a short lie-down, but was interrupted by a shout from the helmsman: 'Land ahoy!'

It was West Spitzbergen, an awesome mass of snow-streaked high ground and black rocks. Then the landscape ahead began to vanish as tendrils of fog drifted past the airship. This was a deadly hazard over mountainous country. One of Nobile's many preparations had consisted of arranging for signal balloons to be flown from the King's Bay landing ground so that they would rise above any fog bank and mark out the goal for a lost airship. As the fog grew thicker, Nobile radioed to Vallini at King's Bay, and had it confirmed that visibility was very low there and that a signal balloon had been sent up.

Keeping the *Norge* under the fog base, Nobile tried to feel his way clear of high ground by creeping along the coast, noting landmarks as they passed but prepared to turn away to open sea if the fog thickened, rather than be trapped inside any of the great fjords or channels between islands. In thickening fog, the airship droned along the seaward, safe side of Prins Karls Forland. Nobile did not make the dangerous turn inland to the east until he had received a further radio message, that the fog was rapidly thinning at King's Bay. At 6.15 they saw their base as a dark patch (the hangar) against a white snowfield at the foot of the hills which rose from the Bay. The airship circled once and then Nobile threw down the mooring rope to the Italians and Norwegians waiting to take it and haul the *Norge* down to the ground. Amundsen and Ellsworth were waiting there, and Nobile's brother Amedeo. There was a Norwegian navy ship also, the *Heimdal*, to act as a floating base.

But there was another ship as well, which flew the Stars and Stripes. This was the *Chantier*. And on the landing ground was the cargo she had brought – a big Dutch Fokker skiplane fitted with three 220 h.p. Wright Whirlwind engines. Its pilot was the American Navy aviator Lieutenant Richard Byrd. His goal was the North Pole.

Chapter 3

THE FLIGHT OF THE *NORGE*

AMUNDSEN, who had originally trained to be a physician, had become probably the most successful polar explorer of all time. He was first to winter in the Antarctic, first to sail the North-West Passage, first to reach the South Pole.

He had borrowed Nansen's *Fram* for an attempt on the Arctic, but was forestalled by an American naval officer, Commander Robert E. Peary, who dashed towards the North Pole first, and claimed to have reached it. As Amundsen himself wrote, to maintain his prestige, he had then needed a sensational success. With remarkable speed, and without notifying Nansen, he had taken the *Fram* south to the Antarctic, and had beaten the British naval officer, Captain Robert Falcon Scott, in a race to the South Pole.

And now, here he was, back again in the Arctic and about to chalk up one more triumph – the first flight over the North Pole – only to find yet another American naval officer getting in a fraction before him.

Naturally, Amundsen proclaimed that although the *Norge* would indeed pass over the North Pole on its way to Alaska, that was entirely incidental to the wider aim of a first exploratory crossing of the Polar sea which might result in the discovery of new lands within the Arctic. But the Norwegian explorer was a highly competitive, ruthless professional very much aware of his reputation; he did want to be first to fly over the North Pole. Just so had Scott, the amateur, really wanted to be first at the South Pole, although he had also a large scientific programme to carry out which supposedly justified the expedition. Apart from Sverdrup, almost the only Polar explorer who really did put science first before geographical 'firsts' was the Frenchman Dr. Jean-Baptiste Charcot, although even he admitted that if he had stumbled on a scientific road which would have led him first to the Pole, he would have taken it enthusiastically. Nobile, it seems, was also ambitious to reach the Pole with the *Norge* before Byrd in his Fokker; but his main preoccupation was with weight and range calculations for the hazardous crossing of the frozen sea.

Byrd had reached Spitzbergen with his ship the *Chantier* some days before Nobile in the *Norge*, but Amundsen had been before them both. When Byrd entered King's Bay, the Norwegian ship *Heimdal*, attached to the Amundsen-Ellsworth expedition, was lying alongside the only quay and taking up all of it, the loading and discharge facilities in Spitzbergen being meagre. So the *Chantier* was blocked off from the quay and thus unable to put ashore the Fokker trimotor Byrd had brought with him. Amundsen stated that the *Heimdal* was not only taking on coal and water but undergoing essential boiler repairs. Those who remembered how Amundsen in 1909 had taken the *Fram* south, when her owner, Nansen, had lent her for an Arctic expedition, and how Amundsen had then trumped Scott at the South Pole, doubted this story, and were to say so.

Whatever Byrd may have thought, he acted as if Amundsen's critics might be right. He did not wait the few days Amundsen said were necessary for the *Heimdal* to complete her business at the quay. Instead he decided to float his aeroplane ashore onto the beach direct, by-passing the obstructed quay. The American had four boats lashed together and boards laid across them to make an aeroplane platform which could be towed to the beach. This has been a standard method among military men for carrying out river crossings for many years (Caesar was particularly adept), but it took Amundsen by surprise.

According to Amundsen, Nobile was very keen to get to the Pole ahead of Byrd. The Italian came to him and said that the *Norge* could be ready in three days. The Norwegian already suspected, wrongly, that Nobile's ambitions went only as far as the Pole and this explained why he had clamoured unsuccessfully for the right to turn back. The Norwegian simply did not understand the tiny margin by which, in the *Norge*, they would either live or die, and consequently that Nobile was preoccupied with the matter of range.

For his part, surprisingly, Nobile found Amundsen in no great hurry to get the *Norge* away on the trans-Arctic flight. Amundsen gave high-minded reasons for this later, but at the time, according to Nobile, Amundsen considered that the snow was much too thick to allow the American to take off in his big tri-motor Fokker, and so there was no hurry to get the *Norge* repaired and ready. Amundsen's opinion on a matter of aviation was worth little, but as ever he was boosted by the beliefs of an aide-de-camp. In this case it was Riiser-Larsen, who did have considerable experience with aircraft, and who dismissed with Norwegian contempt the type of skis fitted to the Fokker. Byrd would never unstick using those, he thought. In a way, he was right – the skis broke. But a Norwegian, Bernt Balchen, made Byrd another pair and these were of the Norwegian type.

On the night of 8th–9th May the blare of three aero engines snarled to a crescendo as the laden Fokker slithered across the snow, the note changing to a deep rumble as the heavy machine lifted on its skis. Richard E. Byrd and Floyd Bennett were airborne and headed for the Pole.

Some 15½ hours later, while Amundsen's party were at dinner, someone remarked that if Byrd and Bennett were ever to return, then they were due now, the distant drone of their engines was heard. The mixed group of Norwegians and Italians rushed out onto the field and surrounded the plane when it had taxied to a stop. Amundsen called for 'nine good Norwegian cheers' for the two aviators, a moment which his own film man caught. Byrd's cine photographer was not present because the American's party were still at table in the *Chantier*, the Fokker having returned unexpectedly early. Consequently, the next day the scene of welcome, starring Byrd, Amundsen and Ellsworth, was re-staged for the benefit of Byrd's cameraman, with only Norwegians and Americans in shot. The Italians were there, watching, but they had to stay out of camera. Nobile did not meet Byrd until next day, when the American invited the four leaders of the *Norge* expedition to dine with him.

The early return was to cause doubts as to whether or not Byrd really had reached the Pole. Could he have done it in the time, considering the known performance figures of the Fokker coupled with the weather conditions? Professor G. H. Liljequist, of the University of Uppsala, was many years later to publish a paper showing that he could not have done. Nobile liked the young American, but also doubted whether he had really got as far as the Pole. Amundsen, tactfully for a change, pointed out what a great feat of sheer navigation had been achieved, an oblique method of expressing disbelief. Later, it was said,

Byrd's co-pilot, Bennett, admitted to Balchen that they had never left the coast of Spitzbergen. Peary, of course, had had no European witnesses at all.

No one knew better than the experienced Polar explorers just how difficult it was to know when one was really at or only near the Pole; and even if weather conditions were perfect for observation, there were greater difficulties ahead in proving that one had actually been there. Most people, including Amundsen, believed that the American Robert E. Peary had reached the North Pole in 1909; although some doubters were never convinced. Very few people, however, believed that his American rival, Dr. Frederick A. Cook, had reached the Pole in 1908. Amundsen himself was able to point out with some glee that his own claim to have reached the South Pole in 1911 was corroborated from the best source possible – the diary kept by his rival, Captain Scott, and found in the death tent afterwards. The British party, heading for the Pole, had homed in on the Norwegian flag planted by Amundsen, a tiny speck in the wasteland. The Norwegians had stayed three days and during that time had explored for a distance of ten miles around it, so as to cancel out any possible small error in fixing the actual position of the Pole.

In the Arctic there are special difficulties in navigation when using a magnetic compass, because the magnetic pole wanders and is usually situated at varying distances on the Canadian side of the geographical North Pole. For this reason, Amundsen had invented a sky compass. With this the reference point from which calculations could be made, was the sun. On the course from Spitzbergen to Alaska, however, use of the ordinary compass might be possible, the solar compass being used as a check at those times when the sun was visible. Position, as distinct from course, would have to be worked out from observations of the sun, when visible, taken with a sextant, which is an instrument really requiring a steady platform for extreme accuracy. A vibrating aeroplane fuselage is not such a platform, nor is an airship car in bumpy air conditions.

If the *Norge* deviated very much from her track because of compass trouble or difficulties in obtaining observations of the sun, then the result was likely to be a series of wild zigzags – the opposite of the shortest route. Over a length exceeding 3,000 miles such errors would result in the actual distance flown being much greater – and the airship would consequently run out of fuel before reaching Alaska. With fairly favourable conditions and reasonably good navigation, Nobile was reckoning on a minimum of 65 hours flying time. That was based on the possibility of meeting head-winds of up to 24 m.p.h., which would cut the airship's speed over the ground in half. But if the head-winds were stronger than this, or if fog caused navigation to be imprecise so that the *Norge* wandered badly from her course, the airship would not have enough fuel to reach North America.

Nobile was trying every way possible to increase the amount of petrol carried beyond the minimum of 130 cwt. Already, he had decided virtually to do without ballast, a very bold move, and convert the four water ballast tanks to fuel tanks. The only way to increase the useful load was to obtain very high lift. This meant that atmospheric conditions had to be just right – that is, high pressure combined with relatively low temperature; and a start at the coldest hour of the night, so that a maximum amount of gas might be put into the cells. Given all this, Nobile calculated on surpassing a figure of 210 cwt. useful load, which enabled him to embark 140 cwt. of petrol and $7\frac{1}{2}$ cwt. of oil.

Nobile now met for the first time Dr. Frantisek (Franz) Behounek of the University of Prague in Czechoslovakia. He was then in his late twenties, very boyish looking for a scientist, and fascinated by the airship. Behounek, whose field was wireless, had come to King's Bay to study the electrical conductivity of the atmosphere in the far north, and he wanted permission from Nobile to fit a small measuring instrument in the control cabin of the airship. 'But who will take the measurements?' enquired Nobile, who was trying to reduce crew numbers, not increase them.

'Oh, I've already come to an agreement with Dr. Malmgren,' said Behounek. Malmgren, a Swedish scientist just turned thirty, of the University of Uppsala, was the meteorologist of the expedition who, with the aid of the wireless operators receiving weather data was to advise Nobile regarding the pressure, temperature and wind patterns which lay ahead. So Nobile consented, and the instrument was installed. Radio was somewhat uncertain in the Arctic and if it was to be used as a navigational aid, the more information about its present weakness's the better.

In addition to technical aeronautical questions and the requirements of the scientists associated with the expedition, there was the purely Polar aspect of survival in the Arctic, if in fact the airship had to come down. The Norwegians were the experts here and their Aero Club had provided 834 lbs. of Arctic survival rations, enough to last one month. To provide beyond that time, the principal resource consisted of two rifles, a good supply of ammunition, and Oscar Wisting, the hunter. In effect, this was the idea expressed by Stefansson, that one could live off creatures like bears, seals and birds, but that there was a lot more meat in a bear than in a bird. Nobile hoped, without much conviction, that if they had to come down it would be in an area of the Arctic where the Norwegians' ideas could be vindicated.

Nobile was determined to keep the crew numbers down to 16 or less, as agreed with the Aero Club of Norway. There were always pressures to increase them and discarding willing volunteers could be unpleasant, particularly if they had governments behind them. Quite a number of people had ridden in the airship between Rome and Spitzbergen, some flying in her only for a single stage. At Spitzbergen there were three journalists, Cesco Tomaselli of the Milan *Corriere della Sera*, Fredrik Ramm, covering the flight for the Aero Club of Norway, and Lebedenko the Russian. Nobile would have liked to eliminate them all, but could only get rid of the Italian and the Russian; the Norwegian had to come because the Aero Club had signed press contracts. But he did get rid of Amundsen's nephew, Gustav Amundsen, no doubt without regret; but it was harder to deprive himself of two Italian crew members, the chief helmsman Lippi and the workman Bellocchi. However, it had to be done. At the last moment, the Russian wireless operator Olonkin was changed for a Norwegian, Storm-Johnsen. That left 16, of whom two, Roald Amundsen and Lincoln Ellsworth, in Nobile's eyes, could probably have been dispensed with; unless of course new land was found and there had to be a token occupation.

At the final count, there were eight Norwegians: Amundsen, Riiser-Larsen, Horgen, Gottwaldt, Wisting, Omdal, Storm-Johnsen, and Ramm; one Swede: Malmgren; one American: Ellsworth; and six Italians: Nobile, Natale Cecioni, chief engine mechanic, Ettore Arduino, assistant chief engine mechanic, Attilio Caratti, engine mechanic, Vincenzo Pomella, engine mechanic, Renato Alessandrini, rigger and helmsman.

There were 24 Italians at King's Bay, aircrew and ground crew, as well as Norwegians who helped on the ground. On 10 May the Italian workmen were busy all day in and around the *Norge*, loading equipment, provisions, petrol and oil, with Nobile supervising this critical part of the preparations. At 10 p.m., with every task completed except the filling of the engine radiators with anti-freeze, Nobile left to go to his quarters and pack. As he stepped out of the hangar, he found that a wind had got up, with gusts blowing diagonally across the hangar's mouth. That was alarming, because unlike an aeroplane an airship is not grounded under its own weight; further the hull area offered to the wind is much greater. Getting an airship out of a narrow hangar in these conditions can be tricky, and, when the wind went on increasing in strength, Nobile called a halt for several hours, hoping that the gusts might die away. He told Amundsen and sent his own men off to snatch at least a few hours sleep.

But at about one o'clock on the morning of 11 May, Nobile's own attempt to rest was broken by a report from Malmgren the meteorologist that the night had become calmer. It was also very cold, which was exactly what Nobile wanted, so he had the engine mechanics roused, the anti-freeze put in the radiators, and sent Omdal to tell Amundsen that the Norwegian ground crew would be required by 4 a.m. to secure a 5 a.m. start to the flight.

At the latitude of Spitzbergen, around this time of the year, the sun never actually disappears. It merely comes very close to the horizon at about one in the morning, when the air is at its coldest, and then begins to ascend slowly, with the air gradually becoming warmer. As it did so, the gas in the cells of the *Norge* began to expand. Soon, Nobile had to begin valving off gas, which would reduce their lift. It was a matter of urgency now that the Norwegians should not be late, but they were. There was no sign of them at 4 o'clock. There was no sign of them at 5 o'clock. By the time 6 o'clock approached, Nobile had had to valve off gas three times and to offset this had had 4 cwt. of petrol unloaded, thus reducing their range. By this time, he was fed up with Norwegians. He had been working all day, had spent a sleepless night, mostly in the cold hangar, and now he angrily threw himself down to rest under a rug on the floor of the control cabin.

Time dragged on until, after 7 a.m., the Norwegian ground crew began to arrive, and much later still the Big Three – Amundsen, Ellsworth and Riiser-Larsen – contented after their breakfast. Nobile, lacking both a night's rest and a warm meal, and seeing that the wind had now risen again and was blowing across the hangar and might wreck the take-off, had generated a head of steam which Amundsen passed off contemptuously as mere 'nervous excitement.' However, he tried to explain to the Norwegians in English that he would wait for a lull in the gusts, and if one came, they would have to move quick to get the vulnerable *Norge* clear of the enclosing hangar walls. Riiser-Larsen took over the task of transmitting the commands in Norwegian and then Nobile, taking advantage of yet another shift in wind direction – this time almost along the axis of the hangar – ordered the movement forward to be begun. There was a tense moment, for him, when the fin nearly touched the hangar walls, for he knew that a minor graze with small damage would mean cancelling the flight. And then the airship was out on the field, with take-off assured.

While Amundsen waited impatiently, Nobile had the airship 'weighed'. There was just enough excess gas to put on board 1½ cwt. of ballast, this consisting of two sandbags and some cans of petrol. Rarely can there have been so slim a reserve of lifting power. The weight of petrol now on board amounted to 137 cwt., less than he had hoped to carry by some 3 cwt., this being the penalty for the loss of valved-off gas caused by the late start.

At 9.50 a.m. Nobile gave the order for the ground crew to let go the ropes holding the *Norge* down to the snowfield. As she rose to 100 feet, he had the engines speeded up and the dirigible went up rapidly to 1,200 feet. It was a bright, cloudless morning and the snow-covered peaks of Spitzbergen glittered in the sun above them. The smaller peaks rose to twice the height at which they were flying, while to the north the white outline of Drygalskikammen soared 4,669 feet into the blue sky. Nobile's fatigue and irritation fell away like magic. Only hours before, he had been shivering with cold. Now he felt light, encumbered by his Arctic furs and would have liked to take them off.

The *Norge* flew down the fjord below the level of the mountains and then turned north with the trend of the coastline which, because of its great height, she must follow. Her speed was 48 m.p.h. and the North Pole was 770 miles away. The effect of the speed was felt almost at once. As the icy slipstream cooled the gas in the cells, they shrank and the dirigible lost lift. She became neutrally buoyant, and then heavy. If left to herself, the airship would go on down until she crashed into the sea, among the ice-flows. Nobile ordered a movement of the elevators to bring the nose up by between 3 and 6 degrees, as this gave dynamic lift.

In a nose-up attitude, as if sniffing the air, the dirigible forced her way forward.

King's Bay had been white with ice, but the open sea was specked rather than covered with ice-flows. Ahead cloud was forming against the blue sky and there was a strange white streak along the horizon, which the Italians were seeing for the first time – the reflection off the pack-ice north of Spitzbergen. The sky began to cloud over as the line of the pack-ice margin grew clearer. Flying at 1,350 feet they had a close view of Danes Island as it went below them, the highest peak there being 1,121 feet. Twenty-nine years before, in 1897, the Swede Andrée and his two companions had set off in their balloon from Danes Island, to drift with the wind over the North Pole, if all went well. A carrier pigeon came back bearing the message: 'All's well on board', and two message buoys drifted ashore years after, but as to whether they had reached the Pole or not, no one knew. No further messages had come out of the north and no trace had ever been found of the three men or their balloon. The mystery was not to be solved until 1930, when a remarkable discovery was to show that the balloon had been forced down for lack of ballast. Exactly the same predicament as that in which the *Norge* now was, except that the dirigible could use engine-power as a temporary expedient to maintain height while she gained lift by losing the weight of the petrol she consumed.

By late morning the airship's shadow was fleeting across the jumbled sunlit surface of the pack-ice, under a sky of pure blue. Nobile took out a stop-watch and measured the speed of the racing shadow below him. The result gave a ground-speed of 33½ m.p.h., instead of their cruising air speed of 50 m.p.h. There must be quite a strong headwind. Low down, because of friction, winds blow less strongly. There was no trouble in getting the *Norge* to lose height, Nobile found. As soon as the helmsman moved the controls to make the airship fly level instead of in a dog-begging nose-up attitude, she sank at nearly 4 feet a second. But the manoeuvre worked. Down at 600 feet, the winds blew more slowly and the airship gained 9½ m.p.h.

From that height a surprising amount of detail could be seen – a white fox, for instance, visible even against the white background, and the double paw-prints of bears, and in pools of water and channels between the ice, the flickering movements of fish swimming below the surface. The last trace of bears, and indeed of all visible life, was seen just beyond the 83rd parallel. Beyond was only an ice desert, a white plain streaked with the grey-blue hues where only a thin covering of ice hid the sea. Plainly, this was a frozen ocean. Unlike Antarctica, which is a real continent, with real land and real mountains, the Arctic so far was proving to be nothing but sea, just water, and not even completely frozen over. Of course, beyond the Pole there was always that distant mountain range which Peary had thought he had glimpsed. If it really existed, now they would discover it. Or, at any rate, very soon now.

By noon, altitude unchanged at 600 feet, the airship was still doing 43 m.p.h. towards the Pole. Nobile thought he saw indications that at height the wind might have changed direction, for often winds blow in different directions at different levels, and ordered a climb. At 3,650 feet, their indicated ground speed had increased to 51½ m.p.h. For eight hours or so they droned on over the sunlit pack at this much greater height. Had there been life below, probably they would not have noticed. The *Norge* was still too heavy, by between 800 and 1,000 lbs., but she was consuming fuel steadily and becoming lighter all the time. There was nothing to worry about.

Cecioni, the chief mechanic, burst into the control cabin to report that the engines were running well. Jubilantly, he cried: 'So this is the terrible Pole!'

'Just wait!' replied Nobile, 'you could be crowing too soon!'

Shortly after this, the port engine stopped. On examination, the trouble proved to be a peculiar and novel form of icing inside the fuel lead to the carburettor, perhaps caused by water-vapour. This happened once more before they reached the Pole.

In the evening the weather began to change, cloud covering the sky almost completely. In 88° degrees of latitude the cloud cover rolled away, but only briefly. Below, the numerous and regular channels in the pack-ice showed that there was only frozen water here; no land at all. At 10.15 p.m. came snow, and then dense fog, accompanied by the formation of ice. It was unbelievably rapid. Within minutes of entering fog, the outer metal parts of the dirigible were a sheet of ice; the celluloid windows were largely covered and vision obscured; and ice began to appear even inside the control cabin. The Arctic was not quite so tame as they had begun to imagine.

Nobile countered this alarming danger, which would first

blind and then force them down, by ordering a climb to 2,000 feet. Still, ice continued to form, and must defeat them if allowed to advance unchecked. Nobile took the *Norge* up to nearly 3,000 feet, where she was poised above the deadly, freezing fog.

The man with the easiest job was Amundsen, as he was himself to point out. As the chief explorer of the expedition, all he had to do was sit in his velvet covered chair and observe. Easily the worst task fell to the rigger Alessandrini. He did a bit of everything, from giving a hand with the steering to inspecting the interior of the airship from bow to stern, not just the control cabin and engine cars but inside the hull; and now and then he had to inspect the outside of the hull to check for the presence of ice and make sure that the gas-valves were properly closed and not leaking away the precious gas. This last job involved squirming through a small window at the bow, climbing up a steel ladder which rose steeply, attached to the outside of the hull, and then, in an icy airstream blasting along the hull at nearly 50 miles an hour, crawl the complete length of the outside of the airship – a distance of almost 80 yards – while clinging for support with one hand to a guide rope. The hull underneath him was not solid – it yielded like a mattress. Few would relish performing such feats in the skies over Naples in summer. To carry them out while rapidly approaching the North Pole in an airship underflying a dismal blank cloud cover and nosing along on top of a thinning bank of freezing fog in an air temperature of 14 degrees Fahrenheit, required nerve and determination of the highest order. But each time he came back and reported to Nobile: 'All's well!' Once, and once only, did the rigger have to report failure. The valves had not been checked because the layer of ice then forming on top of the envelope was too slippery to negotiate (in a howling, 50 m.p.h. blast of air which even under normal conditions would make it hard to keep one's eyes open).

Arduous in a different way were the exertions of Riiser-Larsen, the navigator, who was virtually unable to relax. Even on a little cross-country flight of 100 miles or so, an aeroplane or airship pilot in those days would pick out, say, ten landmarks, noting an estimated time of arrival over each, while he's still on the ground, plotting. The first might be a pond, the second a peculiarly-shaped wood, the third a marked curve in a river, the fourth a railway crossed at right-angles, the fifth a small lake, and so on – all being landmarks which show up well from the air, and spaced

3

about ten minutes flying time apart. On sighting the landmark, the pilot would note the actual time (which would tell him something of what the wind was doing to speed or to slow him), and also his position relative to the landmark, directly above it or off to one side, and which side it was, and by how much, (which would give him further information on any possible changes of wind speed or direction). But there are no landmarks on the pack-ice, the distance to be covered is measured in thousands of miles and not in hundreds, and the time to cover it would be three days instead of an hour or two.

Consequently, Riiser-Larsen had to navigate by 'dead' (i.e., 'deduced') reckoning, corrected by constant checks on drift, and on speed, and on course (as shown by the magnetic compass, verifed or otherwise by the Amundsen sun compass), and on position by measuring the height of the sun, if that was possible, from the difficult, vibrating observation point of an airship cabin. If there was thick fog or cloud above, of course it was not possible.

At fifteen minutes to midnight on 11 May, the log of the *Norge* recorded: Drift – Nil; speed over the ground – $42\frac{1}{2}$ m.p.h.; temperature outside the airship – 14.00°F (approx. 2 °C); temperature inside the airship – 24.8°F.; altitude – 2,350 feet. Only scattered streaks of fog obscured the dead, frozen plain below. The atmosphere had taken on a pearly-grey hue. Inexorably, it seemed, the airship was coming down, the needle on the dial of the altimeter slowly, ever so slowly, creeping round. They were at latitude 89 degrees north. Nearly there. The Pole is of course at 90 degrees. And after that, they would be going downhill – towards North America and a new continent.

At fifty minutes into the new day, 12 May, 1926, Nobile ordered a definite descent, in place of the prolonged fall which the *Norge* had been undergoing. The needle of the altimeter dial began to revolve faster. In ten minutes they were down to 1,000 feet, and within minutes had sunk to 750 feet. Almost there. Riiser-Larsen, crouched at a porthole, the eyepiece of the sextant held steady by his hands, was ready to snatch the altitude of the sun the moment it appeared again from behind the clouds. But no one said a word to disturb his concentration.

Then Nobile called out to Alessandrini, the man who managed everything: 'Get the flag ready!' This was the big flag worn by N.1, before she became the *Norge*, which Mussolini had com-

manded be put into a special casket and dropped over the Pole.
So there was a kind of performance, as the flag was taken from
its casket, unrolled, and attached to its staff, with loving care, by
Alessandrini.

'Hurry up!' said Nobile.

Amundsen said nothing, but what he thought he spilled into
many paragraphs in his book, *My Life as an Explorer*. His own
flag, the banner of Norway, and also the Stars and Stripes
brought by Ellsworth, were only token flags, about as large as a
handkerchief; and this because Nobile had impressed on them all,
continually, the necessity of saving weight.

At 1.30 a.m. the sun was shining in and out, with regularity,
from behind the clouds. It should be possible to check their
position by sextant with fair accuracy. So Nobile ordered the
engines slowed and the *Norge* brought down to within 600 feet of
the frozen sea which was the reality of the Pole. Amundsen and
Ellsworth cheered and threw out their tiny flags. Nobile threw out
a number of flags on behalf of various organisations and, finally,
the large flag – for Italy. 'PLANTED THE ITALIAN FLAG AT
THE POLE', he wrote in the log-book. 'May 12, 1926, 1.30 a.m.'

Amundsen laughed rudely.

Alessandrini beamed his way back into the cabin, and exulted
to Nobile. 'Ours was the most beautiful!' he said.

If Byrd had not reached his goal on 9 May before turning back,
then the men of the *Norge* must be the first to fly over the Pole.
However, this was genuinely a mere prelude to the exploratory
phase of the flight. Peary had said, that from the Pole, he had
thought he had vaguely glimpsed a range of mountains far away
on the frozen horizon. If he had not been deceived, this would
confirm the theories of those geographers who favoured a
'balance' of land masses on the globe, requiring something in
the North to counter the weight and extent of Antarctica in the
South. This was a modern version of an ancient illusion by which
the ignorant geographers of the old world had in the sixteenth
century misled the first practical seafarers to attempt the circum-
navigation of the globe. But if the idea in its most modern guise
proved to be not illusion but fact, then indeed Amundsen would
crown his career with great achievement. Nobile believed that
Amundsen could see himself pointing out from the cabin of the
Norge the first traces of that new territory; and of the airship

hovering low over the snow to lower Amundsen and Wisting and Ellsworth to the ground to take possession. And what would that new land be called? Without doubt, it could be known as none other than Roald Amundsen Land.

At and beyond the Pole the desolation was unchanging, the irregularities of the icy plain wan under a grey sky, picked out occasionally by a yellowish gleam from the horizon. Under them, some 2,000 feet below, there was nothing but frozen sea. Then, between 85° of latitude and 82° 40', the airship was in fog with no sight of what lay beneath. Twelve hours and 540 miles approximately beyond the Pole, and still in fog, a kind of explosion was heard in the control cabin. At least, that was what it sounded like. Nobile suspected that one of the rotor blades for the wireless had broken, making that sharp, sinister noise. That would be unimportant, because the radio had been out of action for some hours, and they were no longer able to receive navigational checks by taking a bearing on the transmissions of known stations. But enquiry showed that the rotor was intact, although a sleeve of ice had formed round the radio antenna.

Then some of the Italian engineers came excitedly to report that they had located both the cause and the result of the 'explosion'. Ice had formed even on the revolving blades of the airscrews, and a sliver of ice from the starboard motor being run by Arduino had broken off and been whirled away at high speed by the rapidly revolving propellor. Like a sling-shot, it had struck the outer covering of the airship and torn it open. It was as if their own engines had, in conditions of icy fog, turned into self-destroying artillery to bring them down. Looking at his notes afterwards, Nobile could see that at this point in the long flight his log-book entries degenerated into rapid scribbles, as brief as possible. For some time, he was hard-pressed to find a remedy.

Alessandrini reported that ice had formed anew on all the metal parts of the hull, but particularly on the front surfaces most exposed to the wind of their passage. There was some 3 mm. on the solar compass, which explained why that instrument also had now ceased to work.

At 3.37 p.m. Nobile jotted down a note that the airship had reached static equilibrium, or neutral buoyancy, when one would have expected her to have become so light as to require the valving off of some of the gas. After 30 hours flying the three engines had consumed about 2½ tons of petrol and oil, but still there was no tendency for her to rise. The *Norge* must be very heavy with the weight of ice on her hull.

As they had now ridden clear above the fog-belt, this did not worry Nobile so much as the thought of the sudden loss of gas from an already heavy airship, which the ice splinters could easily cause. What he did not yet understand was how the pro-pellors could ice up so much as to cause this danger. Alessandrini came in with a further report: the hull had been holed in several places opposite the starboard engine gondola. Undoubtedly, the propellors were causing the trouble. But so far, it was only the outer envelope covering the air chamber which had been holed; the upper chamber holding the gas was still intact.

Now and then came a further sinister noise, as another ice-splinter ripped into the *Norge*. At length, Nobile came to the conclusion that the ice came mainly from the hull, not the air-screws. He reasoned that the wind over the hull caused by their forward motion was tending to break up some of the ice which had formed on the envelope; that some of this ice, as it fell, showered over the engines and pieces struck the propellors, to be violently thrown off, some being deflected into the hull. So there might be a further danger, that these slabs of ice might actually smash a propellor and that flying pieces of the whirling blades themselves might be deflected into the hull, piercing the gas chamber and bringing the *Norge* down onto the pack-ice.

Based on this analysis, he ordered the central engine, which was fairly well-protected from the showers of ice from above, to be run at normal revolutions, while the outer engines, which were receiving most of the ice, should be slowed down and thus reduce the violence of the projectiles they were slinging against the hull. As his order was obeyed, the speed of the *Norge* fell away and a period of calm succeeded the crisis.

Going south beyond 80 degrees latitude, the fog began to open out, giving glimpses of what lay below. It was still pack-ice, heaped and irregular; frozen ocean not frozen land. There were of course no landmarks but it was possible to measure the drift of the airship, now that there was a visible surface underneath them. Their calculations indicated a drift sideways of 13 degrees to the left. The wind must have changed direction and increased in strength, putting the airship off course.

It was 32½ hours since the *Norge* had risen from the snow-field at Spitzbergen. Nobile, most of the Italians and some of the

Norwegians had been on their feet, with little or no rest, preparing
the airship and then flying it, for over two days. Looking round
the cabin, Nobile was appalled at the disorder caused by so many
people having to work for so long in such a confined space. 'The
cabin was horribly dirty,' he wrote. 'The dozens of thermos
flasks heaped on the floor, near the little cupboard where we kept
the charts and navigation books, presented a particularly sad
spectacle: some of them empty, others overturned, others
broken. Coffee and tea had been spilt everywhere, and all over the
place were the remains of food. In the midst of all this mess there
stuck out picturesquely Amundsen's enormous feet, with his
grass-stuffed shoes, his diver's gaiters and red and white gloves.'

They crossed the 79th parallel of latitude at 6.30 p.m. The
promontory of Point Barrow in Alaska lay ahead; and underneath,
through the occasional gaps in the fog, lay only sea ice. Although
the crew of the *Norge* had lost sight of what was below them for
some hours at a time, because of the icing which had occurred in
the thickest of the fog banks, and forced them up, and therefore
they could not say with precision that there might not have been
islands below in that area, there was certainly no extensive
landmass, no new continent. Every time they had seen the ground,
it proved not to be land at all but merely a thin crust of ice on the
surface of a frozen sea – the Arctic Ocean. And they were the first
to cross it. For Amundsen only, was this a defeat.

Of course, the track of the airship allowed them to cover only
a narrow visual path; therefore, there might be isolated land
areas to one side or the other; but no continent. The triumph of
the *Norge* was really to discover a negative. But in the mind of the
public, the primary achievement would appear an aeronautical
one: the flight itself, not the information obtained from it.

Nobile, looking down, noted that the ice surface looked much
rougher than between Spitzbergen and the Pole, but that the
scenic impression was magnificent – exactly as he had imagined
it. A white world veiled in whitish transparent mist, cut by long,
meandering channels coloured grey, streaked elsewhere with
blue. The *Norge* herself had begun to merge into this Arctic
landscape, for an ice coating more than half an inch thick again
hid the metal parts of the hull, while the engine gondolas were
picked out in white along their cables and gangways. This new
ice formation may have looked beautiful but might be deadly
for again they were threatened by splinters of ice.

Above the fluctuating noises of the wind, which at one moment could produce a note like a trumpet, and the next sound like a factory siren blasting off below them, an illusion which convinced Alessandrini for a moment that they must be over an industrial area! Nobile was startled by a most sinister noise inside the ship. On going to investigate, he found a place opposite the starboard engine where the outer envelope had been torn open for a yard. The wind, if allowed to work at this, could strip off much greater amounts of the protective outer covering, and thus allow the next shower of ice splinters to hit and tear the vulnerable gas cells. Cecioni began to mend the tear, telling Nobile: 'The emaillite is nearly finished.' They had used up an unprecedented amount of this sticky stuff because of the unforeseen hazard caused by the splinters. The pack-ice below did not look inviting, impossible to sledge on that, thought Nobile. Even from a height of 750 feet, which tends to flatten perspectives, the surface seemed unpleasantly jagged.

Some hours later that morning Riisen-Larsen called out: 'Land ahead to starboard!' And truly, there in the distance was a line of pearl-grey hills. Alaska, north of the Yukon river. They had done it! A mixture of excitement and joy thrilled the tired men.

That morning Captain George H. Wilkins, the Australian aviator and his Norwegian-American co-pilot Lieutenant Ben Eielson, were at Point Barrow. They had been there for days, hoping to carry out their programme of exploratory flights over unknown parts of the Arctic, but continually frustrated by fog which never cleared for more than an hour or two. The local wireless station had picked up the news that the *Norge* had started and, making their own calculations, they were on the lookout before the expected time. The weather had been very dull early on, but later the cloud cover began to break up, and there, picking its way between the clouds the two airmen saw a small dark object coming towards them – the *Norge*.

'That was perhaps the greatest thrill of my life,' Wilkins was to write, 'because in 1919 I had planned to use an airship to make an Arctic flight.' But no one believed the idea was practical; indeed, the manufacturers both in Germany and in England thought it so dangerous that they would not sell Wilkins a ship at any price, presumably fearing the adverse publicity of a tragic failure. Now, however, he went on, 'as I stood on the coast at Point Barrow watching Amundsen, Ellsworth and Nobile pass, it was the realisation of my plan. Airships had proved useful in the polar regions. It mattered little to me who was at the control or who had organised the expedition, the fact that the machine had safely crossed the Arctic was sufficient.'

But those were precisely the points which were soon to be fought over. Before the quarrels could break out, however, the *Norge* had to find a safe landing ground somewhere in Alaska, a territory not well-prepared to receive airships. As the day wore on, that distant landing ground proved increasingly illusive, and the most dangerous day of the four days flight began. To face its unexpected, heart-breaking hazards, were men blind with weariness, speaking different languages, some with insufficient airship training to be able to carry out their tasks instinctively. When they thought they were almost at their goal, when every sense cried out for rest, they had to go on, and on; and if any one of them made a major mistake, all would die in ignominy.

Chapter 4

'AN EPAULETTED ITALIAN'

THE desire to sleep was an agony. Several times, Nobile saw that the helmsman's eyes had closed and he appeared to be unconscious on his feet. Riiser-Larsen had hallucinations – once, looking out at the landscape, he thought he saw cavalry charging across it. This was the third day during which neither he nor Nobile could relax for more than a few hours at a time. The men at the controls had got some brief rest periods on the second day because the failure of the radio had released Gottwaldt to assist Wisting at the elevator and Malmgren to spell Horgen and Alessandrini at the rudder. Amundsen had more occupation than before, in peering out the window and trying to recognise where they were from the inadequate charts which were all they had been able to secure of this final area, now wreathed in the deadly tendrils of the fog which had kept Wilkins and Eielson grounded for days.

Their landfall, largely due to Riiser-Larsen's navigation, had been accurate. But there was still a minimum of half a day's flying ahead of them, along the frozen coastline of Alaska, until they reached Nome on the Bering Straits. This coastline and its hinterland were wild, mountainous, ice-bound. Unlike the comparatively flat surface of the Arctic Ocean, which posed no dramatic hazard in fog, bad visibility over Alaska could exact the final penalty for a small error. If the *Norge* became mazed in the mountains and struck a hillside, a spark in the wreckage would ignite the hydrogen, and flame would consume her as it had so many other vulnerable airships. Electricity, petrol and hydrogen are a deadly combination. Any survivors would escape from the collapsed structure within the first ten seconds, or not at all.

When they had sighted the coastline near Point Barrow in clear air, there had been a general relaxation, a feeling that they were almost home. It was not for some four or five hours that, soon after noon, fog wraiths began to obscure the ground now and then, and were succeeded by a dense whitish fog which completely enveloped the *Norge*. Nobile ordered the engines throttled back to give him more time for manoeuvre and put the airship into a climb. Up they went to 3,500 feet, but still they could see nothing. The gas in the cells had now reached full expansion. If they went any higher, the automatic valves would blow off the excess hydrogen which would then be lost forever, so that they would be too heavy when they came down again into cooler temperatures. They had virtually no ballast to drop as a compensation. Worse, in the past fog had always been associated with icing. The valves might ice up in the open position so that all the gas would be lost and that meant certain disaster.

It was ignorance of such factors which had made Amundsen so sanguine about the use of airships in the Polar regions, and which he now refused to recognise and tried to blame on Nobile.

Nobile hoped that their altitude of 3,500 feet exceeded that of the highest land in Alaska, but owing to the deficiencies of their maps, he could not be sure. At any time, a mountainside might loom ahead, with seconds only in which to avoid it. A very long hour passed.

Then, although they remained at a constant 3,500 feet the fog bank thinned and finally lay beneath them; above was the sun again. As the fog changed its altitude, so Nobile took the *Norge* up and down, trying to avoid the icing conditions which lay in wait for the airship below and the higher temperatures nearer the sun which threatened it from above. Finally, the fog bank got lower and lower and Nobile followed it down, without entering its freezing depths – until at 6.30 p.m. it began to clear. And there, 600 feet below them, was the frozen surface of the Polar sea.

Nobile judged they might be nearer to Siberia than to Alaska, but this time he was determined not to fly in or above fog if he could possibly help it. Instead, he would try to fly under it, which meant picking up the Alaskan coast once more and sticking to its seaward margin. There were hazards in that course of action, too, but it was the one he intended to take.

After a time they came to the end of the ice. The sea beyond was wild, stormy, foam-crested, blown by a north-easterly gale. The *Norge* bucked up and down for 150 feet or more at a time and Nobile had to take the elevator wheel himself. This wind, if it did not destroy them directly, could drive the *Norge* out helplessly over the Pacific towards Japan. Only as he considered this as a practical calculation did it come home to Nobile how far his little airship had flown from its base at Rome. Utterly weary and anxious, he felt a stir of pride.

At 9.30 p.m. on 13 May they were over the rocky coast of Alaska, with its icy fringe of compressed and jumbled pack and its dense wreath of whitish fog. They turned right, keeping as clear as possible of the fog and trying to follow a difficult coastline. They were somewhere in the Bering Straits, but exactly where, no one on board knew. Staying down under the white wraiths of fog, the *Norge* raced along the coast; over a hutted encampment full of curious Eskimos and terrified dogs; over a village which they circled in hope of identifying it; and all the time the airship was penned between the fogbase and the unknown ground, dodging among the hills, roaring over frozen lakes, driving across an icy bay. Nobile described it as four and a half hours of torment for men whose tired nerves had to rally for a supreme effort. The Italians and some of the Norwegians had worked on the airship in the hangar all day on 10 May. Few of them had had much sleep that night. And few had had much rest since the take-off at 9.50 p.m. on the morning of 11 May. And now it was the evening of 13 May.

Left to himself, Nobile would probably have gone to sleep; only his feeling of responsibility towards the others kept him just awake. Probably this feeling possessed them all. It was the only weapon they had to combat the terrifying dangers of trying to reach the haven of Nome by underflying the fog. What was required was instant decision by the commander and lightning-swift reactions by his crew. And yet they were all drunk as zombies with the all-pervading, aching weariness wrought by sleeplessness.

At this point the navigator, Riiser-Larsen, suggested that it was necessary to check their position, which indeed was desirable, by taking a sight on the sun with a sextant. As it was not a ruler-straight coastline, but mountainous and indented, Nobile had the engines slowed for the climb, so as to make avoiding action easier. The *Norge* now climbed well, so much of her fuel was gone. But this was now a disadvantage, indeed an acute danger, for as the airship rose out of the fog, the dense vapour thinning and becoming luminous, she climbed into the full glare and heat of the sun. As Riiser-Larsen manipulated the images on his sextant, so the gas in the cells expanded swiftly to the maximum. Nobile, alarmed, saw the needles of the pressure gauges rise towards the danger point; he had the valves opened and the gas emitted. But still the pressure rose. The gas was expanding faster than the valves could release it. And the nose was pointed up, for the climb. To get the *Norge* down again, and halt her ascent, the power of the engines had to be used. But not until the nose had been brought down could they be effective in taking her earthwards. And the only way to achieve that, now, was to put extra ballast into the nose. Mobile ballast, human ballast, was what was required and there were two Norwegians in the control cabin who could be spared from duty.

In English, the lingua franca of the North, Nobile told them to climb up inside the hull and go to the extreme tip of the nose.

The two Norwegians stared at him blankly.

The concept he had to put over really required mastery of colloquial Norwegian. Nobile's English, although understandable by an Englishman, did not suffice to express instantly what he meant to two men whose native tongue was Norwegian. The two men, Gottwaldt in particular, looked blankly at Nobile.

The gauges showed rapidly rising pressure – 60, 70, 80 mm. The elevators controls were at hard down, to get maximum dive. But still the *Norge* rose. In moments only, the valves would open automatically to avoid the gas pressure bursting the cells; and the tremendous loss of gas which must result would bring them down in short order just where they were. Wherever that was.

Desperately, Nobile resorted to his native Italian.

'*Subito a prua!*' he shouted, pointing dramatically; and vividly.

The Norwegians got the message then, and complied instantly.

The nose of the *Norge* fell from the heavens to the horizon, and then began to point downwards. The altimeter indicated a descent, the pressure gauges showed that the gas was shrinking, From 5,400 feet the airship fell rapidly into the fog. Nobile ordered a turn away to seawards to lessen the danger of flying directly into a hill. At 600 feet, the ground became visible – and it was land, not sea. They had been lucky. But Riiser-Larsen had got his sun sight, giving a latitude of 67° 5', confirming they were near Kivalina.

Once again, Nobile kept the airship down under fogbase, not

merely commanding it but personally handling the elevator, riding the *Norge* like a horse across the landscape to the coast, jumping the obstacles as he came to them, straining to see out of the cabin window the loom of a hill through the whitish vapour of the fog, in time enough to climb or turn away. Once he came so low that the trailing wireless antenna caught on some obstacle and broke. But if the fog pressed down towards the ground, the airship must go down, too – or be fatally blinded among the hills. Her pilot must have sight of the ground, before the land became sea. The mad ride went on, Nobile staggering with exhaustion, his craving for sleep almost irresistible.

Then came a landmark, a winding waterway they identified as the Serpentine River. At two o'clock in the morning they burst out into a bay, and were over water. The menace of the fog-wreathed hills was behind them. Now all that remained was the easier flight along the coastline to Nome. Nobile was beyond all caring. He had undergone 12 hours of uninterrupted strain on this last day, following three days and nights virtually without sleep. His endurance had been remarkable. Now he was ready to leave the rest to Riiser-Larsen. He sat down in Amundsen's velvet-covered armchair, disturbed his dog Titina who had been sleeping in his fur bag most of the time by wriggling his own legs into it, and stretched out, too utterly exhausted for solid sleep, but even cat-napping was a luxury.

It was the incidents of the last hour or so, when Nobile had been strained beyond endurance but nevertheless had met every crisis and test successfully, which Amundsen was to twist and use against him very shortly. This had been the worst part of the flight for the active members of the crew, particularly Nobile, because instead of a straightforward half-day trip, the sequence of hazards and near disasters they met expanded the time to a full twenty-four, heartbreaking hours. It was of course extremely easy for the quarrelsome, aggressive Amundsen, who had little to do but sit in a velvet-covered armchair for hour after boring hour, to criticise any of the dog-weary men who were bringing him safely through. But as Nobile alone could be his potential rival, it was Nobile he turned on eventually.

The Italian woke up with a start. Riiser-Larsen was shaking him. 'We're getting near, in half an hour we shall be at Nome,' he said. Sick and shaken with fatigue and disturbed sleep, Nobile struggled up to assess the situation. Landing airships could be a tricky business, particularly without trained ground crews or the facilities of a mooring mast; in a high wind, the enormous areas of the hull could make it uncontrollable.

Nobile forced his tired mind to work. The first action was easy – tell Alessandrini to hang out the mooring ropes and prepare for dropping the landing rope. The next was to prepare clear and concise instructions, in a foreign language, to a ground crew who would never have so much as seen an airship before, let alone land it. He left Riiser-Larsen to put the ideas into words. Then, the third stage, assuming the preliminaries had gone well, was to deflate the airship so that the squally winds could not blow her away. Nobile began to work out a sequence of orders to ensure this.

Meanwhile, Amundsen had come to life and was standing beside Wisting at the helm. Apparently, both of them had recognised a place they knew from a previous visit. To Nobile, it looked utterly dreary and forlorn. Certainly, it wasn't Nome. There was a grey, desolate shore; a pale, frozen river; some dark masses, presumably huts; and an abandoned three-masted sailing ship lying on its side among the pack-ice.

The *Norge* circled. Apparently, Amundsen was not so sure after all that he had seen this settlement before. Nome was still probably nearly a hundred miles away. The sky was black, the squally gusts persistent and on the bow. They were making very little headway, with the airship pitching badly, once to 30 degrees from the horizontal. The weather looked as if a full gale was blowing up. Amundsen claimed that it was he who first suggested landing at this place, by asking Nobile if a landing was possible, and then checking with Riiser-Larsen. Nobile says it was his decision and that it formed slowly in his mind. The blackness of the sky was one factor which combined decisively with the other – the utter exhaustion of the crew, most of whom had been working incessantly for four days. It was go down now, or risk disaster.

But once again, his tired brain had to think out solutions. At Nome they were expected and there would be an untrained, novice landing party available. Here, there was no one at all. His first thought was to bring the *Norge* down in the water just off the icy shore. They had inflatable dinghies and would all be saved, although the airship would be lost. Although the *Norge* now belonged to Amundsen and not to Italy, she was his ship and he did not want to lose her. So he abandoned this idea for a better. He explained to Riiser-Larsen that he would descend on the coastal ice nearest to the settlement below and try to bring the airship to a halt; if she would not stop completely but drove slowly along over the ice on her belly, this would not matter much because it would allow the crew to deflate the envelope which would get rid of her buoyancy very quickly.

Amundsen, however, did not trust Nobile's judgement and instead asked Riiser-Larsen for his opinion. This was not merely stupid but insulting, because of the disparity of airship experience between the two men. Riiser-Larsen came up with an emergency scheme he had heard of in England. This was for the crew to cut their way through to the outside of the airship, where they would all hang on precariously, and then all drop off simultaneously on the word of command. Amundsen thought this was a 'very sensible suggestion.' Nobile retorted that it was a 'desperate solution', which would both risk the crew and lose the airship. He called for Cecioni to prepare the 'landing sack'.

Made of cloth, shaped like a large sausage, but open at one end, the sack had an anchor attached outside and could be filled with additional weights. It was to be dropped first, attached to the airship, and would slow her considerably; in effect, it was a brake, particularly useful in the gale conditions now prevailing. Cecioni filled it with pemmican tins and other miscellaneous weights, and eventually had it hanging a hundred feet below the bow of the *Norge*, while Nobile motored in slowly towards the settlement, engines just ticking over. Nobile saw a group of 7 or 8 men standing on the ground, and ordered a burst of throttle to bring the dirigible nearer to them. The motors roared momentarily, the 'sack' touched the ground, its anchor sliding over the ice. The men on the ground saw what was wanted and grabbed the mooring rope which held the sack to the *Norge*'s bow. Nobile ordered gas valved off and as the airship became heavier she sank rapidly. 'Look out for the shock!' he shouted.

The rubber shock-absorber under the cabin made the impact only a slight jolt and bounced the *Norge* into the air again, so that she rose several feet off the ground. Nobile ordered more gas drawn off and the airship touched the ice again – and stayed down. But only for the moment. When 16 men and one dog stepped off, the ship would rise rapidly, might tear the mooring rope from the hands of the small and inexperienced ground crew. Those members of the airship's crew who were also inexperienced might not realise this. So Nobile placed himself in front of the cabin door and in lieu of a complicated English explanation, shouted: 'Nessuno si muova!' And no one did move, so they must have understood.

Then he sent Cecioni down first, his task being to instruct and help the amateur ground crew; and, as he valved off more and more gas, so he sent down the Big Three – Amundsen, Ellsworth, Riiser-Larsen – and most of the others after them. But he sent Alessandrini up aloft to cut the emergency rip-panels to all of the ten gas cells, which would collapse the airship very quickly and thus save her from being blown away by the gale. Looking round to make sure that everyone had gone, he found Oscar Wisting standing beside him. 'Thanks for the journey!' said Wisting, and stepped down. As the Italians got clear, the body of the airship began to sway, then collapsed, overturning the control cabin and covering the engine gondolas. The *Norge* was finally down, damaged, but beyond the power of the gale to carry away. The time in Alaska was 8.30 p.m. on 13 May. By Greenwich mean time, however, it was 7.30 a.m. on 14 May, 1926.

A small airship, built only for flying over the Tyrrhenian Sea between Rome and Corsica, had reached the Pacific Ocean. She had covered 7,800 miles in 171 flying hours. 1,200 miles of that flight had been over unexplored territory, shown as inaccessible on the Arctic charts. They had drawn a line of light across it some fifty miles wide. A question which had been argued for years by geographers and explorers had been settled. There was no continent there, only a frozen sea. A submarine could travel under the ice from the Bering Sea and reach the Pole submerged. (Wilkins was shortly to plan such a venture). Their non-stop flight from Spitzbergen to Alaska, had lasted 70 hours 40 minutes; they had covered 3,180 miles at an average speed of 45 m.p.h. And they could have gone on to Nome and beyond, if fuel had been the only consideration, for there was left at the end $26\frac{1}{2}$ cwt. of petrol and $4\frac{1}{2}$ cwt. of oil.

The tiny settlement where the *Norge* lay was named Teller. Its population totalled 55, of whom only ten were Europeans, the rest being Eskimos. Yet at the height of the gold rush 10,000 miners had camped there. Three days after landing, while he was still superintending the packing up of the *Norge* for return to Europe by sea, Nobile was relaxing in the small wooden house belonging to his host, Captain Petersen. In a corner, he had found a small terrestial globe made of cardboard, and was dreaming over this when Riiser-Larsen, also a guest of Captain Petersen, came into the room and sat down. 'I was thinking,' said Nobile, 'that with that strong tail wind we had, the *Norge* might have gone much further south, perhaps even as far as Seattle.'

With that globe as a crude reminder of reality, they went on to discuss the possibility of flights from Scandinavia across the Arctic ocean to San Francisco on the one hand, Tokio on the other. The distances via the Pole are very much shorter than those involved in simply flying west across the Atlantic to America, which appears the obvious thing to do if one consults merely an atlas. The Italian and the Norwegian were looking a long way into the future, but they were seeing truly.

Then Nobile interjected: 'I think we ought to make a new expedition. After all, our journey has been practical proof that the airship is the best means of exploring unknown country. There's still so much to be done.'

'That's true,' assented Riiser-Larsen. 'But with this enterprise Amundsen has closed his career as an explorer. He has finished – he's going to retire.'

'All right,' said Nobile, 'but we can go on. It would be a pity not to make use of the new hangar at King's Bay, the mooring masts at Oslo and Vadsoe.'

The airship they would need was already under construction, a sister ship to the *Norge*. The money could be raised, given time, said Nobile. He was thinking in terms of 1928. The airship would fly the Italian flag, but if the Norwegian would take part, the expedition could be named after them both. They agreed to talk about the matter again, later; but 'later' never came.

The expedition went by sea the 100 miles to Nome and then on to Seattle, where it dispersed. Nobile had not intended to return to Italy at once, but go on from San Francisco to Japan to help the Japanese operate one of his airships which they had bought. Instead, he received a cable from Mussolini telling him to delay his return home for another reason. There were many Italian 'colonies' in the United States which had been excited by the exploits of an Italian airship; with his Italian crew, he was to tour those colonies. Of course, it was a public relations exercise, for Mussolini as well as for Italy. As members of the Italian armed forces, they could not have disobeyed, even if they had

wanted to; but naturally it was extremely pleasant to be cheered
by crowds of one's own countrymen and women in a strange
land. Nobile and his men made a triumphant progress from
Seattle to New York, via San Francisco, Santa Barbara, Los
Angeles, Chicago, Cleveland, Akron, Rochester, Philadelphia,
Pittsburgh, Boston, Providence and Washington, where Nobile
was introduced to President Coolidge. To Nobile's embarrass-
ment, Titina left a souvenir on the White House carpet. Coolidge,
normally a taciturn man, actually laughed, and after that the
interview went very well.

Next morning, Titina's performance before the President was
headline news in the American press, although not the sort of
thing which would have been publicly noticed in Italy.

Just which American news story ignited Amundsen is not
known. The general effect of the tour was to publicise the Italian
airship, its Italian commander, and those members of the crew
who were Italians. This was natural, given Il Duce's command to
tour the Italian communities in America. It was also a reflection
of the undoubted fact that it was the aeronautical side of the
enterprise which in the event now loomed large. Precisely because
the flight was successful, none of the polar explorers aboard had
been given an opportunity to demonstrate their expertise in
emergency. And because no land had been discovered, there had
been no dramatic landing by Amundsen. This was hard luck for
the famous old explorer, but it was hardly Nobile's doing.

In a book which he was to write later, Nobile had summed up
each man's contribution, as he saw it: 'Amundsen, who had first
thought of it, had brought to it the prestige of his past exploits;
Ellsworth had made it a practical possibility by putting up his
share of the expenses; I had borne the responsibility of preparing
the ship and superintending the flight from Rome to America.'
It was number three, the airship story, which proved to be the
most newsworthy angle in America. And, of course, the *Norge*
was really N.1, an Italian airship designed, built and piloted by
Nobile on the historic flight.

No doubt there were irritating inaccuracies in many of the
newspaper reports, probably there were misquotations, certainly
a report of enthusiastic Italian crowds greeting fellow Italians as
heroes would have an Italian slant; the seven Norwegians might
be momentarily forgotten, also the Swede and just possibly the
American. Among those who have taken an active part in explora-

tory expeditions of some danger, on land, in the air, at sea, or under the water, there is a quick resentment of media inaccuracy which tends to spark off towards rivals rather than at reporters. The same hot feelings occur in war, but then it is usually the reporter (rather than the editor or the printer) who is roasted, innocent or not.

Before Amundsen blew his top in public there had been a build-up of bad feeling in the background. Amundsen and Ellsworth had signed contracts with the New York *Times* for an early exclusive on the flight. Nobile, as the only aeronautical expert among the three leaders, thought he should have had a hand in those articles. Amundsen would not have it. Nobile's own agreement with the Aero Club of Norway allowed him to write concerning only the technical and aeronautical side of the expedition, but even this infuriated Amundsen, who now apparently thought of himself as an aeronautical professional, fully capable of laying down the law on airships.

He wrote a scathing attack for an American publication, denigrating Nobile from half-a-dozen different directions, including the fact that he wore his uniform, and sometimes looked fed up, and used his hands to gesture when giving orders, and possessed bad judgement, and was a poor airship pilot who had been saved only by the quickness of Riiser-Larsen. All these points he made again, more permanently, in the autobiography he was to publish in 1928. In this he devoted ninety-five pages to a denigration of Nobile, designed to put him in the place Amundsen thought he should occupy. He wrote: 'This hired skipper of a Norwegian ship owned by an American and myself shall not be permitted to usurp honours that do not belong to him. This record is written to prevent it.'

The sheer blind-eyed bile evidently on the boil behind this shows how badly Amundsen had been upset, granted that he never was a very nice man in the first place. Nobile was to make a quiet, technical reply to the Norwegian's charges, but he never retaliated at Amundsen's level of denigration (except for a mild hint that Amundsen was a bit of a passenger on the *Norge*). Privately, however, when questioned years later, some months before his death in Rome in 1978, he angrily dismissed the Norwegian's autobiography as just 'Amundsen's lies.' The resentment had lasted a full half-century.

From the beginning Amundsen had intended to keep Nobile

and the Italians in a subordinate position; this was part of his usual system of command which did not fit the facts of this particular case. As a qualified shipmaster he could double this role with that of exploration leader, and so establish unity of command, provided that the vehicle used by the expedition was a ship. When the vehicle was a dirigible designed and flown by another man who was a high-ranking officer in another nation's air force and a director of its airship factory, Amundsen's qualifications were insufficient. There was that much solid basis to the antagonism which grew between the two men. However, it is a fact that Amundsen's irritation rapidly became hatred only after the flight had been completed; almost certainly because he felt that some deserved kudos was being filched from him by Nobile. Yet he can offer no evidence of this, but only trivial accusations springing from ignorance or misunderstanding. In the background was the explorer's stubborn refusal to accept that this had been an aeronautical expedition mainly; that his own previous hard-won experience had been valueless.

He penned his accusations in no coherent order, but merely as he read incoming accounts of Nobile's lecture tour of America, and read them moreover while in his study engaged on writing his own book; the work which was to crown a long career of polar exploration. The chronology is weak or absent, but the first basic clash between the two men, both of them outstandingly talented, took place at Nome. According to Amundsen, Nobile came to him and Ellsworth and demanded 'full recognition as one of the three commanders of the expedition' in the newspaper articles which the other two had contracted to write for the New York *Times*. Contractually, Amundsen may have been right; but some recognition of Nobile's part in the success of the flight could surely have been worked in, had the will to do so been there.

When Amundsen refused him this one-third of a credit then, according to Amundsen, Nobile lost his temper and launched out on a tirade, in which he cried: 'I had the whole responsibility of the flight!' Technically, this was the mere truth. Nobile went on, again according to Amundsen, to claim that he had invented the idea of a flight across the Arctic Ocean and had then designed the airship in which the flight was to be undertaken. In Nobile's own writings, the Italian states that he designed the ship first and later thought that it might be capable of a polar flight; but Amundsen sometimes seemed reluctant to admit that the *Norge* was Nobile's airship. At the start of his narrative, however, he was forced to concede this in order to explain why, in the first place, he was insistent that Nobile himself should pilot it.

To Amundsen, Nobile's resentment was that of a 'strutting dreamer', an 'epauletted Italian, who six months before had had no more thought of Arctic exploration than he had of superseding Mussolini as Chief of State.' His arguments were 'presumptuous nonsense', an insult to the Norwegian and his 'thirty years of labour and achievement in the Polar regions.' 'With furious indignation, I reminded him in no uncertain tones of the pitiable spectacle he would have presented on the Polar ice if the *Norge* had by chance been forced down, and pointed out how preposterous would have been his claims to effective leadership under those conditions.' This was totally beside the point, because Nobile's claims to recognition were as airship designer and pilot, not as potential sled driver or skier or survivor on an ice-flow. The truth of what Amundsen said was to become plain only in another context at a later time. It had nothing to do with the flight of the *Norge*.

Amundsen had concluded that discussion, so he said, by reminding Nobile 'that Ellsworth and I were the leaders of the expedition, that we should never recognise his right to claim a major share in its achievement. . . .' And if they could they would see to it that he published nothing about the flight except technicalities.

In Amundsen's narrative of this quarrel at Nome, Amundsen and Ellsworth are the innocent and aggrieved party. As they are again in the scene at Seattle, when the expedition lands from the steamer *Victoria* to be greeted by cheering crowds on the dockside. While Amundsen and Ellsworth wait, dressed in rough civilian clothes bought at Nome, 'Nobile appeared from below apparelled in the most resplendent dress uniform of a colonel in the Italian army.' In spite of Nobile's injunctions to save weight, fumed Amundsen, Nobile and two other Italians had 'secreted' in the *Norge* 'the bulk and weight of heavy military uniforms!' In his rage, the Norwegian jumped to the most anti-Nobile conclusion he could think of. Both he and Ellsworth had joined the *Norge* virtually at the last moment and therefore did not know, as the other Norwegians did, that the Italians wore their uniforms under their Arctic clothing, in the same way that the civilians wore civilian clothing; the uniforms they had chosen were not their best ones: and they had certainly not been carried separately as extra luggage.

Then followed, according to Amundsen, a minor drama as to who was to get off the ship first (and thus seem to lead the expedition). Nobile, said Amundsen, manoeuvred himself next to the gangplank, while he, Amundsen, held back in high-minded disdain; then an officer of the *Victoria* blocked Nobile and bowed Amundsen and Ellsworth off first. So far so good. But there on the quayside, among the city dignatories waiting to greet the Polar heroes, was a charming little girl in a gay frock, with a bouquet of flowers; and, seeing before her no less than three heroes, two of them in civilian clothes and one in uniform, she gave the bouquet to Nobile! Round two to the Italians.

Once ashore, wrote Amundsen bitterly, they found that the local Italian consul aided by the Fascist squadristi had spread quite the wrong ideas about the flight, for instance, that it had been largely an Italian undertaking and 'that Nobile was, with us, the chief in command of it.' So firmly did this base idea become fixed locally, he complained, that at their very first official lunch he, Amundsen, was given the place of honour, but Nobile was seated second and Ellsworth only third.

The moment the luncheon was finished, Amundsen felt it his duty to call upon his hosts and point out to them unequivocably, how wrong and hurtful their actions had been; and, so he said, they corrected their mistake at later gatherings. Amundsen was experienced in fighting the organisers of public banquets, for he had had a tiff with some already when they were in Nome. There, according to Amundsen, Nobile had made pretentious claims concerning the Italian participation in the flight of the *Norge*, and aided by an interested local priest, had convinced the masses. So much so that he had been the guest of honour at a banquet to which Amundsen and Ellsworth were not invited. Amundsen suspected, probably with some reason, that as he and Ellsworth had been to Nome before, they were no longer a novelty, whereas Nobile was new and had glamour. What Amundsen probably did not grasp, was that it was not just people but vehicles. Aeroplanes were old hat in Nome, particular those that crashed without achieving anything, as his were wont to do. But the designer and pilot of a dirigible – a giant ship of the skies – who had actually crossed the Arctic Ocean from Europe in a successful and spectacular flight, that really was worth a public banquet. Amundsen could not see it that way, and commented bitterly that 'the whole situation revealed bad taste and bad manners on the part of the people of Nome.'

Of course, so far Amundsen had been criticising foreigners: Italians, Alaskans, Americans. Objectively, however, he could find fault with his own countrymen, too. He had a series of rows with the Aero Club of Norway, starting before the flight of the *Norge* and continuing for many months afterwards. The upshot was that Amundsen accused the Aero Club of incompetence, then demanded the resignation of the Secretary, and finally resigned himself. Meanwhile, for their part, the Aero Club issued what Amundsen was to call 'a nasty public statement' . . . in which they came as near as they dared to calling me a thief by indirect language.' This referred to some business matters concerning a film of the flight, but in Norway it must have aroused echoes of Amundsen's previous troubles over money, when he had been sued by his own brother. Indeed, Amundsen was to reveal the awkward fact that at the end of the accounting, the *Norge* expedition was $75,000 in debt. More debts to add to those mountainous obligations he already had! This was not a good time to retire, but for a man in his mid-fifties whose only expertise lay in polar exploration requiring extremes of physical endeavour, there was probably very little option. His lecture fees and book royalties were mortgaged for years ahead; he would never clear off the debt. A sad and burdened old age was the only prospect that faced the explorer who in his great days had received the acclaim of the world, and at the least had deserved well of his country.

Nobile's homecoming was a triumph. Crossing the Atlantic from New York in the Italian ship *Biancamano*, he and his men arrived at Naples on 2 August. It was sunset. The gulf, one of the grandest amphitheatres in the world, flanked by the volcanic heights of Capri and Sorrento to the south and of Ischia, Misenum and Solfatara to the north, with Vesuvius dramatic in the background, was a sheet of vivid blue water speckled white by the sails of hundreds of yachts carrying spectators. Flights of military aeroplanes in formation roared across the sky and northwards, towards Rome, two Italian airships cruised majestically.

After all that, it was galling for Nobile to find himself described in print as an 'epauletted Italian', a 'boastful dreamer', a member of a 'semi-tropical race' unfit even to undertake exploration in the Arctic. More serious were Amundsen's allegations against his technical competence as an airship pilot. In the jealous world of Italian aviation he already had rivals all too ready to denigrate him; and there had been much competition for the post of pilot of the *Norge*. Those critics of N.1, who had prophesied doom if the little airship tried to fly even as far as the French Riviera, might not in their hearts have welcomed its landing in Alaska. At this time, however, Italian prestige was wrapped up in Nobile, and not merely political prestige. The King of Italy asked Nobile to reply to Amundsen's allegations, as they reflected on the Italian armed forces. He did so, and hoped it was the end of the matter, until Amundsen repeated them in his book. He was not to be able to read this until after the flights of the *Italia*, so that it became a particularly painful and poignant experience.

Amundsen's chapter on the *Norge* consisted of ninety-five pages of mostly tedious trivia. They tell one much more about the tetchy character of Amundsen than that of Nobile, and in particular reveal how little he knew of airships. The important charges number three only. In the first, the Norwegian alleged that Nobile made a great fuss about very little, when trying to get the *Norge* out of its King's Bay hangar in what Riiser-Larsen, an aeroplane pilot only, thought was not a very strong wind. There exists a movie film of the American airship *Macon* being caught by a wind and having her lower fin slowly but disastrously crushed, which illustrates exactly what Nobile was afraid of. Linked with this is a charge that it was Riiser-Larsen who actually got the *Norge* out of the hangar, whereas it was Riiser-Larsen who transmitted Nobile's orders, in Norwegian, to a largely Norwegian ground crew.

Accusations two and three follow the line of Amundsen's strictures on Nobile's driving, that it was erratic, dangerous and scared him half to death. Number two is Amundsen's version of the incident over Kivalina in Alaska when, due to the rapid expansion of the gas in the lifting cells, the *Norge* was rising uncontrollably, and Nobile made two Norwegians understand, by gestures and by speaking in Italian, that they must run to the bow. Amundsen confused the rudder with the elevators to start with, and then told how Nobile lost his head completely in this crisis, and with tears streaming down his face, wringing his hands, and screaming, told three Norwegians to run to the bow, which brought the nose down. As Nobile mildly pointed out, 'One might expect that, having lost my head, I would have given a wrong order: on the contrary, it was the right one. . . .'

The third accusation also concerned the last few hours of the flight of the *Norge*, when everyone was tired to extinction, Nobile and Riiser-Larsen especially. In Amundsen's version, Nobile stands 'like a man in a trance' unheeding at the wheel as the airship plunges downwards to destruction and disaster is only averted by Riiser-Larsen taking the wheel himself, thrusting Nobile aside in order to do so. Nobile says that he and Riiser-Larsen were acting in concert, because the view from the wheel was insufficient in the fog; so the Norwegian stood by the window and signalled 'Up!' to Nobile, who had taken over the wheel in the crisis because no Norwegian was expert enough. Of course, Nobile might unknowingly have fallen asleep momentarily at the wheel. Others did so, and with reason. All one can be sure of is that after four days virtually without rest or sleep, he was still capable of making rapid and correct decisions, and despite poor advice from Riiser-Larsen, brought the *Norge* to a landing in very difficult conditions without any loss of life. Even Amundsen acknowledged that.

What was not criticised, now, was the N.1 itself as a polar vehicle. The *Norge* had done what many thought she never could do, so Nobile's reputation as a designer of successful semi-rigids would be hard to attack. Certainly Amundsen never did so; he prevailed, however, simply by calling her a Norwegian airship.

Nobile was feted in Rome and in many other Italian cities besides; but then he had to go to Japan, because the Japanese had purchased one of his airships. When he came back, Nobile found that matters had changed at the Air Ministry. His good friend, General Alberto Bonzani was replaced as Under Secretary for Air by the soldier and airman, Italo Balbo, a member of the Fascist quadrumvirati, and one of the most powerful men in Italy. The new Minister had strong views on airships – he thought that they had no future. Instead, Italy should concentrate on long-distance formation flights by aeroplanes, these formations to be led in person by the Under Secretary for Air. Balbo was immensely ambitious on a scale dwarfing that of Amundsen or Nobile, and his success was to threaten the position even of the Duce himself, who reacted decisively.

General Franceso Pricolo points out that, after his return from Japan, Nobile should have called on the new Under Secretary of State for Air, as a matter of military courtesy, but that he did not do so. And that this was the reason why Balbo was to oppose him. Nobile himself thought Balbo's opposition was due to jealousy of a possible rival, augmented by the fact that Nobile, although he liked and admired the Duce, had reservations about some aspects of Fascism, especially its vulgarity and violence.

It was unfortunate for Nobile that he antagonised Balbo, for he was shortly to feel the need of a friend in high places and instead, found that he had a legion of enemies.

PART TWO
THE ITALIA

Chapter 5

A HEAVY CROSS TO BEAR

THE city sign was a bear – a dancing bear – but in popular terminology the German metropolis was known as 'Red' Berlin. For the Russian visitor, however, it was the luxury of this hotel rather than the revolutionary Communist politics of many of the voters which appeared so incongruous, as the scientist looked up from the chart of the Arctic region which he and his Italian companion had been studying. The hotel lobby swarmed with tourists, many no doubt drawn here by the fabled degeneracy of the German capital which catered for all tastes in the most blatant ways. Many others would be business men, commercial travellers, and the idle rich, for the German economy was booming with unemployment down to less than half-a-million.

It was March, 1928, and Professor Rudolfo Samoilovich (the Germans would spell it Samoilowitsch) was in Berlin to confer with General Umberto Nobile regarding the exciting but dangerous business of Arctic exploration by air. Samoilovich, of Jewish descent and then aged 45, was an expert of long standing, having taken part in no less than thirteen expeditions, dating from before the Great War to after the Revolution. He had served Imperial Russia and the Soviet alike. A geologist of repute, he was now President of the Institute of Arctic Studies at Leningrad and virtually at the peak of his career. The fierce, Stalin moustache Samoilovich wore was at odds with the rimless glasses and balding head, yet truly he was both academic and man-of-action. And he walked a sharp tightrope in the Soviet State, balancing his scientific ambitions, which were mainly geological, against the demands of the Party apparatus for specific minerals. Pure research versus applied research, was in the West, still, a conflict leading only to angry argument. In the East, however, a failure to produce the exact results required by the State could lead to a denunciation as 'an enemy of the people', a verdict from which there was no reprieve. There, the monsters so prolifically spawned by the twentieth century, were already visible.

Not so in Berlin. That year, sales of *Mein Kampf*, a book written by a minor politician rumoured to be a very odd duck indeed, fell to 3,015. In 1927, the figure had been 5,607. The man's attempts to copy the Italian Blackshirt movement of Benito Mussolini did not appear to be proving any more popular with the German people than they had with the founder of Fascism. In 1926, in the whole of Berlin, the National Socialist German Workers Party had had a membership of less than 1,000. That was the year in which the minor politician with the coarse accent and bad grammar had founded the Hitler Youth, adopted the Fascists' salute and some of the Roman-style emblems, and had written personally to Mussolini requesting the honour of a signed photograph. The Duce had coldly declined to have any dealings with this 'unsavoury adventurer'. But the man was nothing if not persistent. In 1927, he had staged his first party rally at Nuremberg. The Fascist salute was widely used, Mussolini's distaste notwithstanding, the Roman Eagles were employed to dignify the swastika, and the Party's storm battalions appeared for the first time in a standard dress. Hitler loathed the brown shirts they wore, but a well-meaning follower had bought up some old militia stocks cheap; and there was no going back from that, as it proved, until the formation of the elite S.S. Meanwhile, Dr. Joseph Goebbels had been appointed gauleiter of Berlin, in the hope that his talent for propaganda would bring in sufficient recruits to make membership top the thousand mark.

Umberto Nobile existed in a different political context, where intrigue was quiet and complicated. The initial noisiness of Fascist street violence was largely over now. Where political opponents were concerned it had been minor thuggery from which only one or two had died; and some of the opponents were themselves no better. True, known members of the Mafia and the Camorra tended to vanish without trace, but they were hardly in a position to object morally. Fascism's emphasis on *dinamismo*, on decisiveness, on efficiency, did actually tend to get things done and although when overdone, it invited ridicule, nevertheless Nobile's projects owed something to being able to harness the support of the Duce. But when other Fascist leaders opposed him, the power inherent in the one-party state became unpleasantly obvious. For injustice, real or imagined, there was no longer redress. The State could stifle. As yet, Nobile had experienced only a hint of this twentieth century malady. Samoilovich had suffered even less, so far. Both were still comparatively free agents, able to help each other.

The previous year, when Nobile was abroad, a friend in the Air Ministry had written to warn him: 'I have been able to discover that an isolating trench is being dug around you. . . . The fact is, an atmosphere of diffidence, hostility and coldness is being created towards you. In short, the construction of a situation intended to render intolerable your presence in the Air Force.' Such tactics were not of course specifically Fascist, but universal, as was the most blatant of the outward measures taken to undermine Nobile's position as Italy's leading airship pioneer. Before leaving Rome in 1927, Nobile had left under construction a much larger and greatly improved airship of 55,000 cubic metres. The N.1 *Norge* had had a capacity of only 19,000 cubic metres, so this new dirigible represented a considerable step forward for Italy in the field of airship construction. Privately, Nobile planned to use it for his programme of continued Polar exploration, if he could gain sufficient support, but in any event its construction was amply covered by an order of the Duce, given to Nobile personally, that he build an airship capable of a flight across the South Atlantic to Rio de Janiero, where there was an important Italian colony whom Mussolini wished to impress with the daring and might of the Fascist mother country. Nobile could reply that he had anticipated the Duce's wishes; such an airship was in an advanced stage of construction. Less than six months later, however, Balbo prevailed on Mussolini to have the whole project cancelled and the airship was broken up, so that no twists and turns on Nobile's part could reverse the verdict. And so it was done.

Later events made Balbo's motive transparent. He was planning preliminary aeroplane flights across the South Atlantic, designed to culminate in 1930 with a formation flight of fourteen flying boats led by himself. Single aeroplane flights were becoming less and less impressive, but the crossing of great oceans by numbers of aeroplanes in mass formation was prestigious for the country with the skill and discipline to carry it out. Although the move was bold, its effect would be to convince most people that air travel was on the verge of becoming routine. Even if some of the aircraft crashed, and they did, and some of the crews were killed, which they were, Balbo felt that the general impression created would be favourable – for the aeroplane, for Italy and for himself.

His reading of popular psychology proved correct. The crash of an airship stunned both authority and the mass mind, whereas an aeroplane accident, even if fatal, was regarded as rather thrilling and tended to increase the hero-worship with which that type of aviator was so frequently regarded. It was probably the sheer size of the vehicle which pushed a crashed airship into the same category of catastrophe as a sunken ocean liner. Certainly, when in 1930 the thoroughly bad British airship R.101 crashed, authority panicked and had the comparatively good British airship R.100 broken up, just like Nobile's new dirigible. Similarly, the loss of the *Hindenberg* in 1937 led to the end of German airship development.

At least, Balbo's decision was not a result of political panic. Against the tide of contemporary technical evidence, which was to continue to favour the airship until about 1933, he believed in the aeroplane for long distance flights. The idea of crossing oceans in formation was not his. The U.S. Navy had tried in May, 1919, sending out Lieutenant-Commander A. C. Read with four seaplanes to cross the North Atlantic in a series of hops via the Azores. Three of the aircraft fell by the wayside but Reid's own machine made the trip, taking just over two weeks. In a sense, this was the first Atlantic crossing by an aeroplane. It was followed within a month by the flight of a British Vickers Vimy bomber, flown by Captain J. Alcock and Lieutenant A. Whitten Brown, which came over non-stop from Newfoundland to Ireland in 15 hours and 57 minutes.

By far the best gauge to the atmosphere of the time were the events of April and May 1927, when airmen had been almost queueing up for the honour of crossing the Atlantic, or at least attempting to cross it. Five of them crashed, and there was no roar of public outrage. Chamberlin and Levine's Bellanca lost a wheel, causing a minor crack-up; Byrd's Fokker, piloted by the designer, Anthony Fokker, crashed on test; Davis and Wooster were killed in Virginia in an accident to the three-engined 'American Legion'; Nungesser and Coli, from France, disappeared without trace over the Atlantic in the 'White Bird'. Most remarkable of all, a prize was offered for the first pilot to make a solo crossing, without radio, in an aircraft powered by an air-cooled engine; but no one saw this as a Roman Circus and when Charles Lindbergh actually succeeded in reaching Paris after 33 hours non-stop at the controls of his single-seater Ryan monoplane, the feat was deliriously applauded.

In Berlin, a futuristic film was soon to be planned, starring the Jewish actor Conrad Veidt, called 'F.P.1', the story of bold aviators pioneering an air service by means of a floating flying platform moored in mid-Atlantic. The airman as hero who accepted all risks was still the public image.

More prosaic was a British formation flight of four Supermarine Southampton flying boats which took off from Plymouth for Australia on 17 October 1927 and reached Australia on 1 June 1928. Essentially it was a 'proving flight', to pioneer procedures where basc facilities did not exist, and by no means to create speed records or take risks. So successful was it, that the four flying boats covered 27,000 miles without any incident worth recording. The average cruising speed was 80 m.p.h., ten m.p.h. faster than the *Italia*'s top speed, but the actual time taken to cover the distance was longer than if the journey had been made by sea and merely stressed the prevailing superiority of the airship over long routes.

But as Professor Samoilovich went over the Italian plans with Nobile in that Berlin hotel, he became increasingly uneasy; a feeling which made the soft chairs in which they were sitting and the general luxury of their surroundings appear downright incongruous. If Nobile's arrangements were faulty, the realities of the Arctic would find them out quickly enough. He himself knew the Arctic very well although he professed no expertise in aeronautics. Even so, it was plain that the scales had already been tipped against Nobile. Now that the really large dirigible which the Italian had been building had been scrapped on Mussolini's orders, at the urging of his rival, Balbo, there was left only another small airship of the 'N' class, basically a slightly more efficient version of the *Norge*. It had little more than a third of the lifting capacity of the airship Nobile had really wanted to use for Polar exploration.

There could be no considerable reserve of lifting power, represented by heavy ballasting, to offset the weight of ice which could accumulate on the hull in unfavourable conditions. Further, the ice which would form on the envelope might become so heavy that it could tear through the fabric and puncture one or

4

more gas cells. Additionally, the power of the three motors, totalling only 750 h.p., was not impressive and might be insufficient to make headway against the strong winds likely to be encountered in the Arctic in the spring and early summer. Apart from all this, Samoilovich, as a scientist, felt that the gondola of the *Italia* was too small for efficient working.

On the other hand, he approved of the aims of the expedition. Vast areas of the Arctic had never been seen by man, let alone scientifically surveyed and examined. Nobile put the figure for unexplored territory at approximately 1,500,000 square miles. He planned, not a single dramatic, record-breaking flight designed to make headlines, but a considerable programme of Arctic flying to be carried out over a period of time from a central base at Spitzbergen. In the balanced judgement of the Soviet scientist, to attempt such a task with a small semi-rigid like the *Italia* was 'extraordinarily risky', but if against all the odds it succeeded the results would be 'very valuable'.

Where Samoilovich jibbed completely was at that part of Nobile's plan which aimed at putting a man, or a number of men down on largely unknown islands such as Nicholas II Land, hoping to pick them up again later when they had carried out their scientific work, or, failing that, expecting them to make their own way back to civilisation by marching to the Taimyr peninsula. He warned Nobile most earnestly of the impracticability of this scheme. It seemed to him that the Italian simply did not realise how extraordinarily difficult it was to even see a man from the air under Arctic conditions. If a party was landed safely, and he had his doubts about that, too, the airship crew would soon lose sight of them and never make contact again. As for walking out from Nicholas II Land, the distance to be covered was much greater than Nobile thought. He explained that no help existed on the Taimyr peninsula, as it was uninhabited. The nearest possible aid might be found 100 kilometres beyond that, by Lake Taimyr, but even that was uncertain because the 'population' consisted of nomads who might have trekked somewhere else at the time their assistance was needed. It was difficult, in the plush surroundings of that hotel, to convey to anyone who had not been there, the unutterable endless expanse of white wilderness which the maps brought by Samoilovich were intended to represent.

On the surface, Nobile had not worked out his plans properly, or so Samoilovich thought, although he considered it not impossible that the Italian was merely playing his cards close to the chest before the flight. However, he co-operated in the fullest possible way by giving Nobile the references to research data concerning Nicholas II Land (now renamed by the Soviets Severnaya Zemlya or 'North Land'), most of which, naturally enough, had been published in Russian; he later supplied charts and maps of Novaya Zemlya ('New Land') and the North Siberian coast, in which Nobile also seemed to be interested. The Soviet scientist formed a sympathetic impression of Nobile, notwithstanding the planning defects he had pointed out to him, and he welcomed the systematic exploration which the Italian intended. But, as they said goodbye, the nagging doubts as to the suitability of the *Italia* remained with him.

Samoilovich was not the first, but the last, to express such doubts. The first had been Mussolini. That had been in the summer of 1927, after Nobile had returned from demonstrating one of his N-class airships to the Japanese who had bought it. Mussolini, with Balbo beside him, had told Nobile: 'Perhaps it would be better not to tempt Fate a second time.' Probably he felt this genuinely, but certainly Balbo would have briefed him, in his own terms, regarding the unsuitability of the *Italia*. But Mussolini went on: 'Still, I recognise the scientific importance of the idea. We'll talk about it again next week.'

No such talk occurred because Balbo had sidetracked any possibility of Fascist government sponsorship for Nobile's project which, if it failed, would recoil most heavily on the Air Ministry, of which he was now the head. Instead, he had suggested to Nobile that he ask the Royal Geographical Society of Italy to be his sponsors; certainly such an expedition would fall well within their terms of reference. Nobile had spoken to the governing Council of that body on 12 July 1927, and received an enthusiastic response. And on 21 July the Mayor of Milan had written to Nobile, confirming an offer made by the City of Milan to raise by private subscription the necessary funds. So Nobile had both sponsorship and finance almost immediately, without committing the Fascist government to anything much beyond friendly gestures. The Air Ministry would supply the airship and crew, but any constructional work carried out in the government airship factory (of which Nobile was the head) would be on payment, the costs being met by the City of Milan. Admiral Sirianni, Under-Secretary for the Navy, was more enthusiastic, and utilising the old stand-by excuse of 'training', promised to loan the *Città di Milano* as base ship and transport and let the sailors learn how to handle the airship on the ground. This solved most of Nobile's needs as regards material and manpower. The question of who was to actually fly in the *Italia* was more difficult and gave Nobile much thought.

When recruiting, he did not conceal his realistic appreciation of the risks; nor did he attempt to assure his financial supporters of inevitable success. In an unscripted speech in Milan shortly before the departure in 1928, Nobile made his basic declaration: 'We have absolute confidence in the preparation of the expedition. All that could have been done to plan the enterprise well has been done. All that could be foreseen has been foreseen – even the possibility of failure or catastrophe. We are quite aware that our venture is difficult and dangerous – even more so than that of 1926 – but it is this very difficulty and danger which attracts us. That is precisely why we are doing it. Had it been safe and easy other people would already have preceded us.'

Nobile even included a barbed reference to unspecified opponents. 'But if our enterprise should be wrecked by one of these mischances, or a complete disaster swallow us up – which is by no means out of the question, in spite of all we have done to prevent it – then you will see all these facile critics come forward, leaping for joy, to tell you that they had foreseen it, that things could not have been otherwise, that it was only natural this should happen. . . .'

What had Nobile done, to avoid disaster but, if it proved unavoidable, to mitigate its effects? The *Italia*, completed in 1927, was some 1,300 kilos lighter than the *Norge* and with three similar power plants had a top speed of 115 kilometres per hour. That was splendid, so far as it went. She was a good ship within the limitations of her size, only one-third that of the airship which had been broken up. All that Nobile could do was to perfect the detail, with particular emphasis on reliable working in Arctic conditions. Experiments were made to find a way to prevent the engine radiators freezing if the motors had to be stopped altogether for some length of time (as they would be if a party was landed on the ice); other experiments were carried out to find a cooling mixture which would not easily freeze; a method of insulating the control cabin against the cold had to be worked out – two layers of canvas with air in between proved to be light and reasonably effective; and the controls of the gas valves were altered to make them less vulnerable to icing. Tests were made to determine the most effective way, within the weight limitations, of protecting the hull in the vicinity of the engines from being pierced by flying splinters of ice from the propeller blades – strips of rubberised fabric proved best. Against the opposite risk – that of fire – Nobile paid attention to the fuel feed system to the engines, so that if a feed line broke, the petrol could not drip down onto an engine; and he tested at low temperatures all the leading makes of fire extinguisher to find those which actually worked in the conditions they would meet over the Arctic. There was an almost endless list of things which had to be enquired into and eventually a decision made and acted upon.

One decision on an apparently minor matter was to have strange consequences later. Nobile decided that he needed a better guide to height than the existing altimeters, which were correct only for the aerodrome of departure and for the atmospheric pressure prevailing there at the time of departure. When you are over the North Pole in June it does no good at all to know how high you would be if you were over Rome in April. So he devised a system of spheres made of glass or light wood and containing a red liquid; these, dropped from the airship, would mark the moment of their impact with a crimson stain; thus their descent could be timed and from the timings the height of the airship could be worked out. For instance, a glass ball which took five seconds to reach the ground indicated that it had been dropped from a height of 100 metres.

To carry complete Arctic survival kit for everyone was impossible, but nevertheless, if weather conditions proved exceptionally good at a convenient time, Nobile planned to land a small scientific party of two or three men who might have to stay in the Arctic for a winter and then walk out. Apart from this, the airship might crash or be forced down; in which case the only hope might be if the survivors were all equipped to make their way back over the ice and snow. At the same time, the payload of the *Italia* was very limited, as was the space inside it for stowage. The decisions made in this field would be both difficult and critical.

Nobile did not blind himself with false patriotism. He enquired as to what kinds of sledge, tent and sleeping bag previous expeditions had used and studied them carefully. He considered the reports of the Norwegians such as Nansen, Sverdrup and Amundsen; of Peary the American and Scott the Briton; and of his compatriot the Duke of Abruzzi. Then he went to Denmark and Norway to inspect equipment and after he had made his choice visited Fridtjof Nansen, the great pioneer of Arctic drift, for his opinion on it. Nansen received Nobile for three hours in his villa at Oslo and said that he would ask Otto Sverdrup, who had been the captain of the *Fram*, to make himself responsible for the preparation of the sledges, sleeping-bags, boats and reindeer-skin suits. Professor Adolf Hoel of Oslo, a leading authority on the Spitzbergen area, was also enrolled as adviser to the Italians, as was Professor Gerard de Geer of Stockholm. This was a very different Nobile to the swelled-headed character Amundsen was then writing about. Further, having profited by the advice of many eminent men, Nobile duly acknowledged having had the benefit of it; rather than boldly taking the entire credit to himself, a proceeding not alas, entirely unknown.

The philosophy behind the choices is recognisably Scandinavian; the concept of survival in the Arctic, with an Italian flavour. Two sizes of sledge were decided on; small for the three-man wintering party, large for the whole crew should a mishap bring the *Italia* down. Nobile toyed with the idea of using dogs to pull them, probably because Peary and then Amundsen had shown their efficiency over mere manpower when harnessed to light sledges; but the weight factor – four or five hundred kilos deducted from the payload – in the end decided him against the dogs. The same principle was used with the boats. One small canvas boat, designed for hunting, to serve with the three-man wintering party; several larger collapsible boats for the whole crew in case of accident. Skis were taken only for those two or three members of the crew who could use them; for the rest, Nobile obtained the small snow-shoes used by the Alpini – the Italian mountain troops.

Clothing was important. Nobile had special three-piece lambs-wool suits made for every man, designed to be wind and water-proof. These were to be worn in flight and might suffice even on the ground, provided that the wearer did not have to remain still for a long time. In case of their having to winter on the ice, more was required and Nobile ordered winter fur-suits of the Eskimo pattern; he was advised by Tryggve Gran and Otto Sverdrup, and Commander Isaachsen supervised the actual manufacture of these suits from reindeer-skin. These, together with their gloves, would go on top of the flight suits and the flight gloves. A selection of footwear was bought for each man. For dry snow, two types were used – the *finsko* of reindeer-skin and the *komager* of reindeer-leather; both to be worn stuffed with dry grass or with slippers. For damp surface, American rubber shoes were to be used; and for rough marching, thick-soled leather shoes would be necessary. This does not exhaust the list of protective clothing; it represents merely the main items.

Nobile decided to obtain one-man sleeping bags of reindeer-fur, with the fur on the outside, which are warmer but not so comfortable as those with the fur inside. Again the Norwegian experts gave advice and supervised manufacture by a Norwegian firm. Nobile discussed with Nansen the type of tent to be taken but decided in the end against a tent of the type the Norwegian preferred, which was extremely light but not ideal protection against cold and damp. He was convinced that for their purposes, a double-skinned tent with an air-space in between, as used by Scott, would be better; and Nansen agreed. The entrance was to be a round hole, easily capable of being hermetically sealed to retain warmth. It was designed to take four men in comfort.

The food reserve, in case of an accident, was provided by a firm in Copenhagen which had already supplied twenty-two polar expeditions. Basically, it was pemmican, which provides a balanced diet in concentrated form, to which water must be added; is best eaten hot, but can be eaten cold. However, Nobile altered the ingredients and proportions of the mixture in order to cater for the tastes of his virtually all-Italian crew: peas instead of rice, oatmeal instead of raisins, potatoes instead of sugar, onions and celery in place of ordinary vegetables; and 70 per cent pulverised meat and fat instead of the 65 per cent preferred by the Norwegians and British.

There had to be cooking stoves, which although made in Nobile's airship workshops, were to Nansen's design. And for the obtaining of fresh food, an absolute necessity to a balanced diet according to the latest Scandinavian thinking, there had to be fire-arms. Again, the philosophy was that of Stefansson, who had criticised Franklin for taking shotguns rather than rifles; a bird, he pointed out, does not hold so much meat as a polar bear or seal. Nobile decided to take three magazine rifles, a Vickers of 8·1 mm (·303) bore and two Krag Jorgensens of 6·5 mm (0·25), as used by seal-hunters; and three 9·7 mm Colt (·38) revolvers. And, of course, ordinary knives and hunting-knives.

Apart from the bulk of the clothing, almost all of the items mentioned represented strictly unnecessary weight. Only if the airship crashed, would most of them be needed. However, Nobile was still not satisfied with the precautions in case of an accident. He asked the Air Ministry – that is, Balbo – for two flying boats to be attached to the expedition. They would be invaluable for search purposes and could airlift provisions to the survivors of an accident, or to a ground party in difficulties, without even having to land; the supplies could be dropped to the men below. For the time, this was forward thinking. There were few precedents for airlifted supplies, apart from the British efforts to help their garrison surrounded by the Turks in Kut-el-Amarna and the really remarkable flight of a Zeppelin, also during the war, from Bulgaria to help the German forces cut off in East Africa (but was ordered back in error when it had reached Khartoum). Nobile's request was turned down. He applied again, for just one flying boat. And again, he was turned down. One can defend Italo Balbo's opposition to airships, disregarding the personal factor, but these refusals seem hard to justify.

Nobile was more successful with a request to a different Ministry for the loan of some Alpini, all expert skiers, to be stationed at King's Bay ready to set out overland to the scene of any accident. A party of eight Alpini under Captain Gennaro Sora were consequently attached to the expedition. Sora was one of the three best ski-instructors in the Italian Army and the men were mostly Alpine born and bred. To back up these professionals there was a further body of young men supplied by SUCAI, the Italian University Students' Alpine Association.

The most vital decisions concerned the crew of the airship. The men to be selected and then asked to volunteer could be divided into three groups. Firstly, there were the scientists, for the purpose of this expedition was to carry out methodical enquiries and experiments during a number of flights. There were three of them and they were all young men. Dr. Aldo Pontremoli, 31, Professor of Physics at the University of Milan, was to study gravity and magnetism particularly. His application had come out of the blue, but it was backed by many scientists; when he met him, Nobile was greatly impressed, for the young man was an all-rounder and prepared to help even with menial tasks about the airship. Dr.

Finn Malmgren, 33, Professor of the University of Uppsala, was to study meteorology and also carry out some of the oceanographical research. A veteran of the *Maud* expedition as well as the flight of the *Norge*, the Swedish scientist was an Arctic weather expert of great operational value to Nobile who was to consult him both on the ground and in the air. Dr. Frantisek Behounek, Director of the Prague Wireless Institute and Professor of the University of Prague, 31, was to study atmospheric electricity and in particular radioactivity. Nobile had met him at King's Bay in 1926, during the *Norge* expedition; he was obviously longing to take part, but all the places were filled. Now he was to have his chance, too.

So the scientists consisted of an Italian, a Swede and a Czech. The rest of the crew, however, were entirely Italian, and Behounek felt sometimes that they resented the two foreigners on board; except, of course, for Nobile who was to be the sole link between the scientists and the other groups which made up the crew.

The second group consisted of the navigators, all of them naval officers recommended by the Admiralty. The two men who were top of the Admiralty's list impressed Nobile also. They were Adalberto Mariano, 30, and Filippo Zappi, 31, both of whom held the rank of Capitano di Corvetta, equivalent to Commander. Mariano had a brevet in navigation; Zappi, although less highly qualified in navigation, had a brevet as second-in-command of airships. The Admiralty also sent two other men, slightly lower down the list, after Nobile had already chosen Mariano and Zappi as ideally qualified both technically and as calm, courteous personalities. Of the last pair, Nobile was particularly struck by a younger, more junior officer, Alfredo Viglieri, aged 28; and he asked for him as well, intending to employ him not only with navigation but at the steering wheel of the *Italia*. This was to prove a momentous choice indeed.

The third group consisted of engineers and airship men generally, service and civilian. Naturally, here Nobile turned to his own associates and particularly those of them who had already taken part in one Arctic flight, with the *Norge*. There were five of these: Chief Technician Natale Cecioni, 41; Sub-Lieutenant Ettore Arduino, 38, as chief motor engineer; Petty Officer Attilio Caratti, 33, as motor mechanic; Vincenzo Pomella, 30, as foreman motor mechanic; and Renato Alessandrini, 38, as foreman rigger. Because these men had been badly over-worked in the *Norge*, Nobile introduced another motor mechanic, Calisto Ciocca, 31. There were really only two major changes. The bulky Cecioni was this time coming along as reserve and to work perhaps only on the ground at the King's Bay base, his position of chief engineer being filled by Arduino. The other alteration, a matter of mild jokes, was the striking increase in the girth of Alessandrini, who had grown very fat. Nobile pulled his leg over this, because a foreman rigger had to have the agility of a squirrel in order to wriggle into all parts of the airship when it was in flight; in addition, the port-hole giving access to the top of the ship was a real squeeze even for a slim man. Alessandrini only smiled complacently, and offered to demonstrate his ability to reach any part of the airship.

Like the navigators, the two wireless operators were now Italians instead of Norwegians, which would produce more rapid comprehension and action; everyone, bar two of the scientists, would be using his native tongue instead of pidgin-English. In emergency, this would be an immeasurable gain not only in speed of reaction but in certainty of comprehension. As Marconi was an Italian also, this was fitting in other ways. The new wireless operators were both Petty Officers: Ettore Pedretti, 34, and Giuseppe Biagi, 31. Pedretti, the senior man, was fair-haired and blue-eyed. Biagi was just the opposite type of Italian – dark, small but massively built.

In a class by himself was Felice Trojani, 31, whom Nobile had known for six years. As a very young man he had enrolled for a course at the School of Aeronautics where Nobile was a lecturer and when Italy entered the Great War he had joined the air force and flown at the front. After the war, he had graduated in engineering and then joined the airship construction works run by Nobile. He had helped with the preparations for turning N.1 into the *Norge*, while at the same time working on the N.3, a similar airship which had been sold to the Japanese navy for scouting purposes. While Nobile went to the Pole with Amundsen, Trojani had gone to Japan to supervise the assembly of the N.3. In due course, Nobile joined him in Japan and it was while they were there that Nobile asked Trojani if he would like to take part in the new Polar expedition he was contemplating. Trojani assented, out of loyalty to his chief, as good a motive as any and better than romanticism. When they returned to Italy, Trojani met Balbo and was not impressed. He was aware that Balbo believed that dirigibles were much inferior to aeroplanes and that neither Balbo nor Mussolini were really enthusiastic about a new polar expedition. Trojani had a few doubts himself, but like all of them was carried along by the wave of enthusiasm which Nobile had generated for his project. Even the scientists felt it, particularly Behounek, who only experienced certain reservations later. They had all been chosen to make history, one way or another, and they knew it.

There were two other members of the expedition who were not part of the crew, properly speaking, and might thus be considered as a fourth group. These were the journalists who were to take turns to fly with the expedition and report on it. They were Francesco Tomaselli, 34, a former captain in the Alpini and now correspondent of the Milan newspaper *Corriere della Sera*; and a younger man, Ugo Lago, aged 28, from the Fascist *Popolo d'Italia*. And there was Nobile's faithful flying companion, Titina, already a veteran of the Arctic.

There were therefore 18 men in all who had a flying role in the project, although in practice Nobile might leave one or two behind for any particular flight in order to save weight. Finn Malmgren, the Swedish scientist, was to remark upon how many of these men did not look like Italians at all, at least not like the popular conception of an Italian as a short, swarthy person with a girth owing something to spaghetti. But, of course, in ancient times much of Italy was a Greek colony and after that there were a number of invasions by various hordes of Nordic barbarians. Today, one can see Goths in almost any street in Italy. Malmgren had a rather fanciful idea that all these fair-haired Italians volunteering for the Arctic were obeying some call from the cold lands of the North.

In March, 1928 the tempo of preparation began to speed up. The various parts of the project were set in motion so that all would converge at the right places at the right moment. On the 20th the navy's base ship *Città di Milano* left La Spezia, bound for King's Bay via Gibraltar, Plymouth, Bergen and Tromsoe; and simultaneously the airship *Italia* was flown from Rome to Milan, which would be the official starting point of the expedition because of that city's backing for the project. On the 24th the 150-ton sealer *Hobby* left Tromsoe for King's Bay, carrying canvas for the repair of the airship hangar there as well as many tons of fuel and spare parts for the dirigible, in case the *Città di*

Milano was late at the rendezvous. The *Hobby* also carried a party of Norwegian workmen and a group of Italians headed by Professor Amedeo Nobile, the General's brother, and including Captain Sora of the Alpini. At the same time, two quite separate groups of Italian workmen left for Stolp in Germany and Vadsoe in Norway, both of which were refuelling stops for the *Italia* according to Nobile's flight plan. This was a commonplace of long distance aviation at this time, when airfields were mostly just that – a grass field with a windsock and no facilities. The amount of sheer organisation that had to be improvised on the ground to allow an aeroplane or airship to even fly from A to B was daunting.

On the last day of March the entire crew of the *Italia* were received by Pope Pius XI, who had asked to be kept informed of the progress of the expedition, in which he was keenly interested. After reviewing the crew, he then had each man introduced to him, before speaking to them all. The Pope referred to the project as a poetic venture which had high and pure aims; he himself appreciated the effort which was being made, at their great personal risk, to gain knowledge of those regions which had already cost so many lives and fortunes. In a gentle tone of voice he told them that in all human undertakings, at a given moment, a higher force intervenes for good or for ill; and that therefore that he would pray for them. Finally, the Pope said that he had a mission for them – to carry the emblem of Christ to the summit of the world. He then showed them a beautiful oak cross which had a compartment containing a document stating that it had 'been entrusted with dedicatory prayers by Pius XI, Pontifex Maximus, to Umberto Nobile and his companions, on the eve of their aerial journey at the charges of the City of Milan, to be dropped by the leader of the expedition, flying for the second time over the Pole; thus to consecrate the summit of the world.'

He added, with a smile, 'And like all Crosses, this one will be heavy to bear.'

Then he was gone, although for a moment on leaving the hall he had stopped, turned and appeared to start back, as if he had not really said enough, or did not find it easy to leave them. The Italians were very moved and comforted by this.

Frantisek Behounek was disturbed by another religious ceremony. When the *Italia* was christened, the Holy Cross was much in evidence. He felt it was almost grotesque. Such ceremonies, he considered, should be confined to the mystical darkness inside churches. In the context of modern aviation, against a background of aero engines, propellers, fins and rudders, the ceremony jarred; it was strange and without harmony. He thought that most of the others felt this also.

Nobile had a final audience with the King and then on 11 April was received by the Duce, who listened affably to Nobile's presentation of the plans of the expedition and the very detailed preparations which had been made for it. 'Good!' said Mussolini. 'You've foreseen everything. That's the way to succeed. To provide for everything – one hundred per cent. That's my system, too!'

Having included himself foremost among those worthy of credit, the Duce then remarked shrewdly: 'This enterprise is not one of those destined to strike the popular imagination, like your 1926 expedition. But it will attract the attention of the scientific world. I see that there is a great deal of interest in it abroad.' He took leave of Nobile with profuse good wishes.

He did not let Nobile see that he was in fact lukewarm on the subject, because that is no way to send a man off on a dangerous enterprise. But the affair had been managed by government with some skill and subtlety. If all went well, they could claim a master share of the credit. But if, as they suspected, a disaster occurred – well, the idea was Nobile's entirely and had been made a practical proposition by support from the City of Milan and the sponsorship of the Royal Geographic Society. All that government had contributed, virtually, was just its best wishes. Could they have done less?

Mussolini's real feelings may have been those he expressed, not at his last meeting with Nobile, but his first, when he had listened to the exposition keenly and then commented: 'Perhaps it would be better not to tempt Fate a second time.'

Chapter 6

TRIUMPH AND FAILURE

THE *Italia* had been at Milan since 20 March, creating great excitement and interest. Because he did not want a vast, surging crowd of well-wishers around during the critical manoeuvre of bringing the airship out of the hangar and onto the field, Nobile had decided on an early un-announced start. This was comparatively easy to bring off, because there was an extremely long flight ahead of the dirigible before she could even get to Spitzbergen and a favourable weather forecast for the first leg to Stolp in Germany was vital; no firm date or time could be given far in advance, although Nobile knew he had to start operations in the Arctic by the end of April or the first week of May at the latest.

On 19 April, although there had been bad weather over Germany that day, conditions were improving slightly. 'If we go, we shall have some excitement!' said Malmgren. 'But we can't hope for anything better during the next few days.' Their Italian meteorologist agreed.

The *Italia* was carrying a fairly full load: 20 people, 1,314 kilos of equipment, 1,735 kilos of ballast, 3,900 kilos of petrol, 315 kilos of oil. About 9,000 kilos in all, some of which was ballast, giving her a better margin of safety than the *Norge* on her trans-Arctic flight. In the early hours of 20 April she was walked out of her hangar and onto the field, the ground crew hanging on to the ropes to hold her down. The engines were started and began to rev slowly. From the control cabin Nobile called out; 'Let go!' As the men released their grip on the mooring ropes the airship rose slowly, looming huge over them in the night. There was a roar as the engines increased power and the dirigible began to climb. Soon her lights were no more than stars in the sky, and then she was gone. Ahead lay the great unseen barrier of the Alps and beyond that the mountains of Czechoslovakia and the Sudetenland, and further away yet the lesser heights of Poland.

2,000 kilometres to Stolp near the German Baltic coast, most of it over high ground and in stormy weather.

Nobile would have preferred to go via Leningrad, but the airship hangar near there had been dismantled. He had to pick his way from the valley of the Po through the mountains over northern Italy, and then over Austria, Hungary, Czechoslovakia, Poland and Germany, while violent squalls swept the valleys, bringing rain, or hail, or ice, or snow, or vivid flashes of lightning; where the winds were calmer, there was fog over the low ground. Beyond Trieste on the Adriatic, the winds screamed at up to 40 kilometres an hour, buffeting and hindering the airship which, with all three engines full out, could only make 115 k.p.h. in still air. Her economical cruising speed was a good deal less. Even so, the gusts set up exceptional stresses on the rigid parts of the great hull. Eventually they broke the left horizontal fin; that is, the projection from the tail to which one of the movable elevators was hinged. Apart from the threat to the control of the airship, if the trouble should spread, one of the steel tubes might break and tear the envelope with a possibly catastrophic loss of lift. Inspection showed, however, that the damage was too local to have immediately serious consequences, and Nobile determinedly carried on with the flight.

The *Italia* passed over Vienna early in the afternoon under a grey and weeping sky which obscured their view of the Austrian capital. Some hours later, while they were flying over Czechoslovakia, the Meteorological Bureau at Prague warned them that bad weather had clamped down over the whole of Moravia and Silesia. Visibility was poor, with a totally obscured sky; at heights between 500 and 1,000 metres the wind was reaching between 30 and 40 k.p.h., and there were many lightning flashes. For men sitting in a control cabin or suspended in engine cars under a great deal of highly inflammable hydrogen gas, this was an alarming prospect. It had occurred at the worst possible moment, for the mountains of the Sudetenland lay ahead. There was no possibility of going up above the weather. They would have to go down underneath it, which meant valley-threading in bad visibility. Or, of course, they could try to go round the weather, or even turn back. The former was hardly practicable because of the size of the storm. Nobile consulted Malmgren, the ship's meteorologist, who advised him to go on, saying he could always turn back in time if serious danger arose.

But they ran into the storm very suddenly, and just as they were about to enter the pass which led through the mountains. A deluge of rain slashed down upon the hull and streamed down the windows of the control cabin. Wisps of cloud streaked by, and then billowing masses of white vapour almost obscured the earth, rendering it unrecognisable. This was followed by violent lashings of hail, the first flickerings of lightning and peal upon peal of thunder. Soon, the lightning streaks were running down the sky all around them and the thunderclaps were deafening. They were in extreme danger.

Nobile took the airship down to 150 metres, as low as he possibly could, and told the helmsman to steer on a patch of sky which seemed to be less dark than the rest of the storm. For half-an-hour they had a wild ride. Sometimes a hill would rear slowly in front of them, seen often at the last minute, and the *Italia* would rise to clear the summit and then go down the other side. At other times the mountain seemed too steep and high for the airship to climb over, so there would be a sudden change of course as the helmsman turned to go round it and the *Italia*, engines roaring, would flee down some dark valley in an unknown direction. It was a bit like a steeple chase, but at 50 miles an hour and in a huge vehicle almost 350 feet long. At last, by steering for that lighter patch of sky when they could, among all the necessary zig-zags, they at last burst out of the mountains and found themselves over a plain with a rapidly clearing horizon in front of them. But where exactly were they?

The navigators were divided. One thought they were over Poland while the other two thought they were still in Czechoslovakia. It had been impossible to keep an accurate track of their erratic twists and turns in bad visibility and much of it at night. The Czechs who had been trying to track them thought also that the *Italia* was over their own soil, somewhere near Brünn. Careful map-reading, however, showed that they were over Silesia. Nobile was in no mood now to risk yet more bad weather, so he circled slowly while waiting for a weather forecast. It was favourable and he turned the *Italia* north again.

Already the sky was clearing ahead and the lights of cities were sparkling in the night as the airship droned over them. Beyond Breslau they had to climb to 2,500 metres to get above cloud; now and then there was rain and also signs of ice formation on the hull. It was certainly very much colder than it had been in northern

Italy, and they began to shiver. The temperature at the height they were flying was —5 °C. some 17 degrees lower than in Milan. At 0750 on the morning of 16 April, after a flight of more than thirty hours duration, they came in to land at Jesseritz, near Stolp, with the aid of a ground crew made up of German soldiers. They had no ballast left, but there was a handsome margin of petrol and oil in the tanks after covering 2,000 kilometres (about 1,200 miles), in adverse conditions. Not only had one lateral fin been broken, they discovered, but the upper fin also, while the propellers were eroded by the impact of the hailstones.

Nobile decided not merely to make good the damage to the broken fins but to strengthen all the fins while they were at it, and so they were delayed ten days because workmen and materials had to come from Italy. The expedition, however, was not delayed because, although the hangar and mooring mast at King's Bay were ready by 28 April, the *Città di Milano* had not got further than Tromsoe, her captain having heard that King's Bay was iced-up. Their time now really was starting to run out and Nobile telegraphed to suggest that the *Città di Milano* begin unloading stores over the ice, without waiting for the little quay to become ice-free. At the same time he and Malmgren were anxiously studying the weather forecasts, looking for a favourable pattern to emerge. They could not expect anything like the easy flight they had had from Leningrad with the *Norge* in 1926, when almost all the winds were favourable almost all of the time, but they did not want to run into another such depression as they had already encountered over Czechoslovakia.

On 30 April the Geophysical Institute at Tromsoe told Nobile that there was a strong wind, Force 5 on the Beaufort Scale, over the Barents Sea, adding that this was as good as one could hope for at the time of year. However, although Scandinavia itself was basking in good weather, there was another patch of rough weather over Stolp. Nobile dared not take the *Italia* out of the hangar. That violent wind continued for two days. At last, on 2 May Nobile and Malmgren decided that a start must be made early next day, although that evening there was a headwind blowing at 50 k.p.h. (30 m.p.h.) at heights up to 300 metres (1,000 feet). This was a tense decision when it was not merely their own lives which were at stake, but the lives of others and the success or ruin of the whole expedition.

Nobile's wife had brought their daughter Maria all the way to Stolp on the Baltic in order to say one last farewell. He told her of his decision while they were out walking. While they were passing a small church, she said to him, 'Let's go in.' Inside it was dark and empty, but she knelt down to pray. She refused to leave his side until the final departure of the *Italia* for the Arctic at 0328 on 3 May. There was a strong north wind of 40 k.p.h. (24 m.p.h.) blowing almost dead against the airship as it rose above the field and with all three engines roaring at forced revolutions, it laboured away towards Stockholm. All the scientific instruments had now been embarked as well as the boats which they would use if forced down into the Baltic Sea or the even more inhospitable Barents Sea.

It was nearly 400 miles to Stockholm, but the Swedish capital was reached after only 7½ hours flying, because Nobile was pressing the engines. Several Swedish seaplanes were waiting for them in the air and formed up on either side of the great bulk of the airship as it rumbled slowly over the islands on which the Swedish city is built. Malmgren pointed out the house where his mother lived and the *Italia* flew majestically overhead, almost hovering so that a letter of greetings could be dropped to her.

That was in the morning. Night found them over Finland, a flat and frozen landscape. Some hours after midnight the first disturbing weather reports began to come in. A depression was moving eastwards across the waters between Spitzbergen and Bear Island. It was advised that they increase speed so as to arrive at Vadsoe and its mooring mast before the good conditions at present existing there deteriorated.

Nobile ordered the third motor started up and higher revs on the other two. The *Italia* droned on through the dark northern night until the spectre of fog over the hills forced her to climb to a safer height. Just before 9 o'clock in the morning of 4 May, thinking that there must now be sea beneath them and that therefore it was safe to descend through the fog without risk of striking high ground, Nobile brought the *Italia* down through the greyish-white vapour – and found that they were still over land. . . . But the coast was in sight and the navigation had been good, for there was the little island that most of them remembered from 1926 and the mooring mast rearing up above it. They secured to it safely although a gust of wind brought the nose into collision with the mast, causing slight damage quickly repaired. Four hours later the expected strong winds began to buffet the *Italia*, swung her round and round her mooring mast, making the flexible girderwork creak audibly. Nobile had two of the engines started and he kept them revving slowly, prepared for any emergency. The wind increased in force until it reached 55 k.p.h. (40 m.p.h.), with violent gusts. Dark clouds raced overhead and snow fell in dense showers.

Fearing that it might freeze, Nobile sent Alessandrini forward to check what was happening on top of the hull. He squirrelled through the port-hole and then came back to report that the violence of the wind was making it act like a brush, it was literally sweeping the fresh snow off the envelope. At midday the wind began to drop, and the whirling snowflakes were succeeded by pouring torrents of rain which ran down the hull and penetrated even into the cabin, soaking everything. And then, even that died away and a meteorological report came in predicting light winds for the first part of their journey, from Norway to Bear Island; strong contrary winds of 35 to 55 k.p.h. for the second part, from Bear Island to Spitzbergen; and winds over the King's Bay landing ground of between 30 and 45 kilometres per hour. Far from ideal for an airship, but if they waited, another depression might catch them in mid-ocean. Malmgren urged an immediate attempt to reach Spitzbergen, and Nobile agreed.

They left Vadsoe, at 8.34 in the evening of 5 May and at 4.30 next morning were in sight of Bear Island, mantled in white. Malmgren suggested they do a turn over the Meteorological Observatory down there as a kind of 'thank you' for the information they had received. After circling, the *Italia* flew on to the north. So far they had met only light winds, as predicted, but beyond Bear Island the winds became as strong as forecasted, but not from the expected direction. Instead of a headwind, the blow came from the south-east, carrying them fast towards Spitzbergen and the Arctic Ocean. Nobile was tempted to accept this piece of good fortune and perform a reconnaissance flight over the ice immediately, without first landing at Spitzbergen. The cruising speed of the *Italia* in still air was only 48 m.p.h. and like a sailing ship it is sometimes best to let an airship do what it wants and not force it in a difficult direction for the sake of a rigid plan. Nobile calculated that he had enough petrol to sail on with this wind for another three days. Then, just as had happened with the *Norge*, one of their three engines packed up, needing major repair work. A Polar research flight now would be rash. They would have to land at Spitzbergen after all.

As they ran along the west coast of Spitzbergen, heading for the inlet of King's Bay, a violent snowstorm engulfed them. The heavens seemed to be in motion, with cloud masses scudding in various directions at different heights but mainly from the northwest. It was a dramatic and magnificent sight, thought Nobile. 'The situation is rather dangerous,' said Malmgren. 'The atmosphere is full of energy.'

This seemed to be an under-statement, for at that moment the wind was so strong that the airship was moving sideways faster than she was going ahead. But the blizzard passed and left them in clearer weather, with better reports coming in from the landing field at Ny Aalesund; wind decreasing, visibility improving. Just before noon, they arrived. Below was the black bulk of the ex-German *Città di Milano*, gaily decked with flags now, making the 150-ton sealer *Hobby* seem small, and there was the hangar and the ground waiting to receive them. At 12.45 Nobile gave orders to drop the mooring cable. Captain Sora's detachment of Alpine skiers picked it up, a mass of sailors from the *Città di Milano* lent their weight, and together they mastered the power of the wind and pulled the *Italia* down towards the earth.

It was too strong to manoeuvre the airship into the hangar, so for the moment the *Italia* had to be secured to the mooring mast. But she was not very secure, because a violent tug by the mooring party had broken a few tubes at the nose and Nobile thought the mooring gear might collapse. He had ropes thrown down and asked an Italian officer below to get fifty of his men to hang on to them in case of a failure of the mooring gear. He was told that he could not have the men for any length of time because Captain Romagna Manoja of the *Città di Milano* would not consent. This was the first but not, as it proved, the last, occasion on which Captain Romagna saw to it that the absolute minimum of assistance was given to the *Italia*. So instead Nobile asked the directors of the Norwegian Mining Company for the aid of their men. When the wind dropped momentarily some forty-five minutes later, a party consisting of the Alpini, a few sailors and a large party of Norwegian miners moved the airship from the mast to the greater security of the hangar. Then at last, after eighty-two hours of continuous duty, Nobile was able to rest.

Nobile's power of endurance was phenomenal. It was a necessity for all the pioneers of long-distance flying of the time. He himself was well aware that he possessed this quality. It was clear even to those who, like Behounek, did not yet know him very well. The Czech scientist was to write shortly afterwards: 'It would have been impossible not to admire the General. He was a highly accomplished leader, ideal for this expedition, who had planned everything down to the smallest detail, and knew how to give an example to everyone through his almost superhuman staying power.'

This second stage of the flight to Spitzbergen, from Vadsoe on the Norwegian coast, had gone very well; the airship had covered 1,332 kilometres in 15½ hours, giving an average speed of 86 k.p.h. The distance from Stolp, their start point on the Baltic, was 3,520 kilometres. In round figures the total distance covered over the ground since leaving Milan was 5,000 kilometres, or approximately 3,200 miles. For a small airship, half the size of a Zeppelin, this was an achievement. Of course, in the *Norge* they had done the same, more or less, but in exceptionally favourable weather conditions. And, of course, with a mixed crew of Italians and Norwegians, whereas this, except for the scientific side, was a purely Italian venture. Nobile was very conscious of it. They all were.

In the flowery phrases which were the common linguistic coin during the years of Mussolini's regime, Nobile wrote down his thoughts next day.

'It is a profound relief to see our ship safely at rest in her shed: the ship to which we have given a soul and a name – our soul and the name of Italy.

'Now we are in the fighting line we can even afford to fall as men die in battle; but it would have been bitter to fall out during the approach march, before reaching our post in the vanguard.

'From Milan to Stolp, from Stolp to Spitzbergen, nothing has been spared us – countless vicissitudes, difficulties, dangers. . . .

'But above all an intangible peril. . . . Two years before I had steered up here a ship with a foreign name: and so, at all costs, I must now bring the ship which bore the banner and the name of Italy. . . . There could be no failure.

'And there has been none!

'During the most critical moments an inner force surged up to give me the necessary strength and will. At the hardest moments of all something within me cried: "*You must not give in! You must overcome even this! . . . We are bound to get up there, on the threshold of the Pole – get there with our ship intact, and get there in time!*" '

The triumph was succeeded by four days hard work. The damaged engine had to be repaired, the other two overhauled. The airship had to be replenished with hydrogen gas, petrol, oil. The scientific instruments had to be checked and put in order. Most of the items required were still in the base ship *Città di Milano* moored out at the edge of the ice sheet in the bay, two kilometres away. All had to be dragged over the snow to the hangar. But all was ready when the Tromsoe Geophysical Institute telegraphed that weather conditions were favourable for an airship flight to Nicholas II Land, renamed by the Soviets Severnaya Zemlya.

As the Soviet scientist Samoilovich had suspected, Nobile did not have a firm plan. Instead he had major objectives which he would attempt in no particular order, but as weather forecasting dictated. He had five routes which he wanted to cover, and so he numbered them and asked Tromsoe to tell him when the weather pattern appeared to be favourable for any of the numbers. Nicolas II Land (North Land in Soviet nomenclature) meant a very long flight indeed to the eastward around the top of the globe, more or less circling the Pole. This was a major objective, covering completely unexplored regions and probably establishing whether or no there was such a place as Giles Land (so called after the Dutch captain Cornelius Giles, who reported it in 1719). The return route would not be the same as the outward flight path, so a vast area would be covered. In addition, Nobile wanted to make one or more flights to the Pole (but not in a direct line) which would enable them to pass over the then unexplored regions north of Greenland and another such area between the 30th and 40th meridians east of Greenwich.

More opportunist ideas were toyed with. A flight to the mouth of the Mackenzie River in North America was on the cards, if conditions were right; a long term drift on one engine, and a possible landing to take sea water samples and depth soundings (there was a lack of these and knowledge of depths in particular was at this time sketchy and inaccurate). Given the susceptibility then of all aircraft to the weather and the impossibility at the time of really guaranteed accurate weather forecasting, Nobile's flexible attitude to exploration seems realistic. Indeed, because much of the world's weather tends to originate in the north, ironically Nobile's scientific programme might enable future weather forecasters to work with increased certainty.

Inherent in that situation was the risk that on such long flights over unexplored regions in a comparatively slow and vulnerable airship, the weather might change more rapidly than forecast, or a change might not be forecast at all, or based on insufficient data, the forecast might be quite wrong. On the other hand, looking at the matter from the perspective of the 1920s, what a great advance exploration by airship was upon the old method of exploration by men on foot with dogs! They had died, too, from bad luck or miscalculation, but no one had blamed them for trying.

Nobile decided to take off on this very demanding flight of at least 3,500 kilometres without refuelling, on the morning of 11 May. Almost at once, there was a minor misfortune. The decision had been taken the day before when the temperature was −10°C (14° F) in the morning, as it had been for some days. This cold contracted the hydrogen gas, so that more of it could be forced into the lifting bags. On the morning of the planned start, the temperature shot up to above zero Centigrade. This curtailed the lifting power of the airship and thus Nobile had to reduce the load she carried. No petrol could be sacrificed on such a long flight; it had to be people. Nobile cut the crew numbers down from eighteen to fourteen. No journalists, no second radio operator, and only two scientists instead of three. Behounek was the unlucky one. Admirably concealing his bitter disappointment, he entrusted some of his experiments to Professor Pontremoli.

At 0755 on 11 May the *Italia* rose above King's Bay, propellers slowly turning; then, speeding up to cruising revolutions, and going out over the sea towards Cape Mitra, prior to skirting round the mountains of West Spitzbergen before turning east for the flight over the Arctic ocean. The Norwegians call the area the Svalbard. The two largest of the many islands of which it is composed are named by the Norwegians Vestspitzbergen and Nordaustlandet − West Spitzbergen and North-East Land. Between these two main land masses runs a broad channel − Hinlopen Strait. West Spitzbergen has much high ground, some of the peaks reaching well over 5,000 feet. North-East Land is smaller but much of the landscape is covered with ice above the

2,000 feet level. For low-powered aircraft and airships these are barriers which it is wisest not to surmount, and so the *Italia* went the long way round, skirting the coast, because a flight low down over the sea was quicker and also made the most efficient use of the gas in her lifting bags. If they went higher up, into thinner atmospheres, the static lift would diminish; but they might have to valve gas because it would expand.

They had not been flying for very long when Alessandrini, the foreman rigger, came to Nobile to report that a wire cable which was a vital part of the rudder controls was badly worn in one place. Loss of rudder control could be fatal, particularly in bad weather, so Nobile went to see for himself. He thought the cable might part under sudden strain, so ordered the worn piece to be reinforced for the moment with a length of fresh cable. This lapse was not a very good omen.

Shortly after, off Barren Cape, they saw patches of ice floating in the sea and, altering course now to the eastwards for Moffen Island, they ran into a low pressure area. A snowstorm battered them for two hours and ice began to form all over the hull; in its turn, the ice collected some of the snow as a rapidly increasing outer covering. Malmgren expressed alarm at this. By now they were approaching the North Cape of North-East Land, beyond Hinlopen Strait, with the weather becoming worse and worse. As the wireless bulletins came in, they predicted bad weather ahead along the whole of the intended route to Nicholas II Land. Nobile was reluctant to admit defeat on his first flight of exploration, but in the circumstances, with a damaged rudder cable and several thousands of miles of bad weather ahead, along the out and return routes, it would be unwise to persist.

But he did not give up. He turned the *Italia* away to the north, seeking for a way round the low pressure area, slight though the chance was. He was soon convinced that the way north was barred also. That left only one of his five intended routes of exploration open: the unknown area off the North Coast of Greenland. If the weather was better in the west than in the east the *Italia* could still carry out part of her programme. So Nobile turned westwards towards Barren Cape, a course which would take him in the direction of Greenland. Meanwhile, Malmgren was trying to get a weather report and forecast for Greenland; but communications were bad because two powerful stations on Spitzbergen were working – Green Harbour and Ny Aalesund –

and for a long time it was impossible to get Tromsoe. When they did, the information was of historic value only.

Locally, they had a dangerously strong north wind pushing them towards the peaks of Spitzbergen, combined with a hazardous drop in visibility. There was no hope for it – they might just as well give up and go home, which they did. At 4.10 p.m. the *Italia* was back again at Ny Aalesund, after a flight of only eight hours or so.

The flight had not been an entire waste of time, fuel and money. Professor Pontremoli had some scientific results to show: 10 observations of penetrating radiations, 5 of the gradient of electric force, 2 of atmospheric conductibility, 4 of radio-activity. Four series of measurements with the Midlingmayer double compass had been made; but three were useless because unreliable. Only one measurement had not been rendered suspect by the continual pitching and rolling of the airship.

Decidedly, an anti-climax.

Chapter 7

ENTER AN UNDERPRIVILEGED JOURNALIST

NOBILE planned to spend only one day on the ground before attempting the next flight of exploration. That would be on 13 May. Its target would depend on what routes were safely available, according to the forecast from Tromsoe. In 1926, during the four days the *Norge* had spent at Ny Aalesund, the weather had been splendid, with blue skies. 1928 proved to be exceptional. On 12 May, snow began to fall. On 13 May it was still falling, and heavily. Worse, the wind had dropped. The snowstorm, arriving on the tail of the *Italia* after her return from the abortive expedition, had swept across King's Bay as a blizzard. It was so thick, that one could lose one's way on the landing ground and even miss finding the hangar. Yet there was a plus factor in the weather, for such a wind did not allow the snow to remain and build up on top of the airship's hull, but swept the structure clean like a broom, as it had done before when they were moored to the mast at Vadsoe.

The moment the wind dropped, the threat to the structure of the airship became extreme. The build-up of snow was rapid, because the 'hangar' at Ny Aalesund had no roof; it was completely open to the storm. Basically, it was a wind-block rather than a hangar proper, which would have been unwarrantably expensive for the Norwegians to build in the circumstances of 1926 – one flight by one airship. It consisted of two parallel wooden walls like a long, high corridor open at both ends, and unroofed. The open ends could be closed at will by dropping canvas curtains. With the wind sideways to the wooden walls, the structure was effective, but much less so when the wind was blowing at one end or the other of the long corridor. Then the curtains flapped violently. From above, there was no protection at all. Sun, rain or snow, all could strike directly at the upper hull of the airship inside. Sun could cause the gas to expand while the

airship was still on the ground; if the cells were full, some gas
would have to be valved off. Snow was the opposite danger.

As the wind dropped, the snow began to accumulate on top of
the hull; it was so rapid that the Italians could see it happening.
Nobile had a snow sample collected in one hour from a flat
surface a metre square: it weighed half a kilo. The amount of hull
exposed to the snow was in excess of 2,000 squares metres. So
every hour, more than a ton of snow was collecting on top of the
airship. Already, the control cabin and the rear engine nacelle
were dragging and bumping on the hangar floor, despite Nobile's
efforts to increase the *Italia*'s lift and to unload some of her
stores. And, ominously, looking high above his head at the
stern structure supporting the great lateral fins, now bowed
under their weight of snow, Nobile could see creases in the
outer covering, evidence that the metal plating underneath was
buckling.

The little white snow flakes, soft and innocuous, falling every
second on the envelope of the *Italia*, would inevitably destroy her
if something was not done at once. The only answer was to
organise gangs of sweepers, to go up on top of the hull and,
walking all over the envelope, brush it free of one ton of snow
every hour as a minimum. And this was not without its own risk
of damage, for the *Italia* was a soft-skinned airship and devoid of
inner framework except for the nose-cone, the stern and the
articulated keel. The upper hull was meant to be inspected but not
walked all over by gangs of workmen for nearly two days. But
this was what had to be done. Nobile brought in sailors from the
base ship as well as Italian workmen and, sweeping continuously
90 feet above the ground, they kept the weight of snow within
bearable limits until the temperature began to rise and the snow
started to melt.

That also brought a risk – the danger that a drop in temperature
during the melting process would freeze both the water and the
remains of the unmelted snow, caking the *Italia* in a sheathing of
ice. This did happen, but only to a limited degree along the keel;
and this ice layer was quickly broken and removed. Then the
snow falls stopped, the sun shone out radiantly, and the water
dripping from every part of the sorry-looking airship dried up.
Nobile at once organised an inspection of the trampled-on upper
hull. Its treatment had looked more severe than it really was:
there were only a few small tears, easily mended, and one large,

abraded area near the nose which Nobile had repaired by sticking down an extra thickness of rubberised fabric.

Starting with the alarming electrical storm which they had encountered over Czechoslovakia on the flight out from Milan, continuing with the unforecast bad weather which had abruptly aborted their long-distance flight to Nicholas II Land before it had hardly begun, and ending with this, the *Italia* nearly destroyed in her hangar by mere snow, bad luck had seemed to dog the enterprise. And yet they had surmounted all these trials.

From the day the *Italia* arrived, however, they had had a critic present, determined to make as much mileage as possible out of the attempts by Italian interlopers to conquer the Norwegian north. The journalist Odd Arnesen, correspondent of a leading Oslo paper, had a difficult task from the beginning. He had virtually nothing to write about. All he could describe at first hand would be the departure and arrival of an airship at King's Bay; for everything else he was dependent on the Italians telling him what had happened and with the sort of detail his own home audience might require. And the Italians could not possibly give him a scoop, for the first news had always to go to Mussolini and then to their home press in Italy. Further, as he was in direct competition with the two Italian journalists actually accredited to the expedition, they had very good reasons for doling out stale and meagre information to their commercial rival. As a good journalist, Arnesen must have envied Francesco Tomaselli and Ugo Lago, his Italian opposition; they had the inside track and, if Nobile was as good as his word, stood some chance of actually going with the *Italia* on one or more of the flights of exploration. As it was, all he could do was look on from the outside, beg for more than an official 'handout' from Captain Romagna Manoja of the *Città di Milano*, who fobbed him off with drinks and excuses, or ask General Nobile some rather obvious and even silly questions, to which the General might have replied in kind. Such as: 'What do you hope to find in Nicholas II Land?' Instead of answering 'If I knew that in advance, I wouldn't bother to go there', Nobile merely said that he didn't know. The Italians must have found Odd irritating but were too polite to say so.

Arnesen suspected that Nobile was saving all the best bits for the articles and books he himself planned to write about the expedition, but nevertheless found that the General was one of the few Italians present who was partly sympathetic to the press and understood their needs. Nevertheless, the *Italia* story was not a string of colourful incidents easily understood by both the press and the public they fed; on the contrary, aviation hazards, especially those concerned with airships, were too technical to be comprehended easily. If the *Italia* did not crash – if there was no disaster – then there was no story. Not for the world's press, at any rate. An Italian airship at Spitzbergen was a story only for Italians and Norwegians, which was why Arnesen and his rivals were there; there was virtually no one else interested (although a crop of local amateur 'special correspondents' were soon to spring up).

If there is no conflict, there is no drama – and no news either. It may have seemed to Arnesen that he might have a story for his readers, who were Norwegians, if he carried on the Amundsen attitude of Italians versus Norwegians in the North. It may even have been suggested to him by reading the report of Nobile's last speech to his supporters in Milan before leaving Italy. The version available to Arnesen had been printed in *Popolo d'Italia*, Mussolini's own newspaper, on 25 March 1928. In this Nobile had outlined the opportunity for aerial exploration – four million square kilometres of unexplored surface inside the Arctic circle; had explained the precautions he had taken but accepted nevertheless the possibility of disaster, and had concluded by saying that the worst danger was, that they would be vilified if they failed. 'There, you see. We warned you. Your race does not breed polar explorers.' Put like that, it might seem that Nobile was referring solely to criticism from Scandinavian countries. What Arnesen could not know were the Italian intrigues against Nobile, the fact that some Italians would be glad if he crashed and ruined himself. The General's closing remarks had been double-barbed.

Still, a convinced critic's comments can be illuminating, particularly when he does not criticise. Above all, it shows how the Nobile expedition appeared to a non-Italian observing it from outside and as part only of an Arctic aviation assignment.

Odd Arnesen left Tromsoe in the sealer *Mina* with three other passengers for Spitzbergen – an American movie cameraman and two Norwegian wireless operators. The first day on leaving the harbour, the skipper collided with another boat and stove in a plank; the second day he got a finger crushed in the engine and the cabin boy was seasick when they ran into a gale. At Green Harbour the *Mina* ran aground, and later when sledging across the ice they managed to get the dogs on one ice floe, the sledge on another, and all the dogs and most of the men ended up in the icy water. After this Arnesen still had the gall to criticise the sailors of the *Città di Milano* for being clumsy in Arctic conditions. According to him, the misfortunes of the *Mina* were due entirely to having nearly sailed on a Friday.

At the Green Harbour wireless station, well to the south of King's Bay, Arnesen had his first interview with Arctic aviators. The two he talked to were Captain George H. Wilkins, the Australian, and Carl B. Eielson, the Norwegian-American. It was this pair who, from Point Barrow in 1926, had seen the silvery shape of the *Norge* as she made the historic first crossing of the Arctic Ocean, and had mentally applauded Amundsen, Ellsworth and Nobile for the feat they had accomplished. Now they had themselves made a crossing, but in the opposite direction, from Point Barrow in Alaska to Spitzbergen, skirting Greenland in a modern American aeroplane, the second Lockheed Vega monoplane to be built. In spite of difficult navigation due to the proximity of the Magnetic Pole, they had flown 2,500 miles of which some 1,300 miles had never been seen before by man. The flight had been almost, but not quite, non-stop; a snowstorm had forced them down on an aptly named Dead Man's Island, off Spitzbergen, for five days. Their flight had been triumphant by a narrow margin; a minor piece of bad luck could have been fatal, many times. Men less well-prepared, ingenious and bold would have succumbed in any case. Wilkins received a knighthood for it.

At the end of their flight, they had overlapped with a Nobile expedition once again. The 150-ton sealer *Hobby* had been up at King's Bay unloading supplies in advance of the arrival of the *Italia*, when on 22 April the Lockheed Vega had landed at Green Harbour with only a few gallons of fuel left. Wilkins was hoping that the little vessel would embark his aircraft and take them on to Norway. Arnesen was still at Green Harbour with the *Mina* when on 6 May he had his first glimpse of the *Italia*, just as two years ago Wilkins and Eielson had first seen the *Norge*. Arnesen was filled with foreboding at what he saw. The polar airship was trying to stem a headwind so strong that it was making her waver like a drunkard from her course; pitching and rolling, fighting the weather all the time, the *Italia* flew over Green Harbour. It seemed impossible that she could land safely at King's Bay let alone be got into the hangar, but although it took many hours, Nobile managed it.

The Norwegian journalist's report confirms the impression left both by Nobile's writings and by meeting the General. Weather conditions and other technical matters are coldly stated, and understated rather than exaggerated. He writes sometimes like a rather finicky and precise lecturer, so that the impact of events is half lost, although there are some fine descriptive passages of Arctic icescapes seen from the air, which clearly thrilled him and was part-motivation for his return to the polar regions. Hyperbole occurs only when he has to describe an achievement in Fascist terms. Even here, unlike Balbo, he does not grovel to the Duce in the writings he published under Fascism. Ironically, when he does admit to having been helped by Mussolini in this or that way, one tends to believe him; whereas with Balbo such compliments appear to be obligatory, perhaps because at one time Balbo became so popular that he even threatened Mussolini's position.

Arnesen gives an amusing description of Captain Romagna's attempts to clear the ice in King's Bay and to bring the *Città di Milano* alongside the quay to discharge the many tons of stores for the *Italia*. He depicts a party of 40 men hauling away while their superiors, with megaphones, shouted out the tempo: 'Forza – forza – piano – forza!' And he contrasts this with the quiet way in which the Norwegians could do the same job of moving an ice anchor with but two men; how the Italians merely blew ineffective holes in the ice while the Norwegian miners created a channel a kilometre long in three days.

The Norwegian journalist called the Italians 'poor ice-men', hailing from a 'soft, smiling and sunny country' who 'were soon found manifestly wanting.' The fact was, that the Italian navy had no ships or crews specifically intended for polar work. The *Città di Milano*, really the ex-German cable-layer *Oldenburg*, merely happened to be available; she was not really suited to the task. Her officers and crew were totally inexperienced; only the Army detachment of Alpini under Captain Sora were used to ice and snow, although not accustomed to solving marine problems. They had to learn while doing. The Norwegian's strictures might seem harsh when applied to the ordinary sailors who were doing their energetic but not very skilful best in unfamiliar circumstances. They are, however, a valuable corrective to the Italian Navy's official history, doubtless based on Captain Romagna's reports, which not merely depicts the work of his ship as immaculate, but seems to imply that, throughout, the *Città di Milano* did everything; there was really no need for anyone else. Navies, much more than Armies or Air Forces, do tend to burnish their image to unbearable (and unbelievable) brightness; by no means is this trait confined to Italy. So it is as well to understand that Captain Romagna was quite unequal to the difficult times which were coming.

For most of the time there was nothing for Arnesen – or any journalist – to do. It was like a war, there was so much waiting. And as most of the actors in the drama were Italians, he discovered that there was plenty of warning when something newsworthy was being contemplated. The tempo of work suddenly speeded up, people ran instead of walked, the tractor carrying loads from the base ship to the hangar was driven at high speed instead of slow; and the Italians *talked* – you could actually measure the increased work tempo by the sound of their voices.

The Norwegian found the Italian sailors to be 'the queerest conglomeration of warring opinions'. Some were fanatical followers of Mussolini. These 'shot up like rockets' to give the Fascist salute whenever General Nobile appeared in camp. Others were lukewarm Fascists, while some were unpolitical and disinterested. Arnesen went around among the Italians untactfully enquiring if they were Fascists and usually got the reply: 'Neva, neva'. When he asked if Mussolini's regime had improved their lot, they turned their thumbs down in the old way of the Roman arena. That they felt free to do so, and were not afraid, was a political commentary also.

The bustle went on, as petrol, gas cylinders, pemmican, furs, sleeping bags – stores of all kinds – were winched up out of the holds of the ship, piled on the quay and later bumped across the snow to the hangar by the tractor or carried up on the shoulders of the Italian workmen. The precise loading for any particular flight, and even the number of men in the crew, were dictated, as we have seen, by the route to be taken, which could not be known long in advance because it depended on the weather, a variable factor; and also on whatever the ground temperature happened to be at King's Bay, another variable. The airship men must have got very tired of explaining technicalities to journalists who wanted a plain, exciting human story, not technicalities.

Nobile gave Arnesen fairly short shift, when the Norwegian accosted him in the hangar where he was extremely busy superintending the loading for what was hoped to be a long flight to Nicholas II Land.

The General, a wary veteran of world press encounters, could not be drawn in to making quotable, but unscientific, speculation regarding his hopes of finding new land east of Spitzbergen. Nor would he give the Norwegian even an approximate start time for such a flight. Disgusted, Arnesen commented that Nobile 'knew very little about anything – everything depended on weather conditions, on Tromsoe, on Malmgren'.

So the Norwegian tried Malmgren. The Swedish scientist shooed him away. 'You get us three or four days of high pressure around the Pole, and then we'll vamoose, to the great joy of you journalists.'

In fact the wait was not long, particularly not to the perspiring workmen, but for unemployed pressmen it seemed endless. Some of their editors were holding them personally responsible. 'Why does not the *Italia* start?' read a telegram received by one journalist. His return message was: 'It really isn't my fault'.

It was then that the snow fell and building up on the *Italia*, threatened the whole expedition. Arnesen described the scene in the roofless hangar as the wet, heavy snow settled on the envelope and every man who could be got was stationed ninety feet up, beating at the stuff with their brooms while the airship's envelope quivered with the impact and from the weight of ten tons of accumulated snow. And then the storm arose and threatened to blow in the shutters and crush one end of the *Italia*. Arnesen wrote that it had been an 'exciting night', which the Italians might well term 'a night of horror', for they had had very real difficulties to overcome. Once again, Arnesen's version is more vivid than Nobile's and confirms the deliberate calmness of the General's writing.

When the sun shone out after the storm, it made people blink, so strongly was it reflected from the overall white of the scenery, the snow on the plain and on the peaks, the ice on the bay. This time, Arnesen sensed from the attitude of the Italians that action was imminent; they acted as if swept by an invigorating breeze. They worked on the airship in the hangar all night, Nobile supervising; they sang happily, Fascist songs and national anthems, as far as Arnesen could tell. In the morning, they were so tired, they

5

fell asleep at their workplaces, ready to carry on if called. Number 3 engine was proving obstinate and Cecioni was trying to fix it.

The cause of the sudden stir had been a good weather forecast for the Polar basin east of Spitzbergen received on the morning of 14 May. Confirmation of the trend was received from Tromsoe at 6 o'clock that evening in the following terms:

'The depression at Jan Mayen will move south-east. The south-easterly wind between Jan Mayen, Bear Island, and South Spitzbergen will increase. The high pressure still extends from Spitzbergen towards Leninland, (Nicholas II Land) and seems to be of a stable character. We therefore still consider the situation favourable for flight on route number one.'

Translated, this meant that the calm weather associated with a 'high' lay over their intended path to Nicholas II Land, and that the 'low', associated with bad weather, was moving away out of the area. Now, weather forecasting is not an exact science; and in 1928 was hardly a science at all, because far too many factors affecting the weather were unknown. But this was a very favourable forecast for the longest flight of all, and well worth a risk. Nobile took it.

The flight to Nicholas II Land was far more difficult and dangerous than that of the *Norge* to Alaska in 1926, although the distances to be flown were about the same – 3,500 kilometres. For the crossing of the Polar Ocean, all that was necessary was to wait for a wind blowing from Spitzbergen to Point Barrow and go with it; rather like a sailing ship, in fact. But the *Italia* could not do this. All her flights from Spitzbergen had to be on an out-and-return basis so that, if the wind was favourable going, it was likely to be unfavourable coming back. To cope with the virtual certainty of encountering headwinds for perhaps half the voyage, Nobile decided to load 7,000 kilos of petrol, enough for 85 flying hours at a cruising speed of 80 km. per hour. The only way to secure this was to cut out ballast altogether, and so Nobile had the last water tank holding 300 litres turned over to petrol instead. The only flexibility he would have lay in the 250 kilos of petrol which the airship would carry in tins; as a last resort, these could be jettisoned. This was an extreme measure, more complete even than with the *Norge* in May 1926. Just how risky it was, only an airship man could really appreciate; certainly the journalists would not be able to convey the sense of hazard to their readers.

Nor would they find much to write about in the complicated process of embarking several tons of equipment; first selecting the priority items and then finding places to stow them where they would be instantly available. Particularly heavy was the gear to assist a landing on snow or ice, to put down a party intending to carry out scientific work; it was a kind of mooring chain with flotation devices, more elaborate than the landing sack used with the *Norge* in 1926. Then, in case of disaster, which could be in the form of accidental damage to the airship or merely running out of fuel due to persistent adverse weather, they had to take with them all the equipment the whole crew would need in order to make a long march over the ice. This included three large tents, three sledges, sleeping bags, heavy clothing for everyone, axes, three rifles with ammunition, stoves, food reserves and so on. And also a portable short-wave radio set with which to summon up rescue.

All these items, plus the scientific instruments, spare parts and food for the flight, amounted to a weight of 2,900 kilos. In addition, there was 7,000 kilos of petrol, 465 of oil, and 1,400 represented by the crew. A total of 11,800 kilos (236 cwt.) for an airship of only 18,500 cubic metres (24,000 cu. yards), suffering from the additional handicap that temperatures had risen to almost zero from the previous sub-zero figures which were most favourable for lift.

Nobile had tried to save additional weight by cutting down the crew figures to 14. But he could not manage it. He decided on 3 navigating officers – Mariano, Zappi, Viglieri; 2 helmsmen for the elevator – Trojani and Cecioni; 1 chief and 3 motor mechanics – Arduino plus Caratti, Ciocca, Pomella; 2 wireless operators – Pedretti and Biagi; and 1 foreman rigger – Allessandrini. Reluctantly, he again refused Behounek a place. Only two scientists would go – Malmgren and Pontremoli. When Behounek was told, he felt humiliated. Everyone had expected him to go and now he had been turned away again. It would have been bad enough if he had been an Italian, but for a foreigner whose only friend was Nobile, the slight was bitter. What made it worse was that this time Nobile was actually taking a journalist along with him. To replace a scientist with a pressman was an insult.

Up to now, Nobile had planned to exclude journalists altogether, but both Tomaselli and Lago had been so furious that he had had to reconsider. The Milanese Committee, the financial

backers of the whole affair, had been urging him to take at least
one of the two Italian pressmen with him on each flight. Nobile
decided for this solution, but still there was trouble, because
Francesco Tomaselli, the Venetian, and Ugo Lago, the Sicilian,
then fell out with each other as to who was to go on this particular
flight. At last, they decided to spin a coin for the honour. Ugo
Lago, 28, won and grinned delightedly. But Nobile intervened.
Tomaselli, 34, and a former Captain in the Alipini, was much the
senior man. He should go on this, the most difficult and also the
most important flight the *Italia* would make. None knew it then,
but Nobile had just decided on a matter of life and death. Life for
the one and death for the other.

Because of the delay with the third engine, the *Italia* was not
ready until almost all the morning of 15 May had gone. The sky
was brilliant blue and the hot sun soon melted what little snow
remained on her envelope, as two hundred Italians walked the
airship out of the hangar and down on to the plateau by the
mooring mast.

While the *Italia*'s enormous bulk loomed high above them,
held down by scores of mooring ropes grasped by the crowd, the
Pope's representative, Father Gian Franceschi, intoned the
explorer's prayer under the blue vault of heaven. A bottle of
sparkling Italian wine was broken against the nose of the control
cabin as it swayed just above the ground, there was leave-taking
all round, Nobile embraced his brother Amedeo in farewell, then
the order to let go was given. As the ground crew slowly allowed
the ropes to slip through their hands, the *Italia* rose almost
vertically to ear-splitting shouts of 'Ala-ala-ala!' As one by one
the motors roared into life, the airship men themselves gave a
series of cheers. Safely up at 300 feet the *Italia* steadied on her
course and began to move away above the snowfield of Ny
Aalesund towards the blue glacier marking the north end of
King's Bay. All this time, a German newsreel cameraman, hidden
in a coal tip, had been filming the start. He could not do it openly
because his company had refused to pay the large sum demanded
for sole film rights.

The miners themselves were now quite blasé about aviation.
What with Amundsen's flying boats, the aeroplanes of Byrd and
the Norwegian Navy, the airship *Norge* and now the *Italia*, they
scarcely bothered to look up as the huge hull passed over, noted

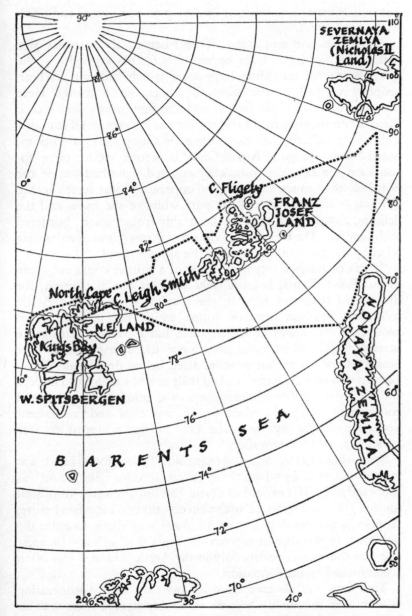

Fig. 1. Flight of the *Italia* to Severnaya Zemlya (Nicholas II Land)

Arnesen. 'Out flying again, is he?' they would grunt, and think no more about it.

Along the northern coast of Spitzbergen the weather was perfect and Nobile took the opportunity for photography, as the quickest way of recording large areas which had not yet been properly mapped. At the North Cape there was a change. Here the sea was completely frozen and the first snowstorm struck them. Even so, they could still see for ten kilometres all round, a welcome peculiarity of snowstorms in anticyclonic conditions, noted Nobile. 'Beyond North Cape,' he wrote, 'clouds came up and soon the sky was completely covered. I looked out of the port-hole then to see the pack, and once more I was struck by the glorious harmony between the pure white of the snow and the delicate, cloudy pearl-grey of the freshly frozen pools, bordered with blue ice. The blending of tints was thrown into even greater relief by the uniform greyness of the sky overhead.

'It was certainly a pity that a poet or a painter could not share in our Polar flights, because only an artist could interpret, for those who have not seen it, the magical sight of this Arctic colouring and the fantastic forms which the pack-ice often assumes. I had always felt this need, but especially during the present flight, when more than once the strange, suggestive beauty of the scene that unrolled itself below drew from me an exclamation of wonderment. And truly it was a delight to the eye and an indescribable exhilaration to the mind to lean out and contemplate the pack, when the air was clear and transparent under the cloudy sky. Even the icy wind that whipped my face only intensified the sensation.'

Somewhere between Spitzbergen and Franz Josef Land was unexplored territory where the so-called Gillis (or Giles) Land was supposed to lie, if it existed at all and had not been just an optical illusion glimpsed by that Dutch ship captain two centuries before. At 6.40 in the evening, just as the *Italia* was about to enter the unknown region, the airship ran into fog. Of all aviation hazards, this was the worst; particularly in the Arctic where it was often accompanied by ice-formation.

This time was no exception. Ice built up with disconcerting rapidity and the airship became noticeably heavy; there was no ballast they could jettison. Nobile was forced to take the *Italia* down below the fog and fly in a narrow band of clear air, only 150 metres high, between the pack-ice and fog-base. In this way, they explored the unknown territory, turning north to go deeper into it, and covering in all some 330 miles without any trace of the 'Gillis Land' shown on a number of maps. Along that path they could see for about 15 kilometres either side, so the area they had checked amounted to some 10,000 square kilometres. It seemed desolate and almost totally lifeless. They sighted a few black birds, coming out of the north, which veered away when they saw the airship; and later, one polar bear, equally startled, which scuttled off southward.

Meanwhile, the journalists back at King's Bay were waiting impatiently for developments. Partly as a safety measure, the *Italia* transmitted a message to the *Città di Milano* once an hour. Arnesen kept a record of some of these messages. One which must have been sent in the early hours of 16 May, contained a note of triumph for Mussolini:

'My promise to guide the *Italia* across unexplored polar territories is now being fulfilled. I send your Excellency respectful greetings from myself and my whole crew. We are now passing the north-eastern point of Franz Josef Land, our course being due north. The ocean is ice-free here. Perfect visibility increases my hope of landing on Nicholas II Land, probably in the course of the day.'

Once past Franz Josef Land's most northerly point – Cape Fligely – Nobile turned the nose of the *Italia* south-east, to penetrate into the heart of another great unexplored area. Visibility became much better, so that they could see for at least 50 kilometres all around. At 11.15 in the morning a strange optical illusion glittered on the horizon – a vague outline, like the roofs, chimneys and spires of a fantastic city of white and blue crystal rising from the ice. At one o'clock a bank of low clouds appeared ahead, reducing visibility to 15 kilometres. At two o'clock conditions worsened further, but at 4.30 they began to improve and at 5.10, as they were crossing a stretch of open water, the sky cleared and the sun shone out. A flock of birds appeared, winging their way over the next area of pack-ice. At 6.5 they were over a large expanse of open water, with a long bank of cumulus cloud in the distance. Malmgren judged this to be clouds over land. Nobile turned the airship's nose a few degrees to investigate, but the open water soon disappeared and another stretch of pack-ice began. There was no telling what might be

here, because even Nicholas II Land, just over the horizon, was
after all a fairly recent discovery, having been found by the
Russian A.I. Vilkitski some 15 years previously, just before the
Revolution. Most school atlases and globes still did not show
it.

It was now nearing midnight on 16 May. They had been airborne for 34 hours, and Nicholas II Land, although not in sight,
could only be an hour or two's flight away. For some time they
had been meeting a sidewind blowing from the north. At first,
it had not hindered them much, but now it was exceeding 40
kilometres an hour on the beam. The airship had to advance
crabwise, angled 30 to 40 degrees off course, and with the fluctuating squalls causing the nose to swerve ten to twenty degrees away.
It was exhausting for the helmsmen continually trying to correct,
and impossible for the navigators to draw an accurate track. As
the cruising speed of the *Italia* in still air was only 80 k.p.h., the
effect of a sidewind of 40 k.p.h. and over, may be imagined.
Further, their outward flight had already lasted ten hours longer
than Nobile had allowed for.

Back at King's Bay, on board the *Città di Milano*, Arnesen sensed
the danger the *Italia* was in from the changed attitude of the
officers and crew. They were what he called his 'barometer', the
centre of the 'instrument' being the wireless cabin and its hard-
working chief, Technical Captain Ugo Baccarini. Around him, as
the messages from Nobile came in, there gathered an anxious
group. Busy with maps and compasses, they discussed what might
happen and what options were open to Nobile, not really aware
that the Norwegian journalist was taking it all in as much by their
gestures and tone of voice as by what they actually said.

The airship was being driven southward, apparently, the
weather very bad. If she was unable to return to King's Bay,
would it be best to make for the mooring mast at Vadsoe? But if
she was driven south of that, what then? Only a handful of places
in Europe were equipped to land airships. She might have to
make an emergency crash landing, as the *Norge* had done in
Alaska. That would be a humiliating end to the programme of
research flights before they had been properly begun.

Arnesen sensed 'considerable anxiety'. The cause, he thought,
was the *Italia*'s continual demand throughout the afternoon of 17
May for radio bearings to be taken and transmitted to her. That

looked as if Nobile was uncertain of his position. That evening, seeing a group of officers, including Captains Romagna and Baccarini, passionately discussing the fate of the *Italia*, the Norwegian edged nearer to hear what they were saying. Baccarini was apprehensive, Romagna taking an optimistic line, however. Then seeing that the journalist was near enough to overhear, he put on an act, dismissing Baccarini with a wave of the hand and a 'Va bene, va, bene.'

It had required a great effort of will on Nobile's part to relinquish Nicholas II Land when it was so near. But the safety of the ship came before prestige. In any event, in this weather there was absolutely no chance of putting a party down on to the ground to carry out scientific research. The only real question was: which way home? To turn back would be unwise, for the beam wind would continue to hinder them just as badly. In consultation with Malmgren, Nobile decided to ride with the wind, like a sailing ship, the long way round, which often turns out to be the most economical route. So the *Italia* was steered away from Severnaya Zemlya, as the Soviets called Nicholas II Land, and headed south-west for Novaya Zemlya, a large long island situated in incompletely explored or completely unknown territory.

This proved to be a happy decision. They covered another 400 miles of pure exploratory flight with the wind actually helping them along and were not much hampered when they left Novaya Zemlya for the long crossing of the Barents Sea to Cape Leigh Smith in North-East Land, the second largest island of the Spitzbergen group. As they were flying along the coast from Cape Leigh Smith to Cape Bruun, the sun came out, bringing exceptionally good visibility. Further, the airship was now light, having used up much of her petrol and oil. Nobile therefore determined to fly over the then almost unknown interior of North-East Land as well as the equally vague interior of Spitzbergen proper. The former proved to be covered thinly in ice, with bare rocks emerging here and there, instead of the thick layer of continental ice shown to exist on many maps; indeed, the Italians saw only one glacier, and that a very small one.

The airship crossed Spitzbergen at a great height, reaching 2,800 metres. Above them, the sky was azure; below them, lay stretched out as on a relief map the fantastic shapes of the mountains, gleaming with ice and snow. It was an exhilarating

finish to their three days in the air. They landed at 10.20 on 18
May, having been airborne for sixty-nine hours and covered
about 4,000 kilometres over the Arctic. In that time, they had
flown over about 48,000 square kilometres of unknown territory,
had disproved the existence of Gillis Land (at least, in the position
indicated on maps), and had suggested the possible existence of
additional land near Severnaya Zemlya.

Arnesen had been out waiting on the field for more than an
hour before the *Italia* had come in sight, a speck high in the
burning blue sky at 8,700 feet. Lightened of her load, she seemed
to have difficulty in losing height and circled repeatedly. At last,
from 300 feet the main mooring rope was thrown down and
grasped by the eager ground crew, their heavy cloaks fluttering
in the wind, as they hauled the ship down to earth, others grasped
the side ropes. There were shouts of 'Ala-ala-ala!' Slowly, towed
by 200 men, the airship was walked into the hangar and secured.

The first to appear in the opened door of the control cabin was
Nobile, with Titina at his heels, whimpering and nervous.
Arnesen called the little dog 'surely the worst gadabout in history'.
Amid the clicking cameras, Nobile posed for the journalists,
'tired and worn, but smiling'; then he went on board the *Città di
Milano*.

Malmgren appeared, short and almost rotund in his warm flying
suit. The journalists surged forward, hoping for better 'copy'
from the Swedish scientist. 'What was the trip like?' they shouted.

'Very pleasant and eventful.'

'What happened, really?'

'Ah, if only you knew.'

'But,' the scientist added, 'if you don't, ask me; we haven't
been over Nicholas II Land.'

'Didn't you see the land then.'

'I'm not sure.'

'Was there fog below then?'

'I can't be definite.'

'But wasn't there sun below you when you were near the land?'

'Well now, generally the sun's up above.'

Malmgren knew perfectly well what they meant and the journalists were well aware that the scientist was bound by contract not
to give interviews; what they were not sure of, was when he was
joking and when he wasn't. It was all a game, but they helped the
chunky little Swede out of his flying suit, pushed an enamel bowl

full of warm water in front of him, so he could wash off the grime
of the long flight, followed by a large glass containing whisky as
a throat-cleanser. They still did not get the scientific results from
him, but that was not what they were after. Failing big exploration news, they needed those little touches which each pressman
could use in his own way, to pad out the official handouts they
would be receiving from Captain Romagna. That sort of thing
made them groan. They were about as newsworthy as a verbatim
parliamentary report, and might just as well be written up by a
writing-machine, if such a thing could be invented.

From unattributable sources, however, came the human interest
stories. Drink was forbidden on board the *Italia*, even wine.
Nevertheless, some of the crew had smuggled on board ten
bottles of chianti. Unfortunately, the cold had been so extreme
that the wine had frozen into blocks of red ice! Their cigars had
crumbled into dust. . . . The water in one of the engine radiators
had frozen, so that the motor began to overheat. The only un-
frozen liquid on board was some still-warm tea in the thermos
flasks, so they had to use that to cool the engine. . . . Thinking to
catch Malmgren off guard, one of the journalists suddenly
interjected:

'You threw down a flag on Franz Josef Land, didn't you?'

Malmgren was not to be caught. 'I don't know. I was asleep at
the time.'

'We know you threw down a flag there.'

'Then why are you asking me?'

However, the scientist volunteered the technically important
information that during the last part of the flight the airship had
been navigating by radio. This was quite lost on the pressmen,
who had taken those constant requests for radio bearings to be
shrill cries of distress. At this time, quite a lot of navigation was
done by Bradshaw; that is, pilots were lost unless they followed
railway lines. That was map-reading, not navigation. But even
those few who actually navigated and flew calculated courses
allowing for known wind speeds and directions, still required
ground checks at frequent intervals, in the form of distinct landmarks, because the winds are inconstant. In the Arctic, however,
there are no distinct lakes of fixed shape, or rivers, or railway
junctions, or power stations, or woods. There are not even any
roads or bridges. To fly over 2,000 miles as the *Italia* had just
done, without any of these aids and in difficult weather conditions,

and still return accurately to base after making a dog-leg down to Novaya Zemlya, showed that the Italians had developed good methods, useful alike in peace or war.

Arnesen did pick up one titbit, an unattributable source who told him that, while flying in fog over Novaya Zemlya at 1,800 feet their trailing radio aerial some 300 feet below them had struck invisible ground, and shortly after they had seen only just in time and so had avoided, a peak rearing up ahead. Arnesen took this to be a sample of Italian inefficiency. If true, it showed rather that the Italians were clever to find Novaya Zemlya at all, when it was hidden in fog, and were not as lost as he made out. The danger of high ground masked by fog or low cloud was an abiding one at the time for all aviators and to a lesser extent is so today. There was and is a premium on rapid reflexes.

What was incontrovertible was the fact that Nobile had successfully carried out a long and difficult flight in the polar regions 'on his own responsibility', as Arnesen put it; meaning, without benefit of advice from Amundsen, Ellsworth or Riiser-Larsen, incredible as that seemed to a Norwegian. But Arnesen still thought it disgraceful that no well-known polar-surface figures had flown in the airship. Malmgren the scientist and Tomaselli the journalist, who had been an officer in the Alpini, were the only two who could handle themselves on skis. It was the old circular argument. As long as all went well, all that mattered was aeronautical expertise; polar survival knowledge counted in the preparation but not in the execution. The Amundsen attitude could be proved correct only if there was a disaster, and, only if the Italian survivors failed to measure up to their fate.

Because he appreciated that he had to play along with the press, part of which was parochial and hostile, Nobile got little rest. After three days in the air, even when lying down in bed, he had to give interviews to journalists tired of hanging around doing nothing. One of these was Arnesen, who sat in a chair cradling the nervous Titina, while Nobile talked over his head about aeronautics. He seemed very satisfied with the performance of the *Italia*, as well he might. He seemed disappointed at not having reached Nicholas II Land, naturally, and particularly regretted not having had the chance to land a scientific party there, which he thought important. Above all, he wanted to forestall the Russians, it seemed – to get there before they did. They had been planning for a long time, but had never got beyond planning because they could not agree among themselves what vehicles to use – flying machines, ordinary Arctic ships or special ice-breakers. To give the Norwegian a useful quote, Nobile said that once the flight to the Pole had been carried out, he might make another attempt to explore Nicholas II Land, At that Titina squirming nervously in Arnesen's lap, terminated the interview. Nobile was long-suffering, but her patience was at an end.

Arnesen gave Nobile full marks for understanding the journalists and the requirements of their work, and doing all he could to facilitate it; but the Norwegian himself had 'tunnel vision'. He was totally unable to see or sympathise with the viewpoint of either an expedition leader or a scientist who has been badly misquoted by the press. He either did not know, or could not appreciate, that when a prominent man or woman is wrongly quoted as saying either a foolish or an inaccurate thing, it occurs to almost no one that it may be the fault of a journalist, a sub-editor or even a typesetter. The public – and the man's colleagues – almost invariably assume that the quote is accurate and that the person who is said to have said it is stupid beyond belief. When the person so misquoted has bitter enemies, the misquote is their most valuable weapon.

Nobile called a press conference a few days before the intended start of the next flight which, it was hoped, would be to the Pole. There were five journalists present, besides the General. Nobile spoke in English, saying that he was sorry that he did not speak that language well, but he hoped that they would understand him. After he said this, he put Arnesen's back up by, in the Norwegian's view, lecturing like a schoolmaster and putting them all on the carpet. He accused Arnesen of having written that he had drunk a toast in chianti before the last flight, and denied that he had ever drunk wine. Arnesen said he had seen him do it (but as he had not tasted the liquid, could not swear that it was wine).

Then Nobile turned to Lars Hansen, a grizzled old fiction writer turned newsman for the occasion. Hansen, he said, had written that they had dropped a flag on Novaya Zemyla, whereas it had been on Franz Josef Land. That was a mere inaccuracy, which the public might ascribe to Hansen, who specialised in polar fiction. But Hansen had telegraphed to the American papers that he had had an interview with General Nobile in which he, Nobile, was supposed to have said all sorts of things which in fact he had never said. As Hansen well knew, because this was the first time they had spoken to each other.

Hansen blustered away, saying that he sent his stuff to Holland and France, and from there it got transmitted to America, and then, well, they all knew what the American press was like. Make a 'big story' out of anything. Then, perhaps aping an American he-man author, he slapped Nobile on the thigh, exclaiming: 'If we should happen to write something which is not exactly according to your wishes, then, being the great man you are, don't you care a damn nickel about it!'

Nobile smiled, but then said seriously that if there was anything they wanted to know, or anything they did not quite understand, they only had to ask Captain Romagna or either of the two Italian journalists, who would be only too pleased to help. But he did ask that any journalist who interviewed him or otherwise quoted him directly should show him the MS. before despatching it so that he could check it for accuracy. This was a perfectly reasonable request. Writers concerned with their reputation – or just the facts – would do this without having to be asked. Arnesen didn't see it that way. He felt the General was treating the Fifth Estate like schoolboys, and resented it.

Of course journalists, unlike authors, are under day-to-day pressure to get a story first, an atmosphere not conducive to accuracy. The flight to Nicholas II Land, for instance, only two days old, was dead and corpse-cold. The new titbits about it which the Italians fed to the pressmen after the conference were contemptuously ignored. The world, they knew, was just not interested. Come to that, a sum total of five journalists, almost all of them fifth-rate or, like Hansen, not really journalists at all, was an eloquent expression of the news value of the *Italia*'s flights so far. This confirmed what Mussolini had said, that a series of scientific flights could not possibly be so popular as the single flight of the *Norge*, although they would attract interest in serious quarters.

The next flight, however, would have news value because it was to be to the Pole, via Greenland. The route out would explore more unknown regions of the Arctic; newswise that was a dead loss, but the words 'North Pole', however, by some alchemy, were magic.

Chapter 8

'ENGLISHMEN WOULDN'T DO SUCH A THING!'

URGENCY and uncertainty now overtook the Italians. Nobile gave his crew a day off to rest, then had them preparing the airship for another flight. Time for their programme was running out. Day by day the temperature was rising; as it rose, so it curtailed the lifting powers of the airship. And as day succeeded day, the time of the summer fogs approached. Nobile even thought of postponing the rest of his programme until the autumn, because there seemed to be no break in the weather. A depression lay over Bear Island and was moving north-east. More bad weather on the way.

It was not possible to load the airship fully until they knew what the objective of the next flight would be; and that would be dictated by chance – by the weather forecast favouring one route rather than another, and also the expected duration of the good weather, for of the two remaining important flights, one was short, one was long. One was fixed, one was flexible.

The short flight was to the Pole via a dogleg to Greenland, with 16 men on board including all the scientists, if possible. The unknown areas between Greenland and the Pole were the main target, but there were scientific experiments to be made near the Pole, particularly if a landing was possible. A good deal of survival gear had to be carried, covering two possibilities – a landing on ice and a landing on water.

The long flight was to cover a route of opportunity. It was extremely daring, yet logically conceived. The need to turn round and return to base shackled the other flights, and made the airship batter forward against headwinds for a day or more. From the long flight there would be no return to Spitzbergen. With the crew cut down to a mere dozen men and one engine only being used at any one time, and throttled back at that, the *Italia* could stay in the air for a week at slow speeds, going more or less with the wind. Whether she went to Nicholas II Land or to America would be decided when actually in the air, in the light of the latest weather reports.

Early on 22 May, the weather changed. A 'high' now covered Greenland, the area they were initially interested in; only south-west of Iceland was there an area of low pressure. At noon, the Tromsoe Institute telegraphed a detailed report and forecast, including the note: 'The favourable situation is not likely to to last much longer, because the warm currents will give rise to formations of fog. The situation is, however, still sufficiently favourable to allow us to advise you to start for routes 5 and 2, provided local weather conditions are satisfactory.'

Route 2 was the track from Greenland to the Pole, route 5 was from the Pole onward to the Mackenzie River on the North American continent. Locally, at Ny Aalesund, there were blue skies and little wind. The temperature was somewhat high, but otherwise conditions were perfect. Malmgren advised Nobile to start.

A crew of 16, was much easier to select than a mere dozen, but even so some of the *Italia*'s normal crew would have to be excluded from the flight to the Pole. Some of the choices were extraordinarily difficult and laden with political overtones. For Nicholas II Land, Nobile had deliberately chosen Tomaselli over the dark little Sicilian, Ugo Lago, because Tomaselli was senior and a representative of the Alpini. But it was also a choice between newspapers, and their backers. Tomaselli represented the *Corriere della Sera*, the influential Milan daily; Milan was where most of their financial support had come from. Lago represented the *Popolo d'Italia*, Mussolini's own paper, and Mussolini was backing the flight, too, albeit with some misgivings. As Tomaselli had already made one flight, clearly it was now the turn of Ugo Lago.

Arnesen had heard that the priest, Father Gian Franceschi, would be going on the Polar flight, to see the Pope's cross properly delivered. But Nobile had no room for the expedition's chaplain. He even halved the number of wireless operators. The tough, thickset little operator, Giuseppi Biagi, would go; his senior, Ettore Pedretti, would stay behind. The reason for the choice was that Biagi had proved himself better able to stand the physical strain of these long flights with their almost endless tours of duty. This trip would be much shorter than the last one, theoretically about a day and a half; even so, 36 hours is a long time for a work shift, even if catnaps could be taken between the hourly transmissions. The General thought that two navigators might suffice, and so the two senior naval officers, the solid, dependable Adalberto Mariano, and the dapper, eager Filippo Zappi, would definitely go in the *Italia*, their junior, Alfredo Viglieri probably would have to stay on the ground. Nobile would make a final decision when the gasbags were full, the ship loaded and the temperature known; on these facts depended the lifting power of the *Italia*.

On this occasion Nobile thought that scientific research with the various sampling and measuring instruments should have priority and that therefore, if at all possible, all the three scientists should go. When he heard this, Dr. Malmgren went to tell Professor Behounek. 'This time, Nobile will take you – definitely,' he assured the Czech scientist.

'I doubt it very much – and even if he does ask me, I shall refuse,' said the embittered Czech. 'He might change his mind again, and then for the third time I'd be in that embarrassing position when everyone knows that Nobile will take me, and then at the last minute I'm left behind. It would be shaming enough if I were an Italian, but for a foreigner like myself, who has been invited merely as a guest, it's even more unpleasant.'

Malmgren, too, was in the same position, one of only two foreigners in a basically Italian project at a time when national pride had an exaggerated importance in Europe. Nobile was the only Italian to whom their nationality made no difference; with the others, Malmgren the Swede felt not entirely at home.

There was one difference between the two scientists, apart from their work, Malmgren as the meteorologist being an important navigational adviser to Nobile; and this was their size. Malmgren was smallish and tidily built. Franz Behounek was enormous – tall, bulky, and ponderous; heavier even than the giant motor man, Cecioni. This gave Malmgren the idea for a joke.

'Under no circumstances can you refuse,' he told Behounek. 'There's a lot of work to be done, and this time I'll be fully occupied with my own and won't be able to carry out yours as well. Then, if we land on the ice, there'll be even more work for us both. You'd never forgive yourself if you hadn't taken this opportunity to carry out your work in person. Besides,' he went on, slyly, 'there's an advantage for all the rest of us if you do come. If we find ourselves stranded on the ice, about to perish from hunger, we'll always have something to live on. . . .'

Behnounek laughed at the reference to his generous girth, then said, thoughtfully: 'Do you really believe that anything like that can happen?'

'Well, they do say it happened with Greely's expedition,' replied Malmgren, 'but then they were practical Americans. Englishmen wouldn't do such a thing, they are gentlemen.'

Malmgren's sly humour tended to disconcert the press. As Arnesen was waiting for the loading of the *Italia* to be completed – a complicated process that he felt was becoming almost a bore – the Norwegian button-holed the Swedish scientist yet again.

'Do you believe there is unknown land in the vicinity of the Pole?' demanded Arnesen.

'Now, one person after another has declared there is no land there, and yet it doesn't seem to help you,' said Malmgren, dryly.

Arnesen's interrogations had already established that Malmgren was going home to get married as soon as the next two flights had been completed; that he thought highly of the *Italia* and of its designer Nobile; and that he was taking part in spite of having been warned against joining by an individual who said that the expedition was not as well prepared as it ought to be – because no one except Malmgren knew the polar ice.

This is identifiable as Amundsen's viewpoint, in which Arnesen also firmly believed. It ignored the fact that in the matter of clothing, rations and survival gear, Nobile had taken the best Norwegian advice. But it was natural for the journalist, for he himself habitually moved about in the snows of Ny Aalesund on skis, and the attempts of the Italian novices, under instruction from the Alpini, to ski down a local coaltip were painful for him to witness; as were the attempts of the General himself. He felt emotionally how vulnerable they would be if brought down in the icy wilderness.

But now, as the loading was completed on the scale appropriate to the polar venture and its hazards, no one had any time off at all. They were all up at the hangar, where Arnesen watched Natale Cecioni testing the new stern motor. Cecioni was a large, impressive looking man, steady, careful and thorough, not to be easily put aside. He could take liberties with the General that no one else could. Nobile was there, of course, highly active as he supervised the final preparations. He went over to Cecioni and told him that he really must finish the testing of the motor; they were due to take-off now. Cecioni waved the General away and carried on for a short while, absorbed in his work, listening to the engine as a violinist listens to the tones of his Strad, as Arnesen put it, until the note was exactly right.

Nobile moved from group to group, busily inspecting, trying to see to it that all their work culminated at the same time, and making the last checks for weight. Of course, it was all his responsibility. The tension must have been considerable, his mind super-active as he weighed the pros and cons. No one except Malmgren, whose advice on the weather could be critical, bore a fraction of the load he did. Arnesen saw him pick up a large package of chocolates, extract a couple of bars, and put some of them in the control cabin. Then, in the same way, he picked up some lifebelts, weighed them in his hands, and discarded half of them. It really was going to be as close as that.

Franz Behounek was wreathed in smiles. This time he really was going. Alfredo Viglieri, most junior of the three naval officers, was looking downcast. His rucksack of personal gear and clothing had already been put on board, but Professor Pontremoli, the physicist, was now bringing it out of the cabin again. It had always been doubtful whether the *Italia* would develop enough lift to take an extra navigating officer; now, it was certain. He would have to remain behind. Suddenly, when the airship was already out on the field, Nobile made a contrary decision. Behounek, watching closely, thought it was the sad expression on the young officer's face which had moved him. The General told Viglieri to hurry up and get on board. Behounek was to remember that scene, so fateful were its consequences.

Now, to make up for the added weight of the young officer, something or someone, would have to be left behind. Airship gear and engine spares weighed 1,449 kilos, the scientific instruments and materials weighed 270 kilos, the reserve food stores 460 kilos, the emergency wireless set (without batteries) only 25 kilos. 480 kilos was the total weight of a mass of recommended survival gear, including tents, sleeping bags, sledges, collapsible boats, snow shoes, skis, stoves, rifles, ammunition, pistol, signalling pistol, medicine chest, fire extinguishers, matches, and so on. It was a very considerable inventory and Arnesen thought sometimes that the Italians ought to have set up a shop outside the hangar, to supply the airship as required. There was, too, on this occasion the cross which the Pope had blessed; that could not be left behind. There was also a Milanese flag to be dropped and, so Arnesen heard, a five-pound note an English lady had given to Nobile for that purpose. Nobile came to a decision, and ordered a few cans of petrol and oil, equivilent in weight to Alfredo Viglieri, to be taken off and left in the hangar.

The engines were already running, ticking over slowly. One hundred and fifty men held the mooring ropes that kept the buoyant *Italia* tugging gently just above the ground. With Viglieri now aboard, they were all at their places. General Nobile, the three scientists Pontremoli, Malmgren, Behounek, the two senior navigating officers Mariano and Zappi, the engineer Trojani, the chief technician Cecioni, the motor mechanics Arduino, Caratti, Ciocca and Pomella, the foreman rigger Alessandrini, the wireless operator Biagi, and the journalist Ugo Lago, representing Mussolini's *Popolo d'Italia*. Sixteen men – and, of course, Titina, the little dog.

It was after four o'clock in the morning of 23 May, 1928. Father Gian Franceschi said a brief, final prayer. The General ordered: 'Let go!' The ground crew released their hold on the mooring ropes that tethered the airship, nose down. A hundred and fifty voices shouted: 'Hurrah!' The roars of cheering intermingled with the thunder of the three engines, as Nobile had them speeded up. The *Italia* lifted her bulk into the frozen sky and nosed towards the entrance to King's Bay. A flock of gulls picking over the camp midden rose screaming, their shrieks sounding like lost souls.

The airship flew along the coast as far as Amsterdam Island, the north-west corner of Spitzbergen, where a strong wind from the north slowed them down. An hour out over the ocean beyond Amsterdam Island, they turned 20 degrees to port for Cape Bridgman on the northern coast of Greenland. Now the northerly wind was tending to drift them south, for which a steering correction had to be made. As they reached the edge of the pack-ice, they found it smothered in fog. It was now ten to seven in the morning and they had been airborne three hours. For the next $6\frac{1}{2}$ hours they encountered continuous dense fog. At first they flew under it, then rose above, an easy matter because the top of the fog did not exceed a height of 500 metres. From 1.15

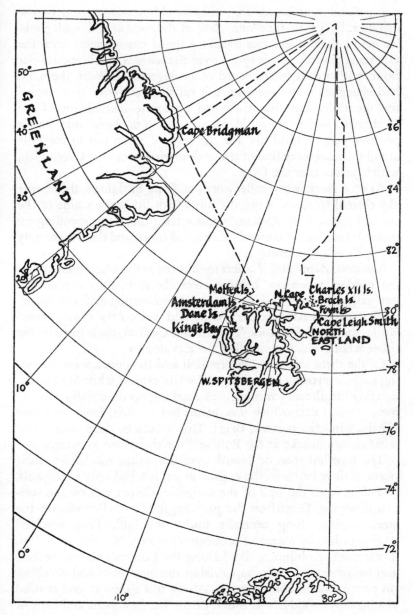

Fig. 2. The Polar flight of the *Italia*

p.m., through thinning fog, they could see Greenland in the distance. By 3 p.m. they were clear of the vapour and, with pack-ice below them, were able to take a speed measurement with the Goertz apparatus. Their speed over the ice was 62 kilometres per hour, with a drift to starboard of 30 degrees. In short, the wind had changed; they would have it on their tail once they turned for the Pole. But first they had to locate and identify Cape Bridgman, which they did about 5.30 p.m. Now they had a positive geographical 'fix' for the start of a run out to the Pole along the imaginary line of the 27th meridian west of Greenwich, which passes near the Cape.

At six o'clock, a few miles north of Cape Bridgman, the cloudy sky cleared to reveal a radiant sun which lit up the inside of the control cabin. With a strong wind astern, they were speeding on towards the Pole. It seemed like a good omen and there were only happy faces to be seen.

Mariano, Zappi and Viglieri took turns at the wheel controlling the rudder; when not helping steer the ship, they carried out navigational duties – taking sun sights, measuring drift and speed, so that an accurate track could be laid out on the chart. Meanwhile, their collaborators, Trojani and Cecioni, took turns at the other wheel, which controlled the elevators.

Of the three scientists, Pontremoli and Behounek were attending to their instruments as if in a calm laboratory; while Malmgren, wearing his glasses for once, was marking up on a wall-chart the meteorogical data which was being fed to them from Tromsoe via the wireless operator, Biagi. This would be their guide as to what course to take at the Pole and for the return journey.

The loneliest men on board were the motor mechanics, their posts of duty being in the engine pods, reached only by catwalk or ladder from the hull of the dirigible. Ciocca was on the starboard engine, Caratti on the port engine; with Pomella on the stern engine, slung centrally under the hull. They received engine orders by means of a telegraph system like that of a ship. Their chief, Arduino, walked along the gangway above the keel and below the gas cells, supervising the mechanics and checking on petrol and oil consumption. Along this gangway and stowed also against its sides was much of the survival gear, and cans of petrol: it was very cluttered.

The foreman rigger, Alessandrini, had already checked every accessible part of the airship and had pulled up and stowed the mooring ropes which, when the ground crew released them, hung downwards from the sides of the ship. This task completed, he had entered the control cabin to spell Trojani and Cecioni on the elevator wheel.

They were now entering an unknown region. The overland route Peary had taken towards the Pole in 1909 lay far to their left, west of Greenland. The route they had themselves traversed with the *Norge* in 1926 lay far away to their right, north of Spitzbergen. The ice-scape over which they now flew had been crossed by no man, and because the visibility had become brilliant, they could now see for 100 kilometres in any direction around them. If there was a landmass in this part of the Polar ocean, they would know; similarly, if they saw nothing, the negative would be definite. In fact, they saw no land; only ice lying on water.

The Pole was now a foregone conclusion, so Nobile dismissed it from his mind. He was thinking ahead about the problems which would arise afterwards, requiring critical decisions. They had a strong tailwind now; if the weather pattern did not change, then they must have a strong headwind for the return. Should they return? Or should they let the wind take them across the Arctic Ocean to North America, as it had with the *Norge*? Nobile already had the required charts for the Mackenzie River area on board with him. It would certainly avoid the exhausting business of trying to fight the weather. A strong headwind slowed the airship by much more than the mere speed of the wind, for it pushed the ship's nose this way and that, and the helmsmen had to correct continuously, causing the ship to make irregular zig-zags and cover much more than the straight-line distance to her objective.

Nobile watched Malmgren marking up the weather chart, tracing the curves of pressure of two cyclones, one over the Barents Sea, the other off the coast of Siberia. Asked for his advice, Malmgren replied: 'Better to return to King's Bay. Then we'll be able to complete our research programme.'

This weighed strongly with Nobile, who had lived with these projects for so long. Already, any idea of landing on the ice was out of the question. Only in calm air could this be done. Consequently, the oceanographic research could not be completed by soundings or samples. That was a pity. Then there were the experiments which it would have been useful to conduct actually at the Pole on the pack ice. Nobile had put a lot of thought, preparation and experiment into methods of landing an accompanied scientist on the ice, and was reluctant to give up all chance of this, which he would do if he did not turn back from the Pole for King's Bay. He would also lose the chance for that week-long drift flight with a dozen men only on board, which was another unfulfilled ambition. Nor had the *Italia* actually flown over Nicholas II Land. All these were factors urging Nobile to agree with Malmgren.

But still he shrank from yet another exhausting battle against powerful headwinds. Malmgren told him not to worry. 'This wind won't last. It'll drop a few hours after we have left the Pole, and then it'll be succeeded by more favourable winds, from the north-west.'

Still Nobile was not quite convinced. A bold possibility occurred to him. Would it not be possible to use the wind currents of the two cyclones to navigate home the long way round, via Nicholas II Land? Malmgren did not agree. He argued persuasively for a direct return to King's Bay, because of the way the weather pattern was shaping up. The strong south wind must die away, a lighter north-westerly wind must take its place. Finally, he convinced the Italian. In his general forecast Malmgren was to be proved right. What he said would happen, did happen. But not when he said it would. Fifty years of forecasting later, weathermen are not proof against such error.

At about ten o'clock that evening, there was an abrupt change in the weather ahead. Although the sky remained infinitely blue, along the line of the horizon now stood up a wall of cloud a thousand metres high with its tops tossed and twisted into fantastic turrets and crenellations. 'That band of cloud, dark and compact, had a menacing aspect which struck my imagination,' Nobile was to write. He thought of it, wryly, as the scenic engineering by which the Pole was defending itself against the curiosity of the airmen; he doubted that they would get through. But it was still several hours flight in front of them. The Pole itself was about 90 kilometres away.

They could not afford to lose sight of the sun, as without it the navigators would not be able to tell them at what time exactly, they were passing over the Pole. So when at length the *Italia* reached the cloud wall, which did not look so menacing now, Nobile took her up above it, to about 800 metres. A rising sense of excitement affected everyone. Nobile, of course, was proud.

He had done it! No one now could pretend that, without Amundsen or Riiser-Larsen to help them, the Italians could not conquer the Arctic. His friend Trojani, the little bespectacled engineer who seemed too frail for such expeditions, was consumed by doubt. Was this a propaganda flight or a scientific expedition he asked himself. If it was scientific, then the ship should have been adequately equipped and the crew trained scientifically. Trojani, who had done most of the experiments in trying to land men and material from an airship, directly, or in a boat, seems to have had considerable doubts, matching those of Professor Samoilovich.

At twenty minutes after midnight on 24 May, the naval officers, busy with their sextants, cried out; 'We're there!'

Nobile took the *Italia* round in a slow circle, still above cloud, and then took the airship down through it until they could see the pack ice of the Pole.

Now Trojani, in spite of his doubts about the basic motive for the expedition, felt a sense of achievement, too, although the Pole appeared to him unimpressive – just a vast expanse of snow and ice.

Also seeing the spectacle for the first time was Franz Behounek the Czech scientist. His mind told him that this moment was of no great importance, because three expeditions had been here before – Peary in 1909 on foot, Byrd in 1926 and the *Norge*, also in 1926. But he was greatly moved, nevertheless, by the sudden thought of all those other expeditions, whose aim had been the Pole, too, but which had ended in tragic failure. Then, as the *Italia* circled slowly, he turned back to his instruments, concerned now with measuring the amounts of electricity and radioactivity in the atmosphere at the geographical top of the world. Beside him, Professor Pontremoli was establishing figures for the terrestial magnetic field at the geographical Pole.

Nobile leaned out of the cabin and dropped the Italian tricolour which fell, fluttering, to the ice, followed by the Milanese coat-of-arms, and a little medal of the Virgin of the Fire which the youth of Forli had begged him to take to the Pole. When it came to the Pope's cross, a certain amount of bedlam developed. As his Holiness had predicted, it was indeed heavy – and so large that Cecioni had some difficulty in manoeuvring it through the door; but finally, at 1.30 in the morning, Nobile could say that he had dropped the cross and could see it below him, lying on an ice floe. Momentarily, he had experienced a wonderful feeling of pride. In the quiet, for the engines were throttled right back, the sound of someone putting a record on the gramophone was startling.

The jaunty notes of the Fascist battle hymn *Giovinezza* filled the cabin and there was a flourish of blackshirt salutes. Ugo Lago, the representative of Mussolini's paper *Popolo d'Italia*, who had put on this record followed it a few minutes later with *Bella Italia del mio cuore*, a well-loved folksong which Behounek, although he was not an Italian, felt was strange and touching, sounding above the dull roar of the engines and framed by the eternal wastes of ice and snow beneath the cabin.

Zappi cried out: 'Viva Nobile!'

And Malmgren came up to shake the General's hand. 'Few men in the world can say, as we can, that they have been twice to the North Pole,' said the Swedish scientist.

In fact, there were only seven. Malmgren himself and six of the Italians.

They drank a toast in a warming, homemade liqueur consisting of eggs, milk and rich wine. Then Biagi began to send out brief messages reporting a successful mission; firstly to the Pope and then to the King and Mussolini.

It was these messages which the journalists back at King's Bay had been sitting up half the night to hear. Odd Arnesen had been getting colder and more irritated every minute of their long vigil. He had gone on board the *Città di Milano* late and been told that at 8 p.m. the *Italia* has sent out a message in cipher which they could not read, although Rome could, but they understood that all was well on board. It was probably a minor linguistic mis-understanding, but it made Arnesen suspicious and he began to wonder if the message had been much more dramatic than the Italians pretended, telling of dangers and difficulties, if not disaster. He was informed, quite correctly, that the airship was expected to be over the Pole at around midnight, but this annoyed him because it meant another night watch and he wanted to go to bed.

Most of the journalists were now tramping the deck of the *Città di Milano*, coat collars turned up, blue with cold, and occasionally putting their heads into the wireless cabin. Two of the Italians stayed up with them, the General's brother, Professor Nobile, and Father Gian Franceschi. About midnight, there was a portent.

Captain Romagna Manoja came hurrying along in slippers and smoking jacket to make his enquiries at the wireless cabin. Seconds later, he came out in a temper, shouting that the pressmen's radio station ashore was too active, its ceaseless transmission of non-news had interrupted an important message coming from the *Italia*.

The newsmen were buoyed up again. Perhaps there had been a landing at the Pole. This was the only news which, for Arnesen at any rate, held any interest. His paper's deadline was in a few hours time, which seemed to him important. Even so, he wasn't going to wait up forever, and would have gone ashore to bed if Professor Nobile had not come up and said: 'I think you ought to wait. There may be some news presently.'

At about three o'clock in the morning the Italian journalist Cesco Tomaselli came in, all smiles, to say that the *Italia* had crossed the Pole at 20 minutes after midnight, and to give them details, including the texts of the various messages sent out by General Nobile direct to Rome. He was asked if anyone had landed at the Pole, although the press assumed that, because the event had not been mentioned, it had not taken place. In this they were, of course, correct. Really, thought Arnesen, the news was meagre – just a few texts. Later, he thought he had got an 'inside' story and published it. It threw doubt on the achievement of the Pole, because this tale was to the effect that at the critical time there was fog and as Mariano and Zappi could not see the sky, they had had to calculate their position without astronomical aid. This was a typical distorted story, based on a single facet of the truth, that there had been cloud over the Pole. It did not mention that the *Italia* had been above the cloud, so that the navigators could take sun sights, before going down through cloud to a view of the icescape from 150 metres. There might have been some slight inaccuracy in the actual dropping position for the flags, the cross and the medal, because of the time spent in cloud and in circling under it, but nothing of consequence.

That the Italians were certain of the achievement was plain to Arnesen when he returned to the base ship after sending his message and resting. There were grins everywhere, high good humour as the Italian workmen rolled more gas cylinders ashore in readiness for the return of the *Italia*. They were talking delightedly and greeted him as a friend. One sailor tried to include the Norwegian journalist in their celebrations by singing: 'Nobile norte polo, croce, croce, norte polo!' to a melody from a well-known opera.

Aboard the *Città di Milano* the saloon was full of Italian officers who were bargaining with some Norwegian hunters who had just returned from their isolated huts among the islands of Spitzbergen with the results of their winter's work. Skins of white fox, blue fox and polar bear were lying on the tables and armchairs; the Italians were trying them on and examining the result in the mirrors. The beautiful skins would make wonderful souvenirs of their trip into the Arctic and the hunters had no difficulty in getting rid of their stocks.

Arnesen's sensitive feeling for the Italian 'barometer' began to work overtime that night. Somehow the atmosphere was not so joyful as it had been before. The messages from the airship became briefer and arrived at less frequent intervals. They spoke of headwinds and handling difficulties, of ice forming inside and outside the hull, of the winds becoming even stronger. Their position was uncertain, and they asked for bearings. Throughout the night there was increasing anxiety.

At 1030 next morning, as Arnesen understood it, the *Città di Milano* received a message from Biagi saying that the *Italia* was north of Moffen Island, off the north coast of Spitzbergen, was meeting a strong wind, was low on petrol, and could not arrive at King's Bay until the evening. He would call them again in two hours' time.

But no call came. At first, so Arnesen heard, they thought that Biagi might be sleeping, worn out after the battle with the storm. But gradually that optimistic thought became untenable. The operators in the *Città di Milano* searched the airways without success, calling up the *Italia* and getting no reply.

Arnesen was reduced to dealing in speculation and rumour. The wind, strong indeed, was blowing from the south-west. The airship, out of fuel, might even now be driving helplessly before it over the pack towards Russia or America. The Norwegian accosted Rosetti, one of the keenest and most hard-working of the Italian ground crew who was always called on to do everything in consequence. Rosetti volunteered his own guess: 'Sibiria, Sibiria!' That accorded with a weather report from Tromsoe.

Subconsciously, Arnesen may not have been too displeased. He recalled Mariano saying something like: 'To fly in the polar zone is like eating bread and butter. In Europe the natural conditions are considerably more difficult. Besides which, it is light night and day in polar regions.' And then had not Nobile, in an interview, told him that the *Italia* was as strong as an airship could possibly be and that practically nothing could happen to it? Again, these sound like distortions of what must actually have been said. In some ways polar flying was indeed less hazardous than trying to corkscrew through Czechoslovakian mountain valleys in a fog and at night, and Nobile did indeed champion the semirigid type of airship as the ideal combination of lightness with strength – which was not to say that it was unbreakable, far from it. To this Norwegian, like Amundsen, the Italians were swaggering Southern braggarts who had no place in the North; it would do them no harm to be taken down a peg or two.

The cold calculation of Balbo was something else again. Nobile learnt that, in giving his consent to the *Italia* expedition, the Fascist chief had remarked to his close associates: 'Let him do it. This way we shall get rid of him forever.' And he refused Nobile's request for one or two flying boats to be attached to the expedition, able to carry out long-distance search flights in any emergency.

Consequently, Captain Romagna was faced with a situation for which he was unprepared both materially and psychologically. The *Italia* had ceased to transmit. And by now her fuel must have been exhausted in any case. But what had happened and where was she? Balbo having forbidden the flying boats to come to King's Bay, he was left with only the *Città di Milano*, a slow ship, her hull unsuitable for barging into Arctic waters along the edge of the pack ice. The ponderous old base ship was perhaps the worst possible vehicle for a search, and one can sympathise with his despondency. But she was all he had, so he ordered her bunkered for a journey to the north coast of Spitzbergen and asked the Norwegian authorities ashore for advice as to what to do. It was all coming true, just as Amundsen had predicted.

For Arnesen and the other professional newsmen, everything was changed, once the *Italia* was posted missing and disaster was feared. Before, it had been hard if not virtually impossible to sell *Italia* stories to the world's great newspapers. Now, they would buy anything and from anyone. People who did not know they were journalists suddenly became 'our special correspondent at

Spitzbergen'. And none of them knew what to write about, because there was no news whatever about the lost airship. There was only rumour, speculation and stories of the slowly gathering international search effort, centred now on Spitzbergen.

Chapter 9

'FERMA LA MACCHINA!'

THE *Italia* spent two hours over the Pole. At 2.20 on the morning of 25 May she began her return flight, following the invisible line of the 25th meridian east of Greenwich at 1,000 metres. Early on, her navigators managed to get a sun-sight, but then the sky clouded over and the airship sailed in a kind of wide corridor between cloud-base above and the tops of a dense, shrouding fog which covered the ground below. Steering only with a magnetic compass, unable to check drift which with such a strong wind must be considerable, was virtually blind-flying. So Nobile brought the airship down through the fog until the grey monotony of the jumbled pack-ice was visible.

Now they could check speed and drift; and the results were not reassuring. Their speed over the ground was 26 m.p.h., which meant that their progress was being reduced by half. The drift was a quite considerable 18 degrees to port, showing that the wind was from the south-west, on their starboard bow.

So strong was the storm that the joints in the cabin structure caused shrill whistling noises as the cold outside air fought to push through. They were all wearing their heavy lambs-wool clothing, except for Nobile, who wanted to be free to move about rapidly, supervising. He had high reindeer boots on, but only uniform trousers with a catskin waistcoat and a woollen jersey. Zappi, Mariano and Malmgren were taking turns at the rudder-wheel and carrying out the running navigation; Trojani and Cecioni shared the elevator-wheel near them and Behounek was working with his scientific apparatus. There was very little talking. After so long in the air, some were looking very tired. It had been one mad rush since leaving Stolp, with little opportunity for any real relaxation between the testing demands of long Arctic flights. And the cabin was very crowded, too small really for a proper scientific expedition. They were all working on top of one

another, and when men went off duty to catch a couple of hours
sleep, they had to bed down in the gangway along the keel,
obstructing the passage of those who had to move about the ship
to do their job, Alessandrini the foreman rigger and Arduino who
was responsible for all the engines. The motormen themselves,
Pomella in the stern gondola, Caratti to port and Ciocca to starboard, were in a different situation, being isolated with their
engines which were connected to the hull only by catwalks and
cables. Their jobs were lonely and monotonous.

All day the airship struggled on, the storm buffetting her starboard side; increasing rather than decreasing in strength, and
with squalls up to 30 m.p.h. or more, making the nose veer uncontrollably from time to time, regardless of whether it was
Mariano, Zappi or Malmgren who was on the rudder-wheel.
They flew through occasional flurries of snow which obscured
everything below them, and so thick and grey were the fog and
cloud layers above that they never saw even a hint of the sun.
Around noon visibility opened up for about 12 or 15 miles; the
pack-ice was colourless and monotonous, and once only did they
sight a large channel of open water, revealing the real nature of
the environment below them. Occasionally, a loud crack like a
rifle-shot announced that another sliver of ice which had formed
on a propeller had been violently flung off and struck the hull.
The rigger foreman Alessandrini was kept busy repairing the
small holes they made. Malmgren, worried that his forecast of a
helpful northerly wind had not yet materialised and conscious of
the danger of these conditions, urged Nobile to put on speed and
get out of this threatening locality. Normally, Nobile used only
two out of the three engines at any one time, and both of those at
reduced revolutions. Responding to the appeal, he had the third
engine started and the other two motors run at higher revs. This
was not economical on fuel, but if the dangerous conditions were
truly local, it would be worth while. The *Italia* thundered on
through the storm, in the grey Polar night.

From 7 o'clock in the evening of 24 May to 3.25 in the early
morning of 25 May, the airship struggled southward; and the
navigators worked out that their indicated airspeed of 60 m.p.h.
represented a speed over the ground of only 37 m.p.h. Nobile
decided that he was burning petrol at an excessive rate for very
little, and had the engines slowed. Malmgren came up to protest.
They were virtually standing still in the air, he said. Here, the

Nobile as a Colonel, 1926. *photo: Nobile collection*

Above: Nobile, Amundsen and Mussolini at Ciampino airport, Rome, before the flight of the *Norge* in 1926.

Left: The *Italia* at Stolp, Germany, 1928.
photo: Nobile collection

Above: At Vadsoe, 1928: two Norwegian officers (in peaked caps) with, l. to r., Malmgren, Mariano and Nobile.

Below: Zappi (centre) with Mariano on his right. Viglieri on his left.

Above: King's Bay, Spitzbergen, in April 1928. *photo: Nobile collection*

Below: Italia in Amundsen's hangar at King's Bay, 1928. *photo: Nobile collection*

Lundborg.

Nobile being helped into Lundborg's Fokker by Behounek. *The photo was taken by Lundborg.*

On June 24·1928, Capt. Lundborg flew Gen. Nobile from the 'Red Tent' to Virgo Bay. On his return to rescue the remaining 5 survivors of the 'ITALIA' he experienced landing difficulties & overturned his 'FOKKER'. After 48 days on the pack-ice the 5 survivors were rescued by the 'KRASSIN' which arrived close-by the 'Red Tent' on 12ᵀᴴ JULY·1928.

The *Italia* commemoration Card issued on the 50th Anniversary.

POLAR EXPEDITION

THE CHARACTERISTICS of the 'ITALIA':

LENGTH	· 106 metres
CRUISING SPEED	· 80 Km
CUBIC CAPACITY	· 19,000 cub.metres
ENGINES	· 3 250 H·P

ESTIMATED COST of EXPEDITION 3½ MILLION LIRE RAISED BY PRIVATE SUBSCRIPTION IN MILAN, & TOOK PLACE UNDER THE AUSPICES OF THE GEOGRAPHICAL SOCIETY

Arrival at King's Bay 6TH MAY 1928

ON 30TH MAY·1928, Dr. MALMGREN with MARIANO & ZAPPI LEFT THE RED TENT TO MARCH ACROSS THE ICE·PACK to BROCH IS & on the 14th day MALMGREN, HAVING ONE FOOT FROZEN, PASSED OVER HIS RATIONS TO HIS TWO COMPANIONS & URGED THEM TO PRESS ON IN SEARCH OF HELP & TO LEAVE HIM TO DIE IN PEACE

DEPARTURE from MILAN 15TH APRIL 1928

MALMGREN (1895-1928)
METEOROLOGIST
OR OF UPPSALA UNIVERSITY

'LATHAM' MONUMENT at CAUDEBEC - en-CAUX

'S MARCHING ACROSS THE
·FERING INCREDIBLE HARD-
IT FOOD FOR THE LAST 12
NO & ZAPPI WERE
THE RUSSIAN ICE-BREAKER
" ON JULY ·12·1928

DV "LATHAM 47"

A DIEV VAT!

s the flying-boat 'LATHAM' left CAUDEBEC-en-CAUX with a crew of 4 : ROALD AMUNDSEN &
TRICHSEN went aboard at BERGEN 16·6·28. The 'LATHAM' left TROMSÖ for SPITZBERGEN
s to search for 'ITALIA' survivors, but beyond N.CAPE it disappeared in the ARCTIC OCEAN

Above: At the 'Red Tent': Behounek, Biagi, Viglieri and the radio station. *This picture was also taken by Lundborg.*

Below: 'Red Tent' and beflagged radio mast seen from Maddalena's S-55, the first aeroplane to sight the castaways.

Above: Maddalena's Savoia Marchetti S-55 (two 600 h.p. Isotta Fraschini). *photo: Nobile collection*

Below: Penzo's Dornier Wal (two 375 h.p. Rolls Royce).

Above: Lundborg's Fokker CVD (450 h.p. Bristol Jupiter) at the 'Red Tent'. Collapsible boat in foreground.

Below: The Finnish Junkers F-13 (185 h.p. Junkers) by the Italian base-ship *Città di Milano,* 6,000 tons.

Riiser-Larsen's Hansa Brandenburg (185 h.p. B.M.W.) on the sealer *Braganza*, 350 tons.

The wooden sealer *Quest*, 400 tons, in pack ice.

The 'Big Three' of the *Krassin*: Air Commander Tchukhnovsky, Professor Samoilovich, Commissar Oras.

At the 'Red Tent' the Newcastle-built icebreaker *Krassin*, 10,630 tons, makes the final rescue.

weather might grow even worse. They must get out of this zone as fast as possible. Reluctantly, Nobile complied. He recalled the storm damage, especially at the stern, which they had suffered during the flight from Milan to Stolp. Forcing the ship in such a gale as this was hazardous, but so was remaining where they were, if Malmgren was right about the weather. Slowly, as the revs. increased, the buffeting grew worse and the gale whined and whistled through the joints in the cabin.

Drugged from a brief three hours of sleep, Dr. Franz Behounek woke up shivering, frozen right through. Awkwardly, he crawled out of his sleeping bag, and came face to face with Professor Pontremoli. The Italian physicist told him that the General wanted his sleeping bag put up with the others on the gangway above, where it would not be an obstruction. Pontremoli said he would take it, because he was going up there for a rest himself, and he disappeared up the aluminium ladder that led into the hull. Behounek wished him goodnight and a good sleep, and then went to a window; there was no life out there, only the endless wastes of the frozen sea.

Nobile was now getting anxious about their navigation. The mountains of Spitzbergen should have been in sight, but there was no sign of them. The violent squalls, making the airship zig-zag drunkenly, in spite of all the helmsman could do, were bound to upset any answers derived from deduced reckoning. No one could plot a track like that. There was no sun for a sextant-check either, so he decided to try to get two radio bearings on the *Città di Milano* by flying westwards; a single radio bearing only gave direction, not position. However, the southerly wind made the airship drift so much to leeward that Nobile stopped the experiment before it could give a reasonably certain result, and steered again to the southward.

At about 9.30 in the morning of 25 May, Behounek noticed that the engines seemed to be faltering; then there was a bang! — followed by complete quiet. Trojani, at the elevator wheel, had made a movement which had locked the elevators in the so-called 'dead' position, nose down. Although the airship was light, having used so much fuel, with the nose pointed downwards and the engines revving at high speed, she was about to dive into the ice from 250 metres. Nobile, standing by the door of the wireless cabin, waiting for news from Biagi, at once shouted for the engines to be stopped. At 80 metres from the pack the downward movement stopped and the ship began to rise slowly of her own accord. Viglieri, who was standing next to Trojani, had meanwhile with one sharp blow knocked the wheel out of the 'dead' position, and Cecioni had jettisoned but without orders four cans of petrol to lighten the ship. Nobile reprimanded him for it, as they were short of petrol and the weight was insignificant. He told him to pay out the ballast chain, a weighty device designed to slow the fall of the airship at once, if she should lose lift. It hung below the cabin, ready for dropping.

But the ship was light and rising, and for the first time in thirty hours or so, there was a thinning of the vapour above their heads that hinted at sunshine. Mariano suggested that they let the ship go up until he could get a sun-sight to fix their position. Nobile agreed. That may have been a momentous decision, but no one will ever know for sure. Watching the pressure gauges as the ship rose, Nobile saw them register a slight increase in pressure, from the expansion of the gas, but oddly, the stern compartment showed a much greater rise than the others. Nobile let a little gas out of that compartment, but not from any of the others. There were automatic valves to avoid the danger of pressure building up too much, but there was the possibility of valve-failure through icing.

They rose into sun and the sight of blue skies at 900 metres and were at 1,100 metres before Mariano and Zappi had made their sextant observations. The engines were still switched off and the *Italia* was rising as a free balloon under the expansion of the gas in her compartments. Cecioni, the all-purpose engineer, was taking the elevator control to pieces to find out if there had been a mechanical failure, so it was physically impossible to drive the ship downwards dynamically, by using the power of the three engines together with the elevators. Cecioni could discover nothing wrong, and when he reassembled the controls they worked perfectly. The pressure gauges were showing a rise; the gas in the compartments was dilating under the heat of the sun, but not abnormally. If, however, the process was allowed to go on too long – and how much was 'too long' was a matter of experience – then the gas would become superheated and be valved off automatically. So that when the *Italia* plunged back once more in the regions of cold just above the pack-ice, she would suffer a catastrophic loss of lift.

Nobile ordered two of the engines to be started up. The time was 0955 by his reckoning, later by Behounek's diary. But before taking the ship down, he sailed on towards the horizon a few minutes more, searching for the highest peaks of Spitzbergen in the far, far distance. But, even through field-glasses there was nothing; nothing except the frozen sea and the freezing fog. He took the *Italia* back into the cloud, and down through the fog, until the pack-ice appeared 300 metres below. And it was going past underneath them rather faster than before, or so Nobile thought. He ordered a speed check, which proved positively favourable. Their speed over the ground had increased. Therefore the wind had died down somewhat, as Malmgren had predicted it would. That cheered Nobile, because it meant that he need not restart the third engine and so force the ship. Excessive speed in storms had damaged or destroyed dirigibles before now, and would again; the vast surfaces they exposed to the wind were much more vulnerable to gale-force torrents of air than were the fabric-covered sufaces of aeroplanes.

Next, Nobile gave his attention to working out their present position. By combining the sun-sight with a radio report at 1000, it seemed that they were 145 miles north-east of the Ross Islands, off the coast of North-East Land, and some 180 miles north-east of King's Bay, Spitzbergen, which they should reach between 3 and 4 o'clock that afternoon. They were now not all that far from home.

Malmgren came to Behounek where he was working in the little 'niche' housing his scientific instruments, apparently very worried. Behounek asked him what was the matter? After all, they would soon be safely at King's Bay. Malmgren replied: 'Yes, but we might go down on the ice at any moment. We are only staying in the air by using the force of the motors and the elevators. The dirigible is too heavy.'

Behounek looked at the altimeter, which indicated 500 metres. No sign there that the ship was sinking. It seemed impossible to him, on thinking it over, that an airship which was really too heavy could stay up more than a few minutes by using dynamic lift. He thought that Malmgren had been too much influenced by the sudden dive of the airship previously, and the jettisoning in a panic of the four cans of petrol.

Malmgren went back into the nose to take over the wheel controlling the rudder, Zappi standing beside him and giving orders. Cecioni was on the elevator wheel, with Trojani standing beside him. At the back of the cabin Nobile, Mariano and Viglieri were working at the navigation table, one of them making speed measurements. Professor Pontremoli was up in the gangway, in his sleeping bag, and the journalist Ugo Lago was also asleep in that long corridor above the keel. Alessandrini and Arduino were on the gangway, too, but on duty. The motor mechancis also were awake. Pomella was in the stern gondola, on the centre line of the ship; Caratti and Ciocca were on the outslung motors to port and starboard respectively.

Nobile ordered a speed measurement at 1030 approximately, Behnounek made it 1100, but the exact time is not important. Nobile then decided to ascertain their altitude by dropping one of the glass balls filled with a red liquid. As he stood there, timing its fall with a stopwatch, Cecioni chimed out laconically: 'We're heavy.'

Nobile, surprised and shocked, turned to the telltale instruments. Yes, there had been a change. The inclinometer showed the ship to be slightly sterndown – by 8 degrees. And the variometer showed that the ship was falling – at half a metre per second.

A rapid succession of orders rippled out. Nobile spoke quickly but quietly. Pomella and Caratti – increase engine revs. to 1,400. Ciocca – well, Ciocca did not need to be told to start up his engine, he had done it already. To Cecioni on the elevator wheel – get the nose up. Pull the airship up by her bootstraps, in other words, by what aviators called dyamic lift, a smooth phrase meaning brute force. And to Alessandrini – run out and inspect the stern valves. The only reason Nobile could think of for their sterndown attitude, like that of a begging dog, was a sudden escape of gas from perhaps a faulty valve, which might be remedied. The foreman rigger raced off to carry out his task.

Having given the only possible orders, Nobile kept his eyes and all his attention fixed on the variometer. If it showed a rise, they were winning. . . . But it did not. The fall continued and, moreover, it was accelerating. So said the instrument, like doom. The crash could not be averted, then. But it could be mitigated. The worst hazard to all airships and aeroplanes was fire. Fire made fatal what might otherwise have been a survivable accident. Nobile ordered the telegraph to be rung: Stop all engines! Then a word to Cecioni, the man most used to the ballast chain – go and release it! Brake our fall! And to Zappi – take over the elevator wheel.

The orders were obeyed with promptitude. But Cecioni was having trouble, fumbling with the rope that held the heavy drop chain in place. 'Hurry up! Hurry up!' shouted Nobile.

Then checking the engines, he saw that the propeller of the port motor, controlled by Caratti, was still working. Leaning out of a porthole opposite, Nobile shouted at the top of his voice: 'Stop that motor!'

Alessandrini was still up above, and Behounek heard that he had reported that the gas escape valves were in order, not blocked in the open position by black ice. The Czech scientist had emerged from his 'niche' and was with Cecioni, trying to help him unfasten the heavy chains which had been designed as an anchor for the *Italia*'s landing manoeuvre on the ice, never carried out. Normally, Cecioni turned a smiling, often laughing face to the world; but now Behounek was never to forget the look of despair he wore at that moment. Meanwhile, Trojani had rung the bell to signal the motormen to switch off the engines, and while Pomella and Ciocca had promptly obeyed, Caratti's was still running. Mariano, the senior naval officer, was bending out of the window nearest to him, screaming: 'Ferma la macchina!' Behounek, leaning out of the same window, and gazing aft, saw that the airship was inclining downwards at the stern, and was beginning to slowly slide downwards in that sternfirst attitude towards the pack. He had a glimpse, from inches away, of Mariano's face. It was completely calm, but seemed to bear a strangely embarrassed expression.

Every man was at his post, except for Pontremoli and Lago, asleep on the gangway inside the ship, when the *Italia* slid sternfirst down towards the pack. 350 feet of airship, a hull as large as that of a destroyer, but far lighter and more frail, came down out of the sky within the space of three minutes.

At the last, Nobile rushed to the control wheels, where Malmgren and Zappi were. He saw Malmgren fling up his hands from the rudder-controls, shock in his startled eyes. Nobile grabbed the wheel from him, as if even now it might be possible to pick a snowfield and divert the ship to that, instead of helplessly striking the unyielding ice of the pack. But no, and there was the pack, terribly uneven. . . .

At the last, Behounek gripped the railing of the cabin with his left hand and looked down directly at the ice. What he saw was horrible. The ice seemed to be flying up to meet them, expanding as it came, and the nearer it came, the more it seemed to change from that height-induced smoothness. From what had appeared a plain, the pack remorselessly grew into hundreds of blocks of ice which had been tossed about in some wild chaos and veined with water channels from the ocean ominously underneath. Instinctively, for protection, Dr. Behounek pulled back his head into the falling cabin of the airship and closed his eys. His mind had already decided: 'This is the end.'

Then came the first impact. And the second. The cabin, with a horrible crashing sound, struck the ice, impacted deeply into the snow covering it, and fell to pieces.

Behounek felt that something heavy was pressing down on him from all sides, as if some great mass was forcing him forward. In fact, it was the snow, which had been forced up into the riven, burst floor of the control gondola and now filled its interior.

Not like a scientist, Behounek made desperate out of control motor movements, trying to free himself from the dimly-comprehended, suffocating masses of snow. To be free, free.

At last, the world around him became lighter. The worst of the darkness had gone. He shook the last snow off him and looked around.

A quiet voice nearby, that of Mariano, said: 'All right, all right, siamo tutti! – we're all here together.'

Behounek's first glance was for the ship, for the *Italia*. She was rising slowly, looking strange. She was still an airship and still airborne, but her silhouette was unfamiliar, odd. The control cabin was missing, so it seemed as if someone had amputated the rump of the airship. And again, the stern engine gondola, the one where Vincenzo Pomella was, that was missing, too. On the bridgework, the catwalk to the port engine gondola, there stood a man; so close, he could see that it was Ettore Arduino, gazing down on the wreckage of the control cabin and its occupants sprawled out across the snow below him. Relieved of that weight, and of the stern motor, the hull of the *Italia* was now buoyant. It rose and drifted with the wind eastward, taking with it six comrades. Renato Alessandrini, foreman rigger; Ettore Arduino, Sub-Lieutenant, and chief motor engineer; Dr. Aldo Pontremoli, Professor of Physics; Attilio Caratti, motor mechanic; Calisto Ciocca, motor mechanic; Ugo Lago, *Dottore in Lettere*, correspondent of the *Popolo d'Italia*, whose turn it was in place of 'Cesco Tomaselli of the *Corrier della Sera*.

Behounek's second glance was for his immediate surroundings and for his companions. They lay surrounded by broken panels and pieces of the control cabin. Behind them across the snow and ice a long line of red dye had been splashed out upon the pack, where one of the glass balls used for height measurement had smashed open on impact, indicating that the control cabin of the airship had been dragged over the snow of the jumbled pack for a distance of at least 50 metres.

Close at hand, only a few metres away, lay General Nobile, sprawled out on the snow with blood all over his head. Mariano was bending down and talking to him with that friendly smile he so often used. Nearby lay the giant Cecioni, unable to move, moaning that his left leg must be broken. It was soon clear that the General had broken a leg, a wrist, and was gashed about the head. Behounek got to his feet. Malmgren was on his feet, too, but with his left shoulder pulled up. 'What's the matter?' asked Behounek. Malmgren replied that his whole left side had been terribly battered in the crash and that his left hand was either broken or dislocated. As they were talking, Behounek saw Zappi, only a short distance away, rise heavily from the snow; it seemed he had a broken wrist. Apart from a few gashes of no consequence, Behounek himself was unhurt. Others had been similarly lucky.

Trojani got up, stupefied rather than afraid. He had thought of how disaster might strike and of what death might be like, as most of them had. Always a crash had been complete and final. He had never dreamed of personally surviving and then finding himself marooned in such a horrible place – an utter, lifeless desolation of white snow and ice, and black, howling gale clouds blowing flurries of white before it. But there they were, he and most of his companions, some hurt or dead, others getting up. Scattered around were tools, instruments, and debris of all kinds from the airship, but mostly the contents of the cracked-open control cabin in which they had been safely standing only a moment before. And the airship itself was being blown fast away eastwards by the gale, smoke coming from it, apparently on fire. The General's little dog, Titina, was scampering about, unharmed and joyfully free.

Nobile had been standing at the front of the cabin which had taken the worst of the impact and then been ground down along the ice by the moving ship, before being torn loose. He remembered experiencing a shocking blow to the head and being thrown forward. Very clearly, he had felt his limbs snap, but without pain. He shut his eyes and mentally voiced the thought: 'It's all over!' Then there was nothing.

When he came to, probably only seconds later, Nobile found himself lying face down on a hummock of pack-ice, in a terrible place – a formless, contorted jumble of ice-crags heaving to the horizon. Looking into the sky, to his left, was his airship – nose up as if praying, adrift. The damage forward was vivid – only the port side of the control cabin remained and from the ghastly rent in the underside of the ship trailed torn strips of fabric, lengths of rope, twisted strips of metal. The envelope of the hull was creased and sagging, losing shape. But on the side there still flared out the black lettering: I T A L I A .

He heard a voice – it was Mariano's – asking: 'Where's the General?' Looking round, Nobile saw Malmgren about six feet away. He was just sitting there, injured and shocked. Beyond, Cecioni lay stretched out, moaning. Next to him lay Zappi. Five men, however, were standing up – Mariano, Behounek, Trojani, Viglieri, Biagi. Tojani's face was bloodstained, but the others appeared unhurt. The grey wreckage of the cabin lay scattered all round on the snow and just in front an enormous patch of red, like a bloodstain, smeared the white landscape. It was only some spilt liquid from the glass balls used for measuring altitude. To the east, the angled hull of the *Italia* merged with the fog and disappeared.

Only then did the pain strike. It hit him in waves. His right leg and arm began throbbing – both were broken. His face and head were gashed and raw. Worst of all was the agony in his chest – the terrible, involuntary convulsions made breathing difficult. But his mind was perfectly clear and calm. It seemed that he had the symptoms of grave internal injury. Death was near, only an hour or two away, perhaps.

He was glad to die, so that he would not see the hopeless struggles of his companions, whom he had led to this spot; they would all perish in the icy wilderness, but he would go first. He started muttering broken phrases of encouragement, ending: 'Lift your thoughts to God!' And with a final effort: 'Viva l'Italia!'

Behounek, among others, was uninjured. As the ice came up at them, he had thought he was going to die. But now he was

alive! It was a marvellous feeling, and so it was with optimism
that he went over to Nobile to assure him that all would be well,
they would be saved. But Nobile apparently needed no consola-
tion, for he replied, smiling, that he hoped so – for their sakes.
The Czech scientist did not then realise that Nobile believed that
he had suffered mortal injuries and would not see the day out.

Malmgren, sitting a few feet away from the badly injured
General, was silent, stroking his right arm, which apparently
pained him. His blue eyes seemed fixed on the horizon and on his
face was a look of blank despair. The plight of the fit men,
marooned on the pitiless pack-ice, was terrible; their chances of
survival nearly non-existent. But for the injured, it must have
seemed, there was no hope at all. Die they must, and slowly.

'There's nothing to be done, my dear Malmgren,' said Nobile,
trying to reconcile the young scientist to his fate.

'Nothing to be done – except die,' was the reply. 'My arm's
broken. . . .'

He got up, stooped, unable to stand erect because of his injury.
'General,' he said formally, and in English, 'I thank you for the
trip. I go under the water. . . .'

'You must not do it!' said Nobile sharply, in English. For a
moment, Malmgren seemed undecided, then he sat down again.
The two men had been close on this expedition, the Swedish
scientist becoming virtually Nobile's second in command. Of
course, he did not give orders, but his was the mind against which
Nobile liked to test his own ideas, a man whose advice the General
valued. He discussed his plans with no one else.

Giuseppe Biagi, alone in the wireless compartment, had had
more time than the others and had probably sensed disaster before
they did. As the airship was actually falling, he had held on to the
small emergency radio set, part of the survival gear which Nobile
had embarked. This had cushioned it from the shock of the crash,
and within minutes of picking himself up from the snow and ice
of the pack, he was busy assembling and testing the set, without
an aerial, to see if it would work. Under his hands, at length it
came alive, and he gave a shout: 'The field station's intact!'

The effect on morale was immediate. Nobile, believing himself
to be dying but that there was now a chance of rescue for the
others, called Mariano over to him, and asked him to take charge.
'Yes, General!' he replied. 'Set your mind at rest, there's still
hope. . . .' He told Nobile that, not only was the wireless unbroken

but that they had found a case of provisions among the wreckage. On it was marked PEMMICAN kg. 18. They would not starve.

The news roused Nobile further. He now saw something familiar in a dark heap lying between two ice hummocks a dozen or so yards away. It was one of the two waterproof bags, containing survival gear, intended for the use of the small party, including himself, which Nobile had hoped to be able to put down on the ice at the Pole. The other bag was gone, still inside the gangway of the *Italia*; this must be the one which had been strapped to the roof of the wireless cabin. He knew that it held vital survival gear – a tent and a sleeping bag as well as provisions. And so it did, in addition to small but important items such as a Colt revolver with 100 cartridges, a Verey signalling pistol, and a case containing many boxes of matches.

Nobile, comparatively thinly clad, and forced to lie without movement on snow and ice, was shivering violently with cold and also from the shock of his severe injuries. Only his lower legs were well protected by the high reindeer boots, but the stiff material was an agonising weight on his fractured right leg. The right arm was fractured also. But the cold was worse, it struck right through to the core. Nobile begged Mariano to bring the sleeping bag over and slide him into it, so that he could die in peace and not in icy shivering convulsions. Getting the wounded man into the sleeping bag involved momentarily greater agony, move the fractured limbs even as gently as they could. But at last it was all over, and with a shudder of relief Nobile drew his head inside the bag and lay motionless, expecting that death would take him and end the nightmare. Titina scampered away, wagging her tail with excitement.

Meanwhile, the less badly shocked of the survivors were busy searching the pack nearby for any useful items which might have fallen from the sky. Mariano led them with optimism and energy, while Biagi pursued his own particular technical trail, searching for cabin and airship structure which might be converted into a radio mast and stays to give his short wave transmitter a chance of being heard by the *Città di Milano* at King's Bay, perhaps 175 miles away.

Almost the last area he covered was where the wreckage of the stern engine and gondola lay on the ice apart from the debris of the control cabin. As he approached the pitiful remains. Biagi noticed Vincenzo Pomella, the 30 year old foreman motor mechanic who normally occupied this gondola. Pomella was sitting down on the ice, motionless, with one of his shoes off. At first, Biagi thought he was merely retying the shoe and did not move because he was dazed from shock. Then, as he came closer, he realised the truth. Biagi called out to Mariano, who was searching nearby, and Mariano passed on the news to the man next to him, Trojani. 'Pomella. Morto.'

There was no time for sorrow, much as they had liked the dead man. Now the roll call read – nine live men on the pack, two of them badly hurt, serious hospital cases. And one corpse – Pomella. Ten in all accounted for. Six men still in the dirigible. Motormen Caratti and Cioca in the gondolas, foreman rigger Renato Alessandrini on the gangway and chief motor engineer Ettore Arduino on an engine catwalk when last seen, professor Pontremoli and the journalist Ugo Lago somewhere on the gangway, where they had been sleeping. Six men missing. Biagi thought he had seen a column of thin smoke or vapour from the direction in which the *Italia* had disappeared. Perhaps they were jettisoning cans of petrol to keep the hull afloat. Perhaps the hull had finally fallen to the ice also. If so, they could not be far away. Not in terms of distance, that is. But, seen at close quarters, the pack was unbelievably jumbled; to cross it would be more like mountaineering than walking. They could not help their lost comrades. They could only survive and hope for rescue themselves.

It was bitterly cold and out in the open they would not survive long; the wind, although not particularly strong now, made the cold seem more intense. They had to have protection or die. Mariano, Viglieri and Trojani discussed the best place to site the tent and then having chosen a fairly level spot, began to erect it. The tent was of the double walled type Nobile had selected, rather than Nansen's, believing that the better insulation justified carrying the extra weight. It had been designed, however, to accommodate four men – not nine. Before they had finished putting up the tent, Biagi had improvised an aerial and had begun to transmit an 'S.O.S. *Italia*' message. There was no reply.

Then the set went dead. In no way could the fault be diagnosed in the open air, in bitter cold. First of all, the tent would have to be finished, so that Biagi could work with bare hands, and repair it, if at all, from the materials lying around them on the pack.

And so passed their first hours of survival on the Arctic ice.

PART THREE
SEARCH AND SURVIVAL

Chapter 10

ENTER AN ELITE JOURNALIST, BY AIR

(25–31 May)

THE last message from the *Italia*, received shortly before the crash, had not hinted at anything more than severe headwinds encountered on the morning of 25 May, which would delay her arrival at King's Bay at least until the evening. Her position, obviously rather uncertain, was somewhere north of Moffen Island off the north coast of Spitzbergen. She was due to report every two hours at a given time – at five minutes to each odd hour. Therefore her radio reports became overdue long before it was clear that, if she was still aloft, the airship could have no petrol left and must be adrift.

Given the two long-range flying boats which Nobile had asked for as a back-up force, an immediate search could have been launched: and with Italian resources. As it was, Captain Romagna had to ask advice from the local authorities in Spitzbergen, and then, when he had finally decided that he had a serious crisis on his hands, the matter had to be referred to Rome. So the Fascist government found itself in the position of having to beg other nations to give assistance in finding an Italian airship, and in at least one case had to negotiate financial terms before aid was given. The reaction in Rome, however, was to blame Nobile, not the air minister Balbo.

The frightening fact was, that there were no air bases anywhere near the Arctic region, and no aeroplanes either. The Nobile expedition having been denied its own support aircraft, based on the *Città di Milano*, there was now no possibility of immediate measures being taken. For two days, nothing happened. There was only speculation. At first, some thought that the wireless aerial of the *Italia* must have iced up, which would explain why she was no longer being heard. Then it was suggested that she might have flown into a mountain, in which case, it was assumed, all aboard were already dead. Others again conjectured that, given the strong south-westerly gales, she might have been blown off course as far as Siberia. But no search measures were undertaken until 27 May when, the thin-hulled *Città di Milano* left King's Bay in an attempt to look for the missing airship along the north coasts of Spitzbergen and North-East Land, if she could get so far at this time of the year, when there was still a great deal of ice about. If, during this time, the crew of the *Italia* did not survive by their own efforts, they would not survive at all.

The crash had occurred just after 1030 Greenwich Mean Time. By 1600 hours approximately, Biagi had connected up his batteries, rigged his aerial and was transmitting the first message to begin '*S.O.S. Italia. Nobile.* . . .' Mariano, Viglieri, Trojani and Behounek were traversing the ice in search of more useful items. Malmgren was sitting up, nursing his injured arm. Zappi, Cecioni and Nobile were lying down, Nobile being inside the sleeping bag, ready to die, and accepting death.

But death did not come. Instead, it receded. Being able to lie quite still, and within the comfort of the bag, the worst of the shivering vanished, and Nobile felt the effects of the shock wearing off. Being temperamentally incapable of resting, he now put his head out of the bag to see what was happening. Cecioni, who had begun to sit up, noticed this and called out: 'I've broken my leg, sir!' Malmgren, gloomily staring into space, took no notice, but Zappi came to life and complained of a pain in his chest, which he thought was from a fractured rib. 'Do you think it's broken, General?' he asked. Nobile said that if it didn't hurt when he breathed, it probably wasn't broken, but that was just an optimistic guess. He could hear Mariano, Viglieri and Trojani discussing the best place to pitch the tent. It had to be got up quick, because the cold was intense, especially for the injured men who, besides being in shock, could not move about to keep their circulation going.

The site chosen was a sheet of ice about fifty yards square, and on a lower level than the ground on which the injured men were lying. They had to be carried to the tent. Nobile was moved first. Waves of agony passed over him as he was moved and the fractured bones ground together, but at last he was inside the tent, at the very back, facing the entrance. Then they carried the heavy bulk of Cecioni, and, slitting the side of the sleeping bag in which Nobile was lying, laid Cecioni beside the General. The two men with broken legs were thus laid side-by-side under the best available warm covering and as far from the icy entrance to the tent as possible, with their feet facing it.

The four active men carried on their search for items lying scattered which, if not found soon, might be covered up by snow and effectively lost to them. By evening on the 25th they had gathered and brought to the tent some 70 kilos of provisons – mostly pemmican and chocolate – which, rationed out at 300 grams each daily, would last them for 25 days. When, late that night, Mariano made the first distribution of a pemmican ration, most of them found it distasteful; the badly hurt men, Nobile and Cecioni, could not eat at all. Nine men, huddled together in a space designed for four, lay down to sleep in a confusion of limbs; and because of their total exhaustion, they did sleep. Outside the bitter Polar wind was howling over the snow and flapping the canvas of their tent in a dull rhythm.

The wind which blew across the pack on the night of the 25/26 May was from the north-west. It had swung round, as Malmgren had said it must and had they still been airborne, would have helped carry them to King's Bay in two or three hours. The crash had occurred when they were almost home. To have lingered on this thought would have been unbearable.

Nobile had slept heavily for hours. Like all of them, he had been exhausted by the long flight and the constant struggle against buffetting headwinds, even before the crash. The accident had not struck a fit, clear-eyed crew, but a collection of desperately tired men and had wiped out their 'home' in a matter of two minutes flinging them all, shocked and defenceless, upon the desolate, relentlessly hostile environment of snow, ice and shivering wind. It was almost as though spacemen had been cast, stripped of their life-support system, upon the bleak surface of the moon.

The wounded, however, could not rest. Intermittently, Nobile's sleep was interrupted by stabbing agony in his broken limbs. With his right arm and his right leg both fractured, and untended, his condition would have been bad enough in a hospital bed. In the constricted space of the tiny tent, there could be no real rest for him or for poor Cecioni. The latter, being a giant of a man, took up even more space; psychologically, probably it was worse for him than for Nobile. A broken leg is not like an inflamed appendix, or toothache, or a sickness, or a headwound in war. When he has broken a leg, a man is felled like a fallen tree. He is condemned in an instant to be horizontal and helpless. Merely to turn from facedown to lying on his back is a long agony. It is hard to adjust to becoming an inert cripple in a fraction of a second. Nobile at least could think and plan to determine the future. Cecioni was now merely a hulk to which things happened.

The waves of dragging agony which washed over the stricken Nobile woke him after several hours. He concentrated his mind upon his surroundings. The inner lining of the tent was pale blue – a restful colour for eyes dazzled by the blinding white of the snowscape all around. The roof of the tent was held up by a pole. The sides were each of them 2·50 metres long – about 8 feet. Nobile had given much thought to the design. Now he was very glad that he had accepted the extra weight of a double-walled tent, with an air layer trapped between two coverings of silk. It was much warmer and more windproof than a single sheet. He was satisfied, too, with the floor covering on which he was lying. He had chosen a solid waterproof sheet, again accepting a weight penalty, which now prevented them all from being in close contact with the pack-ice. The heat of their bodies had soon melted the snow on which the tent had been erected and so, without this flooring, they would have been lying in a shallow pool of water.

The slit-open sleeping bag in which Nobile and Cecioni lay took up one-third of the tent flooring, because they had to lie with their broken limbs out straight. The other seven were huddled close in the remaining space, together with the batteries for the radio. One practical result of Professor Pontremoli's scientific experiments suggested that exposure to extreme cold would cause a rapid deterioration in the life of those batteries which would perhaps determine the length of their own lives, so the batteries too had been brought into the tent for protection. The heat of so many human bodies in the confined space had raised the temperature, so that the razor-keen chill of the Arctic night became more bearable.

In the morning, Mariano took out a further search party, consisting of the youthful naval officer Viglieri, the large and amiable scientist Behounek and the professorial engineer Trojani, to look for more of the gifts which might be scattered upon the snow or flung into the ice crevices. At intervals, one or the other came back with a box of pemmican or a packet of chocolate, tins of malted milk or a can of petrol. The most important discovery, however, had nothing to do with food or drink. It was a cache consisting of a complete navigational kit – several sextants, an artificial horizon, some chronometers, a set of astronomical tables. As soon as the sun shone or the stars became visible, they could calculate their position. Given that the radio was working, and that their messages were picked up, rescue could be vectored in on them. And, within hours, as a result of the concerted efforts at repair of Biagi, Zappi and Cecioni, the little wireless in its wooden box was humming once more. Biagi began to tap out the message, written by Mariano, which started: 'S.O.S. Italia. Nobile. . . .'

A little later, when the navigational instruments had been found and brought in, and a brief burst of sunshine had enabled an altitude to be taken, a position could be transmitted as well. This first sight showed them that they were just north of the 81st parallel of latitude and at between 25 and 26 degrees of longitude east of the Greenwich meridian. Not, in fact, near Moffen Island, but some fifty miles north-east of North-East Land, the second largest island of the Spitzbergen group. They had been delayed by the gale and been blown off course to the east to a greater extent than they had suspected. They were about 180 miles from King's Bay.

Once the radio had been repaired, the injured men were seen to. Zappi on Nobile's instructions, had taken a medical course in Rome before the flight, and although still feeling sick and shaken, he was convinced by now that the rib which pained him was merely bruised and not broken. He was able to examine Cecioni's broken leg and make splints for it out of two wooden boards, tying them to the leg with bandage cut out of varnished cloth from the control cabin. Then he turned to deal with the General's fractures. Having an unskilled person bungle about with broken bones is an agonising process and it is little wonder that Nobile, feeling the fractured tibia move inside his right leg, himself worked it back into position with his unbroken left hand, before letting Zappi fix it in place with a bandage. Like Zappi, Malmgren also felt much better and carried his injured arm in a sling; the shoulder was badly bruised, but apparently nothing was broken. Out of the nine men, only two were truly incapacitated.

After the repair of the radio, a great optimism had flooded through them. A correspondingly deep pessimism overtook the survivors when, after tapping out each S.O.S. message, Biagi put on the headphones of the receiver and listened for a reply. Always, he shook his head. No one had heard the call. Nobile was so depressed that he felt Zappi's medical attentions were the equivalent of bandaging a minor cut on the hand of a condemned man. Now, he felt there was no possibility of rescue and became convinced that they would all die, one by one, from hunger. Although they could not contact the outer world, the radio receiver was working perfectly and that night Biagi was able to tune in to the nine o'clock news from Rome. Part of the bulletin concerned them. No radio signals had been received from the *Italia* for more than 24 hours, said the message from Rome, and considerable concern was felt for the crew of the airship.

The two badly injured men, having to lie still all the time, found it harder to sleep that night, and for many nights thereafter. The weather had been uniformly dreadful and depressing, emphasising the pitiless desolation of the pack-ice. During the night, when vitality is at its lowest ebb, Cecioni's self-control gave way. Had it been the frail-seeming Trojani, such nervous distress might perhaps have appeared natural. But Cecioni was a large, brash, somewhat crude individual of great self-confidence and the transformation was terrible. He kept Nobile awake with the spasm of terror he was undergoing; the thought that he might die out there in the icy wilderness. They were all conditioned by their trade as airshipmen to accept the possibility of death, but most thought of it as something sudden and final. It was the spectre of a slow gradual extinction in the Polar night, with which Cecioni wrestled, and Nobile could do little to calm him.

There was a long vibrating roar and the tent shook. The ice beneath them seemed to move with the shock. Suddenly, they were all awake. Someone shouted: 'Every one outside!' Men grabbed Nobile and Cecioni by the shoulders and dragged them out, too. But now it was quiet again, just a soft snow falling on their faces. Malmgren told them that what had happened was a collision between two ice floes driven by wind and current, the twin forces which served to explain the high, twisted jumble of the pack-ice all around. 'This is a bad place,' he said. 'We ought to look for somewhere safer and move there as soon as possible. Here the ice is so broken and jagged that the winds and currents

can get leverage.' Underneath them was the terror which had
shaken Cecioni; not mother earth at all but the black and icy
fathoms of the Polar Ocean and ultimately the dark sediments on
the floor of the abyss.

In spite of the alarms in the night, most of them snatched much-
needed sleep and woke on the morning of 27 May in better spirits,
determined to survive. They discussed the role each man should
play in the new order of things. Mariano was the team leader on
the ice, organising the searches for provisions and driving the fit
men on. Nobile, lying stricken in the tent, could not possibly do
this. 'The General will decide about meals,' Mariano told the
others. So Nobile worked out fixed hours for mealtimes and
settled the rations: 250 grams of pemmican and a few pieces of
chocolate per man per day. Malmgren spoke up: 'I'll see to the
water!' This was not as easy as it seemed and previous Polar
experience was a definite help. Of course, their whole world
consisted of frozen water – but virtually all of it had originally
been salt water. Malmgren had to seek out and recognise freshwater ice; collect it; and then melt it by putting it in an empty
tin and lighting a petrol fire underneath. There was never to be
enough. When their fuel gave out, there would be none at all.
They would die of thirst, absurd as that sounded, before they died
of hunger.

It was Malmgren also who supervised a vital step forward in
both health and morale – the preparation of hot pemmican soup.
Again, this was not easy because of the primitive conditions in
which the meal had to be cooked. It took two hours to prepare.
But for men who had not tasted hot food or drink for four days,
it gave a tremendous psychological lift. The concentrated mix of
meat, vegetables and fat which, when water was added, produced
a yellowish skilly, had been declined by Trojani's dog when they
had tested a sample back in Rome. Now, the mere odour of the
soup as it heated was delicious; when they consumed it, the taste
of raw peas was delightfully filling, and they could never get
enough of it.

Cooking by petrol in such conditions was a filthy business.
The grime transferred itself to their hands and the improvised
ladles and cups they were using; washing was not possible, let
alone shaving. The formerly elegant young men whom Nobile
had known in Rome now appeared to him as a band of savages,

or uncouth brigands, with beards sprouting from dirty faces and fur caps pulled well down on their heads.

By evening, they had thoroughly scoured the pack for lost items and had added considerably to their food reserves. An inventory was taken. Totted up, their haul consisted of: 71 kg. of pemmican, 41 kg. of chocolate, 9 kg. of malted milk, 3 kg. of butter, 3 kg. of sugar, a small piece of Provolone cheese and one box of Liebig's meat extract. Total: 125 kilogrammes of concentrated food. That meant, that starvation was 45 days away. In a month and a half a lot could happen.

The search had indeed been thorough. They brought in a small picture of the Madonna of Loreto which had first gone with the *Norge* over the Pole before being placed in the *Italia*. If that was an omen, it must be a good one. Another portrait which they found had also travelled in the *Norge* – and this was particularly appreciated by Nobile, for it was of his little daughter Maria. There were also photographs of the Queen of Italy and of Il Duce, discovered in the remains of what had been the starboard side of the control cabin.

Almost the only man who did not assume a new role was Giuseppe Biagi. He was still the wireless operator. But this was now a key post. Once every two hours, at five minutes to the odd hour, he had to be at the transmitter, day and night. He had erected quite a respectably high mast, securely stayed, a little distance from the tent. He had checked that his transmissions really were exactly on the agreed channel for the *Italia* – 32 metres, shortwave. This was the same wavelength as the Rome station, so it was easy to line up. But obviously his calls were not getting through. While a transmission used up a lot of the limited juice from the batteries, having the receiver on used hardly anything, so Biagi was able to do a great deal of listening. The *Città di Milano* came in loud and clear much of the time. At the agreed hour, their base ship transmitted a brief message. 'We imagine you are near the north coast of the Svalbard, between the 15th and 20th meridians E. of Greenwich. Trust in us. We are organising help.'

This was dismaying. Their actual position was 50 miles north of the coast of the Svalbard and, far from being between the 15th and the 20th meridians, it was between the 26th and the 27th, much further to the east.

Even worse was the realisation that the *Città di Milano* was not listening out for them, except at the agreed times. Instead, the base ship's wireless was busy transmitting. The traffic at this time consisted mainly of reporters' copy being sent to Rome, including a piece suggesting that the *Italia* had flown into a mountain. It infuriated them to learn that this rubbish was being broadcast when in fact nothing should have been broadcast. The *Città di Milano* should have been listening all the time, not just at the agreed times, because if a bad accident had occurred, the time-pieces might have been lost or smashed.

There was much argument as to why Biagi's transmissions were not being heard, when they could hear the *Città di Milano* quite well and far-away Rome very well. Zappi thought it was merely because their own transmitter was weak. Biagi suggested that it might be the phenomenon of 'skipped distance' at work. Sometimes, a distant transmitter could be picked up while a nearer one was inaudible. On the nine o'clock news from Rome that night they learnt that the *Città di Milano* was about to leave King's Bay for a search along the north coast of Spitzbergen. This would bring the base ship nearer to them and out of the ring of sheltering hills which surrounded the anchorage.

The *Città di Milano* had last heard from the *Italia* at 1027 (local time) on 25 May. The radio direction-finding apparatus on board had given a crude bearing of somewhere between 30 and 40 degrees north from King's Bay; this line would pass east of Moffen Island in the vicinity of Mossel Bay. If extended considerably it would indeed have passed near to where the airship had crashed. But there was no firm indication of how far along that line the *Italia* had been. In the base ship they estimated some tens of miles perhaps, and so were thinking in terms of the north coast of West Spitzbergen in the frozen area east of Moffen Island, instead of way out on the pack to the north of North-East Land. Captain Romagna had sent a telegram on 26 May to Count Senni, the Italian minister in Oslo, Spitzbergen being officially Norwegian territory since 1925, in the hope of obtaining Norwegian aid for a search. And on 27 May he had received permission from the Ministry of Marine in Rome to carry out a search himself.

The *Città di Milano*, being a 6,000-ton ship with a light hull, was unable to either penetrate ice or come close inshore. She got as far as South Gat near Danes Island and landed a search party. It consisted of two Alpini and two University climbers led by a

Norwegian guide, the celebrated hunter Waldemar Kraemer; they were to make their way along the coast as far as Mossel Bay, looking for the remains of the airship. This plan was distinctly nineteenth century in its approach, but the way north for the ship was blocked by the north wind, which was bringing the ice down upon the coast and with it the fog.

27 May was also the day when Cesco Tomaselli's famous despatch appeared in Milan's *Corriere della Sera*, headlined as being by radio telegram from their special correspondent. Dated from King's Bay the previous day, Tomaselli began by stating simply that after 1600 hours on 26 May, the airship must be out of fuel. Under the bold headline: *L' 'Italia' non e tornata*, sub-editors had given what they took to be the main items of the news: Nobile was not replying to wireless messages: the *Città di Milano* was about to start a search: Amundsen and Sverdrup were hoping to take part with aeroplanes. If the spin of the coin had been accepted, Tomaselli would have gone in place of Ugo Lago on the Polar flight and would himself now be listed as missing. A decision by Nobile to give the Nicholas II Land flight to the senior man, Tomaselli, had probably saved his life.

Late on the evening of 27 May, Davide Giudici, Berlin correspondent of the *Corriere della Sera*, received an urgent message from Milan telling him to join his colleague Tomaselli at King's Bay. He was to leave at once for Norway and the Polar ice-fields. Fortune now left Tomaselli and smiled on Giudici, for he was to be in the right place at the right time with the right qualifications for a memorable scoop. He was a linguist, especially at home in German.

The Milanese paper had acted promptly and decisively, with an urgency lacking in the government at Rome. So hurried was Giudici that he simply threw a few items into a small suitcase and caught the night train for Oslo. As his coach rumbled through the last suburbs of the German capital, Giudici realised that he had forgotten the one item which could not easily be replaced – his passport. It was Whit Sunday, when all offices would be closed, and he had to pass through Sweden. The Swedes took border controls seriously. There was nothing for it – he would have to leave the train at the next stop and go back to his apartment.

At two in the morning on 28 May, Giudici was in Berlin once more, but he was unable to contact Lufthansa until 8 o'clock. The

news was indifferent. There were vacant seats on the flying boat
which plied between Stettin and Oslo, but none on the aeroplane
which connected Berlin with Stettin. Hastily booking a seat on
the flying boat, Giudici caught the 8.30 train to Stettin by the
skin of his teeth. When he joined the flying boat, a Dornier Wal,
he found that the other two passengers had opted out because of
the weather. He therefore had the cabin all to himself, apart from
the wireless operator. Outside, heavy rain was lashing the enclosed waters of the seaplane base, but only when they droned out
over the open Baltic did it become clear how bad the weather was.
The sullen Baltic was a mass of whitecaps, and violent gusts
threw the Dornier off course time and again; its cruising speed
was reduced from 90 to 50 m.p.h. There was only one other
machine in the air, and this was the 2-engined Dornier Super Wal
which worked the Stettin-Stockholm route. The radio operator
was continually monitoring the weather stations and the reports
became more cheerful. At Copenhagen, they found the sun
shining magnificently on the Danish capital.

The Danes, however, were less co-operative. The airport
manager told the Italian journalist that owing to a shortage of
aircraft, it would not be possible to fly him on to Norway. They
would give him a refund and even pay his hotel expenses, but
Giudici would have to continue his journey by alternative means
of transport. 'A very lively discussion' ensued, lasting an entire
hour, between the Italian journalist on the one hand and the
Danish airport manager on the other. Giudici employed the legal
argument that because he had purchased from Lufthansa a ticket
to Oslo, consequently it could be said that a contract had been
entered into. Finally the embarrassed Dane admitted that his
company only had two aircraft and both of them had been sent to
meet the brave Arctic aviator, Wilkins, who with his American
co-pilot Ben Eielson, was hourly expected for a triumphant
reception in Copenhagen. The Italian's sacrifice, he added, was a
matter small indeed when compared with the honours that
Denmark felt she owed to the wonderful trans-Polar flyer.
Giudici countered by threatening to bring an action against
Lufthansa, who had issued his ticket. At length, it was Lufthansa
which capitulated; they authorised the crew of the Dornier which
had taken him to Copenhagen to fly him on alone to Oslo. Once
more, one aeroplane for one passenger. Unfortunately, however,
the three-man crew of the aircraft – the pilot, the mechanic and

the wireless operator – had left the seaplane base; they had joined the throng of thousands in Copenhagen waiting to greet the daring Wilkins. Several motor cars were employed in the hunt to track them down, and at length they were found and hauled out of the crowds. After refuelling, the Dornier took off for Oslo.

Leaving Copenhagen astern the Dornier flew up the Kattegat, with the Viking islands to port and the Swedish coast to starboard. From Gothenburg they continued north across the fringes of the Skagerak and within 30 minutes of leaving the Swedish air base they sighted Wilkins, coming down from Oslo. It was still gusty but a beautifully clear day now and they waved a greeting from the windows of the Dornier as the two machines passed each other. Wilkins, the Australian farmer's boy, was on his way to London to be received by King George V and become Sir Hubert Wilkins.

At about nine o'clock that evening the Dornier came in to alight in Oslo fjord where Giudici was surprised to meet V.I.P. treatment: a fast launch to take him ashore, a helpful official to see him through customs and immigration, and a motor car to take him on into the city. Learning that a flying boat was coming in with a solitary Italian as passenger, the Norwegians had assumed that he must be a senior government official flying to Oslo to assist the resident Italian Minister, Count Senni, in organising aid for the Nobile expedition. Giudici noted with satisfaction that, in spite of all the delays he had experienced, he had arrived in Oslo half-an-hour earlier than the train he had scrambled out of the previous evening in order to go back for his passport.

In Oslo, matters had moved fast. A quite extraordinary coincidence had brought about an assembly of Polar experts at both the right time and at the right place. Messages from the *Italia* had ceased after 1030 on the morning of 25 May, and by evening it was clear that, even if still aloft, the airship's fuel must by now have been exhausted. On the following evening, that of 26 May, a banquet had been arranged in honour of the two Arctic airmen, Wilkins and Eielson, who had just crossed from Alaska and were briefly in Oslo before flying on to Copenhagen (Giudici passing them on the way). The pair were Polar experts in their own right, not merely aviators. As far back as 1919, Wilkins had considered airships ideal for Polar work, but neither the German nor British governments would sell him one because they thought his project suicidal. Earlier still, in 1913, Wilkins had served as photographer with Vilhjalmur Stefansson's ill-fated *Karluk*. Both men, if forced down on the ice, were perfectly capable of climbing out of the aeroplane and walking home many hundreds of miles; and had in fact done so.

Assembled to greet them at the banquet was an array of famous Polar names. Fridtjof Nansen, the pioneer of Polar drift in the pack ice, was out of Oslo that evening but Otto Sverdrup, the man who had captained the *Fram* for him in 1893–96 was present. Also there were Major Tryggve Gran, the Antarctic explorer; Gunnar Isachsen, the geographer of Spitzbergen; Amundsen's old comrades of ice and air, Oscar Wisting and Hjalmar Riiser-Larsen; and of course the little man with the big head, beaky nose and knife-crease trousers, Roald Amundsen himself.

One of the traits which he had developed was an apparent incapacity to stand alone, which contrasted strongly with a deep personal pride in his physical performance despite his small stature, which he had achieved only by strict life-long self-discipline and exercise. But he was easily influenced, and when it came to confronting people he seemed almost invariably to use another person, a rich backer or a committed aide-de-camp as a crutch. He did so now. A telegram was handed to him, telling the news of the lost *Italia*. After he had read it, Amundsen did not stand up and reveal the contents personally to this distinguished audience. He merely turned to Oscar Wisting, another committed friend from his heroic days, and whispered, 'Tell them that I am ready to start a search for the *Italia* at once.'

He did not have the means to do this, being still in debt, nor would the Government support him. What the Government did do was to form a Rescue Committee out of the experts so conveniently assembled in the capital, add to them their own meteorologists and representatives, and hold a first meeting that very night.

At that meeting, it was Sverdrup who had suggested the despatch of an ice-breaker and Riiser-Larsen who had advocated building up a force of long-range aircraft supported by 'mother' ships which could refuel them and accommodate their crews. The aircraft, a Norwegian navy seaplane hurriedly fitted with an additional petrol tank and flown by Lieutenant Lützow Holm, had taken off from Oslo fjord on the morning of 28 May. At the same time the Italian naval attaché for Scandinavia, Captain Quentin, had arrived in Oslo from Stockholm to assist Count Senni organise relief measures. In the evening of the same day Giudici had flown in to Oslo to cover this side of the story. In the course of the next few days he interviewed most of the experts who had been present at the meeting and one or two who had missed it. The advice they gave was strikingly similar.

Riiser-Larsen advocated a systematic air search by long-range planes of the whole of the pack-ice from north of Spitzbergen eastwards to Franz Josef Land, Novaya Zemlya, and the Siberian coast. Norway had no such aircraft but would make do with those she had.

Fridtjof Nansen recommended a similar air search but thought that an airship would be more useful than a great number of aeroplanes; he advocated asking the British government for one of their airships. He reduced the large search area by pointing out that West Spitzbergen could be ignored – survivors could make their own way back from there; North-East Land was more difficult and had fewer hunters and fishermen to assist the castaways; a return of the survivors from Franz Josef Land was impossible without outside help. Siberia merited a lower priority. He refused to accept that the crew of the airship had been wiped out; there would be some survivors, he said, and they could be saved – if rapid, energetic action was taken.

Professor Hoel, the Arctic expert who had advised Nobile on survival equipment, thought that most of the crew would still be alive and would be rescued if prompt and energetic action was taken. He agreed with the air search but was doubtful of the capabilities of the three 'mother' ships so far enlisted. The 6,000-ton *Città di Milano* was totally unsuitable. The 150-ton sealer *Hobby* which was to ferry Lützow Holm's short-range seaplane from Norway to Spitzbergen, was far too small. The 350-ton sealer *Braganza*, which the Italian Government had chartered, was better, but her machinery was inadequate for this task. The only vessel which could quickly reach the northern coasts of Spitzbergen at this season was a large and powerful icebreaker of not less than 10,000-tons and 10,000 to 12,000 horse-power. The Russians were best placed to send such a ship. To operate with anything less involved the possibility of a catastrophe to the rescuers themselves.

Otto Sverdrup severely limited the most likely search area: first explore with care the northern coasts of West Spitzbergen and North-East Land and the area of pack-ice to the north. If that fails, then extend the search to Franz Josef Land, but he did not think that the *Italia* had been carried as far as that. For Franz Josef Land and Novaya Zemlya, an icebreaker was necessary; only one ship would do – the *Sviatogor*, now called the *Krassin*. Sverdrup was exactly right on both counts.

All the Norwegian experts, without exception, pointed to the peculiar difficulties of carrying out search and rescue operations in the area where the *Italia* was believed to have crashed. There could hardly be a worse place, they said. It was neither land nor sea, but drifting ice which could easily sink any ordinary ship. There were enormous distances involved, so that effective air search required long-range aeroplanes and seaplanes; ordinary aircraft would be of little use.

The last Polar explorer Giudici interviewed was the great Amundsen himself, the man whom the popular press delighted to call 'the White Eagle of Norway'. He too urged 'the utmost speed and energy' in bringing help to Nobile. Before the *Italia* was reported missing, Amundsen had said that he would like to see how Nobile and his southerners would conduct themselves if they ever found themselves cast away on the ice. This jealousy he now stifled and said that, from his own experience, he knew that rescue could never come too soon. Besides, the season of the fogs would soon engulf the Arctic. Rivalry should be forgotten. It did not matter who got there first, or who did the most, so long as everyone acted with the greatest promptness.

The old explorer was clearly excited at the prospect of again flying to the Polar regions, which fascinated him. His glance turned to an aircraft model hanging from a beam – it was of a Dornier Wal which he had used in the Arctic. 'If only you knew how splendid it is up there!' he exclaimed to the Italian. 'That's where I want to die. I shan't complain if death takes me in the fulfilment of a high mission, quickly, without suffering.' Then he went on to explain, prosaically but typically, that he could overcome all normal dangers in the Arctic including the worst of them, scurvy, and had proved it many times since his first expedition in 1897 with the Belgians.

By 31 May a large and international rescue operation was shaping up; the Scandinavian nations co-operating closely with one another, the Russians, the Italians and the French being more independent. On that day, Captain Egmont Tornberg of the Royal Swedish Air Force flew in to Oslo to meet Riiser-Larsen and plan combined operations with the Norwegians. He had been instructed directly by General Karl Amundson, chief of the Swedish air force, whose flying activities had begun with balloons in the 1890s. The Swedish force was to consist of seven ships supporting seven aircraft, most of them short or medium-ranged. There were two ships for use far north in the pack, the 400-ton *Quest*, a wood-built, ice-reinforced Norwegian sealer, and the 900-ton *Tanja*, a steel-built Swedish cargo ship. Five other vessels, all colliers, were used to ferry out to Spitzbergen the short-ranged Swedish aircraft; they were the *Inger II*, *Inger III*, and *Inger IV* (named after the wife of the Norwegian who owned them), the *Oddvar* and the *Scard*.

That evening, after a meeting between the Swedes and the Norwegians chaired by Captain von der Lippe, Riiser-Larsen left for Bergen to embark his Hansa Brandenburg floatplane on the collier *Inger IV*, which would transport them to Spitzbergen; there he would join Lützow Holm who had previously shipped another floatplane in the *Hobby* and was now in the Barents Sea. This was the difficulty of the operation, that because the means were inadequate, everything had to be improvised. Most of the aircraft were incapable of flying to Spitzbergen; they simply did not have the range. The ships which were needed to transport them very often did not have either cranes or derricks capable of lifting an aeroplane on board or setting it down on the water again.

Meanwhile the Soviet Government were setting up a Nobile Relief Committee to study the possibility of sending out an ice-breaker carrying long-range aircraft of German design. The Italian Government did possess fast and modern long-range flying boats of the Savoia Marchetti type, but they were under Balbo's command. At length, the city of Milan formed a committee to procure long-range flying boats on its own account and send these to Spitzbergen. The British Royal Air Force possessed long-range flying boats designed for Empire communications, four of which were engaged on a formation flight to the Far East; and they also possessed airships. However, it would have required a political decision before their use could be offered; and possibly there were security considerations also. The Germans decided to help by making one small civilian aircraft available, a Klemm-Daimler flown by the Swedish pilot, Ekman.

For Giudici personally, what sort of story he got depended on how he read the situation so as to be at the decisive point at the right time. For the moment, he stayed in Oslo to cover the organisation of the rescue.

Chapter 11

BREAKING UP

(On the Pack: 28 May–3 June)

O N the morning of 28 May, for the first time in two days, the sun burst clear of the clouds lowering past over the pack-ice under the scurrying north-west wind. The navigators among the castaways were able to get a position. Their immediate reaction to it was shock. Both latitude and longitude had changed considerably. The ice-floe on which their tent was pitched had moved 28 miles to the south-east in two days. So improbable did a drift of 14 miles a day appear to Nobile, that at first he thought that the navigators had made a mistake. But there was no mistake. A distinctive pyramid shape had appeared on the southern horizon, which had not been there before. It was Charles XII Island. This, they knew, lay off the north-east extremity of North-East Land and on the verge of an uncharted wilderness to which, it seemed, the wind was drifting the floe.

'Where will this drift take us?' asked Nobile.

'Towards Franz Josef Land,' replied Malmgren instantly.

They turned to the single book which had, with them, survived the crash. By the oddest of coincidences it was a manual of navigation – the *Arctic Pilot* – the one book above all others of interest to them at this moment. They found what they were looking for on page 264. '*The principal direction of the ice-stream in North East Land is towards the east.*' That is, into the uncharted wilderness they had over-flown in their flight towards Nicholas II Land; and further and further away from the area being searched by the *Città di Milano*.

Later that day, Nobile heard Mariano talking to Malmgren. The naval officer was saying that to stay camped as they were was merely to wait for death. They ought to escape by walking out to Spitzbergen over the ice. 'With them?' queried Malmgren, indicating Nobile and Cecioni. Mariano nodded. But clearly it was impossible. Even if they had had sledges, which they did not, the movement of two helpless men over the jumbled horror of the pack ice was beyond the power of the seven men who could still walk.

Not long after, Commanders Mariano and Zappi came into the tent to speak to the General. They said that the situation was desperate and that the emergency wireless set was too weak to contact the outside world. Nobile, who knew that the set had been chosen on technical advice, objected. Could technicians be so grossly mistaken regarding its range of 700 kilometres? And they must have tested it.

'Yes!' said Zappi. 'They did test it, but under much more favourable conditions.' They had got Rhodes, once, but that had been at night.

What Zappi really meant was, that Malmgren and the three naval officers should attempt to break out from the camp over the pack-ice and bring help. Nobile replied that everyone must discuss this before a decision was made. But first he had to calm Cecioni, who had assumed the logical conclusion, that all the fit men would escape, leaving behind only the badly hurt.

'No! They mustn't be allowed to go! They ought not to abandon two helpless men like that! . . . We should all march together!'

For Cecioni, normally so strong and competent, who always found a way to master machinery, had not yet accepted the full consequences of his broken leg. He was sure that he could construct a sledge and that the others could pull it. Nobile saw further. Sledging was impossible, but if the situation really was desperate, then the able-bodied men should take their chances and try to reach safety. The two abandoned men, he himself and Cecioni, would die, but better that only two perished rather than nine. This assumed that their field wireless was useless, but Nobile, unlike most of the castaways, still had faith in it. There was a difference not merely of opinion but of assumption. At another level it was a matter of personality and temperament; the more active men favouring an active solution rather than a patient and passive role. And, naturally, there were the pressures of being cooped up together, nine men having to occupy the space intended for four.

The discussion took place after the nine o'clock news that evening, when they learnt that the *Città di Milano* had reached

7

the north coast of West Spitzbergen. Although their base ship was nearer to them, they could no longer hear her wireless signals and Biagi once more put forward his idea of the 'skipped distance'. That precipitated the argument.

Nobile invited the two senior officers to define their case. Instead, they turned to Malmgren as their spokesman. The Swede was their ice expert and had inspected with them the state of the pack. He put their ideas concisely. 'All hope of the radio working must now be considered as lost. On the other hand, the drift is carrying us farther and farther from North-East Land. In these circumstances the only possibility of salvation lies in sending a patrol towards North Cape to meet the rescue expeditions.'

'Who would go?' asked Nobile.

'I'm perfectly ready to undertake it,' replied Commander Mariano, the senior naval officer.

'And how many would you be?' queried Nobile.

'At least four,' put in Commander Zappi, answering for his senior. 'The three naval officers and Malmgren, who would be an invaluable guide.'

The large and amiable Czech scientist, Franz Behounek, startled them all with the unexpected crispness of his interjection. 'For my part, I'll willingly remain with the General. But I must insist that one of the naval officers stays with us! We must have someone who can work out our position. Otherwise, what's the use of the wireless operator?'

Trojani said nothing, but was appalled. Their bond of unity, the greatest strength they had, was broken. With the General injured, the next most senior in rank should have stayed, to take his place, he felt; that was the common military ethic everywhere.

Malmgren afterwards told Behounek that he most admired the tranquillity with which Nobile, though sick and crippled, took the news that both the senior officers meant to leave him. 'The General is a truly great man,' the Swede told Behounek. 'Compared to him, all the others seem small.'

Cecioni burst in as soon as Behounek had made his point. 'No!' There was no need for the party to break in two, he pleaded. They should all march across the pack together. From the wreckage of the *Italia*'s cabin, he could make two sledges, one for himself, one for the General.

Then Nobile spoke. He agreed with the idea of building sledges; they might come in useful. But Cecioni was not to

deceive himself; they could never be used to convey injured men
across the ice. A test might be made, in case he doubted that.
Indeed, such sledges would be useful in moving the camp to a
safer place on the pack. That would make the difficulties clear.

To Malmgren and the two senior naval officers, Nobile said
that such a serious decision as splitting up the party should not be
rushed. If they waited a few days, they would see if the drift
really was permanently to the south-east and east, or whether,
instead, it was governed by the direction of the wind. Also, in
that time their S.O.S. signals might be heard. It was not now a
case of the *Città di Milano* only. Biagi had intercepted a message
being sent by some journalist, reporting that the *Hobby* was about
to sail for Hinlopen Strait. In the next few days she would come
very close to them, was bound to have an experienced short-wave
radio operator on board, and might well pick up Biagi's calls.

Next morning, 29 May, the first man out of the tent noticed a
changed landscape. Charles XII Island had disappeared. To the
south-west were two new islands, low lying and close together.
They could only be the Isles of Broch and Foyn. And they were
only ten miles away. Some of the projecting capes of North-East
Land, although unseen, could be only some ten miles further
beyond the islands, so tantalisingly close. The drift was continuing
then, much more to the east than to the south now. They were
rapidly being carried away from Spitzbergen and towards the
uncharted ocean.

So near to land were they, that numbers of seagulls and wild
geese circled above the tent. Biagi wished aloud for a rifle to
match the ammunition they had found. But the rifles must still be
in the hull of the *Italia*. And that brought them to consider again
how close to them the remains of the airship must be. Some of
them had seen a column of smoke to the east about half-an-hour
after the crash, not more than 10 kilometres away. Either it
was Alessandrini and his men jettisoning petrol-tanks to keep
the *Italia* aloft for a little longer, or it was a fire resulting from
the hull and its engine cars falling on the pack. If the latter, the
wreckage was less than 10 kilometres away; if the former, perhaps
20 to 30 kilometres. There was a suggestion that two men be
sent out across the ice to find out, but the hideously broken nature
of the pack-ice caused the idea almost instantly to be rejected.
Steady marching was impossible; one could progress by scramb-
ling, sliding and crawling rather than by walking.

Wireless reception had changed once more. They could again hear the *Città di Milano*, busy transmitting the useless conjectures of newspaper reporters to their editors or private telegrams from members of the crew, assuring their loved ones back in Italy that they were perfectly safe. As usual, San Paolo, the Rome station, although far away, was much clearer than transmissions made by stations near at hand. This had given the castaways the idea of asking anyone who heard them to reply on the same wavelength of 32 metres. Therefore, this day for the first time a brief sentence was added to Biagi's S.O.S. – '*Rispondete via IDO 32.*' 'IDO' was San Paolo's call sign. Still, there was no reply, no suggestion that anyone out there had heard them.

But in fact they had been heard now. Pedretti, listening in the *Città di Milano*, picked up parts of a message. First, the word '*Italia*', followed by considerably distorted sounds, and a final sentence, '*Rispondete via IDO 32 K.*' But no one connected this with the airship *Italia*. It was assumed that the call was intended for Italy from the Italian colony of Mogadishu in Africa. In the *Città di Milano* few seriously considered any longer that there could be survivors from the *Italia*. Consequently the ship's own transmitter, as well as the Norwegian transmitter ashore, crowded the airwaves with messages of their own instead of listening out for faint S.O.S. calls.

Biagi, who had been transmitting every two hours round the clock since the late afternoon of 25 May, was by now thoroughly discouraged. Anyway, the batteries would soon be exhausted, and then their set would fall silent for ever.

The pressure for a march out increased, so that Nobile had to probe its practicalities. Not more than two should go, he thought, not four as had been suggested.

'No! There should be three at least,' replied Mariano. 'Then if one falls sick, the second could stay to help while the third man went on.'

Zappi also wanted four, the three naval officers plus Malmgren, but would settle for three – Mariano, Malmgren and himself.

'How many kilometres a day to you expect to cover?' asked Nobile. 'How many days to reach North Cape?'

'On a pack such as this,' replied Malmgren, 'I think we could manage about 10 kilometres a day. Nearer land, where the ice should be smoother, we might cover 15. Of course, we shall be more tired then, but to make up for it the way will be easier.'

They examined the map. Malmgren traced the route via Foyn Island, Cape Bruun, Cape Platen, Scoresby Island, North Cape. About 160 kilometres. And about fifteen or sixteen days.

'Who wishes to go?' enquired Nobile.

Mariano, Zappi and Malmgren were more than ready, indeed impatient to be off; Viglieri and Biagi were willing to go. Only the Czech scientist Behounek and the engineer Trojani said that they would stay with the General and Cecioni. This, almost exactly, represented the distinction between the able-bodied and the sick or unsuitable. Trojani was small and frail, Behounek was big and clumsy.

Nobile would not give the final word. 'Tomorrow we'll try to shift the camp 500 yards,' he said. 'Afterwards, we'll have to see.'

They settled down for the night. Malmgren took a time trying to find a more comfortable position for his injured arm. Cecioni murmured in his sleep. Mariano lay awake a long time. He seemed to have changed, thought Nobile. In spirit, he had left them and was already striding out for home. Outside, a light wind plucked gently at the tent as they fell asleep.

Tormented by his thoughts and by his injuries, Nobile was awake when on the morning of 30 May the sun shone out, over the pack, a whitish disc when seen through the double silk-walls of the tent. It was an opportunity for the navigators to get another 'fix', to check on their drift into eternity, out of reach of rescue. The General nudged Cecioni, who woke Zappi. Both Zappi and Mariano got up and went outside. A minute or two passed, then Zappi came back, poked his head into the tent and in a very low tone said:

'There's a bear.'

Malmgren, who had been sleeping at Nobile's feet, sat up and said to the General, 'Give me the pistol. I'm going to hunt it.'

The Swede 'broke' the Colt revolver and carefully slipped the fat brass cartridge cases into the chambers. The barrel came back into place with a click.

He crept outside, followed by everyone else. Even Nobile and Cecioni crawled out, helped by the others, so excited that they felt no pain.

It was bitter outside, but not achingly cold because there was only a slight breeze. The sun had gone behind clouds again, but the air was clear and transparent, making the bluish ice-crags stand out dramatically against the whiteness of the snow. Twenty or thirty yards away was the bear.

'Hush! Don't move!' whispered Malmgren. Then he cautiously moved forward trying not to startle the bear until he had got within effective range.

The 'audience' armed themselves. Mariano and Zappi had got the best weapons, a knife and an axe. The others had a file, a nail, and a piece of tubing. They all stayed, as ordered, by the tent, not saying a word; Nobile hugging Titina tightly so that she would not bark.

The bear stared back at them placidly, apparently not at all scared. Except for Titina, all the watchers were frightened, never before having seen a bear outside a zoo: nevertheless, the incongruous scene – with nine more-or-less armed men confronting one animal – struck Nobile as being comic. Malmgren was stalking cautiously forward, while the bear, partly concealed behind a hummock, was slowly wagging its head.

A single shot cracked out. Malmgren ran forward. Two more shots followed on the first, Malmgren shooting as he ran. 'He's hit!' cried someone. Mariano and Zappi were running, too, hard on Malmgren's heels. The bear scrambled away from the humans, and then fell.

The first shot had been enough. At fifteen yards, Malmgren had put a slug into its heart. It was a remarkable performance with a basically inaccurate weapon, which Malmgren had previously stated would be useless for bears. 'You see, the Queen was right!' Nobile told him afterwards, for during the argument he had said that the Queen of Italy, who possessed hunting experience in Spitzbergen, had recommended the heavy Colt as excellent, even for big game. The secret, of course, was to possess sufficient nerve to come in really close before pressing the trigger, so that the 'kick' of the fired weapon had less chance to throw the bullet off.

There was another side to the results of Malmgren's skill. The Italians had tended to think of the live bear as a menace. But the same bear dead represented a fine skin for someone to lie on and some 150 to 200 pounds of fresh meat. 'Skin it and cut it up while it's still warm,' advised Malmgren; 'and it's all edible, except for the liver.' The bear was as good as three weeks rations. No longer would they have to count the decreasing days before starvation would claim them: 40, 39, 38. . . .

Everyone had been surprised by the peaceful disposition of the bear. When its stomach contents had been examined and proved to contain only a few scraps of paper with English words printed on them, there had been some sinister speculations, but finally, by examining the paper fragments more closely, they realised the truth. The pages had come from one of their own navigation books which the bear must have found lying in the snow. So famished was the creature, that it had tried to eat the book.

Later that morning, the sun shone through again and the navigators were able to work out a new position. Shortly after, Zappi came to the General with an impatient demand that the march-out party should depart at once. Nobile was astonished. The killing of the poor bear had so increased their food stocks that the need for an immediate decision seemed to have receded. He said so, but Zappi was too irritated with opposition to hear the argument out. Every demur, he beat down at once. It turned out that this morning's position had shown a further drift of five miles to the south-east, which had brought them very close to Foyn Island. According to their map, it was only about seven miles away now.

After Zappi had left, Commander Mariano came in to insist that the marchers should go at once. Cecioni, who had spent hours making a sledge, protested again. 'Much better we all go together!' he implored.

Mariano turned to him and coldly demolished the idea. 'Last night we tested your sledge by bringing 50 kilos of meat from the place where the bear was killed to this tent. It was barely 40 yards, but it took us over an hour.'

It was clear to Nobile that both Mariano and Zappi were totally convinced that their only hope of life was to break out across the ice to North-East Land, where they expected their rescuers to be. And if they succeeded, that would probably mean rescue, too, for those who stayed with the tent. Nobile did not think they would succeed, but felt it was no longer right for him to stop them. Yet to lose both Mariano and Malmgren together would be a severe blow.

Behounek was of the same mind. 'What will become of us when Mariano leaves? He's been an admirable officer and a help to us all by keeping us hard at work. And what will we do without Malmgren, the only man among us who really knows the Arctic?'

Trojani and Biagi chimed in with their support, particularly as regards Malmgren.

So Nobile called to Malmgren, told him how they all felt, and added his own wish that either Mariano should go, or the Swede should go, but not both together.

Malmgren answered him: 'I think it's essential that the group should have a guide who knows all about the ice. Marching on a pack like this is very tiring and risky. They must have somebody practical.' He paused. 'In any case, I will do as you wish – stay here or go with them, whichever you prefer.'

Nobile asked the Swede if his arm had mended. Was he fit to march?

Malmgren said that he was. The arm was badly bruised but not broken. He could not carry a full load but would manage 15 or 20 kilos without trouble.

Nobile then told Malmgren to be ready to start out with Zappi. He would talk to Mariano after their meal and get him to stay.

This was the first meal of bear broth which they had cooked. It proved tasteless and the few scraps of meat floating in it were too tough for them to chew properly. It was nothing like as good as pemmican soup, because they did not yet know how to cook it; but they would learn. As Mariano got up from this dismaying meal, Nobile told him: 'I want to speak to you alone.' The naval officer did not answer, but merely walked out of the tent, ignoring the General.

Outside, he could be heard talking loudly to Zappi. 'We two should go, as we're such good friends.' That seemed meant for Nobile, obliquely. The two senior naval officers were not to be stopped and they intended to take Malmgren with them. The General gave in as gracefully as he could.

Trojani described this as the ugliest incident of all, the final breaking of their unity; a unity, which for some of them, had been forged as long ago as 1926, on the *Norge* expedition. When Zappi, hoping for encouragement, asked him what he thought of the enterprise, Trojani replied with the blunt truth: 'Ours is a static agony, whereas yours is a dynamic one. The difference is small, the result will be the same.'

Zappi had already made a list of what his party intended to take with them. The food was shared, the clothing was shared, the navigational instruments were shared, and so were the charts. Nobile gave the British Admiralty chart to Zappi and kept the

German chart for himself, both being of the Svalbard. The tent
could not be shared, but what about weapons? The marchers all
wanted the Colt revolver. Cecioni, Trojani and Viglieri protested:
'What shall we do if more bears come along?' Nobile decided to
keep the Colt, and give the marchers the hunting knife and the axe.

'When will you start?' asked Nobile.

'This evening,' replied Malmgren.

Mariano and Zappi left the tent and there was a short silence.
Then Nobile asked Malmgren for his frank opinion of the chances
of survival for both parties, those who went and those who
remained. Malmgren gestured after the two senior naval officers.

'They don't understand how difficult and dangerous this march
will be. A few years ago a perfectly equipped German expedition
was lost to a man on such a pack as this.'

'And what about us?' asked Nobile.

'You have to face the drift. It'll carry you eastwards.'

The Swede paused a moment and then, leaning forward and
speaking in an undertone, said for Nobile's benefit alone:

'Both parties will die.'

Malmgren left to get ready, and the others went with him to
help. Half-an-hour later Viglieri and Behounek came back.
Viglieri sat down, but Behounek stayed by the entrance. Then
Biagi came in, frowning and irritated, and sat down facing the
General.

'What's wrong, Biagi?'

'I'm fit to march, too,' replied the young man.

Behounek did not want to overhear that scene, so he quickly
went outside. As he left, Nobile was pouring out a torrent of
Italian in a raised voice. It was so rapid that the Czech could
hardly understand a word of it. He sought out Malmgren and
told him what was happening in there.

'All right!' said the Swede. 'If Biagi goes, then I stay. I will
not leave the General alone with inexperienced unpractical men
like you, and I will not agree that the only man who can work
the wireless – your last hope of rescue – shall go with us.'

Nobile had admired the way that Biagi, with never a sign of
weariness or impatience, had worked indefatigably day and night
at the wireless. He was one of the staunch, tireless workers like
the dead Pomella and the men who had been carried away in the
airship.

'You've done your utmost to make your radio work,' Nobile

told him. 'If it hasn't succeeded, that's not your fault. You've done your duty, and needn't have any scruples about leaving. Go and get ready.'

As the young radioman stepped outside, no longer sad and frowning, Lieutenant Viglieri, who had been sitting silent, said quietly: 'But then I should like to go, too.'

There was no answer to that. A silence fell in the tent.

Thinking that Nobile had finished, Behounek and Trojani came in again, and Nobile called also for Mariano, Zappi, Malmgren and Biagi. The General was calm once more, noted Behounek, saying that he absolved them from all obligations to him personally; that each one of them had the fullest freedom to stay or to go; and that he had no objection to being left alone with the injured Cecioni and their share of provisions. 'These words were more effective than any order,' Behounek recorded.

Nobile asked each man in turn for his decision. First of all, Viglieri, the youngest of the three naval officers. The Lieutenant hesitated a moment, then gave a composed reply:

'It's been arranged that the three shall leave. I don't think it's necessary to go back on that decision.'

'I'm staying here with the General,' said Behounek.

'I'm staying, too,' put in Trojani.

That meant only four were going – the three and Biagi. To them Nobile said, 'All right! Go and get ready.' Malmgren did not follow them but instead came over and sat down at Nobile's feet.

'If they leave, I stay.'

'But why?'

'I could never go back to Sweden and say that I left the leader of the expedition and another sick man without help. That would be unworthy of a gentleman. No! If Biagi leaves, I remain. He represents the only hope you have.'

A few minutes later, Biagi again came into the tent and sat down, cross-legged and smiling.

'Forgive me, sir! It was a moment of weakness. But I'm not going. You might need me for the wireless.'

The decision made, Malmgren was a different man. The prospect of action braced him. He became optimistic. When he reached King's Bay he would contact Tromsoe and Oslo to work out where the winds and the currents would have drifted the tent party in the meantime. 'Then I'll come back to look for you myself, with Swedish aeroplanes,' he told Nobile. 'Do you think one could land here on the pack? I do. I've seen flat ground; but possibly there'll be a canal, where a seaplane could alight. Mind you keep those balls of aniline dye. They will be useful for colouring some rags red. Put four of those improvised red flags at the corners of a square, 200 metres each side, with the tent as its centre. Then we'll be able to see you better from the air.'

A stream of advice poured over Nobile. 'Keep quite still. Then your fractures will heal sooner. In three weeks you, too, may be able to march and get to Foyn Island. Follow in our tracks, then we'll know where to find you. Eat the bear meat first, it's too heavy for marching.'

'Will the meat keep a long time?' asked Nobile.

'Oh yes! For three weeks certainly. Be careful not to let it touch the ice. You had better hang it up, somehow or other.' The Swede paused. 'Don't use the wireless for twenty – twenty-five days – until we've had time to reach King's Bay and send a ship as near to you as possible. And look out for movements in the ice. If a crack opens under the tent, shift it at once.' Finally, Malmgren said: 'What message do you want me to send to Italy?'

'Tell them that my comrades and I are staying here calmly, waiting for God's will to be done. If we can be saved, so much the better. If not. . . . Only see that they look after our families.'

Malmgren held out his hand.

'All right, General! In any case, remember that the greater number of lost expeditions have been saved at the last moment.'

Mariano asked Nobile for a report to take with him. They would carry this back to King's Bay as well as last letters from those of the castaways who were staying.

'You can report verbally,' replied the General, anxious to write to his wife most of all. Trojani who, thinking the rite of last letters would be perfectly futile, politely handed Nobile his fountain pen. It was very quiet, as they all scribbled away. The stuffy tent became as silent as a church. Young Lieutenant Viglieri was writing to his mother. Behounek to his fiancée and his sister. Biagi and Cecioni to their wives. Nobile was astonished to note that Behounek, the amiable and self-contained scientist, seemingly incapable of emotion, had tears running down his cheeks as he scribbed his last words. The others also. Only Trojani remained impassive. He was with great care wrapping up a little parcel for his wife; it held all the money he had had on him.

Cecioni couldn't write at all; after the first few lines, he had stopped. But those few lines were full of despair. 'No! No!' said Nobile, glancing at them. 'Not like that! It's not certain that we'll die here. So you must write differently. Look! I'll write it for you, and you'll copy it.'

Having done that, the General carried on with his own message. Not wanting his wife to suffer, he added: 'If it is God's will that I die out here, you must not imagine it a terrible end. All will take place with serenity and Christian resignation.' In a note to his daughter, he could be less formal: 'You must keep Mummy from crying, if I don't come back again.' And then there was the question of the dog. . . . He added another line: 'Titina is perfectly happy here, but perhaps she would still rather be at home. . . .'

Commander Mariano made a point of consoling Cecioni. A channel had opened up in the ice near them. If this went as far as Foyn, he told the stricken engineer, we'll come back for you with a raft. If not, why we'll march as fast as we can and bring help.

'Then we helped them load up,' recalled Trojani. 'They took extra clothing, a blanket, a long rope, a large knife, an axe, a bottle of petrol, 55 kilograms of foodstuffs. They also had Pomella's knapsack and what did not go into that was put into parcels. Malmgren, his arm still painful, could not carry his load on his shoulders. Mariano and Zappi reduced the amount of food he carried and tied the remainder round his waist. To me, they seemed to be excessively loaded and uncomfortable. We embraced and kissed. Viglieri, Biagi and Behounek had tears in their eyes.

'After a few steps they halted. One of Malmgren's reindeer-skin shoes had come undone, so Zappi called on Biagi to fasten it for him. This filled us with consternation. If Malmgren was not capable of fastening his shoelaces, he would not get very far.

'They started off again in single file. Zappi, whom Malmgren had entrusted with the compass, led the march. We watched them through binoculars. They moved away towards the island of Broch. Then they stopped; perhaps they intended to spend the night there? The first leg was a short one.

'Next morning they resumed their journey. At one time it seemed that they were returning. We informed the General.'

'They've found the channel and are coming back to tell us!' shouted Cecioni, his eyes shining with joy.

'No, they are not returning, they will not return any more,' answered Nobile, dryly.

'For two days we followed them through binoculars. Then they were lost to sight in that icy wilderness. In two days they had covered about five kilometres. That wasn't much.'

The castaways in the tent felt free at last. No more discussions, insistences, objections; no more impatience, discontent, uncertainty. The strongest had gone, and they were glad. Their destiny was fixed now – to stay and endure.

For Nobile it was a happier time. No longer were ideas, initiatives, wishes set up against his own. The five men remaining besides himself were the most docile, the most acquiescent, perhaps the most affectionate. Morally, at least, he was now able to resume full command; to be obeyed without question by men who trusted his judgement. He was more like a father than a leader. They were more like a family than a group of refugees.

He set himself to reorganise the camp. Viglieri was in charge of stores and making solar observations; Biagi was occupied by the wireless; the cooking was done by Trojani and Behounek, and Cecioni's broken leg did not prevent him using his skilled hands to cut and sew material for new footwear which they badly needed. All were occupied. Nobile himself attempted to make a pair of slippers, but his real role was to think.

He considered Malmgren's advice, to stop transmitting and save the wireless batteries for three weeks or so, until the time when rescue ships might be nearer. But he decided to take the opposite course – to step up the number of transmissions per day and to repeat each message many times, in the hope of at least one getting through. At certain times, Biagi was to transmit continuously for an hour. But first, he got the wireless operator to check that his wave-length was exactly 32 metres. Second, he got him to make his greatest effort on 32 metres at about 8 o'clock (Greenwich time) each evening. That was the time when many people around the world were listening in on 32 metres for the time check from the Eiffel Tower. He wrote out for Biagi a short message which would be the same daily, except for their position, which would change according to Viglieri's last 'fix'. First he wrote out the message in Italian, and then in French. That in Italian, transmitted with their position on 3 June, read:

. . . S.O.S. Italia. Nobile. Sui ghiacci presso l'Isola Foyn, Nord-Est Spitsbergen, latitudine 80°37', longitudine 26°50'. Impossibile

muoversi mancando di slitte ed avendo due feriti. Dirigibile perduto in altrà localita. Rispondete via IDO 32.

Sometimes the message was sent out in English, in which case it read:

. . . *S.O.S. Italia. Nobile. On the ice near Foyn Island, north-east Spitsbergen, latitude* 80°37', *longitude* 26°50'. *Impossible to move, lacking sledges and having two men injured. Dirigibile lost in another locality. Reply via IDO* 32.

Nobile had been assured by the technicians that the set had a minimum range of 700 kilometres. He felt that its signals had not been picked up by the Italian base ship because in the *Città di Milano* they were not bothering to listen very much or for very long, and the weak transmissions were often being blotted out by the ship's own transmitter or the Norwegian one on shore at Ny Aalesund, which were interminably busy with press messages and personal greetings. He accepted the risk that by having Biagi hammer away with their S.O.S. messages, their batteries would soon run down. With the strong-minded individuals gone, there were no counter-arguments and the message beginning *S.O.S. Italia. Nobile* . . . was tapped out time after time into the silent ether. If their own base ship could not, or would not, listen for them, perhaps there were others out there who might hear the faint calls.

Their position now did not change very much, and sometimes there was a reversed drift, taking them back to the west. On 3 June they came back to within four miles of Foyn Island and 5½ from Broch Island. There were plenty of birds and it was from the islands that the bears seemed to come. One night, a bear blundered into one of the wires from the radio set and was only scared off when it was only a foot or two from the side of the tent where Nobile's head lay. Another bear was detected in daylight by the tiny dog Titina, who began barking furiously and rushed at it. The bear lumbered away before it could be shot. When the Italians did use the revolver, they were totally unsuccessful; it proved impossible for them to bring down a bear. Malmgren's Arctic skills were sorely missed.

Chapter 12

RADIO – AND THE 'RED TENT'

(3–9 June)

At half past seven in the evening of 3 June, Soviet time, a radio amateur with the German name of Nicholas Schmidt was sitting by his wireless set in the tiny Russian village of Wossenie-Wochma in the region of Archangelsk. That is, more than 1,200 miles away from the pack-ice north of Spitsbergen on the other side of the Barents Sea. He was listening on the short waves between 30 and 35 metres when he picked up a faint and mangled message in a foreign language. He jotted it down as best he could, and the words came out as:

Itali ... Nobile ... Fran ... Josef ... S.O.S. ... S.O.S. ... S.O.S. ... Terra ... tengo ... Eh H. ... And that was followed by a word which might perhaps be *Petermann*. There was such a place in the Arctic, the so-called Petermann Land, about 100 kilometres north of the Franz Josef Archipelago.

Three days later, on the evening of 6 June, Giuseppe Biagi was sitting by his set with the head-piece over his ears, listening to the news bulletin being broadcast from Rome, 3,000 miles south of the pack-ice. As usual, he had out a notebook and pencil and was transcribing the news. Suddenly, he shouted: 'They've heard us!' As he went on writing, Nobile began to pick out the words:

The Soviet Embassy has informed the Italian Government that an S.O.S. from the Italia has been picked up by a young Soviet farmer, Nicholas Schmidt, at Archangel on the evening of June third. ...

They had been heard at an incredible distance by a 'ham', an amateur operator, listening at a receiver situated more than one thousand miles further away than the professionally-manned naval wireless installation of the *Città di Milano*. They all felt dazed, and Nobile could hardly contain his joy. He suspected that it might be the very remoteness of the Russian receiver which had made the feat possible; he would not have to listen through the interminable wireless traffic of the Italian base ship and the local Norwegian station. Now that the world knew that they were still alive, he hoped, the government in Rome would order an end to all those greetings telegrams and countless press messages with which the *Città di Milano* had been blocking the air waves.

That evening the castaways celebrated with an extra ration of 3 grams of malted milk and 15 grams of sugar; and something to go with it. Nobile kept beside him some alchohol from the compasses, which he was keeping for medicinal purposes; now someone suggested that they use a little of it to drink a toast to an unknown Russian wireless operator.

At 11 o'clock next morning, 7 June, Nobile ordered Biagi to transmit their S.O.S. for an hour without pause, and to add after the word *Foyn* another word, *circa*, to show that the position figures which followed were merely approximate and not exact. Biagi did this and with great zest. Looking at his watch later, to see if the hour was up yet, Nobile was surprised to find that Biagi had exceeded the 60 minutes. It was the first time he had not obeyed an order to the letter. Suddenly he stopped transmitting and began listening. He repeated the words to Nobile:

We have received your call and the word 'Francesco'.

He took off his headphones, thankfully, saying: 'That's the *Città di Milano* talking to San Paolo, I suppose.'

That evening they all gathered in the tent for the Rome news bulletin, all except Trojani who was on guard. As usual, when the news began, Biagi copied it out in his notebook, speaking the words aloud at the same time as he wrote them down. 'A wireless amateur in the United States reports hearing a message. . . .' and then, as the message was given, consternation overtook them. The report bore no relation to anything they had sent, indeed it claimed that the *Italia* had crashed against a mountain and that they were sheltering in the wreckage of it. Still worse, it gave a totally false position, impossibly far north beyond the 84th parallel; the meridian was wrong as well, although not by so much.

They feared two dangers here. Either that the outside world would believe in the message and go looking for them many hundreds of miles away from where they really were; or that the world would realise that it was false and suspect that the Russian message, which Biagi recognised as genuine, was false as well and that the crew of the airship were all dead and not worth bothering over. 'It's enough to drive you mad!' said Trojani, when he came in from sentry-go.

Despite the bitter feelings of the unheard castaways, they were not so callous in the *Città di Milano* after all, at least according to Odd Arnesen, the Norwegian pressman who could hardly be accused of being uncritical of Italians. He described the crew of the base ship during these days as down and out with black despair. He said that the foreign pressmen dared not go aboard, because it would be like entering a house of mourning, and they did not wish to intrude. If they met Captain Romagna on land, he would pass them by, shaking his head repeatedly, to show that there was no news.

Then, he said, the radio amateurs began to start rumours. First, a Dutchman from Huizum called Werkema who claimed to have picked up an S.O.S. in French, then a Russian by the name of Schmidt who had heard something about: *North-west . . . storm . . . S.O.S. . . . . Petermann*. Arnesen bearded Romagna about this and the captain tended to dismiss it. 'In a case like this people hear and see much more than they would otherwise do,' he said, 'and amateurs hear more than anyone else. There may be something in it, but I admit I myself put no great faith in it. But of course we shall look into the matter.'

The chief wireless operator, Technical Captain Ugo Baccarini, certainly toiled away at his set, according to Arnesen; and the Norwegian journalist heard that Baccarini had picked up faint signals which he maintained were in the 'writing' of Biagi. Then halfway through the morning of 7 June the duty wireless operator suddenly jumped up and gestured wildly with happiness. 'It is Nobile! It's the *Italia!*' Everyone, without distinction of rank crowded towards the wireless cabin, shouting '*Italia!* Nobile!' A second radio operator had also been listening and he too confirmed what the first had heard. It was the *Italia* without a doubt.

When the call from the airship survivors ceased, the *Città di Milano*'s radio went on the air, asking for a position, but there was no reply from Biagi. After asking again, there came another indistinct message of which only one word was clear: *Francesco*. The ship replied, acknowledging the word *Francesco*, but adding that reception was poor. Biagi should save his batteries. The ship would call again when atmospheric conditions were more favourable.

Neither operator had really understood the other. Biagi, hearing the reference to that odd word *Francesco*, which he certainly had not sent, assumed that the ship was calling Rome. That morning he had not the least idea that any part of even one of his messages had been heard by the *Città di Milano*. So it was only in the base ship that they celebrated the contact, weak and broken though it was. It was only now that they realised the folly of transmitting so many messages when a weak station was desperately trying to be heard. The energies of their operators would have been better spent in listening.

The excitement among the pressmen at King's Bay was intense. The *Italia* had been missing for nearly two weeks now and for much of that time the journalists had been filling the airways with speculation and the news that there was no news; and so, unknowingly, had contributed to the failure to hear the airship's S.O.S. messages. Now, at last, the penny really had dropped with Captain Romagna, and he sent a sailor up the hill to the Norwegian mining company's wireless station, which most of the non-Italian press used. A swarthy little man burst into the room, recalled Arnesen, flinging wide the door, waving his arms and yelling '*Italia! Italia! Italia!*' while pointing wild-eyed to the *Città di Milano* down in the bay. The Norwegian operator stopped.

In one mad rush, the press went down the hill, bound for the radio room of the Italian ship.

That evening Biagi was at his receiver, listening to King's Bay traffic beamed to Rome. It consisted of telegrams being sent by the Italian journalists with the expedition, giving the news of the day. And the main news was that the *Città di Milano* had at last intercepted fragments of one of Biagi's messages: *S.O.S. . . . Francesco*. There was that word again, which he had not sent! Not until long after did they discover that it was the almost pedantic insertion of the word *circa* into their standard message which had caused the trouble, for the first sentence now ran: *Sui ghiacci presso l'Isola Foyn, circa Nord-Est Spitsbergen . . .* It was *Foyn, circa* which had been mistaken for *Francesco*. Foyn island was minute, but everyone had heard of Franz (or Francis) Joseph Land, so there was the possibility of a serious mistake. That the rescuers, although they might not now be misled by the American amateur and his wild message, would believe that the *Italia* had gone down in Franz Josef Land, hundreds of miles away in a different direction.

Next day, 8 June, Nobile altered the first sentence of the standard message accordingly. It now read:

. . . S.O.S. Italia. Nobile. Long. 28° Est, a circa 20 miglia dalla costa Nord-Est delle Spitsbergen. . . .

It was as plain as he could make it, for it meant simply:

Longitude 28° E., about 20 miles from the N.E. coast of Spitzbergen.

This did away with all the complicated co-ordinates which also might be all too easily misheard, and would certainly change daily with their drift, whether or not they had got a sight of the sun.

That evening they listened as usual to the nine o'clock news from Rome. There was nothing of interest. Biagi took off his earphones to chat for a moment, then put them back on again to hear the press bulletins. Then he gave an exclamation of surprise.

'They're calling us!'

'No, it can't be!' interjected Nobile.

'Yes, it's Rome.' And Biagi began to translate the sound into letters and words. In English, they read:

Italia. Ido. It is exactly 9.55 p.m. At 7.23 p.m., G.M.T., the Città di Milano heard you clearly, receiving your S.O.S. and co-ordinates. The Città di Milano will call you at the 50th minute of every hour on the 900-metre wave length, to ask confirmation of your co-ordinates, and Biagi's registration number as a check.

The Italians hung on every word, for this message was direct to them from 3,000 miles away, from Rome. The homeland was calling them. They had developed a subconscious and perhaps not entirely justified resentment against their own base ship, which this news brought into the open. Why, just now, but never before in all their fortnight on the pack, had the *Città di Milano* heard them clearly? Was it perhaps because before they were not listening? But they were also full of joy, for a Rome broadcast meant that their families would know that there had been survivors from the *Italia*. The bearded, ragged, grimy men were laughing again. They held another special feast – 5 lumps of sugar, 10 malted-milk tablets, 50 grams of chocolate.

Nevertheless, Nobile was quick to get off an answering message because there were three critical points to be covered. The most important was that theirs was only a short-wave set; they could not operate on 900-metres. Then an up-to-date position. And finally, Biagi's number, as proof of identity; that they really were the *Italia* survivors calling and not some crazy practical joker.

Next day, 9 June, Nobile took advantage of suddenly improved communications to make a number of important points in successive messages. The first two were that the positions they gave were accurate but that they were changing all the time. So in the morning Nobile sent:

We confirm that we have checked by solar observation 28° longitude and 80°30′ latitude. We are on the pack, drifting slowly south-east.

At 9.45 that morning Biagi picked up fragments of an interrupted message:

Be ready to make a smoke-signal. Aeroplanes will be. . . .

It was jarring for the castaways to realise that their own messages might be equally fragmented and key phrases jumbled or even lost. So Nobile's reply contained some repetition:

Our co-ordinates have been checked by frequent solar observations. We are on the pack, drifting slightly with the wind. Dirigible lost in another locality towards east. We have two men injured, with broken legs. We will make smoke-signals and fire Verey lights as the aeroplanes approach. Remember that our batteries may run out in a few days, but we shall still be able to receive. We have provisions for 50 days on very short rations. We lack foot-gear, arms, ammunition, medicines, sledges, boots, and a stove. The sky is generally cloudy here, but under the clouds, at 500 metres, there is good visibility. Three of our companions are marching along the coast towards North Cape.

Analysing this, the rescuers would realise for the first time that they had three parties to search for; not just one. And they would have been told that flying was possible and what supplies should be dropped. Above all, they would have been warned that if Baigi ceased sending it did not mean that they had all died suddenly, but that their batteries had become exhausted and it would be a good idea to supply new ones by air.

On this occasion contact was broken off by the *Città di Milano* halfway through the morning because the ship reported a disturbance which made it impossible to receive Biagi's transmissions. They would try again in the evening. Nobile, blackly, suspected that the 'disturbance' was due to the Norwegian station at King's Bay. It was only at 8 o'clock that evening that Nobile could get his message through to the base ship. To this message, he had now added one short sentence:

We have dyed our tent red.

Because they now expected aeroplanes at any time, the castaways had painted the pyramid-shaped tent with wide red stripes, using the aniline dye from the glass balls used to mark the snow and check the airship's height. This when the news reached the journalists, was to create the legend of 'The Red Tent' which was to endure for half a century. In fact, under the strong sunlight of the Arctic summer the red-painted bands faded in a few days and the tent reverted to a drab white colour unlikely to show up well from the air.

At 8.30 p.m., Nobile repeated the main facts about his now dispersed command:

There are six of us here. Three are on the march, as I have said. We know nothing of the others, as they have been carried away on the dirigible, which may be about 30 kilometres away towards the east.

In the Arctic, weather conditions determined absolutely what flying could be done. At the beginning of June, the weather was not too good, but from 12 June there began ten days of perfect flying weather which made Nobile wish that he had delayed his North Pole flight until then. Every day, the castaways expected to see aeroplanes. Once, they thought they heard one – but it was only an Alpini flag attached to the wireless mast and vibrating in the wind.

Chapter 13

HUSKIES AND HEINKELS

(With the Searchers: 4–19 June

TEN Greenland huskies and an ex-German seaplane crowded the deck of the tiny 150-ton sealer *Hobby* as she entered King's Bay on 4 June. The seaplane fitted the space on deck with a mere millimetre or so to spare, and the dogs had taken up their places around its floats. With them was their driver, Rolf S. Tandberg, who normally worked for the coal company at Longyearbyen in Spitzbergen. Standing a little apart was Hilmar Nöis, a well-known trapper of the north who was to act as guide for Tandberg's dog team. They were the coal company's response to a request from the Norwegian Ministry of Defence for search parties to be put at the disposal of the relief expedition. Arnesen heard that the dogs lived on a pound of dried fish a day and a drink of iced-water.

With the floatplane were its pilot, Lieutenant Finn Lützow-Holm and his mechanic, Svein Myhre. They had left the air base at Horten in southern Norway on the morning of 28 May and flown to Tromsoe, which was almost a day's flying time away and then embarked in the ship which would take them across the Barents Sea to Spitzbergen. Arnesen was so justifiably proud of the fact that the first aircraft to arrive was Norwegian that he described it as the 'new *Maake 36*.' New it may, or may not, have been; but the design was old. The curious underslung rudder gave away the fact that it was basically a warplane, this feature giving the rear gunner an uninterrupted field of fire astern. It was in fact a German aircraft of Great War vintage, powered by a 185 h.p. Maybach engine, and with a flying time of only $4\frac{1}{2}$ hours. As it was also very slow (185 k.p.h.), it had not the range to operate from King's Bay and would have to depend on the ability of the *Hobby* to negotiate the ice further north.

The *Hobby* remained at King's Bay only a few hours, while the

Italians from the *Città di Milano* fitted her up as an auxiliary by installing a short-wave radio and five men – an operator for the set, three Alpini and Lieutenant Adalberto Giovannini who spoke English, the lingua-franca of the North. Their orders were to search the north coast of Spitzbergen as far eastwards as the ice would permit, contact any trappers who might have wintered there and keep a look-out for the trapper Waldemar Kraemer who was already guiding four Italians in a search of the coastal areas.

Next day, 5 June, the *Hobby* anchored in Broad Bay, south-east of Moffen Island. While the seaplane was lowered into the water, a landing party went ashore to visit a hut belonging to the trapper Sven Olsson; Kraemer and the four Italians were with him, but none of them had seen any sign of the *Italia*. Lützow-Holm took his Brandenburg off the water at 5 o'clock that afternoon. First, he flew west to make a complete search of the bay before coming back and exploring the twin inlets of Liefde and Wood Bays, as far as the promontory of Grey Hook, due south of Moffen Island. By 8 o'clock that evening, he was back again, having seen no trace of the missing airship. This was the first sweep by an aircraft. It could not be called unsuccessful, because Lützow-Holm's negative report was perfectly accurate. His plane was recovered, Kraemer and his four Italians were taken on board, and by 10 o'clock that night the ship was heading north-east through open ice.

Heavy ice stopped their progress early next morning and they spent most of the day trying to dodge through it. When this proved impossible, the *Hobby* was tied to a large ice-floe and the Hansa Brandenburg was put over the side. It was no longer carrying the extra fuel tank with which it had been fitted back in Norway, because under operational conditions this made the seaplane too heavy to lift off the water. Consequently, Lützow-Holm would have fuel for about four hours. To give himself a margin of safety, he planned to make a three-hour flight only. As before, he went over his intended route in detail both with the captain of the *Hobby* and Rolf Tandberg, the leader of the dog team. At 9.30 that evening, 6 June, the seaplane began its long take-off run, until finally it rose on the step and a wave launched it into the air. Half an hour later, Lützow-Holm and his mechanic were in trouble. A fogbank which was not yet quite down to sea or land level, but which got lower as they flew on, gradually forced the seaplane right down until the floats were virtually touching the ice and the fog was streaming past above the airmen's heads.

At 1 a.m. on 7 June, when there was no sign of Lützow-Holm returning, the *Hobby* began to get worried. By 1.30 they knew they had to report that the Brandenburg was missing. 'This initial set-back filled us with dismay,' said Tandberg. 'If at the very start such a competent pilot as Lützow-Holm should be lost, how many lives would be forfeited before our work was completed?'

Meanwhile Captain Hjalmar Riiser-Larsen and his mechanic Jarl Bastoe had arrived by sea at King's Bay with a second Hansa Brandenburg floatplane. But the weather had clamped down there, too, and they were unable to fly north. The *Hobby* could not move, either, as she was hemmed by broken ice which also made it impossible to put a dog team ashore. For three days the rescuers were helpless. Their frustration was increased by the fact that various unidentified wireless signals which were being heard intermittently were believed to be coming from the *Italia*.

In the early afternoon of 8 June the *Hobby* was able to move again and headed east; a few hours later she met the *Braganza* off Grey Hook. That ship had searched a number of bays and sent a party overland to Verlegen Hook, a long promontory beyond Mossel Bay and both east and north of Moffen Island. They had found no traces of the dirigible or its crew. Between them, the two ships had covered most of the likely places on the north coast of West Spitzbergen right up to the entrance of Hinlopen Strait, the channel which divided the main island from North-East Land.

By the next day, 9 June, it was generally known that genuine messages from the *Italia* had been received giving an accurate position off the coast of North-East Land. Riiser-Larsen radioed from King's Bay asking Rolf Tandberg how long it would take to drive a dog team to Cape Leigh Smith from a suitable landing place on North-East Land. The *Italia* castaways were now known to be some 20 nautical miles north of that cape. Tandberg replied: 'If we can be landed in Lady Franklin's Bay or north of it we can possibly make the round trip to Cape Leigh Smith in 8 to 10 days.' Tandberg and Nöis were elated at what looked like a chance to take part in the rescue, but from a message which Riiser-Larsen sent this day to the Ministry of Defence in Oslo, it is clear that he was by no means inclined to rely entirely on

Norwegian efforts by land and by air. He had, he said, already advised the captain of the *Città di Milano* to ask for a powerful Soviet ice-breaker to bunker at King's Bay and to request the Italian airman Maddalena to hurry up because his machine could carry supplies for dropping to the survivors, which the small Norwegian navy planes could not do.

Early on 10 June the crew of the *Hobby* heard the drone of an aero engine and were surprised to see a Hansa Brandenburg seaplane fly up from the west. It was not the lost Lützow-Holm, but Riiser-Larsen taking advantage of a break in the weather to get as far forward as he could. He alighted at once and was taken on board, because ice was closing in on the ship. All day the *Hobby* tried to force her way eastward and towards midnight found that the wind had loosened the ice sufficiently for her to break out north of Hinlopen Strait into enough ice-free water for the float-plane to take off. Riiser-Larsen was airborne at about midnight and was back 40 minutes later with the good news that he had sighted Lützow-Holm's seaplane, apparently undamaged, in Mossel Bay. Almost certainly, it was out of fuel.

Mossel Bay was 15 miles distant. Tandberg and Nöis loaded a sledge with petrol and set off. The dogs, restless from enforced confinement on shipboard, welcomed the exercise and arrived at their destination hardly breathless. The seaplane was on the shore near a beached smack which belonged to a trapper; and inside the boat, asleep, were Lützow-Holm and his mechanic. While they refuelled the machine, the airmen explained how dense fog had forced them down until they were only 30 feet above the ice. This really meant that all they could see was a small circle of ice beneath the plane – and nothing else. Nothing above, nothing to the sides and, most vital of all, nothing ahead – no horizon. To fly in the fog, not knowing its extent, would almost certainly prove fatal. To fly on and risk the fogbase getting lower still until the machine hit the ice at speed was not advisable. Turning back also seemed a risky course. So Lützow-Holm had reviewed the alternatives and chosen to make a deliberate landing on the ice in Brandy Bay. The floats had acted like skis and he had got the machine down undamaged. There they had stayed for 36 hours until the bay cleared. Then, after no less than than 13 abortive take-off runs on the ice, they had at last got into the air again. Once more Lützow-Holm had been faced by a critical decision. The aborted take-offs had further reduced his fuel. He could turn back and search for the *Hobby*, but her position was uncertain and his margin of flying time small. Instead, he had decided to make for a known search point, Mossel Bay, where he had succeeded in putting down on the beach, the floats again acting as skis. This was a very skilful performance, aided by the fact that, like many of the old-fashioned machines, the Hansa had a low stalling speed and could be brought in quite slowly.

Lützow-Holm took only fifteen minutes to fly back to the *Hobby*. For the dog team the return was a longer process, as they had to be picked up by boats coming in to shore through the wind-drifting ice. Once re-embarked, they heard the latest radio reports from the *Città di Milano* giving a much fuller picture of the position of the survivors, especially their division into three parties – six men on the ice, six men adrift in the airship when last seen, three men making their way across the pack to North-East Land; and one man definitely known to be dead.

For nearly two days the *Hobby* found no wide-open water spaces for her seaplanes to use to get airborne; there was only heavy ice which halted the eastward advance of the ship and then a howling north-westerly gale with snow which packed the ice close against the coast. On the morning of 13 June she turned away into the more sheltered waters of Hinlopen Strait, between the two land masses, and asked the *Città di Milano* to agree to the dog team being put ashore. Tandberg and Nöis would have two objectives: firstly, to lay down a line of well-marked supply depots along the coast of North East Land for the succour of any survivors who managed to get that far; and secondly, to search actively for the three men who were actually known to have left Nobile's camp in a bid to reach that coast.

The Italians agreed to Riiser-Larsen's detailed plan and at 11 o'clock that night Tandberg and Nöis were put down on the sea-ice well inside Hinlopen Strait with their sledge and dogs and skis. The dogs were wildly excited and made good time in spite of the heavy load of 650 lbs. which had been piled onto the sledge. One hour after leaving the ship they began to pass between polar bears. Two large ones first of all and then a she-bear and her two cubs. This little family became intensely curious and from a distance of 300 yards rose up on their hind legs to get a better view and then, as the dog team continued on past them, they clambered up a hummock to watch the odd procession hurry on out of sight. For six hours the two Norwegian skiers followed the frozen floor of the fjord before reaching land and pitching camp by a glacier.

Already they had discovered that the chart they were using was inaccurate and had made many corrections. It was British Admiralty chart No. 2751 of 1913, corrected to 1925, a time when parts even of Spitzbergen were virtually unknown. The original charting had been published first on 5 December, 1865. The latest edition is dated 31 March 1967 and the story of the *Italia* is imprinted on it in the form of new place names, such as Alpini Island, Finn Malmgren Fjord, Albertini Bay.

In the afternoon they went on up the glacier, whose precipices and crevasses they could hardly avoid; they could barely see the leading dogs of their team, and eventually, visibility became so dangerously bad that they made camp until morning. By then the cloud-base had lifted and they could see a mountain ahead. Once over the high ground they were on the descent to an inlet on the north coast where many seals were lying on the sea-ice. This was an incentive to the dogs, who invariably made an attempt to catch the seals, but without success. On 15 June they reached Scoresby Island across the ice and laid their first depot, marking it with a tall pole and pennant. The weather had cleared now and they could see a long way over the ice as far as Cape Wrede.

Next day conditions were unpleasant for sledging, hardly a breath of wind, mild, and with flurries of snow. They decided to make for Cape Platen and set up a second depot there, before conditions got worse. There were many hummocks in the ice, with water lying between, so that the dogs got wet; and after the depot had been placed, they moved a few kilometres away to the shore to find a better camping site. The morning of 17 June was even worse, but later on the sun came out and gave them a brilliant panoramic view along the coast and out to the islands beyond which the *Italia* was understood to have crashed. Tandberg could see North Cape to the west and Charles XII Island to the east-north-east – but no sign of any life at all on the rough ice of the pack.

Cape Platen had been the most easterly depot they had to set up, so now they turned and followed their own tracks westward towards Scoresby Island heading for North Cape, where the third cache was to be placed and marked. It was perfect flying weather, dead calm and warm, but with the snow rather soft for sledging. The dogs, however, saw so many seals and polar bear tracks on the ice that they were as keen as ever. The silence of the white desolation was broken by the distant drone of aero engines and minutes later two seaplanes appeared from the direction of North Cape, flying towards Cape Platen. They were the Norwegian navy Hansa Brandenburgs flown by Riiser-Larsen and Lützow-Holm on their way to search the pack for the Nobile party. Tandberg and Nöis fired a smokeshell to tell them the position of their dog team, then carried on to make camp at Scoresby Island. About 50 minutes later, the two seaplanes returned, flying directly above, the airmen waving to them. They had been airborne about three hours, calculated Tandberg, and must have been dropping supplies to the castaways. In fact, they were returning with a gloomy report – they had seen nothing at all in the area where Nobile's camp was supposed to be.

Next day, 18 June, Tandberg and Nöis reached North Cape and set up the third depot. In the afternoon they heard aero engines and saw an aircraft circling to the west. Closer into the land lay the *Braganza*. They fired a smokeshell to announce themselves and the ship replied with three blasts of her siren. Later the seaplane – it was flown by Lützow-Holm – passed directly overhead and carried on eastward, apparently bound for another search over the pack. In the evening the *Braganza* sent a boat ashore to collect Tandberg and Nöis. There they learned that the *Hobby*'s charter having expired, she had returned to King's Bay and that both aircraft and the dog team would henceforth operate from the 350-ton *Braganza*. Her captain was Ingvard Svendsen, a well-known Arctic seaman from Tromsoe, and as liaison she carried now the second-in-command of the *Città di Milano*, Capitano di corvetta Francesco Baldizzone. An Italian naval doctor, Lieutenant Guido Cendali, had also been placed aboard.

At about midnight, Lützow-Holm returned. Once more, he had seen no sign of General Nobile and the 'Red Tent', nor of the walkout party. The only humans sighted had been with another dog team camped at Cape Wrede. The tracks made by the skis of Nöis and Tandberg and their sledge were quite plain, however. Riiser-Larsen had previously noted that these could seen from 500 metres and easily followed by the aircraft.

Flying boats, seaplanes and ski-planes were now converging from many thousands of miles away upon Spitzbergen, to back up the two Norwegian floatplanes. The man the Italians in the *Città di*

Milano were relying on most was the renowned long-distance flier, Major Umberto Maddalena. Odd Arnesen became rather irritated with the way in which the ship's crew boasted of what Maddalena would do when he arrived. In fact, he was being sent by Milan, not by Mussolini, and he had by far and away the best machine of the lot, the latest Savoia Marchetti twin-hulled flying boat, the S-55, with two powerful 600 h.p. Isotta Fraschini engines and a top speed of 236 kilometres per hour. On 12 June he was reported as having arrived at Copenhagen from Milan, taking off again next day for Stockholm.

On 15 June the Russians began to move. Financial agreements between the Soviet and Fascist governments having been concluded on 10 June and the employment of the *Krassin* approved, the ice-breaker sailed from Leningrad five days later, a remarkable feat as she had not been in commission for two years. She carried dismantled on deck a very large ski-plane, a Junkers G-24 powered by three 300 h.p. Junkers engines giving a top speed of 170 k.p.h. The pilot, the slightly built, even effeminate-looking Boris Grigorevic Tchukhnovsky, was as renowned an aviator inside the U.S.S.R. as Maddalena was in Italy, and further, his experience of flying in the Arctic was immense. In charge of the *Krassin* expedition was Professor R. L. Samoilovich, who had last seen General Nobile in Berlin during the planning phase of the *Italia* flights. A second Soviet ice-breaker, the *Malygin*, was being prepared; she too would carry an aircraft, a Junkers F-13 skiplane, to be flown by Basbuskin. It was on the 15th also that the largest aeroplane of the large Swedish contingent went roaring on and on across the water at Stockholm so heavily loaded with her five-man crew and fuel that many watchers thought she would never 'unstick'. This was a Junkers G-24 powered by three 300 h.p. Junkers engines and with a top speed of 170 k.p.h., hired from a civilian airline, in whose service she bore the name *Upland*. She was virtually identical to the Soviet tri-motor to be flown by Tchukhnovsky, except that she was fitted out as a floatplane whereas the Russian had skis. Also she bore the civilian lettering S-AABG on her wings and fuselage instead of the Red Star.

Next day, 16 June, saw the start of a similar venture, this time from Helsinki, the capital of Finland. At seven o'clock that morning a Junkers F-13 seaplane of Aero Oy, the civilian airline which is now known as Finnair, took off from the waters of the Baltic. The machine had been designed by Hugo Junkers in

1919 as the first real purpose-built airliner featuring all-metal construction and a closed cabin for the passengers. This one bore the lettering K-SALG, the name *Turku*, and was handled by two employees of the Aero Company – Gunnar Lihr as pilot, Uno Backman as mechanic. The Finnish Army supplied the observer, who was also the leader, Lieutenant Olavi Sarko. The machine reached Tromsoe next day, where many of the planes were gathering, and was put on board the steamship *Maritta*. The F-13 was slow – only 160 k.p.h. – and lacked the range to fly to Spitzbergen, as did most of the aircraft of the time.

Also on their way to Tromsoe were some of the remaining Swedish aircraft, all single-engined. There were two Heinkel He. 5 floatplanes, fitted with the 450 h.p. Bristol Jupiter engine and capable of 200 k.p.h. They were three-seaters with a startling resemblance to the 185 h.p. Hansa Brandenbergs flown by the Norwegians; this was not surprising because Dr. Ernst Heinkel had been chief designer to the Hansa company during the war. There were also two Fokker C-VD ski-planes fitted with the 450 h.p. Bristol Jupiter and capable of 184 m.p.h. These were general-purpose warplanes, capable of being equipped as two-seater fighters or three-seater reconnaissance or artillery observation machines.

16 June was also the day when Roald Amundsen and his Norwegian comrades left Oslo by train for Tromsoe to join the crew of a French flying boat which was to take part in the search. Amundsen's dramatic statement, at the Oslo meeting on 26 May, that he was ready at once to go in search of Nobile, had led to nothing. He lacked the money to start an expedition himself and the Norwegian Government doubtless found him embarrassing in the circumstances for his latest book on sale in Oslo contained vitriolic denunciations of the Italians in general and Nobile in particular; he had not been kind to the Aero Club of Norway, either. All he had was his fame, and if he got to Spitzbergen that might be sufficient to win for him the leadership of the gathering international rescue effort, although he might have to fight the Italians for it and it was unlikely that the Soviet would place their forces under an outsider, however eminent in the Arctic he might be – they were proud of their own expertise in the North. Eventually it was France which had placed an aircraft at his disposal.

The machine was a Latham 47, a biplane flying boat of orthodox design; a new machine but old-fashioned in conception. Although powered by two 600 h.p. Lorraine Dietrich engines, its top speed was only 200 k.p.h., well below that of Maddalena's S-55 of equal power. The four French crewmen consisted of Commandant Rene Guilbaud, pilot, Lieutenant Albert de Cuverville, co-pilot, Emile Valette, wireless operator, and Gilbert Brazy, mechanic. Into this comparatively small machine, Amundsen proposed to put as many Norwegian crew members as he could but eventually, in addition to himself, managed one only – Lieutenant Leif Dietrichson, who had piloted a Dornier Wal for him during the polar flight of 1925. It was understandable that the old explorer should want to fly in the company of friends when in a foreign machine but this attitude had led to friction with the Italians in 1926 over the *Norge* flight. Now he was risking it with the French. In both cases, he was risking more – a dangerous overloading of a machine which had only a small margin of safety during any long-distance flight. In spite of his claims, he was not really an airman; he had no real understanding of the element. Mentally, he was booking a ride in a bus – and the bus ought to get there infallibly and without difficulty. That time had not yet come; aviation was still a pioneer, high-risk business.

In his book, Amundsen had proclaimed that his career as an explorer was over. There is no doubt that he meant it and little doubt that he regretted the realities of *anno domini*. He must have welcomed the opportunity to live stirring days again and to play a heroic part. Certainly, Norway felt that, and not the Norwegians only, for he had a tremendous send-off from Oslo Ostbanen Station on 16 June. Not only was there a large crowd, but foremost among them a number of dignitaries and the press. Of course, the Norwegian Government and the Norwegian newspapers were well represented. But Italy had also decided to let bygones be bygones and Davide Giudici recognised among the large crowd the Italian Minister in Oslo, Count Senni, the First Secretary, Baron di Giura, and the Chancellor, Cav. Conti, as well as fellow members of the Italian press. The friends of Amundsen were there, and their hero was accompanied by the aviator Leif Dietrichson and the explorer Oscar Wisting. Dietrichson's wife was there, too, to see him off – a young woman with curly fair hair and fine blue eyes. Giudici noted that the Norwegian pilot, who was to fly with Amundsen, shook his wife's hand rather formally and said 'Goodbye' in so calm and matter-of-fact a tone

that he might have been leaving for the office rather than the
Arctic. And then he promptly disappeared into the railway
carriage. Amundsen, on the other hand, stayed at the window to
the last, waving to the crowds. Probably Dietrichson did not want
to distract from this scene, for it was peculiarly Amundsen's own.
On 17 June, 1903, the explorer had left Norway on his first Polar
expedition which had resulted in the discovery of the North-West
Passage. Now it was 16 June, 1928 – a quarter of a century later –
and still Roald Amundsen was at the centre of Polar exploration.
And that was a world achievement for little Norway as well as
for the man himself. A girl timidly asked permission to shake his
hand. 'Pardon my boldness,' she said, 'but I'm only doing what
thousands of others would like to do. Please be careful, Norway
cannot afford to lose such a son as you.'

As the train steamed out, taking Amundsen and Dietrichson to
their rendezvous at Bergen with the Latham flying boat, Davide
Giudici recalled the dramatic interview in Amundsen's home a few
days before. Amundsen had then been negotiating with Ellsworth
for the money to finance a rescue flight and was confident of
getting it. He had hoped for a Dornier Wal, because it was a type
of machine which he knew, and had stood gazing at the model of
one which hung from a beam in the ceiling of the living room.
That had brought back vivid memories of the Arctic. He had
declaimed to the Italian: 'Ah! If you only knew how splendid it is
up there! That's where I want to die. I wish only that death will
come to me chivalrously, will overtake me in the fulfilment of a
high mission, quickly, without suffering.'

In spite of the drama, the feelings of the man were sincere
enough. He had lived for Polar exploration and now he was too
old. The road, from now on, ran downhill all the way. And he
had many, many enemies, fellow countrymen as well as foreigners.
For an old man, such a death could be a welcome forgetting. And
for his enemies, a last trumpet of defiance. Let it come! And so he
waved from the carriage window, as the train for the north
steamed out of Oslo. First stop, Bergen; then on to Tromsoe in
the Latham and the long crossing of the Barents Sea to Spitzbergen. Giudici turned away. He himself now had a rendezvous
at Bergen, in five days time, with the Soviet ice-breaker *Krassin*.
For Giudici, the die was cast. He would sail with the *Krassin*, the
only Italian in the Soviet ship.

These were pioneering days. There was no central control.

Each pilot picked his own route north. Major Maddalena decided to take the route chosen by Nobile for the *Italia* herself – to Stockholm, to Vadsoe and so out over the wastes of the Barents Sea with Bear Island the only landmark. The Latham, leaving Caudebec-en-Caux near Rouen in Normandy, on 16 June, had made a rapid flight to Bergen, picked up Amundsen and Diet-richson there on the 17th, and then flown on to Tromsoe, where most of the aircraft were assembling. Some had the range to make Spitzbergen in one hop and it might have been safer for them all to fly together. Ex-Sergeant Viktor Nilsson, the experi-enced civilian pilot of the Swedish tri-motor *Upland*, suggested to Amundsen that his own Junkers and the French Latham should fly in company but the Norwegian explorer would give him no definite answer. Then, in the early afternoon of 18 June, with the weather still good, news came that Major Maddalena had taken off successfully in his S-55 from Vadsoe, bound for King's Bay. To a competitive nature like Amundsen's, that news was a cruel spur. He ordered an immediate take-off. Guilbaud and de Cuverville obeyed, and the race was on. The flying boat surged forward through the waves under fully-opened throttles and lifted. She had two engines, so the risk was less deadly than it would have been with one. And the Latham was a flying boat; it could land on the sea – but only if the sea was fairly calm. Even a mini-gale would transform a landing into a dis-astrous break-up. The radio she carried was much weaker than even the emergency set of the *Italia*. Its range was only little over 100 miles, and then, it worked only if the tiny propeller driving a generator was revolving at a fast clip. If an engine failed and the flying boat gradually lost height, perhaps an S.O.S. might be put out during the glide, but after the landing, certainly not. And if the sea was rough, there would be no landing, there would be a fatal accident. Such records as there were showed that if a flying machine came down on the ice, it was likely that most of the crew would survive. The sea, however, was infinitely more cruel than the ice and the snow. Survival was a matter of hours, perhaps minutes, certainly not days, weeks or months. Every airman who flew the Barents Sea faced in his heart this prospect. If an engine faltered, he could be eliminated. Almost certainly, he would be.

On the evening of Monday, 18 June the watchers at King's Bay heard the drone of aero engines at a great height. It was a beautiful sunny evening and they could soon pick out the silver-grey speck of an aircraft flying above the camp. Arnesen estimated that the machine was at 4,500 feet as it crossed over Zeppelin Mountain, losing height until the roar of engines fairly shook the houses and the quay on which he was standing. As it circled the fjord and then steadied for an alighting near the *Città di Milano*, the green, white and red colours of Italy were plain on its twin rudders. It was an S-55. It was Major Maddalena. The siren of the *Città di Milano* blew him a hoarse welcome.

The flight from Norway had taken eight hours, Arnesen was told. They had flown the Barents Sea at between 3,000 and 6,000 feet. One of the motors had given trouble, and they had met fog. But here they were and the position of the Nobile party, with the ice breaking up around them, was full of hazard. Maddalena said one word only: 'Petrol.'

Maddalena and his men went on board the *Città di Milano* for a few hours rest, while 3,000 litres of petrol was pumped into the tanks of the flying boat. Professor Nobile supervised the loading into the machine of supplies intended to be dropped to his brother, the General, on the ice. Inflatable boats (in case the ice broke up), medicine chests for the wounded and the sick, pairs of Arctic moccasins known as *finsko*, clothing, provisions, arms.

The Arctic day had turned into Arctic night and it was 19 June when Maddalena lifted his S-55 off the waters of King's Bay and headed east for the pack and the reported position of the 'Red Tent'. With his long-ranged and fast, modern machine there was no actual necessity to set up a forward base on a ship lying off North-East Land. He could fly direct. Six hours later, the Savoia Marchetti returned. The deck rails of the *Città di Milano* were lined with officers and men eager to hear the results of the flight. The propellers slowed, the wake died behind the twin hulls. Captain Romagna and Professor Nobile closed the flying boat in a motor-launch, revving slowly. Maddalena got out of his cabin to speak to them. He spread his arms, and called out: '*Niente, niente, impossobile vedere.*'

'Nothing, nothing! It's impossible to see them!'

Riiser-Larson and Lützow-Holm had been out, too, from their forward base with the *Braganza*. Nöis and Tandberg had seen them go out to the east once more and before they had even returned, had spotted a much larger machine, the S-55 flown by Maddalena, also fly over to the east. But the two Norwegian pilots also had failed to sight either the 'Red Tent' of the Nobile group or the three men of the walkout party making their way over the ice towards Foyn Island in the hope of reaching North Cape.

Still more machines were coming in. Next day, the big tri-motor Junkers G-24, the Swedish airline's *Upland*, arrived at King's Bay after flying non-stop from Tromsoe. It was followed almost immediately by another Italian – Major Penzo flying a twin-engined Dornier Wal built at Marina di Pisa and named *Marina I*. Powered by two 375 h.p. Rolls Royce engines, Penzo's machine had a top speed of 185 k.p.h., substantially below that of the S-55. Both had been despatched by Arturo Mercanti of Milan. There was one more Italian flying boat still to come, a single-engined Macchi M-18 biplane capable of only 145 k.p.h.; she was named *Marina II*.

The Swedish aircraft-support ship, the chartered cargo vessel S.S. *Tanja* of 900-tons, with a reinforced steel hull, had already reached Virgo Bay on Danes Island. She was carrying three of the smaller Swedish aircraft which had not the range to cross directly by air, and must anyway act from a base further forward than King's Bay. They consisted of two Heinkel He.5 float-planes to be flown by Captain Egmont Tornberg and Lieutenant Bengt Jacobsson, and a Fokker CVD ski-plane to be flown by Lieutenant Einar Lundborg.

Reserve Sergeant Viktor Nilsson, the pilot of the tri-motor Junkers seaplane which had just landed, intended to fly on at once to join the rest of the air group in Virgo Bay as soon as he had refuelled. He refused all offers of rest in the comfort of the *Città di Milano*. However, the big Junkers airliner had hardly come to a stop on the waters of King's Bay before it was surrounded by all kinds of small craft, from motor launches to rowing boats; and their occupants seemed to have one thought only in their minds. Where was the Latham flying boat?

Nilsson looked surprised at the questions. 'Hasn't Amundsen arrived yet? He started yesterday.'

In spite of his keenness to begin the search, and the fact that his large airliner with its three engines and long range was the most suitable of all the Swedish aircraft, Nilsson was able to do little. The former sergeant was now an important man, chief pilot of the Swedish airline, A.B. Aerotransport, but it was rumoured that the Swedish officers recognised only his former status and demanded that he come under their command, as a reserve NCO. Nilsson is said to have replied that, as a condition of its insurance, the airliner had to be flown by himself and that his decisions regarding its employment were final. Unless he approved, the *Upland*'s insurance was invalid. In the event, while the two small Heinkels massed a total of 92 hours 25 minutes flying time, Nilsson was able to log only 26 hours 15 minutes. Even a little Moth was flown for 12 hours 15 minutes.

Chapter 14

AIR DROP

(On the Melting Pack—12–23 June)

'IT's an interesting problem, our rescue!' General Nobile
remarked one evening.

'It's a beastly problem!' retorted Trojani. 'If they don't
hurry up they won't solve it!'

And it was Trojani who gave the alarm on the afternoon of
14 June. Everyone came out of the tent, including Nobile and
Cecioni, who crawled forth awkwardly. Yesterday, a wide
channel had cracked open in the ice not far away, 20 feet or more
across. Today, masses of ice were breaking up and falling into
the gap. It was time to move from their exposed position, thought
Nobile. There was a flat and solid spot some 40 yards away, on
the floe where Malmgren had killed the bear. Nobile decided to
move the camp there. This decision brought him up short against
his crippled reality. Four men would have to shift camp. Two men
would have to lie there and watch them do it and then be dragged
over the ice. It was also only the third occasion on which he had
actually been outside the tent.

While the four fit men started moving the stores, Nobile and
Cecioni sat outside. For the General, it was the nadir of the
eighteen days they had spent on the pack. 'The dreary sight made
a great impression. The ice on which we had been living was
churned up and dirty. Here and there were puddles of water, and
everywhere was wreckages: pieces of twisted tubing, rags, broken
instruments. . . .' The debris of his command. On it from a grey
sky snowflakes were slowly falling.

In vague revolt, because he wished to spare the four men the
further labour of carrying him, and because they seemed so sad
and dispirited, Nobile tried to crawl across the pack towards what
they called the 'bear floe'. In a few yards, with great effort and

229

pain, he found himself lying on the edge of a crevasse. For a humiliated cripple, it was impassable.

Nobile now glimpsed himself with loathing, as some lowly, crawling reptile; no longer a man. He had a mental image from his childhood – of a beggar he used to pass every day on his way to school; very dirty, in ragged clothes, with a long, unkempt beard and withered leg covered with slimy, hideous sores. Better, he felt, that he had died in the crash than be reduced to this.

Then the four men came up to carry him 40 yards. Sweating and out of breath, they had to stop several times and rest – all four of them. Such was their condition – and the condition of the jumbled pack. Then they went back for Cecioni. And after him, for the tent, the provisions, the wireless. . . . And yet, when it was all done, and the tent newly set up and they inside, they all felt better. The snow here was undefiled, white, immaculate except for footprints and the bear's skeleton jutting from the floe and a large, blackish mass which was the creature's liver, poisonous to man. There were no shattered, twisted remnants of the airship lying around.

The wind fell away and with it their drift. Under a pure blue sky, for days on end, their ice floe idled, nearly stationary, close to Foyn Island. It was in daylight, this time, that Trojani put his head into the tent and in the tones of a butler announcing the arrival of a guest to the master of the house, said quietly: 'There's a bear!'

He collected the pistol, and Nobile heard the shots. Then Trojani came back to say that he had hit the bear, but only wounded it, because he had fired from too far away. The beast had begun digging over the grave of Pomella and had actually uncovered an arm. After that, Nobile asked that the body of the dead airman be committed to the sea.

There was still bitterness in their camp towards the *Città di Milano*. The ship only contacted them once a day and then in the evening, when atmospheric conditions were poor and anyway they needed to listen to the nine o'clock news from Rome. When Nobile complained, the number of contacts was increased, but the *Città di Milano* did not seem to want to listen to them. The operator would merely send a routine message: *'Nothing to tell you. Goodbye till the next hour.'* And then those interminable private messages or journalists' reports would begin again. Trojani thought the work of the base ship spasmodic and inefficient.

Perhaps the whole expedition had been too hastily carried out, without paying sufficient attention to the training of crews. The impression was, that the base ship had quite enough to do administering itself, without bothering about such irrelevancies as the survivors of the airship they were supposed to support.

On the afternoon of the third day of wonderful flying weather, that is, 17 June, they saw their first aeroplanes. It was a tremendous boost to the castaways to see the two Brandenburg seaplanes coming up steadily from the south. In wild excitement the men kindled a fire to make a smoke signal and shot off Verey lights. When the two Norwegian pilots, Riiser-Larsen and Lützow-Holm, were within two or three kilometres of the Red Tent they turned away again.

Riiser-Larsen reported from the *Braganaza* to the *Città di Milano* that he had flown along the coast to Cape Platen and then followed a bearing to Nobile's position of 14 June. They had flown beyond it and then both machines had started zig-zagging back towards the Islands of Foyn and Broch, and then around Charles XII Island. 'Nothing was seen of the Nobile group. Searched for one hour, visibility splendid, flying altitude 250 to 300 metres. Ice very rough . . . no landing possibility for aeroplanes if they want to get off again. . . . Followed the ski and sledge tracks to Tandberg's dogteam to Scoresby Island where Tandberg and Nöis were seen in camp. . . .'

Soon Biagi was tapping out a message, telling the *Città di Milano* that they had seen the aeroplanes but that the aviators had not seen them.

Next day, 18 June, they saw a single Brandenburg seaplane and assumed it was Riiser-Larsen making a brave lone flight in a single-engined machine. In fact it was Lützow-Holm, who reported to the *Città di Milano*: 'Made a new flight searching for 75 minutes both sides of bearing 235° off Foyn Il and from 2 to 10 miles off the coast. Altitude only 50 to 100 metres but no result. Four hours in the air. Trying again weather permitting. With present load capacity our machines now can only carry gasolene for 4½ hours.'

Again, Biagi tapped out a message saying that they had seen an aeroplane but had themselves been unseen.

On 19 June, both Riiser-Larsen and Lützow-Holm made a flight in a single Brandenburg, without seeing anything. But they were overtaken on the way by the much faster, twin-hulled Savoia-

Marchetti S-55 flown by Major Maddalena. From the Nobile camp, the castaways watched for 25 minutes while the big flying boat circled away to the north-west, once coming to within 4 kilometres of the Red Tent. This was followed by the appearance of a lone, single-engined seaplane which they followed with their eyes as it flew out from the coast direct for Foyn Island and then began to zig-zag towards them. If it carried on like that, it would be bound to pass over their camp. They fired off Verey lights and made smoke signals, but when another few kilometres would have brought him overhead, the airman turned back.

The *Città di Milano* afterwards received two messages. The one from Riiser-Larsen began: 'Lützow's and my experience after flights in search of Nobile is that results can only be obtained by large aircraft capable of covering large areas very systematically for several hours. Ice conditions around Nobile with thousands of hummocks and thousands of openings of black water make it extremely difficult to find small objects, unless one happens to fly low directly over them. Remember that Nobile has no means of giving smoke signals. It would be a great help if he could erect a flagpole . . . on the highest hummock. Would also be useful for him to provide every man with a shiny piece of tinplate and try to reflect the sun-rays towards the aeroplane, which should zig-zag between the sun and Nobile's supposed position. If possible, Maddalena and Russian ice-breaker should have short-wave receivers on board, so that Nobile can indicate the course. . . . Nobile's camp unsafe as floes may break up into smaller ones. . . . Every day now very precious. Lützow and I are very sorry not being able to do more with our small machines. We have tried our best. Uncertainty about Nobile's position. . . .'

The message from Nobile himself began: 'If you wish to succeed you should carefully follow my advice. Start from Foyn Island and take a true course of 59 degrees. Advance 20 kilometres in this direction, then turn back within 8 kilometres of the island. . . . At least two aeroplanes should be used, flying parallel to each other. . . . Maddalena should have enough petrol to fly overhead for at least four hours. . . . Fix up a wireless on Maddalena's hydroplane, worked by an efficient operator. Observe with the sun at your back. Today we also saw Riiser-Larsen, but he was too far east. Tell him all I have said.'

Another message sent by Nobile was not picked up by the *Città di Milano*, but it was clear that both Nobile and the Norwegians

were thinking in the same terms. A radio set was re-installed in
the S-55 and Nobile's men made reflecting material from tinfoil
and a petrol-can. They could do nothing about making better
smoke signals, as these were improvised.

Maddalena was ready to make a second flight early in the
morning of 20 June. A civilian, Signor Marsano, was brought in
to operate the newly installed radio, although he had never been
up in an aeroplane before. The co-pilot was Lieutenant Cagna
with Rampini as mechanic. Maddalena had spent the best part of
his life at sea; first as cabin-boy, then as seaman, finally as an
officer. He had a long, lean face, dreamy eyes, somewhat stooping
shoulders. Balbo was to write of him that he was 'inclined to be
shy and retiring on land, but was full of self-confidence on the
sea . . . quite a different man, spontaneous, alert, commanding.'

Monitoring the *Città di Milano*, the Nobile group learned that
the S-55 had taken off at 0600 from King's Bay, about two hours
flying time away for this modern machine. Every man had his
task. Viglieri was to fire the Verey lights, Trojani was to light a
smoky fire of petrol, oil, rags and paraffin, Behounek was to
flash a piece of burnished tin from the sun's rays, while Cecioni
would try to do the same with a mirror. Biagi would of course
man the wireless, but the messages would be composed by
Viglieri. Nobile was suffering from an attack of snow-blindness
and had to wear an eye-shade improvised from a piece of coloured
chocolate wrapping-paper.

At 0735 they were in wireless contact with the approaching
flying boat. At 0815 they could hear the throb of its engines.

To begin with, the wireless contact did not seem to be working,
then all at once the S.55 began to obey the orders Biagi was
sending. 'Turn so many degrees to the right'; 'Reverse your
course'; 'Turn so many degrees to the left'. In a few minutes
Biagi had the S-55 heading towards them, like an obedient dog.
'The tent is on your present course, 3 kilometres on. Go ahead!'
The S-55 came on steadily. It all looked very easy now.

In fact, Maddalena thought he had sighted the Nobile group,
then realised it was an illusion. The pack-ice was twisted and
jumbled in many fantastic shapes and in the bright sunlight
there was an ever-changing, weird pattern of different shapes and
colours. All too easily the eye would turn this dark shadow into
a man, that lozenge of colour into a tent.

Then the real men watching by the real tent saw the S-55 nose down into a dive that brought it roaring towards them at 300 feet. Biagi sent 'VVV . . . You are on top of us!' They could see the Italian colours painted on the wings, and as it thundered above them, one or two airmen leaning out and waving their arms wildly. It was a moment of mad excitement, on the pack as well as in the aircraft. Nobile felt his throat grow tight with emotion. Titina was rushing about the ice, barking incessantly.

The twin-hulled machine went on into the distance, its engine roar decreasing, and they expected to see the wings bank into a turn for the return run which should result in a supply drop. But the machine went on, then wheeled in the wrong direction, passed a long way to one side, and began to turn uncertainly. 'Oh, hell!' said someone.

For Maddalena, one moment the men on the ice had been there and the next – as he roared past – they were gone! All he could see were the shifting shadows of the sun-pattern on the pack. It was this phenomonon which Professor Samoilovitch had tried to point out to Nobile as the great practical objection to his plans to put a scientific party down on the ice. The airship would have only to move a short distance away – and the ground party would disappear!

But after half-an-hour of work by Biagi, the S-55 had been manoeuvred back close to the Red Tent and was at last on the right course at the right distance. When it was almost overhead, Biagi signalled 'KKK' – the code for the drop. They could see a man leaning out and starting to drop parcels. Now Maddalena had got the hang of it. He turned and came back again on the right course, and the drop was continued until all the parcels had gone overboard and hurtled down onto the ice and snow.

The S-55 was away from base seven hours, and when Maddalena returned, the journalists at King's Bay knew that he had succeeded. The siren of the *Città di Milano* blew three hoarse blasts that rang along the icy cliffs, there were shouts of '*Evviva Maddalena*!' and as the airmen boarded, a sailor called for '*Silenzio*!' After the pilot had given an impromptu press conference, Arnesen managed to get a few personal 'quotes' for himself. 'It was the grandest experience of my life,' Maddalena told the Norwegian. 'But what a pity I could not slip down and take them all back with me. Imagine being only a few metres from safety – I could almost touch their heads.' Maddalena's face, which had been 'simply one large joyful smile', now darkened at the thought of his helplessness. There had been no stretch of water large enough for the flying boat to alight, and to come down on the ice was to crash. Back at the tent, most of the supplies had been picked up now. Broken and useless were two rifles, several batteries for Biagi's radio, and some 30 eggs. But there were two collapsible boats, in case the ice broke up and they had to take to the water; there were six pairs of leather shoes – a vital item – and all were happy except Viglieri, whose feet were exceptionally large. There were also smoke signals, two sleeping bags and some provisions. The food did not please Nobile because it lacked bulk; mainly it was bananas, oranges, lemons, cocoa, marmalade, biscuits. A load of pemmican and chocolate would have been a more effective supply, he thought – more nutrition for less weight.

He began to compose another message for the *Città di Milano*, partly in anger at the nagging thought that the base ship might not bother to listen. He listed the further supplies they needed. He warned that the rising temperatures of the last few days, which were approaching zero, were breaking up the ice pack on which they lay. He advised them to put Amundsen in charge of rescue operations, as he was expert in these matters. He stated his own opinion, that the six of them should be airlifted off the ice one by one as rapidly as possible, before the ice melted, the fogs came back, or the floe drifted further away. He suggested that their aeroplanes should also watch over the sledge party led by the Alpini Captain Sora, which was reported to have set out on 18 June to try to find the Malmgren group; his brave march across the pack was likely to be halted by the large channels which were now opening in the ice. He urged them to have Cecioni at least taken off by air, as a man with a broken leg could fatally hinder the fit men, in case of their having to make a rapid move to avoid a rupture in the ice. And he added that they had seen three Swedish planes in the distance that evening, circling some kilometres away before turning back. Some delicacy prevented him from saying that he also was helpless and a dangerous hindrance to the fit men.

Riiser-Larson and Lützow-Holm had also been out that day in a Brandenburg, and had been seen by the Nobile party but had failed themselves to sight either the 'Red Tent' or the three men of the walkout party. What had been plain to them, however, was that the ice between Cape Bruun and Foyn Island was in such a deteriorating condition that it would be dangerous for Captain

Sora's search party to attempt to sledge across it; if they did, and got into difficulties, the Norwegian seaplanes would be unable to help them. Therefore, next day, 21 June, Lützow-Holm set out with Myhre as his observer to locate Sora's team and drop a warning message to them. The team had originally consisted of the tough little Alpini captain, Gennaro Sora, who had a distinguished war record, Sjef van Dongen, a large, tough Dutchman with a prodigious appetite, and the civil engineer, Ludvig Varming, who was Danish. This international trio had a sledge and nine huskies. But very soon they had become two parties instead of one, because Varming was put out of action temporarily by snowblindness, and was forced to return on his own from the Cape Platen depot; unfortunately, Varming was the experienced Arctic man upon whom they were relying for a modicum of caution.

Lützow-Holm took off at 1215, picked up the snow tracks of the party near Cape Platen, and followed them to Cape Bruun, where he found them in camp and dropped the warning message. It was badly needed, as he could see from the tracks that the team had made two attempts already to go out over the treacherous ice towards the islands beyond which the castaways from the airship were awaiting rescue. The warning did not deter them, however, and shortly after the two men set off over the ice towards Broch Island and actually reached it. Meanwhile, Lützow-Holm turned back towards the *Braganza*, their base ship, which was trying to dodge a sudden fog bank which threatened to blanket the whole area. She found a little patch of still-clear sky in Beverly Sound, which would probably not remain open much longer. Lützow-Holm reached it just in time at 4.40 p.m., when his fuel was almost exhausted and the fog was about to engulf the ship. This was the last flight made by the Norwegian airmen in search of the Italians, because on this day the Norwegian Ministry of Defence asked them both to search for the Latham flying boat which had been bringing Amundsen to Spitzbergen and had now been missing for three days.

On 23 June the Italians offered the temporary use of the *Braganza* to ferry the short-range Norwegian floatplanes back to King's Bay to begin a new search which would be carried out south-east of Spitzbergen for Amundsen instead of north-east of North-East Land for Nobile. It was almost a repetition of Amundsen's abortive North Pole flight with two Dornier Wals in 1925. One of them had been flown by Riiser-Larsen with Amundsen as navigator, while the other had been piloted by Leif Dietrichson with Ellsworth as navigator. Both had been forced down and had been missing for twenty-six days. Two Hansa Brandenburg seaplanes had been sent to Spitzbergen to look for them, when a single Dornier Wal, carrying all the airmen, at last returned. Now Amundsen and Dietrichson were missing again, but Riiser-Larsen had changed roles and was flying one of the Brandenburgs.

The search for Amundsen gathered momentum. The little sealer *Hobby*, which had been taken away from the search for Nobile because her charter had expired, came back onto the scene. The new charterer was an American, Miss Louise A. Boyd, who had intended a hunting expedition near Greenland. But as it happened she was a tremendous admirer of Amundsen and so offered the use of the ship for a search directed at finding the missing Latham flying boat. Shortly, there was a second, for the Norwegians sent their largest warship, the *Tordenskold* with a 250-man crew and two small Sopwith Baby seaplanes. Then there was a third, for the Soviets diverted their ice-breaker *Malygin* from the Nobile search to a series of sweeps east of Spitzbergen into an area where it was thought the Latham might have come down. By 25 June, a forth major unit had joined the search, for on that day the French cruiser *Strasbourg* left Cherbourg for Spitzbergen. And there were innumerable smaller vessels keeping a lookout for the lost Norwegian hero: the *Heimland*, the *Quentin Roosevelt*, the *Pourqoui Pas?*, the *Michael Sars*, the *Vesslekari*, the *Durance*, the *Svalbard*, the *Gustav Holm*. From fishing smack to oil tanker, all on the alert. Unfortunately, no one knew what Amundsen's plans might have been. He had been reported as saying that the men carried away in the hull of the airship were likely to be in worse plight than those who had been cast away upon the ice, for they at least had a radio. Was it possible that the Latham had set course for where Amundsen believed the *Italia* had possibly come down?

If so, he was probably the only one – apart from Nobile – who regarded a search for the hull of the airship and possible survivors in it with any urgency or seriousness.

Before the *Braganza* moved to King's Bay, Tandberg and Nöis urged that their dogteam be allowed to leave the ship and carry out an extensive search for the walkout party. The *Braganza* therefore left the two Norwegians on the ice, together with two Italians, Albertini and Matteoda, who were members of the Studenti Universitari Club Alpino Italiano – that is they were students, not soldiers of the Alpini Corps like Captain Sora. They would try to look into areas not covered by Sora's dogteam and both teams would later be picked up from Beverly Sound by the *Braganza* on her return. On 23 June, early in the morning, they were duly put ashore and the *Braganza* steamed off for King's Bay with the Norwegian airmen and seaplanes aboard.

Meanwhile, Italian and Swedish aeroplanes had been circling over the 'Red Tent' like flies around a honeypot. Gone now were all the difficulties of finding the right place. Radio, familiarity, and probably the use of proper smokepots which had been dropped to the castaways made easy what only days before had been difficult or impossible. For safety, they flew in groups, highlighting the risks which the Norwegians had taken in their unsuccessful searches. The Brandenburgs were single-engined machines and the engine of one of them had given so much trouble during this period that on a number of occasions either Lützow-Holm or Riiser-Larsen had to risk a flight with just one seaplane on its own. One of the few people to note this fact and admire their icy courage was Nobile, who painfully jotted it down in the logbook he was keeping, in spite of his broken arm.

The long sorties made by the S-55 on 20 June prevented it from coming back again the same day, as Nobile had hoped. The crew required rest and another list of supplies needed to be made, then the actual items had to be found, prepared with improvised parachutes where necessary, and packed into the aircraft. On the 21st there was a good deal of local fog over the pack, the same fogbank which had nearly trapped Lützow-Holm on his last flight. The weather was not uniform; there were many local variations; forecasting was often largely guesswork. So on the night of 21/22 June, the *Città di Milano* asked: '*Tell us what weather you are having, and what visibility.*' In reply, Nobile had Biagi send the message: '*The weather here is perfect and the visibility exceptional. Come at once.*' For the fog had cleared where they were by evening.

Nobile got ready to receive another airdrop by marking up his camp as vividly as could be done with the materials to hand. Maps and charts had fallen from the cabin of the *Italia* as it split open; and some of the red aniline dye containers had not broken. So he had the stiff white sheets stained with red dye, hoping this would be more permanent than the short-lived attempt to colour the tent fabric red and the maps were placed on the sloping sides of the tent. Red and white flags were fastened to the wireless aerial, Behounek stood with a red flag on a hummock of ice, like a corpulent early traffic warden ready to lead a primitive motor car on to the highway, the new smokepots were prepared by Viglieri, Biagi was by his radio set ready to guide in the aeroplanes, and Nobile crawled out on to the ice with a bearing compass in order to plot the direction of fall of the various items. Trojani, who was ill with gastric fever, stayed in the tent.

Biagi was in touch with the approaching aircraft from the time they reached North Cape. Fifteen minutes later, they were in sight. This again was an Italian drop, but using both the big flying boats – Maddalena's twin-hulled Savoia-Marchetti S-55 and Penzo's Dornier Wal. Both of them had the same engine-configuration – twin motors in tandem, one pulling, one pushing. They came straight to the tent without trouble, made a couple of circuits for each pilot to get his eye in and adjust speed and altitude appropriately, and then made their runs. 'Down from the sky rained every gift of God', recalled Nobile. Some packages came down like rocks, others drifted down under opened parachutes, others again had faulty parachutes. One heavy box nearly annihilated Nobile and Cecioni, while a smaller missile grazed the tent where Trojani was lying, ill. The furthest away, estimated Nobile, was 100 metres distant, but many fell as close as 20 metres. It was a creditable drop in the circumstances, because an object loosed from an aeroplane flying at, say, 100 m.p.h., does not fall vertically; it leaves with a forward velocity of 100 m.p.h. and descends in an arc, to a point which is ahead of the position of the aircraft at the time of release. Calculating this for odd-shaped parcels of differing weights, some with parachutes and some without, is not easy.

Oddly enough, for their different reasons, Trojani and Nobile felt that the drop was degrading to them. The flying boats came so low that the men leaning out of them could be seen clearly and one of them, noted Nobile, was turning the handle of a cine camera. That brought home to him the reality of their present state – half-starved, living in abject misery and squalid filth, objects of pity and curiosity. Trojani felt an illogical irritation at Nobile's calls to the world for help, to which this was an answer. After all, he argued, the *Italia* project had been a voluntary mission; no one had been ordered to go. To have to make appeal after desperate appeal for help seemed to him degrading.

It took several hours to find and bring in all the supplies, few of which had been lost. Degrading or not, they now had extra provisions to last a further twenty days on short rations; they now had a medicine chest and a stove; for the smokers, cigarettes; and for Viglieri two pairs of shoes so enormous that they fitted him. Only now, when they had a full medical kit, did Behounek ask for his right arm to be looked at. He had not told anyone that it had been hurt in the crash and had endured stoically. Viglieri and Biagi asked if there were laxatives in the medicine chest. Most of them had suffered in the same way as ship survivors often do when cast adrift in lifeboats. Viglieri had tried butter as a purge, without much effect; Biagi had had better results with drinking seawater.

Eighteen packages had been collected from where they had fallen on to the snow, into crevasses or into the water. The aeroplanes had left for King's Bay shortly after 11 o'clock in the morning. On the same day, at 7.30 in the evening, there was another air drop, this time carried out by two Swedish seaplanes, Heinkel He.5s from 2 Flying Corps, Stockholm, using a base just set up in Murchison Bay inside Hinlopen Strait. The air drop was very neat, skilful and well-thought out. The two small machines homed in on the smoke signal and dropped five packages only, each one under a red parachute, and containing very well-chosen items. Most important, there were five dry batteries for Biagi's wireless set, two medicine cases with equipment for splinting broken limbs, a collapsible boat with oars, a rifle and ammunition, cigarettes, oranges, and two bottles of whisky. All arrived intact with the exception of one of the whisky bottles. That the red parachutes had a second useful purpose was made clear by a message in English attached to one of the packages:

'*If you can find a landing-ground for aeroplanes fitted with skis (min. 250 m.), arrange the red parachutes in T-shape on the leeward side.*'

Trojani and Viglieri had already prospected a landing ground of this size, with an excellent flat surface, about 150 metres away from the tent. So it needed only to be marked up with a landing 'T' made out of red cloth. How long the ground would remain serviceable was doubtful – the temperature was rising.

The order of rescue had also been thought out with some care, and was based on logic rather than precedent. Nobile laid down that they would be evacuated in the following order:

1. Cecioni (because badly injured).
2. Behounek (because heavily-built and clumsy on ice).
3. Trojani (because suffering from fever).
4. Nobile (because badly injured).
5. Viglieri (last but one, because the senior, uninjured officer able to use a sextant to fix position).
6. Biagi (last, because he was the radio operator).

If the logic had been absolutely strict, Nobile would have been evacuated first, as he was the most seriously injured. In any emergency resulting from melting of the ice, the two men who could not walk were a potentially dangerous burden to the others. But, probably from a wish to command on the ice to the last practical moment mixed with a recollected sea tradition not really valid in this context, the General had put himself down as the fourth to go, not the last, that would have been absurd, because he could not move to the landing ground, let alone climb into an aeroplane, without the aid of at least two fit men.

It was the logical approach which had guided Captain Egmont Tornberg, the head of the Swedish air group. He had decided that if a landing was possible, then the two injured men, Nobile and Cecioni, must be saved first. But he had a further reason, which it was not politic to air at the time. The Norwegians and the Swedes were co-operating well, but the Italians were vacillating and unreliable. Sometimes the *Città di Milano* would keep the others informed as to what the Italian airmen were doing, and sometimes not; often the Scandinavians had to push for information. Nobile had received exactly the same impression of Captain Romagna's inexplicable inactivities. But while Nobile had thought Amundsen should be brought in to co-ordinate all rescue efforts, Tornberg had come to the conclusion that Nobile should be brought out to do that job. Physically he was a cripple, but there was nothing wrong with his mind and he above all knew best the plight of the parties on the ice.

On the evening of 23 June, the castaways heard the sound of aero engines but could at first see nothing because of their high, jumbled horizon of ice. Nobile ordered a smoke signal lit and told Viglieri and Biagi to go to the landing ground and lay out a 'T'. Then three aircraft appeared, two Heinkel He.5 floatplanes and a Fokker C–VD fitted with skis, from 3 Flying Corps, Linköping. If things remained as they were, the Fokker could land but the

Heinkels could not; if the ice split and formed a wide channel, the Heinkels could alight safely but not the Fokker; what they all feared was an in-between state of melting when no aircraft at all could get down.

The aeroplanes separated. The Heinkels stayed high up and began to wheel in slow circles round the encampment. The Fokker was losing height towards the landing ground. It came so low that now and then it vanished behind an ice hummock, then there was a renewed blare of its engine and it rose again to make a circuit of the landing ground. It went round several times, very low down, and it seemed to Nobile that the pilot was inspecting the surface of the ice most thoroughly before deciding to land. The biplane glided in again, losing height slowly until it seemed almost to skim the snow. Nobile held his breath. Yes, it was down; running smoothly over the surface and slowing to a stop. 'Thank God!' exclaimed Nobile to Cecioni. Three or four more landings like that, and they would all be taken away, their sordid misery ended.

One man remained in the machine, keeping the engine ticking over all the time, while the other accompanied Lieutenant Viglieri and Biagi to the tent where the General was waiting, supported by Behounek. As the airman approached, Nobile could see that he had a frank, rather rugged face and blue eyes.

'Here is the General!' said Viglieri to the stranger.

'I am Lieutenant Lundborg of the Swedish Air Force,' the airman replied, in English, saluting. He added that he was happy to be the first to succeed in landing.

Nobile thanked Lundborg and, with the aid of some of his men, stood up and embraced the Swede.

'If you want to do something for us,' Nobile said, 'take that man,' and he pointed to Cecioni.

To Lundborg, the engineer appeared a 'large, powerful man with a stately, typically Italian appearance.' What he meant was, that Cecioni appeared to weigh about 16 stone. He had been $15\frac{1}{4}$ stone before the crash and had put on weight from eating bear meat and fat. Nobile had been $9\frac{1}{2}$ stone originally and had lost weight from incessant thinking and worrying about methods of rescue.

'General, I have come to fetch you all,' replied the Swede. 'The landing ground is excellent and I shall be able to take away the lot of you during the night. But you must come first.'

'But that's impossible!' protested Nobile. And he pointed to Cecioni. 'Take him first.'

'No,' said Lundborg firmly. 'I have orders to take you first, because we need you to advise us how to search for the other two groups who are missing. Our base is not far from here. I can come back quickly for the others.'

It seemed a very minor point to him; but not to Nobile, who continued to object.

'I have decided on a different sequence,' he said. 'First Cecioni, then Behounek, Trojani, Viglieri, Biagi, and finally myself.'

'I ask you to change the order only so far as you yourself are concerned,' said Lundborg. Pointing to Cecioni, he went on: 'No! I can't take him now, he's too heavy. I'd have to leave my observer here with you, and I won't do that. But after I've taken you, I'll come back for him tonight. Trust me. Besides, it would take too long to carry that man to the plane, and we've no time to lose. Do please hurry up!'

This dialogue, which was carried on in English, was understood by everyone except Cecioni and Biagi, for whom the issues had to be explained. Behounek could see that Nobile was disconcerted and uneasy about the whole thing; he gazed round at them all uncertainly. Behounek himself was impatient with any delay; it was clear to him that the most important thing to do was to relieve the party of the two people who were incapable of walking and so tied them all to the same spot. They could not march to safety without abandoning them, and not one of the castaways now contemplated that. As to which of them went first, well Cecioni did not seem to mind going second, and his was the only opinion which counted.

Nobile was still doubtful. The logic of what Lundborg said was overwhelming; there could be no counter-arguments. But at a deeper level, instinct struggled against it. So he asked the others what they thought. Viglieri and Behounek pressed him to go, and quickly.

Biagi said: 'You had better go first. It will set our minds at rest.'

The injured Cecioni said: 'You go! Then, whatever happens, there will be somebody to look after our families.'

Lundborg did not understand what these two men said, as they spoke in Italian, but he saw that Cecioni was crying. The Swede tried to tell him that they had established a forward base on North-East Land, so that, after taking Nobile, he would be back within hours for Cecioni, and this time he would not bring his observer, Lieutenant Birger Schyberg. But the Italian understood only the gesture of comfort.

Nobile crawled into the tent to question Trojani, who replied: 'Yes! It's better so. You go!'

But he did not really mean this, and became uneasy at the thought of the General, the commanding officer, being rescued first. He had certainly heard Lundborg put a persuasive case, telling them all that Nobile's presence in the *Città di Milano* was essential for the rescue of Malmgren, Mariano and Zappi, of whom no one knew anything. But were the Swedes being quite open about their motives? Were they perhaps thinking of the glory which would reflect upon them if they brought back Nobile, the chief of the Italian Polar Expedition? Had Lundborg received positive orders to that effect?

He had, of course, been told to do just that; and the reasons he had given were valid, every one of them, so far as they went. He had fought in Finland and Estonia with the White Army, during the Russian revolution, and had gained a reputation for daring. But he thought it unlikely that the Fokker would get airborne in the short distance available with both Cecioni and Schyberg as passengers. Indeed, his nerves were screwed up tight already at the thought of just trying to get off with only Nobile aboard. A take-off run is much longer than a landing run. And if anything went wrong, there was no 'blood wagon' waiting to reach the site of the crash with a doctor.

These were very real fears. Lundborg himself as well as Maddalena and Penzo, were all to be killed afterwards in flying accidents.

When Nobile crawled out of the tent with the *Italia*'s logbooks and his record of the messages Biagi had sent from the ice, but without his heavy topcoat or boots, Lundborg was quick to say: 'You don't need to put any more clothes on; the lighter we are, the better.'

Nobile embraced his comrades and was then helped across the ice by Viglieri and Biagi, assisted by Lundborg and Schyberg, who had left the plane. When they were exhausted, Nobile tried to help them by crawling. It took three-quarters of an hour to cover a distance Lundborg estimated as 200 yards; and Schyberg was dead tired and dripping with sweat from his exertions. Halfway across, Lundborg had left Nobile and hurried onto the Fokker alone, because it was untended and with the engine idling. He got into the front cockpit and waited for the others to arrive. Then he had them swing the Fokker into the wind and while he waited for them to lift Nobile with difficulty into the back seat, Lundborg ate a piece of Swedish chocolate. This calmed his nerves and put him in excellent form for the nervous tension of the take-off. Titina had got in before the General and was snuggled down in the rear cockpit; Schyberg and Nobile were got as far forward as possible so that the tail would lift early, Lundborg asked the Italians to bring Cecioni across the ice to the landing ground as soon as they could, so as to avoid any delay when he returned.

Lundborg tensed, pushed stick and throttle forward together, feet on the rudder-bar combatting the torque and the unevenness of the ice. The skis began to hiss across the ice, and the tail came up. Now, would she or would she not, lift off in time?

Chapter 15

THE PRISONER OF THE *CITTA DI MILANO*

(With the Swedes and Italians: 23 June–2 July)

THE hissing of the skis stopped. The ride became smooth rather than bumpy. Nobile leaned over the side to look down. The terrible distorted surface of the pack was moving away downwards and flowing past behind them. The Fokker was safely airborne. Where was the tent? He could not see it, until Schyberg pointed it out – and then it seemed a wretched little object, a scrap of soiled material nearly invisible in the vast white wilderness of ice. The only sign of life was the flutter of white and red flags hoisted on the wireless mast.

The night air at height was bitterly cold in the open cockpit, but Nobile felt it as a cleansing of the dirt and stubble on his face. He looked down again at the pack – a few stretches where an aeroplane could land, but mostly broken by crevices and channels. And then the two islands, Foyn and Broch, twin lighthouses of hope almost throughout their drift on the floe. On hilly Foyn the grey rock showed through the snow here and there, to prove it was truly land. Schyberg pointed. 'There, south of the island, we once saw human footprints. They went on for miles, then vanished. In their place we saw now many tracks made by polar bears.' Could the human prints have been made by Malmgren, Mariano and Zappi wondered Nobile, before huddling down in the cockpit out of the icy air of the slipstream. He held Titina close to him, so that she should not risk getting caught in the control cables, which ran inside the fuselage from the front cockpit to the tail. They moved slightly from time to time as Lundborg corrected. After less than an hour the motor's roar died away to the whisper of a slowly-turning propeller, the control cables moved again, several times. There was a jerk underneath them, then the swish of skis. The Fokker had landed at the newly-established forward base of the Swedish air force.

The advanced landing ground was just an expanse of snow by the shore. A driftwood fire was burning merrily, and sleeping bags lay around. Food was being warmed on a petrol stove. Offshore, two Heinkel seaplanes were moored and further out there was room for the base ship when she arrived, the 400-ton sealer *Quest*. To follow their prey, sealers had to work in the ice – unlike whalers or cargo ships. The larger 900-ton *Tanja*, merely a strong steamer, remained at Virgo Bay, the Swedish main base. In her hold she carried a dismantled Fokker C–VD as a reserve aircraft. She had brought out most of the Swedish aircraft, but as there was a regular shuttle service by colliers between Tromsoe and the Spitzbergen mines, some of these were used to carry supplies and occasional aircraft. The *Ingerto*, *Ingertre*, *Ingerfire*, *Oddvar* and *Scard* were so used. In all the Swedish air group now numbered 28 men – pilots, observers, mechanics and ground staff – split between Virgo Bay and this new base situated in the sheltered waters of Hinlopen Strait, which had been in existence for less than twenty-four hours.

None of the Scandinavian nations had ships tailor-made for the purpose of operating seaplanes, with heavy cranes, aircraft workshops, fuelling facilities, and so on. The British navy possessed two such vessels, the seaplane-carrier *Ark Royal*, originally an oil tanker, and the converted railway packet *Pegasus*, which had operated in the White Sea in 1919. And they also possessed the seaplanes and flying boats to go with them. It would have been easy for Britain to have offered effective help immediately, had the government desired, and a better public-relations gambit than many which they did authorise. 'Showing the flag' was an accepted use for many an expensive British warship.

The Russians had already done so with their old ex-British icebreaker. The Swedish-flown Fokker had lifted Nobile off the ice at 1030 p.m. on 23 June. A bare three hours later, at 0130 on the morning of 24 June the *Krassin* steamed out of Bergen to the rescue of the Italians, burning Welsh coal in her British boilers, but with the Red Star blazoned on her two tall, yellow smokestacks. On her deck she carried a German-designed aeroplane licence-built in Russia. A few hours later another ship brought to King's Bay the Finnish airliner *Turku*, which was really another German aeroplane. This was put into the water and flew forward to Virgo Bay the same day. This day also, which was Midsummer's Day, the *Citta di Milano* steamed into Virgo Bay. The newsmen followed in hired boats, noting that the remains of the shed used by the Swede Andrée for his balloon flight in 1897 still showed above the snow, reminder of that earlier tragedy of Arctic aviation. Andrée and his companions had not yet been found, but soon would be; they had not vanished forever as everyone had assumed. Now the mystery of their disappearance was linked with similar unresolved questions. Where are Amundsen and his companions? What has happened to the hull of the *Italia* and the six men in it?

While Lundborg took a brief rest after his flights, Captain Tornberg, the leader of the Swedish air group, explained to Nobile the forward movement of the ships, the *Città di Milano* to Virgo Bay, the *Quest* (hourly expected) to Murchison Bay in Hinlopen Strait. He explained that they had had difficulties in organising a proper search for all three of the lost groups – the Red Tent, the Malmgren party, and the men carried off in the *Italia*. But now that Nobile was at hand, he expected that things would go better.

Nobile turned to Lundborg: 'When are you going?'

'Very soon,' the pilot replied. In a moment or two he got up, said 'I'm off', and walked towards the Fokker. With luck, Cecioni would be with them on the landing ground in two or three hours. After that, perhaps two more flights, with two men brought out each time, and the 'Red Tent' would be empty. That would certainly be a resounding success for the Swedes, whose slick efficiency deserved success. Half a day more, and all the castaways from the tent would have been brought out. There would be a great deal less for the Russians ice-breakers to do, so they could concentrate on the walkout party and the *Italia*, and have that much better a chance of succeeding. His mind racing, Nobile dozed off into a fitful, jerky half-sleep. He was hardly aware of the actual take-off.

Nöis and Tandberg, however, who were out with two Italians and a dog team near Cape Platen, searching for signs of the Malmgren group, heard and saw two planes go over that night, heading east. They were in fact Lundborg's Fokker and its escort, a Heinkel He.5 floatplane. Some time later they saw one plane come back. In fact, this was the Heinkel. They never saw the Fokker in flight again.

Back at Murchison Bay, Nobile woke with a start – he had heard the throb of an engine – Lundborg returning with Cecioni?

But only one machine appeared, and that was fitted with floats. Lieutenant Einar Christell got up to enquire. When he returned, he told Nobile casually, 'The Fokker has overturned, the pilot is unhurt', got into his sleeping bag, and dozed off, unperturbed.

Nobile felt literally sick, misery succeeding joy. Desperately, he turned to Tornberg, the Swedish leader. 'What are we to do now? Do you have any other planes with skis?'

'No, none of our own. But the Finnish floatplane which has just arrived can be fitted with skis. But the best thing is to send for some little sporting planes. The De Havilland "Moth" is a suitable type. They can be got in England. You ought to ask the Italian government for them at once. And you can count on the Swedish government, too, doing everything in its power.'

Tornberg was not making empty promises to a worried man; but he did not explain why he did not intend to make use of the reserve Fokker carried by the *Tanja*. It was officially known that this type of machine became nose-heavy if flown without an observer and if operated in slushy snow was likely to tip over. This, he must have suspected, was what had really happened to Lundborg on his second landing – without an observer – by the Red Tent. Instead, Tornberg asked for the loan of a D.H. 60 Cirrus Moth from a Swedish flying school; a German flying club offered a Klemm-Daimler L-20 without being asked. Both these aircraft could be safely flown solo with the pilot sitting in the rear cockpit and using the trail-trimmer to compensate for the empty front seat. The Moth was a light biplane designed to carry two people and two suitcases; it had a stalling speed of around 40 m.p.h. Its performance, as the saying went, would not pull the skin off a rice-pudding, but it could be force-landed into almost any field and got out again. The engine was the 80 h.p. Cirrus II. Later versions would have variants of the more powerful Gipsy engine. The Klemm was a monoplane with a 50 h.p. Salmson engine, almost a powered glider and well-suited also to landing in a small space. The Moth was a typically British sports biplane, of which there were a number of types, all nearly ideal for this particular task; but none were obtained from England. Nor were any obtained by the Italian government. Once again, it was Swedish initiative which was to produce the machines and ship them to Spitzbergen.

Nobile would have done better to wait for the *Quest* and discuss further rescue measures with the Swedish group, as Tornberg suggested. In ignorance of the reception that was awaiting him in the *Città di Milano*, and believing that once aboard the Italian base ship he could take command and direct the search more effectively, Nobile asked to be flown to Virgo Bay. Tornberg and Christell took him there in a Heinkel seaplane, but Nobile did not remember much of his arrival because he was a sicker man than he allowed himself to believe. This, however, was not fully understood by some people who were present at the time.

For instance, Maddalena had reported after his first successful flight, that he had seen Nobile himself down below, wearing a white jumper and standing on a hummock of ice. At the time, Nobile had been lying down with a bearing compass; he was unable to stand without being supported. Maddalena had simply made a mistake. Odd Arnesen, without checking, repeated this story as being the literal truth and he also added, for who knows what reason, that 'Cecioni was much more seriously injured than Nobile.' This was utterly untrue. In fact, Nobile did not fully recover for 20 years. He had not rested his broken limbs, but had moved and kept writing down messages for Biagi to send. Finally, Arnesen said of Nobile's arrival at Virgo Bay that 'here it was obvious that the General was not so badly hurt but that he was able to climb up the side of the *Città di Milano* without aid.' He made it sound as though he was a witness, but turning back a few pages of his narrative, it appears that the press party did not arrive until later and then had an altercation with the officers of the Italian ship because they wanted to rush on board and plunge down into Nobile's sick berth for interviews.

Less-biased Norwegians reacted differently. Riiser-Larsen was to write: 'Great was our horror when we heard that Captain Lundborg had rescued Nobile. . . . It was a disservice that had been rendered Nobile. The world at large turned upon him, and things went so far that one of his countrymen at Spitzbergen declared that there was nothing left for him to do but to shoot himself. He had, however, been coaxed out on false premises.'

Captain Romagna floundered as ineptly here as he had over the rescue measures. In his first report he included the tactless phrase: 'It is not yet known what the reasons were for taking General Nobile off first.' Then he tried to undo the damage by including a statement that the General had a broken leg. A journalist heard a report that 'General Nobile injured his leg in an ice crack.' And his enemies in Italy began gleefully to spread the story that Nobile had run so fast across the ice in order to be first at Lundborg's plane, that he had slipped and broken his leg.

Shortly after Nobile had been carried below, Romagna came into the cabin and said: 'People might criticise you for coming first, General. It would be as well to give some explanations.'

This attitude came as a thunderbolt to Nobile, whose mind was concentrated on working out relief measures for the castaways at the tent and search plans for the walkout party and those with the hull of the *Italia*. He had also just seen himself in a mirror – his face covered in 32 days of bristle and grime. In the enclosed warmth of the ship's interior, Nobile could for the first time actually smell the stench that came off his unwashed body and filthy clothes. It was revolting and demoralising. He needed a bath before he needed a doctor. What he could well do without were red hot press interviews and slurs upon his courage.

A film was taken while a doctor was bandaging Nobile's leg. When he saw it, Arnesen commented that this 'showed quite a new Nobile, very different from the General who departed from Ny Aalesund early in the morning of 23 May. The unhappy sufferer in the bed was a broken man. His eyes were wide, stiff, and staring, his voice lower and more quiet than usual – almost colourless. The fate of the rest of the men weighed heavily on the General's mind. The criticism of the hapless expedition had hit him hard, and there had been a controversy between him and the Commandant of the *Città*, the General wishing to direct all efforts to the rescue of the six men with the balloon, while the Commandant would not listen to the suggestion.' This certainly was an issue which tortured Nobile and from his sickbed he fought to remedy some at least of Romagna's errors or inactivities.

Romagna did, however, keep the foreign press at bay initially, although not in the most tactful manner. Correctly, they were intercepted at the head of the gangway and not allowed to barge on board and swarm down to Nobile's cabin, as they wished. But then they were told that Captain Romagna could not see them for an hour, which eventually turned into three hours. When he did appear, he barked: 'What do you want?'

Arnesen spoke out. 'I want to ask for an interview with the General. The whole world is waiting for news, especially details of the rescue. As I am also representing a Swedish paper, and it was the Swedes that rescued the General, the Swedish nation would much appreciate it – and indeed they feel entitled to know how it all happened.'

Romagna said he cared nothing for any newspaper at all, and pointed to the *Tanja*, lying also in the bay. 'If the Swedes want news, their own ship is there. You can go and do what you like there, but I have nothing to say. There will be no interview with the General – he is in his cabin with a broken leg, and is both unable and unwilling to receive anyone.' Arnesen tried various trick questions which Romagna parried: until finally the Captain turned his back on the journalists.

Arnesen was reduced to telling a story of how Titina had frightened off a polar bear by getting up on her hind legs and barking furiously. One strange thing about the dog, was that her coat had turned brown. Before, her markings had been black.

At the same time as Nobile was vainly trying to reassume command of the expedition and so justify by deeds his return to the *Città di Milano*, so Captain Romagna, on orders from Rome, was deftly stripping him of his authority bit-by-bit. First, Nobile's messages were sent, but his signature was removed, so that the men on the pack would believe he had deserted them. Then Romagna's signature was substituted, without informing Nobile. The Italian airmen were forbidden to co-operate with him in working out rescue procedures, and then when Nobile turned to foreign airmen, such as the Finns, they too were tipped off to the fact that Nobile no longer commanded and that they should have nothing to do with anything he suggested.

While this slow process of erosion was being carried out, Nobile was in a pain-racked rage with Romagna's complacency. The Captain was happy with everything that had been done so far. He was utterly impervious to Nobile's criticisms of the ship's radio procedures and the General's ideas for improving them. Indeed, he looked shocked every time Nobile made a point. Very quietly, Nobile explained why it was important to keep in frequent contact with the castaways at the tent – now known as the Viglieri group. The ship should listen far more frequently than it had done in the past and if it was necessary to stop all electrical machinery to improve reception, then that should be done. Romagna looked at him with the surprise of a man who believes that the wireless of his ship had provided an immaculate service to the castaways on the ice.

Nobile was forced to ask why then had the ship's wireless

failed to pick up Biagi's transmissions and it had been left to a
Russian amateur far away on the other side of the Barents Sea to
do so? Remorselessly, he reminded Romagna how the ship had
put out formal messages every two hours, telling the castaways
that a search was being efficiently carried out between the 15th
and 20th meridians – which was nowhere near their real position –
and then had switched off, failing even to listen, so that no one
heard the desperate messages from the men on the pack, saying
that they were alive and giving their real position. The ship had
made them waste the limited battery time of their emergency
radio in fruitless calls and also convinced some of them that none
of the S.O.S. messages would ever be heard. The three men who
had walked out of the camp – and were now lost and missing
somewhere on the pack – would not have done so if the *Città di
Milano* had picked up even so much as one fragment of a message
from Biagi. If they died, then Romagna was responsible.

'But my dear General,' protested Romagna. 'If logic is to count
for anything, then we were perfectly right in imagining – as we
did – that it was impossible for you to transmit, and so it was a
waste of time to listen to you.'

This particular remark, which was made on the first day of the
General's return, took Nobile's breath away. Even in his
weakened and depressed state, he was able to beg the Captain
to explain why he had made this colossal blunder.

'Well, look here, General – our last wireless communication
with the *Italia* was at 1030 on 25 May. Then, all of a sudden, there
was silence. We put our wits to work. Could this silence be
explained by some damage to the transmitting station? No! that
was improbable, because there was an emergency set on board.
So it was not a question of damage to the apparatus. Then how
was it that you had not even managed to send out an S.O.S.?
It was plain as a pikestaff! The wireless operator had been unable
do it. So we came to the conclusion that Biagi was dead.

'And how could that have happened?' went on Romagna, while
Nobile lay speechless. 'You see, we thought Biagi had leaned out
of the porthole, and at that moment the screw of the wireless had
come loose and cut off his head.' The lethal mechanism he was
talking about was really just a small fan which served to actuate
the motor of the wireless. This limp explanation, employing
'logic', almost certainly concealed a basic error of assumption.

The most popular fate for the *Italia* at King's Bay during the waiting period had been that the airship had crashed into a mountain and been totally destroyed and everyone in it killed instantaneously. So – no survivors, no S.O.S. That *would* be logic. At least, to a naval man who knew nothing about airships. Also, it would be comforting in that the naval man would now not have to do anything drastic. A purely formal radio procedure, a few gestures of search 'for the book', so that all could be explained away if any questions were asked later. No need for anyone to lose sleep, work overtime, or actually think. Any airman, of course, would have ridiculed the whole idea. Almost always, from an airship disaster – no matter how total – there are survivors, sometimes many survivors, especially if the airship strikes land, however violently, rather than the sea, however gently. From impact with a mountain, even if the airship caught fire, many men would probably escape. Inevitably, some would be badly injured. Undoubtedly, they would require speedy rescue. That was the real logic of the affair.

These were the revelations given to Nobile on the first day. But later, talking to the wireless operators, he realised that the junior radioman Pedretti had indeed picked up parts of a message from Biagi on 29 May, many days before Nicholas Schmidt the Russian 'ham'. He had got the first word *Italia*, capable of misunderstanding because of course it could mean the country as well as the airship. But he had also picked up the last words, which definitely identified it to Nobile. These were: *Reply via Ido 32K. Ido* was the code for the San Paolo station in Rome, 32 was the wavelength, *K* was their own code for '*Hurry up! Answer!*' Pedretti had leapt out of his seat, seized Captain Baccarini by the arm, and cried: 'The *Italia* is calling us!' Baccarini, who was the senior radio officer on board, had replied: 'Nonsense! It can't be! It's probably Mogadishu.' That station did in fact call Rome every day. Had there been the slightest shred of optimism on board, the *Città di Milano* could there and then have called Mogadishu, to see if any such message had been sent by them. And the reply must have been NO! As it was, Pedretti noted down '32' as the possible wavelength of the *Italia* survivors, but in face of scepticism by his superiors, dared do no more.

At that time Signora Nobile had been in Rome, anxiously waiting for news of her husband, but it was not until 4 June that she was told by the Under-Secretary for the Navy that a Russian amateur had picked up an *Italia* distress call the previous day.

She looked so doubtful at this news, that the official had said it was perfectly possible that the *Città di Milano*, so much nearer to the scene than Archangel, might well have missed many distress calls. He had discovered that on 3 June, the base ship had logged some 400 private messages. 'But now,' he told her, 'I have given orders to stop these transmissions and concentrate attention on listening-in. I have also had another wireless station set up on land at King's Bay.'

But now, three weeks later, Nobile found the same indifference shown to receiving calls from the Viglieri group on the ice. Eventually he was able to get more frequent contact made, not only in listening out but in the sending of messages, partly for their information, but above all for morale reasons. Nobile realised how important was the factor of hope. He managed to get an air search under way for the remains of the airship, but this met fog and so proved abortive. Here also the authorities in the base ship had simply written off another six men without even half-trying to find them.

Not only did it prove impossible for Nobile to re-establish his command of the expedition, but little-by-little he became a virtual prisoner in the base ship. He was unable now even to exert pressure for this or that measure to be taken. He saw how vital it was to establish a forward air-base, as the Swedes had done at Murchison Bay; but Romagna would not hear of it. It was impossible to ginger him up. Rome now disapproved of Nobile, and he would follow suit.

Amundsen and his party had not been found either. This had two adverse consequences. It caused a diversion of search planes and ships to the south and east of Spitzbergen, thought to be the most likely areas where the Latham might have come down. And it prevented the possibility of Amundsen himself taking over the control of all search and rescue operations from the separate national organisations handling them to produce instead an integrated effort. Even if his had proved impossible, he could at least have got proper objectives agreed and planned realistically.

On 2 July both Riiser-Larsen and Lützow-Holm came to see Nobile. Nobile was very touched by this, and broke down. He felt unable to express the feelings of comradeship he had with anyone who had flown with him in the *Norge*, and was now also involved in the *Italia* tragedy. Now he had had no option but to defend himself against the charges made by Amundsen, but infinitely regretted that the incident had arisen. (At this time, Nobile had not yet read Amundsen's latest book, *Mitt liv som polarforsker* (*My Life as a Polar Explorer*), which was more virulent even than the magazine articles to which he had been officially ordered to reply.

Riiser-Larsen radiated confidence and cheer, entering the cabin with a 'How do you do, my dear Nobile!' And after the preliminary expression of emotion, going on to enquire about the survivors still to be found – the three men of the Malmgren group for whom he and Lötzow-Holm had searched for so long. 'What provisions had they when they left your camp?'

'Just over 52 kilos of concentrated food – pemmican and chocolate.'

'Oh, that's all right then!' said the Norwegian. 'You needn't worry about them. They have enough for 45 days.'

Nobile enquired about Amundsen. Riiser-Larson expressed complete confidence. The search would certainly succeed. He was going with the *Hobby* to search the west coast of Spitzbergen, although it was possible that the Latham had come down on the east coast. That area would be covered also. No need to worry about Amundsen either. Probably Riiser-Larsen's confidence sprang from his own experience with Amundsen in 1925, when they had gone missing for three weeks, and not merely survived but had escaped from the grip of the ice entirely by their own exertions and without calling up a great international gathering of rescuers.

Now the rescuers were coming anyway. The Soviets alone were sending a small fleet of ice-breakers equipped with aircraft, one of which, the *Sedov*, would cover Franz Josef Land and to the south-west of that area; another, the *Malygin*, would search east of Spitzbergen for a great distance out over the Barents Sea; while the most powerful of them all, the *Krassin*, would come up the west coast of Spitzbergen, and pass round to the north of North-East Land in an attempt to break through to the Viglieri group.

Chapter 16

'THE *KRASSIN* IS A VERY STRONG SHIP'

(On board the Ice-breaker: 24 June–12 July)

IT was 1.30 in the morning of a windy, rainy day at Bergen in southern Norway. The squat bulk of the ice-breaker *Krassin*, 10,630 tons, loomed above the dozens of spectator boats which crowded around her. Her tall yellow funnels, emblazoned with the red star, reared high over the quay which was crowded with Norwegians anxious to see her off. On her deck was an enormous crate containing a tri-motor Junkers airliner. Those parts of her upperworks which were not obstructed by this incongruous packing-case were encumbered by mountains of Cardiff coal and stacks of aviation fuel in cans. The entire ship was filthy since she had been out of use for two years. Only five days had been allowed to assemble a crew from somewhere and get her to sea. She also was now covered in the black slime left by the deposition of another 2,000 tons of coal into her bunkers in addition to the 1,200 tons already there.

As the stumpy-looking vessel moved slowly away from the quay there came a roar from the crowd gathered there: 'Save Amundsen!' The spectators in the boats echoed the cry. Other ships in port saluted with blasting sirens and the passengers in a German tourist liner waved their hats and their handkerchiefs in a frenzy of enthusiasm.

It was 24 June and the Soviet Nobile Relief Committee, under the chairmanship of Unschlicht, Vice-Commissar for War, and with the authority of Kamenev, Chief of General Staff, Stalin's and Malinowski's right-hand man in the Revolution, had in two weeks got the ice-breaker from her laid-up berth in the River Neva to the beginning of an Arctic voyage from Bergen. With 'energy, discipline, staying power, zest and courage on the part of all', wrote the Moscow Committee in its final directive, 'there must,

257

be unconditional success.' They didn't add: 'Or else . . .' but the thought must have been there.

The *Krassin* had been built at Newcastle-on-Tyne in 1917 for the task of keeping open the ports of Archangel and Murmansk to Allied shipping. She could reach fifteen knots at sea (i.e., 15 nautical miles per hour); her speed through ice varied naturally with the thickness of the ice and the depth of its snow covering. An average for two or three feet of ice would be 1 to 1½ knots. She was fitted with a radio supposed to have a range of 500 to 1,000 nautical miles (a sea mile being a trifle longer than the statute mile).

The crew of the ice-breaker numbered 110 ordinarily but she was now crowded out with 136 men and 2 women. The extra personnel included aircrew, four extra wireless operators, and eight journalists. Of the seven Russian journalists, one was a woman, the slender and charming Ljubow Woronzowa; the eighth was the Italian, Davide Giudici, Berlin correspondent of the *Corriere della Sera*, Milan. Professor Adolf Hoel, the Norwegian Arctic expert, was also on board. The crew were not the normal crew because they had been dispersed when the ship was laid up two years before. Indeed, one of the 'oldest' members (in terms of service with the ship) was Xenia Alexandrowitch, a waitress.

The former captain of the ship had believed it impossible to bring her back into service in five days, so the post had been given to the captain of the slightly less powerful ice-breaker *Lenin*. He was 35-year old Karl Pawlowitsch Eggi, born on the Estonian island of Oesel. He was almost the only man aboard who could not speak at least two foreign languages although he did possess a single sentence of English; 'The *Krassin* is a very strong ship.' Many of the crew were of German origin, or from the Baltic states, or had served with international companies and so Giudici had no language problems anywhere, except with the captain.

Apart from Eggi, who ran the ship, its moves were guided by a three-man directorate who were fluent in several languages. The head of the expedition was the geologist, Professor Rudolf Lazareywich Samoilovich, who was already acquainted with Nobile; 45-years old, and President of the Institute of Arctic Studies at Leningrad, Samoilovich spoke German, French and English. Two younger men were almost equally important. Paul Oras, from Reval in Estonia, had studied at the Marine

Engineering School at Kronstad. He was 31 and was the Commissar, representing the Party on board the ship. Group photographs taken on board almost invariably show the others keeping slightly apart from Oras, as though shrinking away from the Commissar. The third director was Boris Grigor'evic Tchukhnovsky of Leningrad, aged 30; a very experienced aviator and engineer, he was to fly the Junkers G-24 tri-motor. He spoke German and French fluently, but Oras was master of more languages than any of them.

Giudici noted that the leaders completely dispensed with normal etiquette at mealtimes, sitting down at the first vacant place, among the ratings. There appeared to be a kind of 'large family' feeling which prevented discipline slackening; indeed, he was told that all aboard had, from the start, voluntarily waived the eight-hour day which he understood to be an irrevocable edict of the Revolution. But politics were never mentioned and even the Anniversary of the Soviet Constitition was celebrated with extreme simplicity and one small glass of vodka.

The good temper of everyone aboard was amazing, considering the appalling overcrowding in a ship not designed to take any passengers at all and now thronged with them. Hoel and Giudici, honoured guests, were awarded a sofa apiece on which to sleep in a corner of the messroom; others had to sleep up in the bows or out in the passage ways. The bows and the messrooms were almost the only clean places aboard for the first few days. Only when the coal left lying on deck had been used up in the boilers and the decks hosed down with rain did a semblance of cleanliness appear. Before that, wrote Giudici, 'one literally wallowed in black mud on the main deck and on the bridge'. Worse, for the first few days clouds of evil-smelling vapour arose from the crannies of the ship, particularly from the holds, which appeared to have been closed down for years.

The Russians had an almost English addiction to tea, and it was excellent tea, but during those first few painful days it was made from boiler water; and probably the boilers had not been cleaned for some time. Food was plentiful, consisting of bread, butter, cheese, potatoes, dried fish, and sausage; and prepared by a single kitchen so that officers and ratings fared the same. Although to an Italian palate it was not very tasty, Giudici found that the greatest hardship was the lack of freshwater, either for drinking or for washing. To distil freshwater from seawater meant using up coal, and the mission of the *Krassin* was critically dependent upon coal. Amazingly, apart from one or two cases of minor poisoning, there was no illness on board.

The *Krassin* lurched northwards, making an average $11\frac{1}{2}$ knots, and once beyond Tromsoe kept special watch for any sign of Amundsen and Guilbaud's Latham flying boat. Lookouts were posted in the tops and on the iron ladders mounted on the two tall funnels. The approach to Bear Island was marked by fog, which usually meant ice. There had been fog when Major Maddalena had landed there with engine trouble ten days before; and Amundsen's last radio message had been to enquire about conditions in this area. But although Bear Island was sighted in the distance on 28 June, the lookouts saw no signs of the French flying boat.

Ice indeed there was, but with much water in between, so that the *Krassin*'s speed was reduced only by half, to about 6 knots. At this rate she thundered and banged her way ahead with a noise which deafened Giudici. The high, armoured bows rose up over the ice and broke it under their formidably weighted impact. Spray rose to the height of the bridge, and broken pieces of ice slammed against the tanked steel sides of the ship as on sounding boards. If one was below, the series of impacts sounded like artillery 'drum-fire', echoing madly because of the emptiness of the special tanked compartments which are built in to ice-breakers to enable them to be rolled first this way and then the other.

Early on the morning of 30 June, the Soviet ship was passing Virgo Bay where the *Città di Milano* lay at anchor, and where General Nobile was virtually imprisoned. Captain Romagna would not allow him to contact the Russians to discuss rescue measures, claiming that his decision was based on medical grounds. Samoilovich could not take the ice-breaker into Virgo Bay because it was too shallow. The *Krassin* therefore rounded Amsterdam Island and entered the first of the close-ice, the forerunner of the pack. Now life took on a Polar appearance, the officers and seamen putting on sheepskin clothing and heavy jackboots. The temperature, however, remained mild – several degrees above freezing point – and there was a golden sun throughout the twenty-four hours; except for those few days when a bitter north wind blew, or a gale howled over them, it was possible to stay on deck.

Now was the time, as they approached North-East Land and the position of the Viglieri group, that wireless communication was important. Before leaving Leningrad, a small short-wave radio station had been installed in a hurry; this proved to be totally useless. Therefore there was no possibility of communicating directly with Russia. The only set which worked was one which was old when it was first put into the ice-breaker in 1917; now it could manage 500 miles by day and perhaps 800 or 900 miles on a favourable night. So a message for Murmansk would have to be sent to a Norwegian station which would then, hopefully, re-transmit to Russia. The process was painfully slow. According to Giudici, the transmission of a 1,000-word telegram from the *Krassin* sometimes took as much as twelve or even eighteen hours. Of course, it was the Italians – not the Russians or the British – who had invented radio and it was to be expected that their apparatus would be much superior. According to Odd Arnesen, on 'gala days' Tomaselli alone 'despatched between ten and 12,000 words by wireless'. It was all this activity which interfered so much with the reception of messages from, first, the Nobile group and then Viglieri group. Like Arnesen, Giudici was subject to censorship; unlike him, he accepted that his hosts must inform their Government first, and his despatches were so objective that not one word of his was altered.

According to Arnesen, there was a 'pirate radio' ship, a Norwegian sloop hired by two German journalists, which lay off Spitzbergen intercepting traffic and even 'high-jacking' the telegrams of other pressmen. Half the inhabitants of Spitzbergen, he said, had turned to journalism. A doctor represented one American press agency, while a works manager wrote for its rival; a student was writing for a string of papers. Their outpourings to the world helped overload the weak Norwegian wireless stations. And just as the castaways at the Red Tent had tuned in to Rome to learn what was happening at King's Bay on their behalf, so in the *Krassin* they tended to get their news by listening to Swedish broadcasts. However, frequent references to their own ship made clear how important was the part they played, and this made the crew readier than ever to put forth great efforts when required – and they were to be required – far in excess of the 8-hour day.

The *Krassin* could not come in as close to the coast as shallow-draught ships like the *Braganza*, particularly as soundings were very uncertain; and so was not able to take advantage of easier ice conditions inshore. At first all went well, the ship fully justifying the faith the Soviet had put in her. Under her weight and mass, the ice field gave way and shattered with a loud report, like a sheet of glass, thought Giudici. Channels opened, great blocks of ice plunged into the green waters and grated angrily down her sides, the pack-ice crumbed for hundreds of yards around, hummocks being pushed up and then overturning in a fury of foam; the whole expanse convulsed as if by an earthquake. Meanwhile, her siren sent out piercing blasts at ten-minute intervals in case the three men of the walkout party should be within hearing distance somewhere on the pack.

In the great bay between North Cape and Cape Platen, in the middle of which sits Scoresby Island, the Newcastle-built ship met her match. Here the wind had driven the pack-ice firmly against the land, so that it was high-piled and virtually immovable. Captain Eggi turned away to the north in the hope of finding easier conditions. They saw their first polar bears that day, 2 July, the Russians calling out delightedly *'Michka pliachet!'* ('Here's Dancing Michael!') The ice they now met was in process of melting. It was so soft that the bows of the *Krassin* compressed it into solid walls which built up and stuck to the sides of the ice-breaker without even allowing open stretches of free water to appear. Three times in 12 hours Captain Eggi had to resort to the extreme expedient of filling and blowing the lateral tanks. As those on one side were filled, the great ship rolled over, shattering the accumulated ice on that side; when those tanks were blown and the tanks on the other side filled with swirling seawater, the vessel heeled the other way, completing the fracture and giving the ship renewed freedom of movement. Captain Eggi said some words in Russian which Giudici was told meant: 'It's all a matter of patience and coal – if we've got enough of both, we'll win.'

Giudici gained the impression, however, that the Captain was trying to cheer them up because there was something badly wrong with the ship. The *Krassin* no longer seemed capable of dealing with the ice as decisively as she had before; the journalist sensed this but could not confirm it. Eggi gave up the attempt to find a northern route and steamed south, but by noon next day, 3 July, a strong north wind had further compressed the ice and virtually locked them in. Four hours steaming that evening consumed 20 tons of coal and advanced the ship by a mile only. This tiny gain was almost wiped out by the fact that the current was drifting the ice westward.

In the distance they could see the twin masts of the *Braganza*; she too was blocked by the ice and unable to move. They heard that the ice-breaker *Malygin* was similarly halted on the far side of North-East Land. Her aircraft, a Junkers F-13 flown by M. S. Babuschkin, disappeared soon afterwards on a reconnaissance flight. The Latham carrying Amundsen was still missing. So was the hull of the *Italia*; so were the three men of the walkout party. There was no news of the two men who had ventured on to the dangerous ice in an attempt to reach Broch Island – shortly Captain Sora and his Dutch companion van Dongen were to be declared missing also. The Swedish Fokker was down – and Lundborg was sitting, fuming, on the ice by the Red Tent, putting forward one reckless scheme after another in his impatience to break free. But now, all transmissions from the Red Tent had stopped and banks of fog prevented flights in that area by the two big Italian flying boats or of machines from the Swedish air group.

For nearly four days the *Krassin* was locked in the ice which on examination turned out to be 2½ metres thick with a layer of snow on top 80 cm. deep. Something like 9 feet in all. The sailors council applied to the Commissar for permission to go out on the ice, hunting; Oras himself went with them. Giudici took care not to go off the smooth ice near the ship, because it was in the cover of hummocks that the bears lurked and the wild shooting of the Soviet sailors was equally intimidating.

On 5 July a diver was sent down to make a thorough examination at the stern of the *Krassin*. He wore heavy underwear, socks and gloves under his suit because he would be operating in the bitter temperatures of the freezing level. The deeper you went, the warmer it was, as Professor Beretskin, the expedition's hydrographer, had established. At 100 metres the temperature was one degree Centigrade above freezing point, while at 30 metres it was 0·5 of a degree above. Sergej Sheludjew was the diver's name, and what he had to report explained the *Krassin*'s apparent loss of efficiency. A blade of one of the three propellers had broken off, the steering had been damaged and some of the rudder fastenings were smashed. The ship's First Officer, Paul Ponomarew, put on a diving suit and went down personally to check. This damage was probably the result of the many reversing manoeuvres that had been used to break a way through the pack. Moscow was notified that the power of the ship had been reduced by 1,000 h.p., and asked if they ought to attempt repairs, either at sea near the Seven Islands, or back at Advent Bay.

Moscow's reply arrived next morning, Friday, 6 July. 'No return; find a stretch of ice sufficiently smooth to allow the aeroplane to take off and descend without serious risk; the airman Tchukhnovsky to be allowed to attempt the rescue of the Viglieri group by air; continue the work of rescue with the utmost activity until there is on board only 1,000 tons of coal necessary for the return voyage.' That was the sort of determined directive a captain needed in this situation. Almost simultaneously with the receipt of the order, the wind began to blow strongly from the south-west and broke up the pack; the *Krassin* broke out of the ice and began to search for a large stretch of floating ice which would make both a dock and a natural aerodrome. They found it within a few hours and the crew began to construct a ramp down from the ship's deck to the ice 'dock'. The tri-motor Junkers was to be moved down this and, once on the ice, the wings would be fitted. All night, they worked feverishly at this task.

Realising that a crisis was upon them, Giudici asked Professor Samoilovich what he planned. The Professor explained that, back in Leningrad, all the polar experts who did not know Spitzbergen intimately had judged that the *Krassin* would break through to Cape Leigh Smith fairly easily; those with local knowledge had strong reservations. It was still too early, by some weeks, to attempt polar exploration with ships. Tomorrow, Tchukhnovsky would fly a reconnaissance over the ice; what they did would depend on his report and on the weather, for the state of the ice could change in their favour. In any event, they still had 1,700 tons of coal. 1,000 tons were required for the return to Advent Bay, the only place in Spitzbergen where a big ship like theirs could re-bunker. That left them 700 tons of coal with which to reach the Viglieri group – and the *Krassin* consumed 120 to 140 tons per day. In brief, if conditions did not markedly improve soon, within days they would have to return to Advent Bay.

The Viglieri group had just had another series of supply drops by Swedish aeroplanes. A Heinkel single-engined seaplane had dropped pemmican, chocolate, medicine, a bottle of whisky and some Swedish newspapers for poor Lundborg, who was twitchy with boredom by now. The big Junkers tri-motor floatplane, the *Upland*, similar to that of Tchukhnovsky's, had dropped more food, a stove, a mouth organ, and letters. And radio messages told them that on 4 July a D.H. Cirrus Moth had arrived from Sweden and would soon try to make a landing by the Red Tent. On 6 July, very early, the castaways saw two aeroplanes appear. One was a Heinkel floatplane and it was escorting a Moth fitted with skis and flown by Lieutenant Birger Schyberg.

Lundborg's departure in it was almost a 'panic' flight, Franz Behounek was to write. The unfortunate Swede had told him privately that if he had to stay on the ice much longer, he would commit suicide. All the Italians had been through this period of nervous depression soon after the crash, but they had encountered it together and overcome it together. Einar Lundborg had the worse fate of experiencing it alone. Also, while all the others had become accustomed gradually to the state of filth and misery which tent-life in the Arctic necessarily imposes, Lundborg came to this degradation fresh and clean from a brisk Swedish military society. Above all, the terrible, mind-beating boredom. The waste. What might have been just bearable if it had happened to a small group of Swedish comrades was so alien that it was impossible. When the Moth bumped to a stop by his own overturned Fokker, Lundborg left most of his own personal belongings behind. Arnesen wrote that Lundborg hurriedly climbed on board, so that no discussions might arise as to who should first be saved, 'as one never knows what wrecked men may do.' Behounek, who was one of the wrecked men, wrote that the Swedish pilot 'fled almost in panic,' although promising to come back next day and fetch them all. The Czech scientist admired Viglieri for merely thanking the Swede for his good intentions and disdaining to beg for help. It showed how good their morale was now, he thought.

But Lundborg did not come back, nor did Schyberg. The Italians, particularly those in the *Città di Milano*, were critical; there were accusations of cowardice against Schyberg. The report of an outside party, the Finnish aircrew flying the Junkers *Turku*, recorded very bad flying weather between 6 and 12 July. But also General Nobile had a long talk with Captain Tornberg, the leader of the Swedish air group. Tornberg was quite frank. The thaw was making landings more and more hazardous, but at the same time would make things easier for the ships to get through.

Why risk more men and machines when a sea rescue seemed imminent? Nobile did not agree, as he had been told by Lundborg (less frankly) that the reason for the crash had been, not the deteriorating state of the ice and the dangerous nose-heaviness of the Fokker in those conditions, but engine failure. Lundborg now said, with much greater experience of the pack, that in low temperatures a landing was possible. Biagi should report the temperature each night, as well as visibility. But not only did the weather change for the worse, with much heavy local fog, but from 7 to 11 July some strange atmospheric effect prevented the Red Tent party hearing any outside station at all, so that they became dejectedly convinced that their own radio set must have failed and was now useless.

But Lundborg had left a legacy behind him. Like Malmgren, Mariano and Zappi he was a restless do-er. The ice floe carrying the castaways was drifting in slow circles, coming as close to the mainland as a mere 4½ miles. It was tantalising and he had constantly argued for a march, which would mean abandoning Cecioni. The Italians were glad to see him go, so that they would be freed from exhausting, useless arguments. But his views had now infected Captain Romagna, who brought them to Nobile. 'No! You won't do it! You'll have the whole civilised world against you!' Nobile remonstrated. Instead, he sent a telegram to the *Krassin* that evening, 6 July, asking for news of progress.

Samoilovich replied with news of the intended air reconnaissane of the ice by Tchukhnovsky on 7 July, and asked for the plans of the other expeditions. Romagna, who had brought this message to Nobile on the evening of 7 July, immediately began to draft a reply, citing the efforts he was making with the *Braganza*, and what the Swedes planned. Nobile saw how fatal this might be and interrupted. 'No! Not like that! The Russians might think that the Swedes and the *Braganza* have great chances of success, and that therefore they need not risk their ship in a dangerous advance. No! We must write quite differently.' And he dictated a brief appeal: *All our hopes are centred on the Krassin. We beg you, therefore, to do your utmost to reach the tent as soon as possible.* This chimed exactly with Moscow's instructions.

On the morning of 8 July the three engines of the Junkers skiplane were started. Their roar sounded over the pack, punctuated by shots from the hunting parties out on the ice. They had got one seal, which they had cut up as bait for the wary bears, but apart from that all they could bag were a few seagulls. This part of the Arctic was not very friendly. Tchukhnovsky, who had worked all night and been able to snatch a few hours sleep in the morning, opened his throttles and the big Junkers began to slither forward over the snow. First one ski dipped into a pocket of fresh water hidden under the snow, then the other; the wings waggled dangerously as the pilot kept his engines at full power, correcting each time a wing dropped. At last she was airborne, circling slowly over the landing ground before heading towards Charles XII Island. When he returned, the spectators could see the results of that bumpy take-off – one ski was hanging vertically downwards. Men rushed forward, waving their arms frantically. Tchukhnovsky understood and came in for a careful touch-down, the tail of the damaged ski brushing the ground first and being forced back into position. Then both skis were touching and neither had broken. There were one or two sharp releases of breath.

Tchukhnovsky did not have the rugged look which was the conventional image of an airmen. He had a delicate, diffident, even intellectual appearance which concealed his inherent toughness of character and physique. He explained his plans to Giudici so that they sounded very simple and easy of accomplishment. Tomorrow he would make a brief two-hour flight to Charles XII Island and Cape Leigh Smith, off which the Viglieri group were now reported to be drifting, very close to land. His main object would be ice reconnaissance. Firstly, to see if a further advance by the *Krassin* was practical. If it was not, then to see if it was possible for him to land close to the Red Tent and eva-cuate all the castaways by air. He would need to drop a message, in Italian, explaining what he wanted in the way of information regarding the condition and extent of the landing area and giving a code for a set of answers, to be traced out in the snow. Giudici translated this message for him, and three copies were made. To it was attached a note which, if received, would alleviate the anxieties of the men on the ice:

'*P.S. We know that for two days you have been unable to communicate with the Città di Milano. Do not worry. It is the result of an inexpli-able general disturbance.*'

Next day, 10 July, the three copies of the message were attached to three of the big packages which the Junkers was to drop. After the supplies for the castaways, Tchukhnovsky took on board a complete survival kit, including a tent and a stove, plus rations for fourteen days for his own crew of five men. The other four men were George Straube, second-pilot, Alexander Schelagin, mechanic, Anatolij Alexejew, observer/navigator, and Wilhelm Bluvstein, cine cameraman. At 4 p.m. that afternoon the engines coughed into life one by one, and were slowly warmed up. Up to now, the weather had been fine, but even as the engines were started a fogbank appeared on the western horizon. Dr. Adolf Hoel, the Norwegian Arctic expert, warned that in less than three-quarters of an hour, the whole area would be blanketed with fog. Tchukhnovsky might take-off, but he would never find his way back to the *Krassin* again. However, the Russian airmen were impatient. Tchukhnovsky pointed out that they would be flying east, into clear weather, and could complete their task; as for the return, the ship was a very large object and if she made smoke, this would rise above the fogbank and mark her position.

How large a part was played in this decision by the unconditional determination shown by the Soviet government's order, and how much by General Nobile's alteration of Romagna's message to suggest that the Russians were their sole hope now, cannot be known. Beyond that, there must have been the pilot's own personal prestige as a factor, a matter of professional skill. But it was with uncommon tension that the spectators watched another bumpy, hazardous take-off from unfavourable ground, followed by a couple of climbing circuits to gain height to 600 feet over the ship, before the tri-motor flew east towards Charles XII Island about 12 miles away. The high ground of that island could still be seen as a reddish mound through the first banks of fog, which changed the golden sunlight to red. Now a speck in the distance, the Junkers began to zig-zag in a search pattern to the south of the island. Then distance and the growth of the fog made them lose sight of the aeroplane. Giudici looked at his watch. It was 4.40 p.m.

Three minutes later, the *Krassin*'s radio operator logged the message: '*Approaching Charles Island.*'

Samoilovich sent back: '*Heard you clearly. Good luck.*'

Then there was a wait of more than an hour until 5.50, when the *Krassin* logged a disappointing message: '*Camp not yet found. Camp not yet found.*' After a further half-an-hour had passed, came the final disappointment. The Junkers was signalling: *'Coming back. Coming back.'* It was 6.18 p.m.

It was not until 6.45 that another message came in from the aircraft. This time, their wireless operator, Alexejew, was sending his message very slowly indeed, instead of rapping it out.

'The Malmgren group –'

Samoilovich was thunderstruck. They were expecting news of the Viglieri group, known still to be alive. Malmgren and his two companions had walked out of the camp on 30 May, nearly six weeks ago, and nothing had been heard of them since. They were almost certainly dead.

Eleven minutes later, the *Krassin*'s operator picked up a single word more from whatever it was that Alexejew was trying to send. The word was: 'Charles'.

Charles XII Island, obviously. Whoever they were, the men whom the airmen had seen must be near there. Possibly Sora and van Dongen, the Alpini captain and his Dutch companion, who were now missing on the pack? Unlikely. Or could they be survivors from the Latham flying boat? Perhaps it was Amundsen and his companions? Surely not survivors from the hull of the *Italia*?

Shortly after, a complete message came through: *'Cannot find Krassin in fog. Seen Malmgren group. Looking for landing place near Seven Islands.'*

Samoilovich sent back: *'Have understood. Firing a rocket every five minutes. Burning signal fire on ice.'*

Then he rushed out of the wireless cabin, where he had been since the Junkers took off, to order the signals to be made and to tell everyone the good news of success. The rockets were fired, the bow searchlight lit, a fire of tar and logs started on the ice, and the boilers made smoke. But there was no sign of Tchukhnovsky, not even the faintest drone of his engines. After quarter of an hour or so, the *Krassin* heard the Junkers asking *'What visibility have you?'*

That was at 7.16 p.m. Samoilovich replied: *'Visibility bad. Signal fire burning on ice.'*

After ten minutes of silence, Samoilovich sent: *'Have you understood?'*

At 9.10 p.m. the *Krassin* asked: *'Where are you, what's wrong?'* and went on asking every half-hour, except that on the odd half-hour the message was changed to *'Why don't you reply?'* The rest of the time the operator spent listening. But there was no sound.

Then Samoilovich decided to call at minute intervals: '*Where are you? What's happened? Why don't you answer?*'

That also failed to raise any reply, so at 10.53 p.m. Samoilovich sent a final message, saying that he was listening out and awaiting their call. Still there was nothing.

Then at 11.30 p.m., seven hours after Tchukhnovsky had taken off, the wireless man turned to Samoilovich: 'Here he is!'

'Where is he?'

'Sssst . . .' and the operator began to write down the letters that were coming in. '*KM*'. The code for *Krassnyj Medwjed*. A series of difficult contacts established that the Junkers was down on the ice near Cape Wrede and had damaged the landing gear.

An hour or so later, at 1.10 in the morning of 11 July, Tchukhnovsky was able to send a detailed report. The Malmgren group had been sighted at 80°42' N., 25°45' E., on an ice-floe surrounded by open water. Two of the men were standing up and waving, a third man was lying on the ice. After circling them five times the Junkers had carried on with the search, but bad weather made the pilot come down some 40 miles away, damaging the undercarriage and smashing two propellers. Tchukhnovsky's message ended:

'*No one hurt. Food for two weeks. Don't stop for us. Go to Malmgren's aid soonest.*'

Those three men were somewhere between 15 and 18 miles away, concluded the officers of the *Krassin*. In fact, the real number was unsure. What happened was that the mechanic, Schelagin, had rushed into the cockpit excitedly, shouting: 'People . . . People!' and pointing. Alexejew, the navigator, looked in that direction and thought he saw at least five people (enough to make up the crew of the Latham or the men missing with the hull of the *Italia*). Straube, the co-pilot, saw two men. Tchukhnovsky himself had seen only a single individual standing on the ice and making flag signals.

The leaders in the *Krassin* decided that an all-out attempt must be made to reach them. If the ice were very thick, they might cover only five miles a day, but reach them they would. The crew worked all night and half the morning without cease to clear all the heavy equipment off the ice and bring it on board, including the loading ramp. It was 10.25 before the *Krassin* could make a further attempt to force a way through the pack. Everywhere, the ice was very thick, in excess of 6 feet. Average rate of progress was 1½ miles per hour.

With the ship moving at less than walking pace, the sighting of five polar bears during the night sparked off a hunt across the ice – after a fusillade of rifle fire from the deck had failed to halt any. The bears scrambled away among the tall hummocks of ice and only a single she-bear was shot down, to be hauled aboard the ice-breaker and eaten.

At midnight they had passed beyond Charles XII Island and found broken ice to the east. By 1.30 on the morning of 12 July, stretches of open water were appearing and the ship began to move appreciably faster. Apart from the few men on duty down below, everyone was on deck and the ship was crammed with lookouts – up the masts and standing on the funnel-ladders. 100 roubles had been promised to the first person to sight the marooned men. The incentive was hardly necessary. A tremendous tension gripped the ship in the long silences between those times when the siren gave its shrill wail of greeting to anyone out there. At 5.20 a.m. there was a loud shout from the second mate, August Breinkopf.

'A man! A man!' he bellowed so forcefully that he went red in the face. 'I can see him!'

It was 20 minutes before Giudici, his eyes searching among the many black shapes which were sometimes seals and sometimes pools of water lying on the ice, saw for himself that the second mate had been right. The ship's siren gave a long blast and the figure moved quickly. It was incongruous to see a human being in all that desolate expanse of Arctic ice, the forbidden end of the world. As the ice-breaker thundered on, smashing the ice-floes aside, it became clear that there was another man there, lying down on the ice, for the erect figure every now and then bent down and appeared to be talking to someone. Who were they? Did they come from the wrecked *Italia* or the missing *Latham*?

As the *Krassin* ground slowly on to within a hundred yards, the active man stepped forward to the edge of the floe, apparently to watch the effect her bow wave was producing. Tall, his face burnt almost black from the glare of sunlight on snow, with a shaggy beard and long, uncombed hair – he was unrecognisable. Then he made a commanding gesture with his hands: 'Stop!' The ship was obviously endangering the little ice-floe he was standing on. It measured no more than 24 by 30 feet wide, although some 15 feet protruded out of the water. Behind him, the prostrate man momentarily showed signs of life, attempting to sit up and watch, but sank back immediately, very far gone indeed. Of the third man mentioned in Tchukhnovsky's report there was no sign.

It was now 6.40 a.m. The man standing on the ice made a megaphone of his hands, and shouted up at the ship: 'Krassin. Welcome!'

Rescue was not immediate. A plank and rope ladder was put over the side, but the ice was so uneven that the sailors had to bring planks to bridge the gaps. Of the leaders, the expedition's secretary, Iwan Iwanow, led the way, followed by the doctor, Anton Srednjewsky, and Professor Samoilovich. Iwanow was the first to speak to the man who was on his feet:

'Malmgren?'

'No, Capitano Zappi.'

'Where is Malmgren?'

Zappi said something incomprehensible in Italian, and let his hands fall helplessly to his sides in an expressive gesture. He appeared to be a big, powerful man swaddled in layers of Arctic clothing.

Dr. Srednjewsky did not bother with him, but went on to where the other man lay prostrate. His eyes were burning with fever as he looked at them over the edge of a totally soaked blanket. He was lying in a depression in the ice, sheltered from the wind but lying actually in icy water which had collected in the hollow. Every stitch of clothing, the rags he was lying on, and the blanket which covered him, were sopping wet. The Russian doctor bent down and put his hand behind the suffering man's head, but the head fell again once the support was removed, although the lips seemed to form the words, 'Thank you.'

A few yards away on another ice-floe strips of rags and cloth had been laid on the snow to spell out four words in English:

'HELP. FOOD. ZAPPI. MARIANO.'

Nearby a pair of trousers was laid out so as to draw an airman's attention. This, probably, was the 'third man' seen by one crew member from the Junkers.

Mariano was placed on a stretcher, carried to the Krassin and the stretcher swung up and on board. Then it was lowered again for Zappi. Defiantly, he did not wait for it but managed to struggle up the 15-feet ladder. Swiftly, Mariano's stretcher was carried to the sick bay, the sailors baring their heads as it passed. His soaked clothes were stripped off and he was warmed; massage was begun and a little hot broth administered. He had a raging fever, gangrene in one foot as the result of frost-bite and was completely starved and suffering from severe constipation. Dr. Srednjewsky considered that had he remained on the ice-floe, he would have been dead within the space of ten to twelve hours.

Zappi, however, was well enough to be taken straight to the mess-room. He was in a very excited, not to say nervous state; rather like a soldier coming out of battle unwounded to the totally different undangerous world behind the lines. He had given himself up for dead, and now he was alive. He was consumed with his own thoughts and hardly cared to follow the line of reasoning of his questioners. He answered indifferently in various languages – he spoke good English and French – and in short bursts, jumping from thought to thought.

Samoilovich asked the question they all wanted answered: 'And Malmgren – where is Malmgren?'

'C'était un homme!' said Zappi. 'He's been dead for a month.'

After a short silence, he said: 'Give me some food, I'm very hungry.'

Samoilovich refused. The doctor was busy with Mariano and until he came back and examined Zappi, the Professor thought he ought not to have anything.

Zappi grew impatient. 'I'd like some hot, very hot, coffee. For twelve days I have not eaten anything. Since 30 June I have not had a warm drink.'

There was no coffee on board, but Samoilovich let him have a cigarette, while he waited for the tea to brew. Zappi, with a steady hand, wrote two telegrams – one to his mother, the other to Captain Romagna of the *Città di Milano*. When the tea came, he swallowed it greedily, and asked for biscuits. Samoilovich said he would have to wait for the doctor to authorise food. When Srednjewsky came in from dealing with Mariano, he took Zappi's pulse and allowed him one biscuit, just one.

'But why?' said Zappi, devouring the biscuit with a couple of bites. 'You save us from death by starvation and now you won't let us eat!'

But now it was his turn for the bathroom. The expedition

secretary, Iwanow, showed him there and as Zappi's hands were too sore for the Italian to divest himself of his sodden and frozen outer clothing, Iwanow did it for him. With difficulty, he undid the wet laces of Zappi's boots. Underneath the Italian was wearing another pair of boots, fur this time, and these were drier. Under this, Zappi was wearing two pairs of woollen socks.

The inner piece of headgear Zappi was wearing was so wet that Zappi could not remove this unaided, either. As the Russian assisted him, Zappi touched the cap and said: 'Malmgren.'

When the outer, anorak-type garments had been got off, there were more layers of clothing to be removed. A fur vest over-lying a knitted woollen vest, and linen trousers over fur trousers. Finally, when Zappi stood there in fur trousers and woollen vest, the Russian gestured to him to empty his pockets. Zappi pulled out a compass, said: 'Malmgren' and added a few words the Russian couldn't understand. (Later, he was to tell Oras that the compass had belonged to Malmgren, who had asked him to give it to his mother.) After the compass, Zappi pulled out a wallet, three letters and two watches. (Behounek later testified that two of these letters were his, and that he had given them to Malmgren.)

The undressing was not finished yet. When Zappi stepped out of the grey fur-lined trousers, he proved to be wearing yet another pair underneath; these were of dark brown material. Then under that a warm pair of longjohns came into view, and after that Zappi really had nothing more but skin. He got into the bath happily, crying 'Karascho! Karascho!' This rather jolted the secretary, for Zappi was now calling out 'Good! Good!' in Russian. In very broken Russian, Zappi tried to explain that he had visited various towns in Russia, by reciting the names.

After the bath, Zappi was put to bed in the sickbay next door and Iwanow heard him call: 'Mariano! Mariano!' followed by a rapid burst of Italian which the Russian couldn't understand. The two men had been friends for fifteen years, which made more extraordinary the discovery which the Russians had now made – they had two complete sets of clothing, that belonging to Mariano, and that belonging to his friend Zappi. And they were not the same. Zappi was wearing twelve items, Mariano only five. The Russians listed them carefully, photographed them, and took the two sets back to Leningrad for display in their museum. For you had to see it to believe it. The lists were bad enough.

GARMENT	ZAPPI	MARIANO
Fur cap	1	–
Linen coat with cap	1	–
Fur vest	1	1
Knitted vest	1	1
Linen trousers	1 pair	–
Fur-lined trousers	1 pair	–
Cotten trousers	1 pair	1 pair
Fur-lined boots	2 pairs	–
Warm socks	2 pairs	1 pair
Warm longjohns	1	1

To cap it all, Zappi was talking much too loosely and with a hint of hysteria. Everyone wanted to know about Malmgren, who had died early. Nobody seemed to want to know what it was like to survive on the pack without a tent above you or a groundsheet under you; not for a few hours, but for a month and a half. No one knew the pressures they had been under. Who believed him when he said that he had not eaten for twelve days?

The Krassin's doctor did not. According to Professor Hoel, the doctor took samples of Zappi's faeces and concluded that he had last eaten within a day or so. But a similar test with Mariano proved that this unfortunate man had had no food for about eleven days. Hoel's only disagreement with the Russian evidence was a small one; his recollection was that Mariano, as well as Zappi, was wearing a fur cap when he was brought on board.

Chapter 17

RED STAR TO RED TENT

(With the *Krassin*: 12–23 July)

O UT of suspicion, the Russians questioned Zappi; but cautiously and with the reservation that, even if what they suspected was true, they themselves might act no better under the similar alternatives of life or death. Zappi was eager to talk, to tell what he and Mariano had endured and how they had conducted themselves. He put on a heroic tone. Just before they were saved, he said, when they had seen the big Russian tri-motor flown by Tchukhnovsky, but it had failed to come back, they had not fallen into despair. No. Instead, so stoically resolute was the dying Mariano that he had whispered to his friend:

'Zappi, when I die, you must hold out. Begin to suck my blood, then eat my brain. Try to make your stomach accept it . . . one of us must survive.'

A few Russian skins crawled as they listened. Nobile, when he heard, was intensely irritated with what he considered to be Zappi's foolish and blatantly theatrical bragging. Of course, he knew Zappi and the Russians didn't. He also knew how the rations had been divided between the two parties – those who would stay behind and those who would attempt to make the coast (uselessly, he had thought). The three men had carried 55 kilograms of concentrated food – pemmican, chocolate, malted milk, butter. That would have given them 550 grams per day, more than Amundsen, Riiser-Larson and the other survivors of the Dornier Wal had had in 1925. As for Zappi not having eaten for the last twelve days before being picked up, he did not believe it; it was just more boasting. The Russians had reservations, too, and more than one thought that the explanation lay in the fate of Malmgren, rather than the rations General Nobile had shared out.

276

Professor Hoel, the Norwegian, spoke to Zappi several times and got a brief, factual account. Zappi volunteered the information that they had only one pair of snowgoggles between them, and that he, Zappi, had worn them; so Mariano had been snow-blinded twice. After seeing the clothing worn by both men, one would have been surprised at any other division of vital survival gear. When they were rescued, he went on, Mariano had been lying on the ice for one-and-a-half weeks; and they had been without food for thirteen days. If Mariano had been without food for thirteen days, his collapse and present condition were sufficiently explained.

The man to whom Zappi talked most was Davide Giudici, the correspondent of the Milan *Corriere della Sera*. Anything he said to the journalist was likely to get into print, so here it was worth making an effort to make the best case possible, not only for him-self personally, but for the whole breakout attempt, which Nobile had resented, objected to, and opposed as long as he could. Nobile had maintained, their best hope lay with Biagi's radio and remaining with the tent, in a group, to be rescued. The three activists had thought, to the contrary, that the wireless set in its little box was just so much useless lumber; no one would ever hear its signals. And they had almost succeeded in getting virtually the whole party to leave the injured men and attempt to break out to safety over the ice. They would have taken Biagi with them, if they could – the only man capable of operating the radio, and Viglieri as well, if possible, because he too was a strong man and useful. Behounek was too clumsy and would have to be abandoned; Trojani was not really very effective for an assault on the pack.

'As nobody had heard our wireless calls,' Zappi told the reporter, 'Mariano, Malmgren, and I were charged with the task of reaching North East Land, and possibly North Cape. . . . The only way of saving the Nobile group was to make our position known. The only means of communicating it was by sending someone to re-establish contact with the outside world. Malm-gren, who warmly favoured this project, was chosen, as the one expert in Polar conditions, and as he thought the group should consist of at least three persons, Mariano and I were chosen by General Nobile. . . .'

That had been on 30 May, forty-three days ago. They had had food for 30 days; no leather footwear – only light Eskimo boots;

no change of clothing; and no tent – only a wool blanket. No arms – except an axe. But because of Malmgren's damaged shoulder, the Swedish scientist could not carry his share of their supplies, and so it fell to Mariano and Zappi to be beasts of burden, too heavily-loaded to move fast over the pack. They had reckoned on reaching North Cape in eighteen days, but so difficult a surface did the pack-ice prove that they managed no more than two miles a day over it for the first 14 days and then, because the ice itself was moving with the wind and the currents, they were actually further away from their destination than when they had started, as they could see from the position of Broch Island. They were also much weaker, moving more and more slowly. Because it was impossible to cook, they had no warm food. Because they had no tent, they were always chilled. Because they continually slipped and fell on the snow or into pools, they were wet to the skin; and they had no dry clothes to change into.

It was on that fourteenth day, almost exactly a month ago, that Malmgren collapsed – from the injuries he had sustained in the crash, from the privations he had endured after that, and from the evident failure of his project to break out over the pack and summon help. This last, thought Zappi, the anguish of being proved wrong in a matter where so many lives were at stake, had been as critical a factor in the scientist's plight as his failing physical powers.

'I can't go on,' he had said, 'but you must. You must save the others.'

After that, Malmgren had refused further food, asking Zappi to take from him also the compass with which he had been leading the march and give it to his mother together with a final message from her son.

At this point in his narrative, noted Giudici, Zappi's voice became 'hoarse and almost inaudible'.

Mariano and Zappi then left Malmgren to die in peace, as he seemed to wish, but walked no further than a hundred yards, so that if he changed his mind about the food he had given them, it would not be too late. They remained there about twenty-four hours, loathe to leave, until they saw Malmgren's head rise above the trench they had dug for him. They thought he might now be desperate with hunger and want to rejoin them. Instead, the Swede put his hands together and implored them to go on,

'Quickly! quickly!' Then he raised one arm as if pointing onward. Those were his last words. Mariano and Zappi accepting the sacrifice now got up and left him.

Carrying the remainder of Malmgren's rations, the lives of Mariano and Zappi were significantly extended. But because Zappi was wearing the only pair of snowgoggles, Mariano went blind and Zappi had to lead him by the hand, stumbling and falling, across the white devastation, climbing over great blocks of ice, trying to jump across water-filled fissures or lying down, exhausted. Once, they dug a trench out of the soft snow and lay huddled there for five or six days, unable to go on. One day succeeded another in a daze, and events merged and jumbled together in recollection. Zappi thought it was on 16 June that they had left Malmgren for the last time, and that it must have been 20 June when they saw the first aeroplane.

The mists and fogs had cleared and the sun had shone through, picking out Broch Island for the first time in days; it was much closer now. They heard the seaplane's engine clearly and as it passed above them, they took off their caps and waved them frantically. But the airmen did not see the two men below. For the next five days or so they saw one or two aeroplanes every day, each time waved their arms but at no time were they seen. Greenish water appeared between the ice, as the pack began to break up, and they were so near to land that Zappi thought he might soon be able to jump across on to Broch Island. Mariano, blind again, and with a twisted ankle, would never be able to do so. The blind man told Zappi: 'Save yourself – save our comrades.'

Zappi decided that, for a weak and laden man, such as he was, the gaps were too wide to jump. So he chose a large ice-floe covered with hummocks, the most solid in sight, and led Mariano there. In the *Krassin*'s sick bay, Mariano listened to all this in silence, except when Zappi turned to him to ask a question, as he did now:

'Mariano, how many days did we stay on the floe?'

'Five, Filippo,' said Mariano quickly, in a firm voice.

Then on 10 July, in the evening, they had heard engines again. Knowing that this really was the end, if they were not seen, Zappi had dashed out of their 'cave of ice', wildly waving a fragment of cloth in lieu of a flag. To his utter surprise, the aeroplane did not this time just fly straight on in to the distance, but came down low and circled them. Zappi shouted out to Mariano with joy, and they started to calculate how long it would take for the aeroplane to reach King's Bay, refuel and come back again. For King's Bay was where they assumed it had come from. Unlike the men at the Red Tent, with the wireless they had thought useless, Mariano and Zappi knew nothing of the Swedish and Russian relief expeditions; since 30 May, they had had no news at all of what was happening in the outside world. So they became very depressed when the aeroplane did not come back for them next day.

When Zappi first heard the siren of the *Krassin* howling across the waste of ice and snow, he thought it was just some grinding movement of the pack as it disintegrated around them inexorably. But as he looked in the direction from which the noise had come, there seemed to be a stain across the sky which might have been smoke. He climbed on top of a tall hummock and looked out – and there it was, the last thing he expected to see – a steamship. But had the steamship seen him? Frantically, he waved the rag in his hand again and again and again, until there was a sudden, answering blast of the *Krassin*'s siren. And then he knew that he was going to live.

Picking up Mariano and Zappi had delayed the *Krassin* by an hour and twenty minutes; but by 8 o'clock that morning she was under way again and heading south-east towards the last reported position of the Viglieri group. At around 11 o'clock she was passing well to the north of Foyn Island when both Jakob Legsdin, officer of the watch, and Paul Panomarew, the first mate, reported movement there. Two men waving a pole with a flag on it. Yet more passengers to be picked up. After so many frustrating days locked in the pack, now that the 10,000-ton ice-breaker was really on the move she was being hailed by groups of castaways as if she was a taxi. The Russian leaders talked it over and decided not to pick up these men yet, partly because they were on land – firm ground unlikely to melt underneath them. The other reason was the probable identities of the pair. It must be one of the two dog teams known to be searching the area for the Malmgren group: either the Alpini captain, Gennaro Sora and his Dutch driver, Sjef van Dongen, or the two Norwegians, Hilmar Nöis and Rolf Tandberg. All experienced men, unlikely to be in real trouble. The *Krassin* signalled to the men on Foyn Island that she would pick them up on her return (they did not receive the message, however, and gazed rather dumbly after the steamer as it passed on into the distance).

The *Krassin's* radio report to the Swedish seaplane support-ship *Quest* was received, and shortly after acted upon. Two Swedish Heinkel seaplanes and *Turku*, the Finnish Junkers, preparing for another air drop to the Red Tent, were told to look into Foyn on the way back. Samoilovich also informed Nobile and asked for the latest position of the Red Tent. So Nobile called for Baccarini, the wireless chief, and pointed out that the *Città di Milano* must act as intermediary or radio relay-station between the Viglieri group, who had only short-wave, and the *Krassin*, which had only long-wave. Since they could not com-municate direct with each other, the *Città di Milano* must do so for them. Baccarini objected; he had important telegrams to send to Rome. Romagna was sent for, and backed up Baccarini. But after Nobile had cogently argued that the *Krassin* might easily fail to find the tent, and that no wireless message they could send could be more important than those ensuring that she did not, the Captain at last consented.

At 2.55 that afternoon, the first hourly message went out to the Red Tent, telling them that when they saw the *Krassin* they should report it at once to the *Città di Milano*. When the next message went out at 3.55, Nobile added that they ought to be ready to make smoke signals for the benefit of the *Krassin*. At 4.55 Biagi sent the message:

'*We have sighted the Krassin about* 10 *kilometres S.W.*'

But the *Krassin*, as Nobile had anticipated, had not seen them. The ice-breaker, with her enormous yellow smokestacks, was a bulky object. The Red Tent and the overturned Fokker were not nearly so easy to see. The *Krassin* was zig-zagging, with the crew divided into groups, each group watching a clearly defined space; but there seemed to be nothing there. At 5 p.m., the *Città di Milano* relayed Biagi's message received five minutes earlier by the Italian ship, and the *Krassin* was turned nearly at right-angles to her previous course, now heading north instead of east. She would have missed the tent by an increasingly long distance, had not General Nobile prevailed over the normal Rome-oriented routine of the Italian ship. The Red Tent was far to the north and it was not until 8.15 that evening that the officer of the watch reported a big column of smoke some four or five miles ahead. Siren echoing shrilly over the white wasteland, the *Krassin* thundered into the pack, regardless of her damaged helm and broken screw. As she smashed aside the ice to within a hundred yards of the strange encampment on the floe, Captain Eggi telegraphed to his engine-room:

'*Stop!*'

Biagi tapped out his final message: '*It's over! Krassin's here! We're saved!*'

While a gangway was being lowered on to the ice for the *Krassin*'s leaders to descend, a tall man broke away from the group of castaways below and made his way to within 20 yards of the high steel sides of the ice-breaker. It was Lieutenant Alfredo Viglieri. Giudici called out to him the good news about Mariano and Zappi, the sad fate of Finn Malmgren. Behounek was now approaching, followed by Trojani. Samoilovich, Oras, Eggi and Iwanow went down the gangplank and embraced them. Behounek told Samoilovich that the sound of the *Krassin*'s siren was the finest music he had ever heard. Aboard the ice-breaker, Xenia the waitress was making the mess-room warm and comfortable for the men who had endured on the ice for so long. The other woman on board, Madame Woronzowa, was in the sick-bay, nursing Mariano, who was still very ill.

Now permission was given for the journalists to go down on to the ice and inspect the encampment; and finally the crew generally were allowed off the ship. Giudici shook hands with Viglieri and then went on towards the tent. On the way, he met Cecioni the engineer, limping slowly along with the aid of two oars (from one of the rubber boats) which served him as crutches. His leg had knit, but not correctly. Giudici told him (in Italian, of course): 'Wait a minute, and we'll get you a stretcher!'

'A stretcher!' replied Cecioni. 'Oh no, I'm going on board by myself.'

But Giudici called to a Russian officer, who detailed two sailors to support the injured man over the ice and up the gangway. Cecioni thanked Giudici and added: 'Let me pay you a compliment. You speak Italian as well as we do!'

'Oh, my Italian's not bad,' said the journalist modestly, 'but if you heard my Milanese, it would really surprise you. . . .'

'What? Are you an Italian then?' said Cecioni, taken aback.

A few steps further on, and it was Giudici's turn to be astounded. Standing beside the wireless station was a short man with a thick beard, wearing the cap of a General in the Italian

Air Force. 'What's this – another General!' thought Giudici, approaching the mysterious personage warily. The 'General' stuck out a hand and said, 'Biagi.' Grinning, he explained that General Nobile had asked for the loan of his own woollen cap, before he was flown away in the open cockpit of the Fokker, because it was warmer than a General's cap. So they had exchanged headgear. 'When I get back to the *Città di Milano*, I'll have them all jumping to attention – just you see!'

In minutes, Biagi was surrounded by spectators, for he had become as popular in the *Krassin* as he was in Italy. He had to explain to Iwan Eckstein, the chief wireless operator of the ice-breaker, the details of his little set and pose for photographs. Duly appointed guide, he showed the spectators over the floe, pointing out the sites of the three different camping places they had used. The condition of the ice was still fairly good, but would probably not remain so much longer, two or three days at the most, thought Giudici. Biagi showed them the two rubber boats dropped by Maddalena and how these were ready and stored for the water in case the ice opened up. He also showed them inside the tent, where they had at last improvised a flooring from wing sections of Lundborg's wrecked Fokker. On top of it they had made bedding out of the skin of the bear shot by Malmgren, and no longer had they had to sleep in melting snow and sometimes water.

Nobile had asked the Russians to save at least the Red Tent and one or two instruments, the first being of historic value; but they did better than that, bringing off everything they could find, from part of the rudder of the *Italia* to the remains of Lundborg's Fokker. This process took several days and cost the Russians the credit for the rescue of the men on Foyn Island.

Between the 6 and the 12 of July, that is, between the time of the rescue of Lundborg by the Swedish air group and the rescue of both the walkout party and their comrades at the Red Tent by the *Krassin*, fogs had prevented the Swedes and the Finns attempting further air operations from their forward base in Hinlopen Strait. Deceptively, it was not uniform; sometimes local, often it could be general. Only the Russians, flying from their ice-breakers, attempted to carry on; and both their machines were forced down. Both Babuskin, flying a Junkers from the *Malygin*, and Tchukhnovsky from the *Krassin*, were missing – but known to be all right. Tchukhnousky, however, could not

take off again, even if the weather improved, because of landing damage. So, when the message came through that Foyn
Island was now 'inhabited', only the Scandinavian air group was
operational. The Finnish Junkers' crew, who had joined the
Swedes on the 5th, had had a most disappointing time. From the
day of their arrival at King's Bay, which had been as far back as
23 June, their aircraft's landing gear had kept steadily out of step
with the changing weather. When they fitted floats, the sea froze
and there was no open water; when they changed the floats for
skis, the snow melted on the landing grounds; and they had to
change back to floats again. Then, when at last they got forward
to Murchison Bay, fog clamped down over the area of the forward
base.

But at 10.20 on the evening of 12 July, Gunnar Lihr opened
his throttle and took the Junkers F-13 screaming across the Bay.
With him were two other seaplanes, Heinkels of the Swedish Air
Force; Tornberg, the Swedish leader, was flying one of them.
Their task was to drop supplies and have a look at Foyn. *Turku*,
the Finnish Junkers, was an ugly, square-looking aircraft with a
car-type radiator; but as a small civilian airliner it had more
cargo capacity than the Swedish-built Heinkels, which were
warplanes.

At twenty-five minutes to midnight on 12 July, they were over
Foyn. The scene had a new look about it, for summer was on the
way, and a channel some 500 metres wide had opened in the ice
along the coast of the island. No one had expected this, but the
opportunity was too good to miss. The two aircraft without radio,
Turku and one of the Heinkels, throttled back and planed down
towards the wide stretch of open water, while the second Heinkel
remained above. If anything went wrong, its radio could notify
the *Quest* back at base. Things very nearly did go wrong, for the
ice began to close the gap rapidly. The two men on the island
came hurrying down to the shore, leaving their sledge and their
two surviving dogs behind. They proved to be the bandy-legged
little Alpini captain, Sora, and the wild young Dutch youth, van
Dongen. Five of his dogs had died during their epic but unsuccessful journey, and two they had eaten. Some Norwegians
had refused to believe that they could make Broch Island at that
time of year, let alone Foyn; but they had. The effort was wasted,
because although some of the *Italia* survivors had been trying for
more than a month to get there, they had failed. Very probably,

they had been within sight of the Red Tent itself on one occasion, for Viglieri thought he had seen men moving about in the distance, and then dismissed it as a trick of the eyes or of the light. It was a very gallant effort, but because their goal was a drifting ice floe, the odds against their success had been immense. 'Stupid and futile,' said one critic later.

With one passenger in each of the two planes, their take-off runs would be longer – and the ice channel was narrowing. The Heinkel's Bristol Jupiter radial roared healthily, and it sped over the water; but the car-type Junkers engine refused to start. It was half-an-hour before Uno Backman, the Finnish mechanic, had it going properly, and his pilot, Gunnar Lihr, lifted *Turku* into the air when he was within a hair's breadth of the ice.

In less than twenty-four hours, three groups had been rescued – Mariano and Zappi, the five members of the Viglieri party, Sora and van Dongen. Nine men in all. The survivors from the airship had been out on the ice 48 days, the sledging party half that, having left camp on 18 June. There remained only four groups to be found and saved – all of them with aircraft. Babuskin was believed to have come down somewhere near King Charles Land (far to the south-east), while vainly trying to help the Red Tent party and Tchukhnovsky was definitely down safely in Rijpsbucht, a long inlet of the sea into North-East Land which was teeming with game. There had been no word from Amundsen since 18 June, and the whereabouts and fate of the Latham flying boat were still unknown after 24 days. The main hull of the *Italia* with Alessandrini and five other men had not been seen since the crash on to the ice on 25 May, but was likely to be within 15 miles of the present position of the *Krassin* inside an arc to the east from the Red Tent.

Back at King's Bay, Nobile composed a telegram for Samoilovich, asking him to look for the *Italia* within 10 to 15 miles eastward of him. The sending of this message was delayed for many hours by Captain Romagna. Eventually, the Russian replied that he now had no means of air reconnaissance and that the *Krassin* was too low on coal for a purely ship search to be worthwhile. A little later, he had thought of a solution and telegraphed to the Italians: '*Please tell me if you are going to search for the airship group with flying boats. In that case we will wait here by the tent.*' Nobile could no longer order. He had to beg Romagna to send the big Italian flying boats; it was the last right moment for such a search, Romagna having missed all the other opportunities, particularly the long spell of fine weather in June, ideal for an air search. Such a large object as the hull of an airship nearly 350 feet long, with a diameter of 64 feet, was likely to be more visible than a tiny tent 8-feet square, even if it had caught fire or deflated without burning. But Romagna hesitated at so bold a decision as to instigate a search for the airship he was supposed to support, and clutching at any excuse to avoid action, seized on a reported remark of Zappi's aboard the ice-breaker, that the *Italia* must be considered destroyed with all those on board. Just as he had written off Nobile and the Red Tent originally, so the captain of the *Città di Milano* finally wrote off the *Italia*. There never would be a better opportunity, because the fixed start-point for the search, the place where the airship had struck the ice, was actually marked by an ice-breaker. Once the *Krassin* moved away, the variable drift of the ice-floes would make calculations more and more inaccurate and confused.

The *Krassin* waited all day on 13 July by the Red Tent floe and all night through, while a decision was reached. The survivors had bathed, shaved, and put on the civilian suits which had been brought for them. Biagi spent many hours taking down personal telegrams which had been received in the *Città di Milano* and intended for the castaways. He was expecting a message himself, reporting an increase in his family, but this was not among the telegrams received that day. There was one official communication addressed to him, however, and this was from the municipal authorities of Rome, informing Capo 2nd class Biagi, G. 86891, that as he had failed to pay his Dog Tax, unless the bill was settled immediately, the Municipality would have no alternative but to seize some of his household goods in lieu. Sitting at his radio set, Biagi was tempted to reply at once: 'Am awaiting you on pack-ice at 80°38' North, 29°13' East.'

At 3 o'clock in the morning of 14 July, a steady rattling and clanking noise showed that the anchor was being raised. Giudici, who had been asleep only for a couple of hours, went on deck, and asked Professor Samoilovich where they were going – east or west?

'For King's Bay,' said Samoilovich, adding that they had to pick up Tchukhnovsky and the Junkers, and after that to take in water and coal, and also repair the damage to their propeller and rudder. It would take less than a week, then they would be back

again to search for the six men from the *Italia* who were still
missing.

After taking his noon sight, Commissar Oras came over to the
Italian journalist and asked 'Do you know where we are?'

Giudici looked at the land. 'I can see Foyn, and beyond that,
Cape Platen.'

'We are now precisely at the spot where the day before yesterday we rescued Mariano and Zappi. The winds from the south
and east have dispersed the ice, and if we had delayed a single day,
most probably the two men would not have been saved.'

A factor in Samoilovich's decision to return was the condition
of Mariano. One foot was so far gone with gangrene that it
would have to be amputated and the facilities for such an operation were better in the *Città di Milano* than in the ice-breaker.

Zappi was restless and feverish, not eating well. 'Professor'
Trojani was in the sickbay, too, with foot trouble; he lay in the
bunk above Mariano, reading books about Polar exploration.
Franz Behounek, a real professor, also had foot trouble, although
less severe, so that he could spend much of his time writing up
his scientific notes. His records and apparatus for measuring
cosmic rays had survived the crash and he had collected a great
deal of invaluable scientific data while actually on the pack.
Nobile had intended this, of course, but not quite so drastically
as it had turned out. Viglieri was writing up the expedition notes,
while Cecioni was experimenting with a pair of real crutches
which he had found in the *Krassin*'s medical store. Biagi was the
fittest of them all, partly because, while all the others wore the
warm but light Eskimo footwear, he had had on leather boots at
the time of the crash, the wireless shack being not so cold as the
main cabin. For moving on snow and ice, leather footwear was
infinitely superior. Indeed, he had refused an offer by Malmgren
of a gold watch and chain for the boots, just before the Swedish
scientist left with Mariano and Zappi. This was not selfishness,
because, unlike the others, Biagi had to be much on the move,
walking through the snow continually from the tent (where the
receiver was) to the transmitter outside by the aerial.

The *Krassin* was heading past Cape Platen and between Cape
Wrede and Scoresby Island in order to enter the long fjord of
Rijpsbucht; and here, in a sudden blinding snowstorm she once
more encountered very thick ice. At 4 o'clock in the afternoon
of 15 July, a north wind opened up to view a coastline of low

glaciers, very interesting to Samoilovich as a geologist; and a dark speck on the ice a few miles away which must be the stranded Junkers. As the ship was able to move only at a walking pace and the thickness of the ice seemed to be increasing, the *Krassin* was brought to a stop and two skiers sent off to contact Tchukhnovsky and his four companions.

Two hours later, figures began to appear from the fog. There was a whole bunch of them. Giudici counted eight at first – one more than the total of the crew of the Junkers and the two skiers from the *Krassin*. Then more and more men appeared from the swirling vapour, until he could count eleven. Had Tchukhnovsky found the survivors from the Latham? Then there were loud shouts – in Italian! What on earth were Italians doing here, in this uncharted area of Spitzbergen?

They proved to be a party of skiers who had gone to visit the stranded Russian airmen from the Italian-chartered sealer *Braganza*, which was nearby, locked in the ice. They were led by the Norwegian hunter, Hilmar Nöis, who spent his winters out in the wilderness, operating from a simple cabin; there were only three or four men like him in Spitzbergen. With him was Sergeant-Major Gualdi of the Alpini and two of the University students, Albertini and Matteoda. The inexperience of the two latter men had hampered a previous trip by Nöis and Tandberg, the Italians making up for it by their courage and good humour. Like most amateurs, they tended to be high-spirited and eager to press on when the going was good, but would fret and tire easily when obstacles were encountered. The steady, unruffled, apparently plodding pace of the Norwegian hunter actually covered a great deal more ground more rapidly, because he had been doing this sort of thing almost every day for thirteen years. For him, these were the easy conditions of summer, with the temperature around freezing point. In the winter, it could sink as low as 35° or even 40° Centigrade below freezing-point. To Giudici, Nöis appeared a wild man, 'semi-barbaric', and was rumoured to have killed more than 150 polar bears during his hunting career, some at close quarters. But he was also very shy, and anxious to keep up with world events, enquiring of Giudici how the trial in America of Sacco and Vanzetti had ended and if the 'two Frenchmen' (Nungesser and Coli) had managed to fly the Atlantic. No, they were dead. Or rather, missing. Like Amundsen.

During the five days Tchukhnovsky and his crew had spent on

the ice, they had shot two reindeer, which had provided them with abundant fresh meat; and they had with them the food and clothing they had intended dropping to the Red Tent. So they had done rather well, though Tchukhnovsky grieved because he had forgotten the salt; if he had remembered to bring some, his arrangements could have been regarded as perfect! Now, sledges took spare parts out over the ice to the aeroplane, the engines were started, and Tchukhnovsky taxied the machine the two miles across the ice to the *Krassin*. Early on the morning of 16 July it was hoisted on board and the ice-breaker set off to join the *Braganza*, to collect the Italian doctor for a second opinion regarding Mariano's foot. He, too, decided for amputation.

On 19 July, the *Krassin* rounded Cape Mitra and, bedecked with Soviet flags, steamed into King's Bay, anchoring in deeper water than the *Città di Milano*, which had returned from Virgo Bay on 17 July. A grey launch carrying Captain Romagna left the Italian base-ship and sped across to the *Krassin*, circling as a gangway was lowered. The *Braganza* was three days behind, once more locked into the ice, and would not reach King's Bay until 21 July; aboard her were most of the men who had searched the coasts on foot, including Varming (now cured of his snow-blindness), except for Sora and Van Dongen who had been flown back. So when the grey launch left the Soviet ice-breaker it brought with it only Viglieri, Behounek, Trojani, Biagi, Cecioni, and Zappi. Mariano was transfered as a stretcher case in another boat. The Russian officers had dressed in their best uniforms, as for a gala occasion, and little Madame Ljubow Woronzowa, instead of her sheepskin coat, was wearing an elegant black silk dress. Until now, Mariano had been in her care. He was to lose his leg next day, in the *Città di Milano*, painfully, under inadequate local anaesthetics.

The men of the *Città di Milano* crowded the decks to welcome the survivors. General Nobile had left his sickroom to greet them. Cecioni hobbled aboard, then dropped his crutches to embrace the General. They were all very moved. The only one who even attempted a smile was Professor Behounek, whose sister had travelled to Spitzbergen to be among the welcoming party. Of course, six men were still missing, and two were definitely dead – Malmgren and Pomella. Eight survivors had now been rescued and brought to King's Bay – exactly half the sixteen-man crew of the airship.

10

Even so, this was an infinitely better result of the great international search and rescue operation than had been expected by
some pressmen recently. Nine days ago, on 10 July, 'graphic
messages' had been received from the Arctic, among them
'details of the pitiful death of Signor Cecioni', who had been 'left
under the open sky all night. His wounds were frozen, and death
soon followed.' Later the same day, a further report was headlined:

DEAD, MISSING, OR IN DESPAIR

This piece included the statement that: 'The search for Professor's
Malmgren's group, and for Capt. Sora, has been definitely
abandoned, and Professor Malmgren, Sig. Mariani [*sic*] and
Appi [*sic*] and Capt. Sora, with both sled drivers, Van Dongen and
Warming [*sic*], are regarded as dead.' This was on the day before all of them, with the exception of Malmgren, were saved
(Varming had never been in danger). That special correspondent's
report had concluded: 'Moreover, the five Italians in the Viglieri
group must be abandoned to their fate, unless they are rescued
within the next very few days. Their physical resistance is reduced
and they are in a state of despair.'

What now? The only striking speculations left for the more
exciting realms of journalism were those concerned with the death
of Malmgren – had he been eaten and, if so, by whom? And with
the air-lifting of Nobile by Lundborg – had the Italian General
deserted his men? And with the fate of Amundsen – would the
great Norwegian now be found?

Behounek ceased smiling when he realised how the world – and
particularly Italy – had turned against Nobile; people were
actually scared to defend him. So Behounek took care to go on
record that no one had any right to an opinion, even, unless he
had been present at the Red Tent: 'We – the only human beings
who had the right to pass judgement – had judged it right and
fair that Lundborg rescued him first, because his state of health
prevented him from fulfilling efficiently the responsible post of
our actual leader.' He took issue with the newspapers who compared Nobile with the captain of a sinking ship. A more valid
comparison, he thought, would be with Captain Robert Bartlett
of Stefansson's *Karluk* in 1914, who had left his ship to get help
for his crew – and had succeeded.

But he came down hard on Zappi, less severely on Mariano.
What they said about Malmgren's death was in character with the

Swedish scientist he knew; he could perfectly believe that he had
sacrificed himself for the two fitter men. Their acceptance of that
sacrifice was a different matter. Worse, had been Zappi's treatment of Mariano, his friend and comrade for 15 years. He must
have accepted both food and clothing from his stricken comrade
in order to carry on with that 'pointless march'. In Italy, the
Fascist papers were making a great thing of it, as the *Heroic
Mercy March*. Behounek thought that ordinary human kindness
had been driven out by primitive instinct under the extreme
conditions of the Polar wilderness.

Professor Samoilovich had the same view of Malmgren, and
compared his sacrifice to that of Captain Oates, during Scott's last
expedition, when the British team had been wiped out after
Amundsen had succeeded. He believed Zappi's story that Malmgren had died a month previously; and if so, there could be no
question of cannibalism, because the two men still had a good
deal of food with them. But to him, the hero had been Malmgren.

Nobile felt bitter towards Mariano and Zappi and remained
bitter to the end of his life. He thought they had deserted him –
and for nothing. All they had achieved, was the death of
Malmgren. If they had all remained at the tent, as he had wanted,
all would have been saved. As it was, they had wanted to take
Viglieri and Biagi with them, leaving two men with broken
legs behind to be looked after by Behounek and Trojani, neither
of whom was really fit. And, of course, they would not have been
able to use the radio – and so not one of them would ever have
been found. The crew of the *Italia* would have been wiped out
completely. As for their conduct on the march, they should have
stayed with Malmgren, because it must have been clear by then
that at the rate of two miles a day, they would be unable to reach
the mainland.

He thought he had misjudged Zappi. Under that surface charm
of manner one could now see a 'strong man, energetic and
resolute, but also a trifle selfish.' But at the moment, his
experiences had left him overstrung, and now in the *Città di
Milano* he was repeating to journalists eager to lap up any taste of
possible scandal, his bragging, exaggerated version of the macabre
agreements he had entered into with Mariano in the event that
the other officer died first. Nobile was quite sure that Zappi
was out to heighten the heroic side of his march across the
pack.

The unfortunate Mariano, who had bravely born the lengthy operation to remove his foot, now asked to see Nobile. He wanted the General to propose Zappi and himself for the military gold medal for valour, in recognition of their conduct during the breakout attempt. Although Nobile realised the severity of the ordeal they had endured, he had to refuse politely, on the grounds that it had not been a military achievement. In fact, of course, there had been no achievement. And medals are normally awarded for success, not failure.

A few days later, on 22 July, the *Città di Milano* left for Narvik to take the survivors on the final stage of their journey home. On 23 July, the *Krassin* also left for Norway, but for water, coal and repairs to her damage, which was more serious than at first thought. After that, she would return to search for the remains of the hull of the *Italia*, and other Soviet ships would help. But the delay turned out to be much longer than anyone thought.

The *Krassin* had hardly left Spitzbergen when she received yet another Arctic S.O.S. The German cruise-ship *Monte Cervantes*, carrying 1,500 passengers, had been holed by ice, had her fore-peak flooded, and was in urgent need of assistance with no other large ship anywhere within reach. The *Krassin* and her divers spent ten days giving assistance to keep the liner afloat and then escorted her to Norway. Each day's delay made more difficult a precise return to that drifting ice-floe where the *Italia* had struck and the hull had soared up again into the air.

It was on 23 July also that Mussolini complained of the international press coverage. 'We cannot but protest against the inhuman and anti-Italian wave which has been demonstrated against the protagonists of this unfortunate enterprise, the Nobile Polar Expedition,' the Duce was reported to have told his Cabinet that day. 'The men who set out on this undertaking,' he continued, 'knowing the risky character of their enterprise, have shown their courage and should, therefore, merit universal respect.'

In terms of public relations, Italia had suffered a stunning defeat. Her airship lost, her general apparently abandoning the survivors, the men themselves apparently abandoning a stricken comrade to the bears; a failed, pitiful group of Italians having to be rescued by Russians, Swedes, Finns, Danes, Dutchmen, Norwegians, Frenchmen. . . .

Almost simultaneously, at some level in the Fascist government, it must have been decided to cut all losses by disowning Nobile, finally and forever. He had many enemies, anyway. It should not be too difficult.

Chapter 18

DEATH COMETH SOON OR LATE

(1928–1978)

ISSUE No. 162 of the Communist Party newspaper *Pravda*, which appeared in Moscow on 14 July, carried a 'leader' article on the front page headed:

THE '*KRASSIN*'S' SUCCESS NOT JUST LUCK

'We do not wish to concern ourselves at this present time with the question as to whether the Italians should have sent an air expedition to the North Pole at all, since at that time the Italians had no polar base and no means of rendering assistance should their airship crash,' the article began. Nobile might have agreed – he had wanted to take two flying boats with him for that purpose. In the event, the writer went on, the main group of survivors was picked up by the Soviet ice-breaker *Krassin* and he had good reason to suppose that the search for Amundsen would meet with equal success. 'We can now speak without false modesty of the brilliant qualities and outstanding accomplishments of our sailors and airmen as well as those of our scientists and all who are engaged in research into Arctic conditions.' The foreigners, he said, had less to be proud of.

'It would be extremely harmful to the interests of science and the future of Polar exploration if we were to remain silent about the muddle, lack of planning and ill-concealed hostility displayed by the international organisation of relief for the Nobile expedition.' While admitting that great courage had been shown and much unselfish work done by foreign scientists and airmen, the rescues could have been carried out with less cost and sacrifice, 'had it not been for the criminal indifference of some European governments and the rivalries among some of the others.' In his next paragraph he made clear the identity of the chief 'criminal' government.

'From the very first our government used all the means in its power. It did not use the opportunity to make a "good thing" out of it, as did the English government in 1920 when it went to the help of the Soviet steamship *Malygin* in Norwegian waters and demanded 200,000 roubles. However, alone of all the maritime powers, England sent neither ship nor aircraft to help Nobile, since she has no aircraft suitable to Arctic conditions. Our scientists, our pilots, our sailors did not waste time talking about "humanitarianism", but quickly and carefully made their preparations for the long and dangerous journey to the Arctic ocean. Interest in scientific achievement, a high feeling of human solidarity, a sensitive response to heroism – all these features for which the working masses are noted, enabled the Soviet rescue expedition to carry out its difficult task speedily and successfully.'

The 'criminal' government was of course England, which in 1919 had sent a naval force to Archangel to support the Whites against the Reds. Norway, very anti-Red, was probably one of the 'rivals' and certainly Italy was. The Italian official history (*Storia Della Campagne oceaniche della Marina Militare*, Vol. IV, Chap. 10, Rome, 1960) claims most of the credit for the rescue for Italy, in that it was Italian airmen who located the Red Tent and were the first to drop supplies. This is true. More doubtful are the claims for the work of the *Città di Milano*, which in this version rank before that of the *Krassin*. These, of course, are claims made by the 'management' – respectively the Soviet Government and the Italian Navy.

At a lower level, that of direct involvement, was a report made by Captain Tornberg, leader of the Swedish air group, on his return home. 'The operations of all these groups were not co-ordinated under a joint management or command. However, the Norwegian and Swedish groups reported to the *Città di Milano* flights carried out and missions planned. From the *Città*, reports were received on Italian pilots' activities and the position of the Nobile group – but far from regularly. We often had to push for information. Between the Swedish and Norwegian groups and, later, between the Swedish and Russian groups, good mutual communication was maintained, so these groups were well informed about their respective activities and plans.' Tornberg would not have agreed with the writer of the *Pravda* leader regarding that wasteful muddle he had alleged.

'In my opinion it is questionable whether efficiency would have been improved a great deal by super-imposing a joint command: the objectives and the area of operations were well known; each group was informed of the others' intentions, and I am convinced that they were all used to best advantage in competition with each other. Besides, aircraft equipment of the various groups was so heterogeneous that it was hardly feasible to organise search formations or other joint operations.'

Tornberg's personal papers became available for study for the first time in March 1978, when they came into the hands of Lieutenant-Colonel Rolf Westerberg of *Svensk Flyghistorisk Förening*, the Swedish Aviation Historical Society. Westerberg, looking at 1928 documents from the standpoint of 1978, concluded that the most vital factors affecting co-ordination of the rescue efforts were seven in number:

(a) Weather conditions, with rapid changes in local visibility.
(b) Poor weather forecasting.
(c) Radio communications – poor equipment, over-loaded nets.
(d) Language difficulties.
(e) Interference from journalists and spectators.
(f) Distances of approach to search areas – as an average about 450 km from base.
(g) Logistic support more or less improvised, although Norwegians and Swedes seemed to have made the best preparations.

'There was no doubt,' he wrote (personal communication, 1978) 'a large influence of national prestige. The Italians were sensitive – the *Italia* venture was a flop. The Russians claimed know-how and were anxious to gain more of the Arctic region exploration, which perhaps can explain their tremendous effort.'

Equally important, in the political context of 1928, was the propaganda gain in terms of an impending world revolution to be led by the U.S.S.R. International admiration and sympathy could be important; but in turn the feeling that foreigners admired their government, might be of home use also. On page 2 of the 14 July edition of *Pravda*, both these objectives were aimed at in a general article on the rescues supported by an imposing round-up of praise from the European press. Not all the newspapers quoted were Communist, Socialist, or Liberal, but many of them were.

In Rome, in Paris, in London, in Berlin they all seemed agreed that the hero of the hour was Tchukhnovsky. Only in Stockholm did the Conservative *Aftonbladet* refer to Samoilovich, although not by name: 'The whole world must recognise the heroic feat which has been performed by the *Krassin*'s rescue party and its leader. Fate has given him the opportunity to accomplish his task and all honour must be paid to the energy and drive of those who took part in the expedition.' *Pravda*'s own correspondent in Berlin supplied what must have been the intended keynote: He reported: 'The Central Committee of the German Red Front-Line Troops asks the Soviet Union to convey to the gallant commander of the *Krassin* and to all Soviet workers the heart-felt congratulations of all the German Front-Line Troops on the rescue of the Malmgren group and the Viglieri group. Our Soviet comrades acted at a time when others were merely talking about it. This heroic exploit has heightened the sympathy of the whole world towards the Soviet Union.'

Almost immediately following the heartening paragraphs from Berlin was a Tass report from London headlined:

ENGLAND DID NOTHING TOWARDS THE RESCUE OF
THE NOBILE EXPEDITION

The news item below it read: 'Speaking in the House of Commons, a member of the Labour Party, Wedgwood, asked a question – bearing in mind the fact that the English government did not lend any support to the organisation dealing with the search for, and rescue of, the crew of the *Italia*, did this not cast aspersions on England? The Minister for Aviation, Hoare, answered that the English government had informed the Italian and Norwegian governments of its readiness to send an English aircraft. However, this offer was declined because of the unsuitability of the English aircraft for Arctic conditions.'

A popular English airwoman had condemned the British government for taking no interest in aviation. As an example, she had referred to the fact that England was almost alone in not sending help to the crew of the *Italia*.

The last item of all was a lengthy piece from Berlin headlined:

'BERLINER TAGEBLATT' CRITICISES NOBILE

In fact, it turned out to be the German newspaper quoting a *Pravda* special correspondent in Tromsoe. It stated that Nobile's report on the disaster, 'cleverly glossing over the most important points, has occasioned a great deal of surprise here.' In short, they did not accept his story of how the cabin broke off after the airship struck the ice. 'Even more inexplicable is the behaviour of the crew' (of the *Città di Milano*). 'As I learned from reliable sources, Nobile brought back with him a notebook in which had been recorded all the messages which had been received since the very first day of the disaster. His radio had not been out of action for one moment. The question arises: Was it possible that the *Città di Milano* did not receive these messages or did the Italians conceal the fact until the disaster was known about, thanks to their radio messages having been intercepted by amateurs?' One can see how the suspicion arose – if the amateurs far away could hear Nobile's radio, why could not the professionals in the Italian base ship which was so much nearer? But this was a question that all the survivors themselves had been asking, and with fury. The answer had much to do with Romagna, a little to do with atmospheric conditions in the Arctic, and nothing at all to do with Nobile. 'Yet another question arises,' went on the reporter. 'What induced Malmgren to walk out over the ice? Nobile gives no logical explanation of this point. It is not easy to understand why Malmgren went on foot and gave no notice of his intention by radio. One can only suppose there was a bad relationship between Malmgren and Nobile.' Nobile gave no logical explanation, simply because there was no logical explanation. Malmgren, Mariano and Zappi marched out because it was in their nature to act rather than to wait passively. It was this psychological background which made them believe that the radio was useless and that the messages would never be heard.

What was printed and re-printed were the baseless suspicions of ignorant men; and each one was formulated as a criticism of Nobile.

Italian officialdom read, noted, and did not see it in that light at all, for they had suspicions of their own regarding this wealth of strongly-slanted stories. Cesco Tomaselli was to write in 1961: 'When the *Italia* crashed and Nobile accepted Lundborg's invitation to board his rescue plane, he laid himself open to all the criticism which has lasted for several decades. His enemies, whom the Fascists saw as their own enemies, had driven him into doing what was labelled as a cowardly action. A similar dismal view was taken by the Italian government. It was felt that Nobile had been manipulated by Italy's enemies, and he was relieved of his command.' Trojani saw deeper roots: 'Nobile had always been unpopular with the Fascists because he was considered a left-winger and disloyal.' The government had already decided to disown him, but it proved at first not so easy as they had thought. On 26 July, the *Città di Milano* reached Narvik. 'Two railway carriages had been specially sent from Paris to meet us and take us right through to Italy,' wrote Nobile. 'A gangway from the ship allowed us to pass straight into the train. Our orders were – not to speak, not to stir, not to leave the carriages: a form of detention. It was only natural that the wildest legends should spring up in the minds of foreign journalists – amongst others, that of the "sealed railway carriages". All this was utterly sickening. . . . Then at Vindeln, the first Swedish station where the train stopped, a little fair-haired, blue-eyed girl came towards me, smiling sweetly, to offer me a bunch of flowers. It was like a ray of sunshine piercing the clouds in a sky still darkened by a hurricane that had swept it unawares. Shocked with emotion, I thanked her, stammering.'

There were similar sympathetic scenes through Sweden and also in Denmark. 'And then we crossed into Germany. In the north, where the campaign of slander had taken more grip, we met with a cold and distant reception. I bought a newspaper. A caricature showed our train with the carriage windows barred and the doors padlocked, with horrible allusions to the accusations of cannibalism. The German people had believed these things – still believe them, perhaps. I have a very vivid recollection of a great, hulking man who ran beside our train at Halle, gnashing his teeth. But in Bavaria, things changed, and once more there were demonstrations of affectionate sympathy.'

On and on across Europe rolled the train. In the early hours of 31 July, they crossed the Brenner; and late that night they were in Rome. No official receptions awaited them, but all the way tens of thousands of friendly, emotional people had thronged the railway stations to see the men of the *Italia* go by, and speak to them if they could. By now, the compartments were full of flowers handed up by well-wishers. When finally their carriages came to a halt in the Rome terminus, it was estimated that an enthusiastic, unofficial crowd of 200,000 had gathered in and around the station. Nobile, they said, at that moment looked like a ghost – a distant gaze in his eyes, as if he was staring out into the Beyond. If so, it was prophetic, for ahead of him was fifty years of a living death. There was little his enemies could do to him now – for the moment. The thing would have to be most carefully set-up and stage-managed, if the hero was to be toppled convincingly. But these are matters in which politicans are expert.

Some of the hatred at the top was genuine. Earlier in the month the Fascist, Denti di Piraino, had suggested to Mussolini that General Nobile be tried by courts martial aboard the *Città di Milano*, and shot. Balbo's newspaper, *Corriere Padano*, had published a report that Nobile had broken his leg when running across the ice to be first at Lundborg's Fokker. Others again, doubted that he had hurt himself at all and demanded that X-rays should be taken of Nobile's supposedly broken limbs. Nobile was well aware of Balbo's attitude, for while he was still in the *Città di Milano* he had been visited by Arturo Mercanti, the influential Milanese who had forced Balbo to agree to sending two flying boats, and Mercanti had shown him part of a letter he had received from Balbo. As Nobile recalled it, the key phrases had gone like this: 'The Royal Air Force is not responsible in any way for this expedition. On the contrary, I had foreseen the disaster. . . . This expedition in the false guise of a scientific undertaking constituted only Nobile's personal revenge. This does not alter the fact that everything possible will be done to save Nobile's unfortunate companions. . . .' The letter had been written about 3 or 4 June, but Balbo's sentence about rescue was purely for the record; he did not act upon it, and so presumably did not mean it. Balbo was not merely 'passing the buck'; he was probably actually glad that the tragedy had occurred, because it might be thought to prove his point that the future of long distance flying lay with the big flying boats such as the S.55s, for which he had the most grandiose plans.

The 'personal revenge' which Balbo alleged as Nobile's motive for launching the *Italia* expedition was a reference to Amundsen's libels against him. On 31 July, the day of Nobile's return to Rome, the Latham flying boat had been missing for six weeks, utterly without trace. The first definite news came a month later, on 31 August. On that day the sloop *Brodd* was off the rocky and barren Fuglöy islands, near Tromsoe, when the lookout reported a large floating object. It was riding high and looked like a barrel, or perhaps a buoy come adrift. When a boat was sent away to retrieve it, the object was found to be made of light metal, painted blue-grey and about seven feet long, but much battered. Its shape suggested a wing-tip float of the sort fitted to flying boats. The object was sent for examination by naval air force experts serving on the ship *Michael Sars*. There it was shown to one of the mechanics who had worked on the Latham at Bergen. He looked closely and found a tiny detail – a small copper repair plate, welded on to seal a tiny puncture. 'That's mine!' he said, in effect. 'I welded that on myself.' Looking at the condition of the float, the experts were agreed that it had been 'wrenched with great violence from the flying boat, probably at the moment it crashed into the water.'

Later a fuel tank, probably also from the Latham, was found floating. Certainly, Amundsen was dead, with all his companions. Their machine had hit the water, not the ice. Even in the area of the Gulf Stream current, where the wreckage was picked up, life for men in the sea would be a matter of hours at most. Amundsen's polar skills were of no avail here. And that completed the progression of the argument between the two men. Nobile and his Italians had indeed come down on the pack, but Amundsen did not live to see his prediction falsified. The Italians had done reasonably well as Polar survivors; the only casualty from Arctic conditions was the Swede, Finn Malmgren, who was also the only man among them who was a polar expert. As for Amundsen himself, he had been killed by an aeroplane, by a failure of the technology of which he had claimed to be an Arctic pioneer. But he had not died, as he had wished, once more in the ice regions which he loved and where he had made his name. He had gone to his grave in the sea. But it was in the course of a Arctic rescue attempt under the eyes of the world; no bad end for the old explorer, and a quick one, as he had desired. Or so it was thought at first.

During the official Norwegian investigation the second recovery from the sea – the petrol tank – also revealed signs of what at first glance looked like a repair. But the repair to the wingtip float had been a professional job carried out in a workshop. This was not. A hole in the fuel tank had been filled by a wooden plug rough-cut to fit with a pocket knife. The inference was obvious. The Latham had come down on the sea, either because of engine trouble or fog, and had lost a wingtip float in the process. The crew had tried to replace the lost float by an empty petrol tank. This was the Latham's lowest tank, the easiest to remove. And it was known that the Latham's co-pilot, de Cuverville, had reported favourably on a subordinate for getting out of a similar situation by exactly this ingenious method, when they had been serving in the Colonies. That piece of rough-hewn wood told a lot about the last hours of Amundsen, but not whether the Latham had crashed on take-off or been overwhelmed by rough seas before repairs had been completed. By a bitter coincidence, Maddalena in his S-55 had been forced down on the sea on the same day and in the same area, but had repaired his engine and got away again. And it was his departure which had spurred Amundsen to leave at once, forgetting Nilsson's offer to accompany the Latham to Spitzbergen with the tri-motor *Upland*. Not Nobile, but Amundsen's own character had caused his death.

Another missing airman, Babuskin, forced down by fog on 11 July, had eventually managed to fly back to the ice-breaker *Malygin*; he had simply waited on the ice until the skies had cleared. The only major mystery remaining was the central one – the fate of the *Italia* with the six men it had contained. The *Krassin*'s damage proved worse than anticipated and she had to go south to Stavenger for repairs. But in September the Soviet sent her back to the Arctic to co-operate with the ships still searching the disintegrating pack-ice. The principal ones were the Italian-chartered whaler *Braganza*, carrying the airmen Penzo and Crosio, with their two small flying boats; two ships working for the French, the *Veslekari* and the *Heimland*; the sealers *Viking* and *Hobby*. They were spread out covering a very wide area as far east as Franz Josef Land. The *Città di Milano* returned to King's Bay as liaison and communications ship and stayed there until 15 September. By 19 September the *Krassin* was as far east as Giles Land, shown here on nautical charts since 1707 and removed from them a few months earlier by one of General Nobile's flights with the *Italia*. The *Krassin* was able to confirm that Giles had been mistaken; they found 380 metres of water over the site. But after this the temperature fell and ice conditions became so bad that they threatened to imprison the *Krassin* for the whole of the long Arctic winter. Although ordered to continue until 30 September, the ice-breaker's captain decided on 24 September to abandon the search and make for open sea as quickly as possible. No sign had been seen of the airship, not even any tracks of men having walked across the ice.

From the airship, the dead or missing numbered seven Italians and one Swede; from the Latham flying boat, two Norwegians and four Frenchmen. Fourteen in all. Then, on their return flight Major Penzo crashed in France and was killed together with two other members of his Italian crew, Tullio Crosio and Giuseppe della Gatta. Oscar Wisting had been lucky; there had been no room for him aboard the Latham. So it was Dietrichson's blonde widow who wept.

More than a year later, on 9 July 1930, Captain Theodor Grödahl of Tromsoe went ashore from his ship at White Island with two companions. This place, eastward of Broch and Foyn Islands, has also been called Giles Land or Gillis Land; but unlike the non-existent, larger land similarly named to the north-east, there really is land there under the covering of ice and snow. At this time of the year, much of the low-lying shoreline was clear of ice although there were patches of snow about. Captain Grödahl was looking for the hull of the *Italia*, for the remains of the keel, the nose-cone, the gasbags and the fuel cells. Had they come down on the melting pack, they could conceivably be at the bottom of the sea, but here was firm land. Looking for traces of human occupation, Grödahl found them. There were piles of brushwood lying unnaturally, as if heaped up deliberately. Then, 150 yards from the shore, he found the remnants of a rusted sheet-iron box and a hand-made wooden peg. And that was all, although he sent out a second search party that night.

In August, 1930, a month afterwards, Dr. Adolf Hoel came to White Island with a combined scientific and commercial expedition on its way to the Franz Josef Islands. The scientists went ashore to make geological investigations and then returned to the ship; but walrus were sighted and the commercial hunters went off after them. Two of the hunters got very hot with the exertion and went looking for a drink of freshwater. They found a brook, then wandered a few yards beyond. They were both youngsters, Olav Salen being 17 and Karl Tusvik being 24; and possibly they were a good deal more alert than the scientists and certainly, unlike them, free to look around generally instead of scientifically. They found the lid of an aluminium pot by the brook. Searching further, they saw a dark shape sticking out of a snowdrift. It was a canvas boat. They called urgently for the other walrus-hunters and an intensive search was begun. The next major discovery was made just beyond the boat. There they found a 'human body which lay leaning against the slightly sloping wall of rock.' Captain Peder Eliassen directed their search and they soon identified the site without doubt. A number of the artefacts they uncovered were labelled:

Andrée's Polar Expedition 1896

So perfect was the preservation that the log of the three-man crew was found also as well as exposed film which, when developed, produced printable negatives.

The log of their balloon, the *Örnen* (*Eagle*), showed that in Andrée's 1897 attempt to be first at the North Pole, he had drifted across what was to be the southward track of the *Italia* returning from the Pole; and that his balloon had come down well to the north-east of where the *Italia* was to crash. The three-man crew had been unhurt and had sledged and hunted their way south across the drifting pack ice and forced to winter at White Island. They had not died of hunger, so many people assumed they had died of cold; Stefansson thought the fumes from their stove, inside their hut, had sent them to sleep forever. But a Danish doctor, E. A. Tryde, was able to identify *trichinosis* – a disease caused by eating bear meat which has not been properly boiled.

Other human remains and artefacts were found in the Arctic during 1930 and 1931, but these items were all associated with wooden sailing ships. Most were definitely identifiable as coming from survivors of the Franklin expedition of 1845, some of whom seemed to have lasted as long as 1849. There appeared to have been a few cases of cannibalism of the normal type; that is, eating the dead, not actually killing to eat, although in at least one case the weaker men had ganged up against the man who was eating frozen human flesh and murdered him. A number of skulls had neat shot-holes in them. The British raged against the accusations of cannibalism because they believed they were above that sort of thing. To make it worse, the accusers were often Americans, none of whom were gentlemen.

But of the *Italia*, nothing was ever found. To the time of writing, which is December, 1978 – half a century later – there has been no trace. The fate of Alessandrini and his companions is still one of the great unsolved mysteries of the Arctic.

Early in August, 1928, shortly after the return of the survivors to Rome, Mussolini asked Nobile to call on him at his official residence. He was affability itself, asking various questions about the expedition. But when he rose to indicate that the interview was at an end, Nobile stood his ground. He had come prepared with documentation of the slanders which Balbo and others had made against him publicly. He grew so indignant as he recited them, that he raised his voice, forgetting that it was some years since anyone had spoken to Il Duce like that. Mussolini went pale, walked over to the table, sat down, took a sip of water from a glass, and pressed a button. Nobile thought the glass held a medicine of some sort, which it probably did, because Mussolini suffered painfully from ulcers. An usher appeared, in answer to the buzz. 'Show the General out,' said Mussolini. And that was that, for the moment.

A few days later, Viglieri came to warn him that he ought to pay a formal visit to Balbo. Nobile assumed that this was well-meant and based on good, private information; but he did not call on Balbo. Indeed, he never saw either Mussolini or Balbo again.

In September, General Crocco, chief of the Aeronautical Engineers, sent for Nobile and told him that he had been recalled to the Service (during the expedition he had been on loan to the Geographical Society). As a consequence, he must not move about, speak, write, or go to the theatre! Then Nobile found his office at the airship factory sealed up. And finally, he discovered that he was being watched and shadowed by two men, probably from the OVRA, the not-so-secret police of Italy.

The more deadly work, however, lay in setting up a commission of enquiry into the disaster, of packing it with some of Nobile's most bitter enemies; of pretending it was to consider matters like the death of Malmgren; and of continually leaking 'information' to Nobile that the findings of the enquiry were likely to be favourable to him. He was to be kept off guard until it was too late to speak out and defend himself. On 4 March 1929, therefore, when the findings were published in the newspapers, Nobile was shocked to find himself branded guilty without chance of reply. He was held resposible for a manoeuvring error which was said to be the cause of the crash and that his departure with Lundborg could be explained but not justified by his physical and mental condition. All this was suddenly in the newspapers, as an accomplished fact. Nobile felt so bitterly shamed and angry that he acted without due thought and resigned his rank and position as if it could be a slap in the face to Balbo and his enemies, rather than exactly what they wanted. The resignations were accepted with alacrity.

On the other hand, this set Nobile free to write two books about the expedition, the general history and the results of the scientific work. Some censorship was exercised by the Fascists and naturally no mention could be made of the current political intrigues against him. The general history, *L'Italia al Polo Nord*, was published in January, 1930. Behounek, Lundborg and Samoilovich also published books at this time, basically favourable to Nobile, Behounek's particularly so. But, of course, they were in foreign editions and in foreign languages.

What had been published in 1929 was merely a summary of the findings; the full report of the Commission of Enquiry, before which Nobile had not been allowed to appear, was not published until 30 January, 1930 – and then it was widely distributed as a booklet and headlined in the Italian press as if it was red hot world news. This was the final act in the careful manoeuvres to utterly discredit Nobile and thereby distance the regime from his failure. As an accident report it lacked standing: firstly because it concerned airship flying in the Arctic, of which Nobile had logged 243 hours, which was precisely 243 hours more than anyone on the Commission; and secondly, because the hull of the *Italia* had not been found, let alone examined by competent experts. In the circumstances, it was not possible to be certain about the cause of the crash; even Nobile himself could not be sure. And that is the situation still. The airship was brought down by a serious and sudden loss of lift, and that is all that is known.

The report was issued, and heralded by a world-wide release from the Stefani Agency in Rome, to coincide with the date of a lecture Nobile was due to give concerning the *Italia*'s achievements to the Swedish Geographical Society in Stockholm. The Swedes applauded and then, very pointedly, awarded to Nobile the Andrée gold medal, given only four or five times before to persons of distinction in polar exploration. A Swedish publication, *Nya dagligt allehanda*, commented on 18 February:

'Nobile has been here in Stockholm, and has been – not condemned (that is neither our right nor our duty) but – judged, and our judgement was to the effect that he had made a grand attempt, and that, if it had failed, this was nothing worse than what had happened to our own Andrée in 1897. . . . Nobody in Sweden, however, has ever said one word against Andrée on account of his ill-luck. The worst that has been said about him is that he was "an optimist", but this is not usually considered a reproach. . . . And so Nobile became Italy's Andrée. Upon his departure he was as great a hero as our own aeronaut. Now, in the age of Fascism, all Italy is attuned to great achievements, the more fantastic, the better. And then the enterprise failed. Such a thing is never pardoned – except that we pardoned Andrée. If Nobile too had died, he would probably have become one of Italy's saints. . . . The main point is, that Italy's haughty ambition to set up scientific North Pole records was frustrated; and whoever fails to live up to great expectations is condemned. The only man who seems to have avoided this fate is Andrée.'

In neighbouring Norway a pertinent comment came from consul Saether of Tromsoe, who had been involved in some of the rescue organisation: 'I find it a terribly unjust sentence. 95% of his flights were successful. If we other mortals were to be judged on the basis of 5% ill-luck, not many of us would remain uncondemned.'

The campaign against Nobile was not finished, however. It was necessary to exclude him from public life and stifle any possible publicity which might remind his countrymen of either the *Norge* or the *Italia*. Consequently, when Nobile was invited by the French Air Ministry to assist at the unveiling of a monument at Caudebec-en-Caux to the men who had died in the Latham, the Italian Air Attaché said that he would stay away if Nobile took part in the ceremony. Nobile had to promise the French that he would not. Instead, he turned up merely as a spectator and, of course, was recognised and given a great welcome by the French.

This was in June, 1931. On his way back Nobile went to Berlin because there was a possibility that he would be invited by Dr. Hugo Eckener to take part in a programme of scientific research to be carried out in the Arctic by the *Graf Zeppelin*. There, he discovered that the Italian embassy were putting pressure on Eckener to prevent his participation. Nobile's German friends told him of this and his Russian friends found an answer. It took the form of a telegram from Professor Samoilovich inviting Nobile to leave for Russia at once to join the ice-breaker *Malygin* which was to take part in the same scientific programme that summer as the German airship.

The *Graf Zeppelin*, named after the inventor, first flew in September, 1928. She was 776·25 feet long (236·6 m.) and had a range of 7,456 miles (12,000 kilometres) on four of her five 580 h.p. Maybachs. Her top speed was 79·5 m.p.h. (128 km/hr), while her cruising speed of 68 m.p.h. (110 km/hr) was nearly as fast as the top speed of the *Italia*. Her useful load of over 160,000 lbs. compared to the *Italia*'s restricted capacity of less than 20,000 lbs. She was a huge ship of the type, not better than the *Italia*, but in a different and very much more expensive and powerful class; because of her great range and carrying capacity, she was far more suitable for scientific exploration. Count Zeppelin had dreamed of making an Arctic flight in one of his airships before the Great War – that idea was not an Amundsen patent – and it was coming true. With such costly ships, finance was the main problem. The first practical scheme was to have been funded by Randolph Hearst as a newspaper stunt, *Graf Zeppelin* to rendezvous at the North Pole with Sir Hubert Wilkins (now knighted) who would go there in an American submarine. The submarine got as far north as Virgo Bay, but with so many machinery faults that Wilkins had to give up. Then German finance became available. So instead the rendezvous was with the Soviet *Malygin* off Franz Josef Land on 27 July 1931. Among those present were Samoilovich, Lincoln Ellsworth, Umberto Nobile and the young Arthur Koestler, then a science correspondent. The *Graf Zeppelin* actually landed on the water, the feat Nobile had wanted to achieve with the *Italia*, and the survey work carried out during her single flight of 71 hours, it was estimated, would have taken a traditionally-equipped expedition two years. But she did not detour to the Pole, because the insurance companies were against it, and this became her sole Arctic flight. It was to rank as a landmark in her long career, but far less had been achieved with a ship of far superior performance than had been done by Nobile in his small and cheap semi-rigids.

In return for this grandstand seat, the Russians had asked Nobile to remain in the Soviet Union for a month or so in order to advise them on airship construction. Then, while Nobile was still in Moscow, they asked if he would be prepared to settle down in Russia on a four-year contract (later extended to five years) in order to initiate and direct a programme of airship construction. His contacts had to obtain approval from Stalin personally and Nobile had to do the same with Mussolini. Stalin approved and Mussolini was probably glad to have Nobile out of the country. The reasons for Stalin's approval are fairly clear.

Germany led the world in the big rigid airships, but Italy was supreme with the more utilitarian semi-rigids. From the end of the Great War until 1927 she had exported these ships to major powers. Four were sold to Spain, two to the U.S.A., two to the Argentine, one to Holland, one to Japan. All had been built by the Stabilimento di Construzione Aeronautiche, the group of which Nobile was the most brilliant engineer. The Soviet intended to use these small practical airships in opening up large tracts of Siberia by carrying perishable freight, medical supplies, instruments, etc., and for survey and photography. Other Italians, including Trojani, joined Nobile, who was to write: 'This long stay in Moscow constitutes one of the happiest periods of the later twenty years of my much-tormented life.' He was happy, principally because he was working at the creation of airships; he is believed to have built nine in all for the U.S.S.R. And he was among sympathetic friends, one of whom was Professor Samoilovich.

Then, in 1932, came the assassination of Kirov. This was followed by the first of Stalin's purges. People simply disappeared and no one knew what happened to them. A number of people concerned with the *Krassin*'s rescue mission vanished from sight around this time. Nobile was followed. Then one day Nobile's private secretary, a Russian, was taken away to prison and never heard of again. In 1937, shortly after Nobile had left Moscow, Professor R. L. Samoilovich, Director of the Arctic Institute, was declared 'an enemy of the people'. A purge of geology in the Institute had begun, starting with the killing of its director. The professor's wife fled to America but returned later when her dead husband was rehabilitated.

Nobile's wife had died in 1934 and his daughter Maria had been constantly imploring him to return home; at Christmas, 1936, it was all too much for him and he went back to Italy, exchanging the GPU for the OVRA. Gianni Caproni, the aircraft designer, tried to help Nobile by offering him a suitable post, but Balbo was able to hinder this. As Air Minister, he had already scotched Italy's airship development. Ships in process of construction, which might have been sold off to the Japanese or the Russians, were simply destroyed and their remains sold as scrap metal. Balbo was making quite sure that his massed formations of flying boats would have the world's headlines to themselves.

In 1927 and 1928 the British R.A.F.'s Far East Flight of four

Supermarine Southamptons had leisurely flown 27,000 miles in
14 months; and without trouble, almost without incident. This
was acclaimed as a tremedously significant feat of aviation. Balbo
approved of the general idea. He thought that the era of dramatic
flights by single aircraft piloted by heroes was over; people were
getting bored with it, even when the heroes fell into the sea, as
they often did. What was required was evidence of reliability;
of a standard performance rather than an exceptional, or exceptionally lucky, feat of derring-do. So he planned to up-stage the
British by mounting impressive long-distance flights by really
large formations. This was much more difficult to do than may
appear. The most obvious place for the first attempt was the route
to South America pioneered by the *Graf Zepplin*, because it was
semi-commercial in competition with surface transport which
took two weeks.

Balbo intensively trained the crews of fourteen S.55 flying
boats and personally led them off from Orbetello on the
Tyrrhenian Sea on 17 December, 1930, towards their first stop at
Baloma on the coast of North Africa. They were to cover 6,450
miles in all to Rio de Janiero. Having refuelled, they took off for
the crossing of the South Atlantic. In flights of threes, heavily
laden with petrol, the big machines went surging away across the
waves. The first flight was led by Balbo – they had black identifica-
tion markings on their wings. After him came the second flight –
they had green markings. The third flight of threes had red
markings. All the flying boats being so heavily laden, took a
long time to get airborne, their take-off runs seeming to go on
for ever. But at length the third flight began to lift off one by
one. As they were skimming the wave-tops one machine lost
flying speed and stalled back into the sea. There was a spurt of
spray, which slowly subsided around the crumpled, floating
wreckage. Three of the four-man crew escaped, the mechanic
drowned.

The next flight roared ahead for the take-off, surging across the
water – they had white-marked wings. Twin engines blaring, the
big flying boats went bouncing over the wave-tops; at last unstick-
ing, they flew low while picking up airspeed, then climbed away
for South America. Number two of this formation may have had
an engine cut out at this critical point – airborne and climbing,
nose up. Half her power gone, the machine's nose dropped and
it dived at speed into the water. There was a ball of flame and

gouts of smoke, extinguished almost at once as the sea closed over the wreckage and the four men hopelessly trapped inside it.

Twelve got off, two crashed, five men died. Balbo ordered two reserve machines to take the place of the fallen. Seven Italian warships had been strung out over the South Atlantic to form a rescue chain, if need be. They were needed. Both the reserve machines suffered engine trouble and had to come down on the sea, one sank after colliding with a rescue ship; but no more lives were lost. Balbo led a squadron of twelve Italian flying boats in formation into Rio de Janiero on 15 January 1931. The main ocean crossing had taken just over 17 hours. It was the staging which had consumed the time. The flight was regarded as a great success, which it was. And if there is success, with world acclaim, the dead don't matter.

Balbo was careful to give credit to the Duce, describing a message from Mussolini as 'like a lightning flash rending the dark clouds of the future', adding, 'his words confirmed me in my determination and marked out the goal for which I aimed!' In Fascist Italy, this homage was obligatory, more or less. His real debt, he acknowledged, was to 'the traditional policy of old England of scattering her naval squadrons over all the waters of the globe with instructions to unfurl the proud flag of the country wheresoever the sea provided them with an opening or a landing'. Mussolini would not object to that. Like Balbo, Il Duce had a rather naive admiration for certain aspects of England's past; as he saw it. Of the current leaders, he was to say: 'These men are not made of the same stuff as the Francis Drakes and the other magnificent adventurers who created the British Empire. They are the tired sons of a long line of rich forefathers and they will lose their Empire.' Mussolini and Balbo were image-builders, firstly for themselves, secondly for Italy. In their eyes, Nobile had tarnished Italy's image and threatened to rival Balbo's. In a sense, Nobile had been trying to design and construct airships in a theatre.

For his next drama, Balbo chose the grey North Atlantic, grave of so many lone heroes, culminating in a triumphant entry onto the internationally floodlit stage of the Chicago World Fair, which had as its motto 'A CENTURY OF PROGRESS'. If two-dozen twin-engine flying boats, having just flown over both the Alps and the Atlantic from Italy, were to arrive over Chicago in mass formation on the right day, this must have an immense impact in terms of public and technical publicity; particularly if they then flew back in formation to make a double-crossing of the killer ocean.

In 1933, he did just this, using the latest type of S-55 with more powerful engines giving a top speed of 180 m.p.h. and a cruising speed of 140 m.p.h., far in excess of the speediest airship. The outward route totalled 6,065 miles which they covered in some 48 flying hours; but this time was spread out over more than two weeks while they waited for good weather at this stage or that. The return took more than three weeks, for the same reasons. Balbo was being very cautious, with so much at stake; possibly the example of the *Italia* was in his mind. Nevertheless, he lost two machines and two men, not counting Maddalena (newly promoted Colonel) who was killed during the training period in 1931, a month after the death of Captain Lundborg in another flying accident.

The total of Balbo's losses on all four of his Atlantic flights was therefore five big flying boats and the lives of seven airmen. These four flights were acclaimed in Italy, and by the world, as outstanding feats of pioneer aviation. Yet Nobile was condemned outright, with a very similar record, for he had carried out four Arctic flights with two airships and had lost one airship and eight men. In fact, it was a better record, because Balbo would have lost two more machines complete with their crews had they not been picked up by Italian rescue ships stationed at intervals along his routes. And, of course, it was Balbo who had forbidden the use of support and rescue aircraft by the *Italia* expedition.

Partly, it was because Nobile was out of favour with the regime to start with, that he was blamed; and partly because his accident had resulted in an embarrassingly large international search and rescue operation, which reflected on the capacity of the Italian government. But also it was because of the vehicle he was using. The drawback to airships was that too many eggs were in the one huge basket. When an airship went down, the disaster was likely to be appallingly total, with immense repercussions bordering on panic.

Even so, Nobile was most unfairly singled out for blame when in context his accident was just another in a pattern of risk and resulting tragedy. The years 1930 to 1937 saw no less than four of the big rigid ships destroyed. First Britain, then America, and finally even Germany gave up. Britain's last two rigids were R.*100* and R.*101*, both of them bound to be commercial failures in terms of lift, but useful for Empire prestige purposes. Even after modification, their percentages of useful to total lift were, respectively, only 36 and 35. They were bound to lose money, because 45 was required. The *Akron*, a German-designed American ship, achieved this; *Graf Zeppelin* comfortably beat it at 47. In 1930, R.*101* was sent off on an immensely long flight to India after insufficient tests, with a tired crew under constant political pressure; she flew no more than a few hundred miles, to a hillside near Beauvais in France, where she killed by fire 48 out of the 54 men aboard. It was a ghastly failure, insufficiently camouflaged by the whitewash of the usual official enquiry, according to a number of experts. That was the end of the British airship programme.

The U.S. Navy had two big German-designed ships, the *Akron* and the *Macon*; they were intended for scouting purposes in war. In 1933 the *Akron* was forced down into the sea by storm with the loss of 74 men out of 77; in 1935 the *Macon* also crashed in a storm, after suffering structural failure, only two men being lost out of 83. It was thought that the real cause in both cases was human carelessness; e.g., previously weakened parts not having been replaced. But after that, America built no more of the large rigids. However, she continued to operate much smaller non-rigid ships filled with non-inflammable helium gas instead of hydrogen; and does so to this day.

In 1937 the German *Hindenburg* crashed in flames while mooring in America; 35 out of 97 people were killed, plus one person on the ground. The Germans had made a commercial success out of running long-distance airships in competition with ocean liners and although they could not obtain helium and had to use the inflammable hydrogen, had until now successfully overcome the fire risk. This disaster, which was filmed by newsreel cameraman and decribed 'live' on sound radio, effectively killed the German airship programme. In any event, Herman Göring, the new German Air Minister, like Balbo, believed in the aeroplane.

Balbo had killed the Italian airship programme, both rigid and semi-rigid, in favour of his successful flying boats; but only in Italy. Russia continued her programme of building semi-rigid airships, based on Nobile's *Italia* design and intended for use as freighters rather than passenger-carriers; and still does so. But,

except for limited uses along the coasts of the U.S.A. or over the
vast wastes of Siberia, the airship was finished; rapidly, it was
being overtaken by the aeroplane. Nobile had been right in the
short term; but Balbo had read the future correctly.

In Italy, the programme against Nobile had been believed by
too many people. He had become a partial outcast, scorned,
hated even. And he was forbidden to publish any reply, or to
state his own views. While publicly abused, his desire to hit back
was stifled by the State. A not-uncommon predicament of the
twentieth century, where government possesses hitherto unheard of means for both spreading its own word and suppressing
that of others. When, in 1939, Nobile received an offer from
Cardinal Mandelein of a modest post at the Lewis Holy Name
School of Aeronautics in Chicago, he accepted with alacrity,
intending never to return, hoping that his daughter Maria would
be able to join him when she had completed her studies. In June
he left for America. Once in the United States, he had to be careful not to be trapped by journalists into making openly anti-Fascist
statements which might be interpreted in Italy as being anti-
Italian. This predicament is not exclusively twentieth century,
but is certainly very common. Further, his daughter and other
relatives were still living in Italy, and might suffer for any words a
newspaper man might care to put into his mouth.

Almost a year later, on 29 May 1940, there was a gear-shift
which changed history and was to alter the future completely for
Umberto Nobile. On that day, Mussolini received news that the
Belgian Army had surrendered. Holland, Denmark and Norway
had already gone (Riiser-Larsen escaped and was shortly to be
appointed Naval Attaché for Free Norway in Washington). Il
Duce called for his Air Force Marshal, Italo Balbo, and his Army
chief-of-staff, Marshal Pietro Badoglio, and told them that he was
declaring war on the Allies next week. Badoglio protested and
Balbo looked shaken. France was clearly doomed and numberless
people, friends, neutrals and enemies alike, had written off the
British. Even so, these two men knew the real state of Italy's
armed forces and were aware that she was not ready for a serious
war. Mussolini imperiously quelled their doubts. 'I can tell you
that everything will be over by September and that I only need a
few thousand dead so that I can sit at the peace conference as a
man who has fought.' Next day, both Marshals were trying to
arrange for that to happen, so far as it lay within their power. Of

the three men present at that meeting, one only survived Mussolini's decision – Badoglio.

Sensing a political competitor, Mussolini removed Balbo from
the central stage of war-direction by sending the Air Marshal to
Africa as Governor of Libya, where he died, his aircraft shot down
by Italian guns – in error, it was said. In England, he was remembered for his friendly visits during the Schneider Trophy
seaplane races over the Solent and with admiration for the
exploits of his massed armadas over the Atlantic. In 1940, when
technically he was an enemy, the R.A.F. incorporated him in
their slang – the current term for a big formation was 'a Balbo'.

Nobile's fate was harsher and long drawn-out. In wartime, the
call of his own country became stronger. It became irresistible
only when Italy began to experience serious setbacks. In 1942, he
returned to offer his services but even in defeat the regime would
not have him. So Nobile went to neutral Spain where he remained
until the downfall of Mussolini in July, 1943. After the war his
name was cleared, he was given back his rank and allowed to
publish his side of the story. But to publish is not necessarily to
convince. The previous regime had spent time and money
appropriating Nobile's achievements with the *Norge* for themselves, by making him an honorary Fascist hero; and then shown
equal care in disowning and denigrating him when the *Italia*
crashed on the last lap of her third Arctic flight, and he was the
first to be saved. How many times since then must he have
wished that he had dug his heels in and refused to alter his
previously-decided order of departure beyond what was now
plain, that Cecioni and Behounek were too heavy for the first
flight? Perhaps it should have been Trojani, who was a small man
and suffering from a fever? And if it had been, would it have
altered the future?

In Italy it had not been plain that the initiative had lain with
the Swedish pilot and that he had been determined to take Nobile
first, because those were his orders. Lundborg's book was not
published in Italy, although he repeated the story to any who
questioned him. One of these was Stefansson, who summarised
what the Swede told him personally: Lundborg had 'found
Nobile demanding, in the best "grand opera" tradition, that all
the others should be saved first and he himself be removed last.
Lundborg replied that this was no grand opera, that he was in
command, and that the rescue would be conducted as seemed

best to him and his associates.' Nobile had not been in a strong position to stand up to that, even had Lundborg's arguments been weak. They were not: all logic and reason was on his side. This was what had finally overwhelmed Nobile. A cruder, less intellectual man might have resisted more stubbornly over what must have seemed at the time a trifling matter of precedent, for they had all assumed that the Swedish plane would be able to make repeated flights and evacuate everyone the same day. And so he had to suffer fifty years of ostracism, patiently, knowing he had been right, and seeking always to prove it in books and articles.

Just conceivably, something of the sort might have happened to Amundsen, had he been unable to obtain support from the French government for his rescue flight. He had neither the money nor the influence in Norway to persuade his own government to back him – but would the Norwegian public have accepted that as the plain truth? Arnesen had thought not. If, for whatever reason, Amundsen had been unable to fly north, then 'the trend of popular gossip' would have been: 'Oh-ho, he is funking it – that is not like him!' Although it cost him his life, Amundsen was probably lucky to have been given the Latham at the last. The fate of Nobile, who survived, was much harder; and the qualities required to endure it, very great. Truly, as he said, his life had been 'much-tormented'.

The approaching 50th anniversary of the *Italia* disaster had nothing to do with my choice in 1977 of this theme. It was the story I liked – conflict between men of brilliant talents and powerful personalities. That I had some points of contact did count. I had visited Italy in 1926, the year of the *Norge*. I had seen the most famous airship of them all, *Graf Zeppelin*, passing low and by night over our home at Southsea. I had learnt to fly myself in the early 1930s on Cirrus and Gipsy Moths, going solo for the first time when I was a 15-year-old schoolboy. All those years after, I could still recall the thrilling atmosphere of open cockpits, few instruments, and grass aerodromes, which was aviation in Nobile's time.

1978 turned out to be the last year in which one could make direct contact with the people involved. Rolf S. Tandberg, who had made those ski and sledge journeys over the ice of North-East Land, was admitted to hospital just as we began corresponding and he had sent me his booklet on the subject: *The 'Italia' Disaster: Fact and Fantasy*. He died later in the year. In the spring, I was able to meet Umberto Nobile in Rome. The General was then 93, and his second wife, Signora Gertrud Nobile, had warned me that a thirty minute talk would be about the limit. In fact, the General was able to give my wife and I twice that time, before tiring.

The period was that of the Aldo Moro kidnapping and the machine-gunning, in daylight, of all his bodyguards. But, entering the General's room, one went back fifty years. The walls were hung with airship photographs and mementoes of the *Norge* and the *Italia*. Nobile was still living those days, which helped the interview, conducted in English and German. There was a particular reason for this. With the 50th anniversary of the disaster about to be celebrated, Nobile was a celebrity once more. My wife and I were just two of many interviewers. A special commemorative stamp of the *Italia* expedition, a special air mail envelope, and a commemmorative postcard were on sale; a number of official ceremonies were soon to take place, honouring Nobile, the men of the *Italia*, and their rescuers. A full fifty years afterwards, the General had been fully rehabilitated.

Of course, I came not merely to ask questions but to see what kind of a man Nobile was and what he might have been like fifty years before. His intellect was still formidably sharp and he still possessed a considerable personality; perhaps he had been as much a prima donna in his time as Balbo. Unwillingly, I was forced to ask questions about Amundsen and the various criticisms he had made. I had to put them to Nobile, because Nobile was alive and Amundsen was not. Quite a number he dismissed angrily as 'Amundsen's lies'; and I believed him. The General clearly bore some resentment still against Malmgren, Mariano and Zappi, for in effect deserting the others; he emphasised that their march had achieved nothing whatever. He made only one boast – that his powers of going without rest or sleep had been unusual. This was a necessary qualification for all long-distance flying at that time; the sheer physical endurance required by these flights was phenomenal, and is often not fully appreciated. A deeper insight into character lay in Nobile's explanation of why his broken arm did not heal properly. He had carried on writing with it, while lying in the Red Tent, so that it was unable to knit; instead a kind of hard tissue formed between the broken ends of the bones. The kind of worrying willpower required to do this must be rare.

On the anniversary of the *Italia*'s reaching the North Pole – on 24 May 1978 – the Italian Air Force held their commemorative ceremony at the Museum of Military Aeronautics at Vigna di Valle by Lake Bracciano. Representatives of the countries which had helped in the rescue also attended: France, Norway, Sweden, Denmark, Holland, Russia. Nobile did not want to attend, so bad was his physical condition now, so that he almost had to be propelled there by force in his wheelchair. 'Still,' wrote Signora Nobile, 'it was a great day of satisfaction for him and he was thankful to live it'.

Two months later, on 19 July, he died, aged 93. The obituaries gave him his proper status as 'the Italian airship designer who had a spectacular career in polar exploration'; others added that he was 'the first person to fly over the North Pole'.

The week after, the anniversary of the abandonment of all hope of finding Amundsen was recalled, as that of a 'gifted pioneer who challenged the unknown with all the intrepidity of the old Vikings'.

In January of the same year the shade of yet another pioneer explorer long dead had been evoked by the maiden voyage of a 1,119–ton oceanographic vessel belonging to the Arctic & Antarctic Research Institute, Leningrad. She was named the *Rudolf Samoilovich*, after the disgraced professor of geology and former 'enemy of the people'.

SELECT BIBLIOGRAPHY

including the principal works by witnesses

AMUNDSEN, ROALD:
My Life as an Explorer (Heinemann, London, 1927); with
LINCOLN ELLSWORTH, JOH. HOVER, HJ. RIISER-LARSEN,
GUSTAV AMUNDSEN, FINN MALMGREN, B. L. GOTTWALD: The
First Flight Across the Polar Sea (Hutchinson, London).

ARNESEN, ODD:
The Polar Adventure (Gollancz, London, 1929).

BALBO, ITALO:
My Air Armada (Hurst & Blackett, London, 1934).

BEHOUNEK, FRANTISEK:
Sieben Wochen auf der Eisscholle (Brockhaus, Leipzig, 1929).

BIAGI, GIUSEPPE:
Biagi racconta . . . I miracoli della radio nella tragedia polare
(Mondadori, Milan, 1929).

CHRISTELL, EINAR:
Kring Murchison Bay för 30 år sedan ('Orlogsposten', No. 4,
1958).

DITHMER, ELISABETH:
The Truth About Nobile (Williams & Norgate, London, 1933).

DONGEN, SJEF VAN:
Vijf jaar in ijs en sneeuw (Scheltens & Giltay, Amsterdam).

FINNISH AVIATION YEAR BOOK 1928 (SUOMEN ILMAILU):
Article: Suomalaisten Huippuvuorten-Lento Kesållä 1928.

FLYGHISTORISKT MANADSBLAD Nr. 5–6 Maj-Juni 1978 (Swedish
Aviation Historical Society, Stockholm): Complete Anniversary
issue).

GIUDICI, DAVIDE:
The Tragedy of the *Italia* (Benn, London, 1929).

GRIERSON, JOHN:
Challenge to the Poles (Foulis, London, 1964).

HOEL, ADOLF:
'Krassin'-ferden. Tillegg i boken 'Roald Amundsens siste ferd'
av GUNNAR HOVDENAK (Gyldendal Norsk Forlag, Oslo, 1934).

319

KRAEMER, WALDEMAR:
Italienere pa Svalbards ismarker ('Middagsavisen', Oslo, July 1928).

LUNDBORG, EINAR:
The Arctic Rescue (Viking Press, New York, 1929); with KNUT STUBBENDORFF: Det Store Polardrama (Hagerups Forlag, Copenhagen, 1928).

MADDALENA, UMBERTO:
Lotte e vittorie sul mare e nel sielo (Mondadori, Milan, 1930).

NOBILE, UMBERTO:
With the *Italia* to the North Pole (Allen & Unwin, London, 1961; & Dodd, Mead, New York, 1931). My Polar Flights (Muller, London, 1961; & Putman, New York, 1961). Posse dire la verità (Mondadori, Verona, 1945). La Verità in Fondo al Pozzo (Mondadori, Milan, 1978).

PRAVDA, Moscow: June and July 1928.

RIISER-LARSEN, HJALMAR:
Femti år for Kongen (Gyldendal Norsk Forl., Oslo, 1958).

SAMOILOVICH, R. L.:
S-O-S in der Arktis (Union Deutsche Verlag, Berlin, 1929).

SORA, GENNARO:
Con gli alpini all' 80° parallelo (Mondadori, Milan, 1930).

STEFANSSON, VILHJALMUR:
Unsolved Mysteries of the Arctic (Macmillan, New York, 1939).

STORIA DELLE CAMPAGNE OCEANICHE DELLA MARINA MILITARE:
Volume IV, Chapter 10: La *Citta di Milano* nella spedizione del dirigible *Italia*, 1928 (Ufficio Storico della Marina Militare, Rome, 1960).

TANDBERG, ROLF S.:
The *Italia* Disaster: Fact and Fantasy (privately printed, Oslo, 1977).

TOMASELLI, 'CESCO:
L' *Italia* non e tornata (despatch in *Corriere della Sera*, Milan, 27 May 1928).

TROJANI, FELICE:
La coda di Minosse (Mursia, Milan, 1964).

VIGLIERI, ALFREDO:
48 giorni sul pack (Mondadori, Milan, 1929).

Tandberg's booklet contains a most useful 13-page bibliography.

INDEX

PROPER NAMES

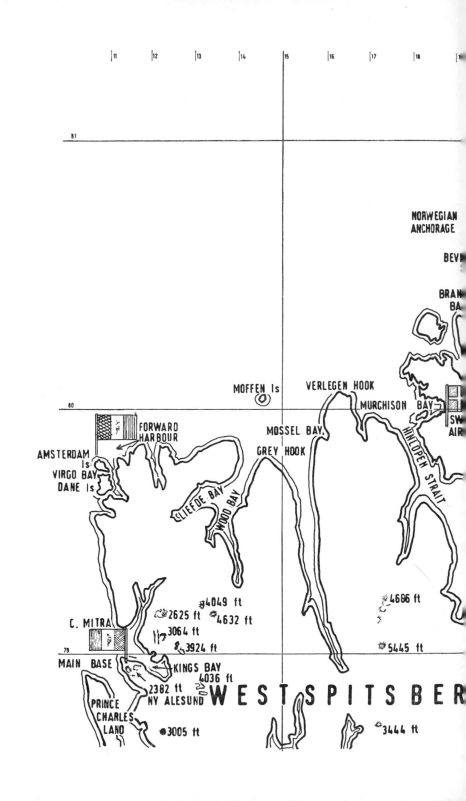